WIRELESS SENSOR NETWORKS AND THE INTERNET OF THINGS

Future Directions and Applications

WIRELESS SENSOR NETWORKS AND THE INTERNET OF THINGS

Future Directions and Applications

Edited by
Bhagirathi Nayak
Subhendu Kumar Pani
Tanupriya Choudhury
Suneeta Satpathy
Sachi Nandan Mohanty

A▲P APPLE ACADEMIC PRESS

First edition published 2022

Apple Academic Press Inc.
1265 Goldenrod Circle, NE,
Palm Bay, FL 32905 USA
4164 Lakeshore Road, Burlington,
ON, L7L 1A4 Canada

CRC Press
6000 Broken Sound Parkway NW,
Suite 300, Boca Raton, FL 33487-2742 USA
2 Park Square, Milton Park,
Abingdon, Oxon, OX14 4RN UK

© 2022 Apple Academic Press, Inc.

Apple Academic Press exclusively co-publishes with CRC Press, an imprint of Taylor & Francis Group, LLC

Library and Archives Canada Cataloguing in Publication

Title: Wireless sensor networks and the Internet of things : future directions and applications / edited by Bhagirathi Nayak, Subhendu Kumar Pani, Tanupriya Choudhury, Suneeta Satpathy, Sachi Nandan Mohanty.
Names: Nayak, Bhagirathi, 1963- editor. | Pani, Subhendu Kumar, 1980- editor. | Choudhury, Tanupriya, 1986- editor. | Satpathy, Suneeta, 1978- editor. | Mohanty, Sachi Nandan, editor.
Description: First edition. | Includes bibliographical references and index.
Identifiers: Canadiana (print) 20210124822 | Canadiana (ebook) 20210124881 | ISBN 9781771889612 (hardcover) | ISBN 9781774637951 (softcover) | ISBN 9781003131229 (ebook)
Subjects: LCSH: Wireless sensor networks. | LCSH: Internet of things. | LCSH: Internet—Security measures.
Classification: LCC TK7872.D48 W57 2021 | DDC 681/.2—dc23

Library of Congress Cataloging-in-Publication Data

Names: Nayak, Bhagirathi, 1963- editor. | Pani, Subhendu Kumar, 1980- editor. | Choudhury, Tanupriya, editor. | Satpathy, Suneeta, editor. | Mohanty, Sachi Nandan, editor.
Title: Wireless sensor networks and the internet of things : future directions and applications / edited by Bhagirathi Nayak, Subhendu Kumar Pani, Tanupriya Choudhury, Suneeta Satpathy, Sachi Nandan Mohanty.
Description: First edition. | Palm Bay, FL, USA : Apple Academic Press Inc., 2021. | Includes bibliographical references and index. | Summary: "Wireless Sensor Networks and the Internet of Things: Future Directions and Applications explores a wide range of important and real-time issues and applications in this ever-advancing field. Different types of WSN and IoT technologies are discussed in order to provide a strong framework of reference, and the volume places an emphasis on solutions to the challenges of protection, conservation, evaluation, and implementation of WSN and IoT that lead to low-cost products, energy savings, low carbon usage, higher quality, and global competitiveness. The volume is divided into four sections that cover Wireless sensor networks and their relevant applications Smart monitoring and control systems with the Internet of Things Attacks, threats, vulnerabilities, and defensive measures for smart systems Research challenges and opportunities This collection of chapters on an important and diverse range of issues presents case studies and applications of cutting-edge technologies of WSN and IoT that will be valuable for academic communities in computer science, information technology, and electronics, including cyber security, monitoring, and data collection. The informative material presented here can be applied to many sectors, including agriculture, energy and power, resource management, biomedical and health care, business management, and others"-- Provided by publisher.
Identifiers: LCCN 2021003363 (print) | LCCN 2021003364 (ebook) | ISBN 9781771889612 (hbk) | ISBN 9781774637951 (pbk) | ISBN 9781003131229 (ebk)
Subjects: LCSH: Internet of things. | Wireless sensor networks.
Classification: LCC TK5105.8857 .W576 2021 (print) | LCC TK5105.8857 (ebook) | DDC 006.2/5--dc23
LC record available at https://lccn.loc.gov/2021003363
LC ebook record available at https://lccn.loc.gov/2021003364

ISBN: 978-1-77188-961-2 (hbk)
ISBN: 978-1-77463-795-1 (pbk)
ISBN: 978-1-00313-122-9 (ebk)

About the Editors

Bhagirathi Nayak, PhD, is a highly results-oriented professional with experience of 25 years from IIT Kharagpur, India, in the areas of computer science and engineering, academics, administration, database design and development, and pedagogical activities. He is presently associated with Sri Sri University, Cuttack, India, as Head of the Department of Information and Communication Technology and Professor in-charge of the Enterprise Resource Planning (ERP) System. To date he has published more than 40 articles in reputed international journals and has written four books. He has holds five patents in the area of computer science and engineering. Dr. Nayak won the prestigious Dr. A. P. J. Abdul Kalam Professional Excellence Award in Data Science from the Dr. A.P. J. Abdul Kalam Research Centre. He was also honored with the Best Professor of Data Science in Odisha, India Education Award 2019 at Bangalore. For his significant contribution to the field of data science, he awarded a Best Researcher Award by the Technological Conclave 2019, Bhubaneswar, Odisha, India. He also received the Research and Innovation Award of the Year on the occasion of the National Summit 2020 on 17th January 2020 at New Delhi in the august presence of Shri Nitin Jairam Gadkari (Honorable Minister of MSME). Four PhD scholars have been awarded and presently six PhD scholars are working under him. He did many more projects in the works, such as on bioinformatics with the Department of Biotechnology, Government of India, MSME & Paradip Port, Odisha, India.

Subhendu Kumar Pani, PhD, is a Professor in the Department of Computer Science and Engineering and also Research Coordinator at Orissa Engineering College (OEC) Bhubaneswar, India. He has more than 15 years of teaching and research experience. His research interests include data mining, big data analysis, web data analytics, fuzzy decision-making, and computational intelligence. He is the recipient of five researcher awards. In addition to research, he has guided two PhD students and 31 MTech students. He has published over 50 international journal papers (25 Scopus indexed). His professional activities include roles as associate editor, editorial board member, and/or reviewer of various international journals. He is associated with a number of conferences and societies. He has more than 100 international publications, five authored books, two edited books, and ten book chapters to his credit. He is a fellow in Scientific Society of Advance Research and Social Change and a life member in many other professional organizations, including IE, ISTE, ISCA, OBA. OMS, SMIACSIT, SMUACEE, and CSI. He received his PhD from Utkal University, Odisha, India, in the year 2013.

Tanupriya Choudhury, PhD, is an Associate Professor in the Department of Computer Science and Engineering at UPES Dehradun, India. He has nine years of experience in teaching. Recently he has received the Global Outreach Education Award for Excellence and Best Young Researcher Award at the Global Outreach Education Conference and Awards 2018. His areas of interests include human computing, soft computing, cloud computing, data mining, etc. He has filed

14 patents to date and received 16 copyrights from the Indian Ministry of Human Resource Development for his own software. He has been associated with many conferences in India and abroad. He has authored more than 85 research papers and has delivered invited talks and guest lectures at several universities in India and elsewhere. He has been associated with many conferences throughout India as TPC member and session chair, etc. He is a lifetime member of IETA, member of IEEE, and member of IET (UK) and other renowned technical societies. He is associated with corporate, and he is Technical Adviser of Deetya Soft Pvt. Ltd. Noida, IVRGURU, and Mydigital 360, etc. received his bachelor's degree in CSE from the West Bengal University of Technology, Kolkata, India, and master's degree in CSE from Dr M.G.R. University, Chennai, India. He has received his PhD degree in the year 2016.

Suneeta Satpathy, PhD, is an Associate Professor in the Department of Computer Science and Engineering at the College of Engineering Bhubaneswar (CoEB), Bhubaneswar, India. Her research interests include computer forensics, cyber security, data fusion, data mining, big data analysis, and decision mining. In addition to research, she has guided many postgraduate and graduate students. She has published papers in many international journals and conferences in repute. She has two Indian patents in her credit. She is an editorial board member and/or reviewer of the *Journal of Engineering Science, Advancement of Computer Technology and Applications, Robotics and Autonomous Systems, and Computational and Structural Biotechnology Journal*. She is a member of CSI, ISTE, OITS, ACM, and IE. She received her PhD from Utkal University, Bhubaneswar, Odisha, in the year 2015, with a Directorate of Forensic Sciences, MHA scholarship from the Government of India.

Sachi Nandan Mohanty, PhD, is an Associate Professor in the Department of Computer Science and Engineering at the College of Engineering Pune. Pune, India. He has published 94 journal papers and has edited and authored fifteen books. He is actively involved as a fellow of the Indian Society Technical Education, the Institute of Engineering and Technology, the Computer Society of India, and as member of the Institute of Engineers and senior IEEE Computer Society. He is currently a reviewer of many journals, including *Robotics and Autonomous Systems, Computational and Structural Biotechnology, Artificial Intelligence Review,* and *Spatial Information Research.* He has been awarded a Best Researcher Award from Biju Pattnaik University of Technology in 2019, Best Thesis Award (first prize) from the Computer Society of India in 2015, and an Outstanding Faculty in Engineering Award from the Dept. of Higher Education, Government of Odisha in 2020. He has also received international travel funds from SERB, Dept. of Science and Technology, Govt. of India, for chairing several sessions at international conferences (USA in 2020). Dr. Mohanty received several best paper awards during his PhD at IIT Kharagpur from the International Conference at Bejing, China, and the International Conference on Soft Computing Applications, organized by IIT Rookee, India, in 2013. Prof. Mohanty's research areas include data mining, big data analysis, cognitive science, fuzzy decision- making, brain-computer interface, and computational intelligence. Dr. Mohanty received his postdoctoral degree from IIT Kanpur in the year 2019 and PhD from IIT Kharagpur in the year 2015, with an MHRD scholarship from Government of India.

Contents

Contributors

Ajay
Amity Institute of Information Technology, Amity University, Noida, India

Rajeshri Aneesh
Department of Computer Engineering, Faculty, PHCET, Navi Mumbai 400705, India

Archana Arudkar
Department of Computer Engineering, Faculty, PHCET, Navi Mumbai 400705, India

Varinder Kaur Attri
Department of Computer Science & Engineering, CT Group of Institutes, Jalandhar, Punjab

Silki Baghla
JCDM College of Engineering, Sirsa, Haryana 125055, India

Parveen K. Bangotra
Department of Space, Semi-Conductor Laboratory, Mohali, Punjab, India

Abhinav Bhandari
Department of Computer Science and Engineering, Punjabi University, Patiala, Punjab, India

Jasmeen Kaur Chahal
Department of Computer Science and Engineering, Punjabi University, Patiala, Punjab, India

Alka Chaudhary
Amity Institute of Information Technology, Amity University Noida, Noida, India

Shivani Chaudhary
Department of Computer Science & Engineering, CT Group of Institutes, Jalandhar, Punjab

Vivek Chauhan
Department of Mechatronics Engineering,Chandigarh University, Mohali, Punjab, India

Tanupriya Choudhury
Department of Computer Science and Engineering, University of Petroleum and Energy Studies, Dehradun, India, Email: tanupriya1986@gmail.com

Tarun Gulati
MMEC, MM (Deemed to be University), Mullana, Ambala, Haryana, India

Aman Gupta
Department of Mechatronics Engineering,Chandigarh University, Mohali, Punjab, India

Abhilasha Jain
PTU GZS Campus, Bathinda, 151001 Punjab, India

Pulkit Jain
Department of ECE, Chandigarh University, Mohali, Punjab, India

Swati Jindal
PTU GZS Campus, Bathinda, 151001 Punjab, India

K. Kathiravan
Department of Computer Science and Engineering, Easwari Engineering College, Chennai, India

Amanpreet Kaur
University Institute of Computing, Chandigarh University, Gharuan, Chandigarh Group of Colleges, Landran, Mohali, Punjab, India

Divjot Kaur
PTU GZS Campus, Bathinda, 151001 Punjab, India

Harleen Kaur
Department of Computer Science and Engineering, Baba Farid College of Engineering and Technology, Bathinda, Punjab, India

Jashanpreet Kaur
Punjabi University, Patiala

Jaspreet Kaur
JCDM College of Engineering, Sirsa, Haryana 125055, India

Mandeep Kaur
Computer Science and Engineering, SLIET Longowal, Punjab, India

Manpreet Kaur
Department of Computer Engineering, Punjabi University, Patiala, Punjab, India

Pankaj Deep Kaur
Department of Computer Science & Engineering, Guru Nanak Dev University Regional Campus, Jalandhar, Punjab

Sarabjeet Kaur
University Institute of Computing, Chandigarh University, Gharuan, Chandigarh Group of Colleges, Landran, Mohali, Punjab, India

Upinder Kaur
Department of Computer Science, Baba Farid College, Bathinda, Punjab, India

Arun Kumar
Maharishi Markandeshwar (Deemed to be University), Mullana, Ambala, Haryana

Satyasundara Mahapatra
Pranveer Singh Institute of Technology, Kanpur, Uttar Pradesh, India

Monika Mangla
Department of Computer Engineering, LTCoE, Navi Mumbai, Maharashtra 400709, India

Prashant Kumar Mishra
Pranveer Singh Institute of Technology, Kanpur, Uttar Pradesh, India

Sachi Nandan Mohanty
Department of Computer Science and Engineering, ICFAI Foundation for Higher Education Hyderabad, India, Email: sachinandan09@gmail.com

Vishal Nagar
Pranveer Singh Institute of Technology, Kanpur, Uttar Pradesh, India

Bhagirathi Nayak
Department of Information and Communication Technology, Sri Sri University, Cuttack, India
Email: bhagirathi.n@srisriuniversity.edu.in

Maninder Pal
Liverpool John Moores University, United Kingdom

Surya Narayan Panda
School of Engineering, Ajeenkya DY Patil University Pune, India 412105, Chitkara University Institute of Engineering and Technology, Patiala, Punjab, India

Subhendu Kumar Pani
Department of Computer Science and Engineering; Research Coordinator. Orissa Engineering College (OEC) Bhubaneswar, India, Email: skpani.india@gmail.com

R. Radha
School of Computer Science Engineering, Vellore Institute of Technology, Chennai.

K. Vinuthna Reddy
Department of Computer Science and Engineering, Koneru Lakshmaiah Education Foundation, Hyderabad, India

Suneeta Satpathy
Department of Computer Science and Engineering, College of Engineering Bhubaneswar (CoEB), Bhubaneswar, India, Email: suneeta1912@gmail.com

Komal Saxena
Amity Institute of Information Technology, Amity University Noida, Noida, India

Satnam Singh Sekhon
Department of Mechanical Engineering, BFCET, Bathinda, Punjab, India

Jyotsna Sengupta
Punjabi University, Patiala

Riya Sharma
Amity Institute of Information Technology, Amity University Noida, Noida, India

Sharad Sharma
Maharishi Markandeshwar (Deemed to be University), Mullana, Ambala, Haryana

Gurpreet Singh
Department of Computer Science and Engineering, PIT, MRSPTU, Rajpura, Punjab, India

Gurinder Pal Singh
Department of Space, Semi-Conductor Laboratory, Mohali, Punjab, India

Karandeep Singh
Department of Electronics and Communication, BFCET, Bathinda, Punjab, India

Manminder Singh
Department of Computer Science and Engineering, SLIET Longowal, Punjab, India

Parmpreet Singh
Department of Computer Science and Engineering, Punjabi University, Patiala, Punjab, India

Sukhwinder Singh Sran
Department of Computer Engineering, Punjabi University, Patiala, Punjab, India

Amit Sundas
School of Engineering, Ajeenkya DY Patil University Pune, India 412105, Chitkara University Institute of Engineering and Technology, Patiala, Punjab, India

Mayank Verma
Department of Mechatronics Engineering, Chandigarh University, Mohali, Punjab, India

Rajat Verma
Pranveer Singh Institute of Technology, Kanpur, Uttar Pradesh, India

Abbreviations

ACL	access control list
AGVs	automated guided vehicles
AI	artificial intelligence
AODV	ad-hoc on-demand distance vector
API	application programming interface
API	application performance indicator
BCT	blockchain technology
BDP	bandwidth delay product
BEB	binary Exponential back off
BEMS	building energy management system
BS	base station
CA	collision avoidance
CH	cluster head
cIoT	cloud IoT
CNs	core networks
CoAP	constrained application protocol
CSMA	carrier sense multiple access
CTS	clear to send
DDoS	distributed denial of service
DER	distributed energy resources
DNS	domain name system
DoS	denial of service
EC	eddy current
EIoT	enterprise IoT
GDPR	general data protection regulation
HVAC	heating ventilation and air conditioning
IBC	identity based cryptography
ICMP	Internet Control Message Protocol
IDE	integrated development environment
iIoT	industry IoT
IoMT	Internet of medical things
IoT	Internet of Things
IRC	Internet relay chat
iTCP	intelligent TCP

LBCAR	load balanced congestion adaptive routing
LF-RFID	low-frequency RFID
LOS	line of sight
LPWAN	low-power wide-area networking
MAC	media access control
MA-MEC	multi-access mobile edge computing
MANET	mobile ad hoc network
MGDEV	metric for garbage data evaluation
MiTM	man-in-the-middle
MSW	municipal solid waste
NAV	network allocation vector
NDT	nondestructive testing
NFV	network function virtualization
PDR	packet delivery ratio
PEC	pulsed eddy current
RAN	radio accessed network
RF	radiofrequency
RFID	radio frequency identification
RTS	request to send
RTT	round trip time
SAW	surface acoustic wave
SDN	software-defined networking
SGS	smart garbage system
SSL	secure socket layer
SVM	support vector machine
TCP	transmission control protocol
TFRC	TCP friendly rate control
TLS	transport layer security
UDP	user datagram protocol
UE	user equipment
WCD	weighted channel delay
WoT	Web of Things
WSN	wireless sensor network
WXCP	wireless explicit congestion protocol
ZC	zombie computer

Preface

Today, the world has grown to be a smaller place with the maturity of the concept the "Internet of Things" (IoT), which makes use of sensors to firmly join digital communication expertise with smart physical devices such as smart grids, elegant homes, well-groomed water networks, and intelligent transportation. The number of Internet-connected objects grows, giving a paradigm shift in the digital age where smart embedded devices, people, and systems are connected. The junction of digital information technology, Internet, and digital communications fastened with modern engineering advances is making concrete the way for inexpensive sensors, capable of achieving a better accuracy. In such perspectives, wireless sensor network (WSN) technology consisting of an album of sensor nodes coupled with wireless channels and proficient in providing digital interfaces to the real-world things is becoming an indispensable constituent of IoT. With the IoT concept, one is able to shrewdly manage, monitor, and control the smart network devices.

Wireless sensor networks are networks consisting of a substantial number of sensor nodes with each sensor node having the capability to sense different physical properties, like light, heat, and pressure etc. These sensor networks have brought a revolutionary change in the world of communication to assemble the heterogeneous information and fuse it to improve the reliability and efficiency of digital infrastructure systems. Further the WSNs having the characteristic features as infrastructure-less, fault-tolerant, and self-organizing capabilities has provided the opening for economical, easy-to-apply, rapid, and flexible installations in unattended and harsh environments in various prospective applications.

Nowadays, WSN applications are also considered as IoT applications, forgetting the eminent new features that characterize the denomination because as it takes place in IoT. WSN networks are also ruling an extensive number of appliances in different domains, like healthcare, enhanced smart living scenarios, agriculture, logistics, wearable computing, industrial and production monitoring, control networks, and many other fields. Further the development of IPv6-enabled WSN protocols and their wide variety of applications have made it an integral component of IoT. So in today's scenario, in contrast to wired systems, wireless systems providing better flexibility is becoming the key factor for IoT. Hence, WSNs are amalgamated into the IoT, where sensor nodes are united with the Internet dynamically to cooperate with each other and carry out various tasks.

The peculiar features and motivational factor for academics and industrial research work has enabled WSN to make revolutionary changes in digital information technology to play a vital part of our lives. This book describes the historical revolution of WSN along with the wider application of IoT. The book also investigates the technological characteristic features of WSN to be assembled with IoT, including data fusion, data association, correlation, and data aggregation. The application areas of WSN with an eye on its standard features enabling its design requirements for digital information infrastructure are also reviewed.

Further, the mysterious ideas and concepts of wireless sensor networking along with IoT applications for modern living styles have always opened a pathway for cyber scammers to swindle the systems response, which leads to a variety of digital crimes that misuse the technology. The up-to-date view on the problem of security is also focused on in the book with an idea that protective mechanisms and corresponding technical enhancements must be integrated into it.

Lastly the illustrations of various challenges and the corresponding design factors of WSNs along with their IoT applications can give a deep insight to explore work in the related areas in search of appropriate solutions. Though WSN is open to unlimited real-world application, on the other hand it poses many challenges for researchers to satisfy the rigorous constraints due to its weird characteristics, like scarcest energy sources, unattended and harsh deployment environments, insecure radio links, changing network topologies, heterogeneity of nodes, and multihop communications enabling the need of the development of new paradigms.

PART I

Wireless Sensor Networks and Their Relevant Application

CHAPTER 1

Intelligent 5G Networks: Challenges and Realization Insights

UPINDER KAUR[1*], and HARLEEN KAUR[2]

[1]*Department of Computer Science, Baba Farid College, Bathinda, Punjab, India*

[2]*Department of Computer Science and Engineering, Baba Farid College of Engineering and Technology, Bathinda, Punjab, India*

Corresponding author. E-mail: drupinder2016@gmail.com

ABSTRACT

5G is the future generation network offering the variety of changes in the architecture of the core network. The network function virtualization and software-defined networking provide unconditional support to the emerging 5G network. This chapter highlights the evolutionary changes from 1G to 5G networks. Then it covers the important aspects for the realization of the 5G networks comprising the management of radio network, providing network service, mobility issue, and so on. This covers the complicated configuration issues and challenges for the future 5G network. Then it also creates a vision to solve the issue and overcome the challenges in 5G network by using the artificial intelligence (AI). Including the AI concepts to empower the 5G networks to meet the challenges of future generation networks. So, the main focus is to empower the 5G network with AI to acclaim intelligent 5G as a reality.

1.1 INTRODUCTION

The emerging mobile network system from its pervasive coverage and fundamental Internet of Things (IoT) system provides innovation in terms of advanced network applications and new venture of creativity. The 5th generation networking withholds the new opportunities in the era of future technology like IoT, virtualization, big data, and virtual reality services. It involves the massive deployment of networking devices which will cross more than 75 billion by 2025 [1]. In contrast to the present technologies, 3G, 4G, and 5G networks support high frequencies and high spectrum efficiency. The evolution of 1G to 5G is shown in Table 1.1. There is a need of new procedure and policies for managing, signaling to support new application. 5G networks can provide extensive connectivity to the massive heterogeneous networking devices.

The objectivity of the 5G networks is to provide scalability and high speed for next generation technologies like IoT, AI and virtual reality, autonomous driving, smart cities in a sustainable and economical fashion. It requires the architectural modifications, new communication platforms, algorithms for proper utilization of the network function virtualization (NFV), edge computing, software-defined networking (SDN), and big data analytics. Some researchers have shown their promising result to support 5G networking requirements in Refs. [2–8]. The ongoing transactional changes in various domains originate new perspective for technical and management for 5G networks.

This chapter mainly addresses the challenges of 5G networks in different applications. We can demystify the challenges of 5G architectural changes in support of smart cities, IoT, big data, and so on. Some research work on the new opportunities for 5G to support the future prospective of technologies in various application domains can enlighten the path for development of 5G networking. The main objective of this chapter is to classify the new application domains for 5G. It may include the low latency, bandwidth requirement, communication range, better reliability, security, and privacy measures. We also discuss the challenges and ongoing experimental testbeds among different universities, network companies, government organizations, and so on. The remaining article provides the structure of 5G networking in Section 1.2. Section 1.3 provides the requirements and demands of the 5G networking. Section 1.4 provides the challenges and innovative projects with the conclusion and future prospective.

1.2   THE FUTURE GENERATION NETWORKS: 5G NETWORKING

The recent advancement in networks has created a multifarious application to enhance the lifestyle and include better mobility, social networking, e-health,

TABLE 1.1 Evolutions of Network Generations from 1G to 5G

Technology/ Generation	Time	Bandwidth	Technology Used	Network	Multiplexing	Switching	Primary	Variations
1G	1970—0	2 kbps	Analog	PSTN	FDMA	Circuit	Analog Devices	Mobility
2G	1990–2004	64 kbps	Digital	PSTN	TDMA/ CDMA	Circuit & Packet	Digital Devices & SMS	Security and Acceptance
3G	2004–2010	2 Mbps	CDMA 2000, UMTS, EDGE	Packet NW	CDMA	Packet	Phone Calls, Data and SMS Services	Reliable and better services
4G	NOW	1 Gbps	Wi Max, WiFi, LTE	Internet	CDMA	Only Packet	All Services	Faster broadband and low network latency
5G	SOON	Higher than previous	WWWW	Internet	CDMA	All Packets	Advance and High Capacity data broadcast services	Better connectivity, better offloading and reduced latency and many more

and so on. Nowadays, Internet services have seen a rapid development over past times. The emerging technologies, for example, IoT, mobile and social network, fog computing, big data, and so much, are completely dependent on Internet application. This exhibits requirement of technological evolution in the present Internet services.

The evidence forms the conventional data exchange among p2p, www, social, and mobile networks with the emerging technologies and forthcoming tactile Internet [9–11]. 5G networks involve integration of physical devices and the digital data, covering the use case of many IoT devices. So the required service of 5G networking demands the high available speed, reliability, security, ultra-low latency, context aware services, and so on [12].

Further, the smart cities concept linked with the context of 5G networking. The smart cities integrate existing information sources with modern information sources and support the communication network for the unified access to services for the smart city administration and their residents. Thus, the main focus is associated with the enhancement of the use of current resources with the improvement in quality of services and reducing operational cost, for example, smart cities, automation vehicular network, IOTs, big data, and so on. Table 1.2 represents the requirements, application areas, and the proposed solutions for the prospective of 5G networks.

TABLE 1.2 Describes the Requirements, Proposed Solutions, and Application Areas of 5G Networks

Requirements	Proposed Solutions	Application Areas
High Network Capacity with Data Rate	Densification FDD, CRN, mMIMO,D2D, FULL DUPLEX	Better connectivity, usages, virtualized homes, smart grids, better health care services, IoTs, industrial services
Ultra-Low Latency	Cache management, D2D connectivity, self-heal, smart reduced cells	
Better Handoff	SIC, CRN, detection and decoding, multi-rat handoff	
QoS	Delayed bound QoS, Quality service management	
Scalability	NFV, SDN, C-RAN, CONCERT	
Environment Friendly	C-RAN, VLC, mMIMO, D2D Communication etc	
Connectivity	Multi-Rat, CRN, CONCERT, RAN, densification	
More Secure and Reliable	Better services and advanced encryption and decryption	

1.2.1 THE CHALLENGES AND ADVANCEMENTS FOR 5G

The four technology advancement that can focus our interest in 5G, including lightweight virtualization, software-defined network, blockchain inspired distributed ledger, and mobile edge computing, are shown in Figure 1.1

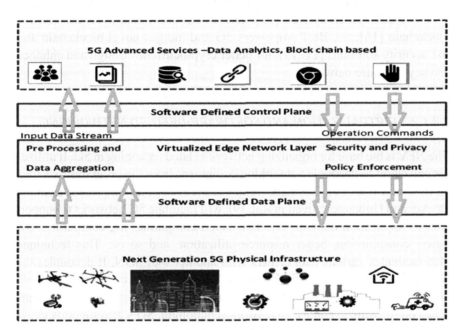

FIGURE 1.1   Architectural View for 5G networking [40]

1.2.1.1 BLOCKCHAIN TECHNOLOGY-BASED DISTRIBUTION LEDGER

Beyond keeping user privacy on the Internet, General Data Protection Regulation (GDPR) is also accelerating the development of distributed ledger technologies (i.e., blockchain technology [BCT] based protocol design). So, it gives rise to the strong demand nowadays to unify the data management across companies, government, and end users. Here it provides the congruous meaning to fulfill user request, for example, receive, track, and update the data when requested by user.

BCT enables us to store historical record for each transaction in a tamper proof format to enhance data security. So it has more visible role in the various data driven services in 5G. BCT also keeps information at different locations and the history cannot be removed and further information can be accessed when the node possess it [13]. The main concept used in BCT and distributed ledger technology enables each participated node that has access to shared ledger at distributed locations [14]. All the transactions stored in ledger and information are copied to all the participated nodes. The blocks are timestamped in batches to validate the transactions and each block contains the information of hash value of previous block. Mining means generation of new blocks given by Ref. [15]. The blocks are linked by chain, formed blockchain [16]. So, BCT empowers 5G and merges novel blockchain and IoT security solutions [17–19], for better cryptocurrency design and enhance privacy in future networks.

1.2.1.2   VIRTUALIZATION AND SOFTWARE-DEFINED NETWORKING

The NFV is the base for organizing network-related reckoning in 5G. It utilizes virtualization to decouple networking equipment from the programs executed on their machine [20]. The light weight virtualization technique, for example Docker and Unikernels given in Ref. [9], will facilitate 5G networks to support various application domains like IoT, cloud computing, fog computing, low power consumption, better resource utilization, and so on. This technique also facilitates various data centers with another tool SDN. It decouples the data and control plane to control all the functions using centralized network controller. It eliminated the need of vender-based hardware and its designs based on software to control all network functioning. SDN also supports large-scale distribution of 5G services [20]. The main application will be visible in smart cities, IoT, fog computing, and many more [21, 22].

1.2.1.3   MOBILE EDGE COMPUTING

Emerging of 5G technologies provides solution to many recourse hungry applications, broad paradigm application like IoT, big data, and huge computation applications. The border term mobile edge computing envisioned challenges to bring the cloud resources closer to IoT devices and highly optimistic technology to benefit potential of IoT. This will help in visualizing the emerging technologies' real-time video/audio surveillance, smart city, smart e-health, smart transport management system, IoT, Internet of Vehicles. Multi-access mobile edge computing (MA-MEC) explores the integration of wireless technologies in 5G. The design of MA-MEC evolves the deployment of ultra-dense small cells—femto/pico/micro cells—to increase the capacity of mobile network connections [23, 24] facilitating the dual connectivity in future 5G networks to communicate with traditional macro cells and manage data between macro and small cells, respectively [25–27]. They provide the existing edge offloading techniques with further improvements with respect to speed and low communication latency.

1.2.1.4 EDGE COMPUTING 5G NETWORK SERVICE FRAMEWORK

The new edge-enabled platform proposed to merge new technology with 5G to manage huge amount of data along with the cyber-physical network deployment. The mobile edge computing brings us benefits with 5G networks.

- Fast processing of data with IoT devices.
- Ultra-low latency for real-time data sharing between cloud and IoT network management.
- It enhances the better privacy and security.

The edge computing platform provides efficient access to the upcoming computing style for real-time data management. Some researchers exhibit the better utilization of SDN framework [20], Kafka framework, and IoT management [28, 29].

1.2.2 RESEARCH CHALLENGES FOR 5G NETWORKS

The SDN, NFV, and edge computing are the promising techniques to fulfill the requirement for new applications. While the implementation of 5G undergoes many other challenges,

- The major concern deals with the privacy and security, Ref. [30] has discussed the pervasive encryption and also discussed the issue with ISPs, cloud service provider, standardization units like ETSI6 and IETF5.
- Issue related to the troubleshooting and management at various network layers in 5G networks. This also focuses on the unencrypted data management to provide high data privacy on the Internet [31].
- Operational challenge related to the management of existing technologies and creates a balance between both convectional system data and real-time web traces [32].
- Less response time in 5G is required to support new emerging technologies like IoT, edge computing, fog computing, big data, and so on.

- Provide efficient computational and storage resources at the application domain, mobile edge devices, radio resource allocation, and so on.
- Combine optimization between the convectional technology and 5G technology with the minimal cost, for example, adequate use of wireless channels when user move across the cells with respect to the storage and computation resources.

1.2.3   CHALLENGES BY THE GOVERNANCE POLICIES

With the growing demand of the Internet, it becomes the common pool resource. So the requirement to efficiently regulate the services ensures fair usage of bandwidth, scalability, interoperability to different applications. So the standard regulation is required in 5G future. Back and recovery plans are also regularized. Ultra-low latency application will be developed to handle run-time vehicular network in 5G. Governance policies are required to ensure the proper functioning of 5G components with the restriction limits. Proper allocation of the spectrum is required as the failures are critical in certain applications. Proper fault tolerance is needed in mobile edge computing to avoid network failure. Strong security measures are required so that the security cannot be breached by the hacker. Major governance is required related to the interoperability between different computing and platforms. Handoff management at very small cells is required for the proper functioning of the vertical applications in multiple 5G providers [33, 34] that discuss on the data protection laws. They discuss the GDPR for the management of the huge amount of data collected at the cloud and user applications. So the major concern is related to the privacy of the data and standardization needed for implementing 5G network in smart cities [35].

1.3   AI IN 5G NETWORKING

AI support the 5G mobile network to provide knowledge to get self-administrative techniques for network, for example, to configure 4G network hyperbolic to 1500 from 500 hubs at network in 2G and 1000 hubs required in the 3G network [36]. So the AI imparts intelligent support system to 5G network with previous knowledge that is used to train the 5G standard hub network with more parameters at least 2000.

The application of 5G network, that is, eMBB (enhanced Mobile Broadband), URLLC (Ultra Reliable Low Latency Communication), and mMTC (massive Machine Type Communication), required new sort of advance services for system administration. The new services continually evolve and the existing services also change to support the technology change. In this manner, 5G network required services for self-configuration, self-healing, and self-optimization to intelligently take decision and administrate, and to appropriate supply system to proper provisioning mechanism and provide new network slice.

Another issue, in emerging cellular network systems in 5G, is that it depend intensely on SDN, and still need more flexibility and robustness under the evolution of new heterogeneous and progressively complex cellular 5G networks. To self-regulate these networks, automated built-in network slice for the future networking services, network management, environment variations, identify uncertainties, particular response action plan, and proper network configuration are required. The desired features for the future networks solved the emerging of AI with 5G network because this solves the problem of classifying issues, interaction with environment variations, and many other uncertainties.

Today AI is evolved as the future technology and also support multidisciplinary techniques, for example, machine learning, meta-heuristics, theory optimization, game theory, control theory, and so on. [37]. The AI learning technique is classified as three main categories.

1.3.1 SUPERVISED LEARNING

The supervised learning is based on training the system by the existing inputs and their desired outputs and also specifies the rules to determine the desired output using inputs. So the supervised learning had widely been applied to solve the uncertain network issue, and effective channel utilization. Thus, the supervised learning assumes to be using the probabilistic methods to solve the characteristic equations and take the advantage of well-known Bayes learning methods. For example, Kalman filtering is used for optimizing cellular networks.

1.3.2 UNSUPERVISED LEARNING

Here the system has the prior inputs but not fed with the desired outputs. Therefore, the leaning agents were made self-capable by embedding the intelligent system or pattern in its input. They work on by finding out the hidden patterns and resolve it by correlating this with the input data. This layer of AI has wide scope to estimate the hidden layer using the neural networks. They enhance the importance of deep learning methods in AI. Here, the 5G nonorthogonal multiple access receivers perform on the same graph-based factors to achieve low-bit error rate. It also uses the *K*-means algorithms to detect the uncertain network anomalies.

1.3.3   REINFORCEMENT LEARNING

The controlled theory and the lean psychology, the new evolved technique is reinforcement learning. Here, the agent is trained to attain the intelligence by interacting in the dynamic environment. The agent should take action according to the situation. This learning enhances through the strong pattern recognition ability. Few researchers that show the evidence of cognitive radio usually method for dynamic transition of spectrum [38, 39].

Table 1.3 provides the detail of AI support for intelligent networks and Table 1.4 summarizes the AI algorithms for cellular networks. It supports the AI for various tasks in cellular networks, network traffic management, user demands, resource utilization, coordination between the base stations (BSs), and other network entities.

Figure 1.2 presents the architecture for intelligent 5G networks empowered with AI. It contains the AI controller on the top of Open Network Operating System and it is independent entity; it can convey with the radio accessed network (RAN), global SDN controller, and core networks (CNs). The role of AI center is to keep the record of service level agreements and also keep check on the requirement rate, area coverage, failure policies, data redundancy, and so on. The User Equipment (UE) level information in AI center handles the receiver category, network level information, quality of service, schedule maintenance, the in-fracture level information, that is, CPU, memory, storage, and so on, from the global controller. The AI center manages the embedded modules (sensing, mining, prediction, and reasoning) for the network management and provides feedback result for traffic management. The AI center, sensing module, keeps the track of local UEs and focuses on the mobility patterns in the networks. The reasoning and proactive module records the UEs to track the location and prepares handover functions with managing the mobility cost. Thus, the merging of AI in the working of 5G networks helps in controlling the uncertainties and maintains normal working of networks under non-normal conditions. AI center helps in periodically exchanging the information between the global controllers and

TABLE 1.3 Changes in Intelligent 5G Networks

| Types | 4G Network | 5G Network | AI-Based System | | | Smart/Intelligent 5G Networks |
			Sense	Mine	Predict	Reason	Service -Support
Services	MBB	eMBB, mMTU and urLLC	Y	Y	N	Y	Service-Aware
RRM	Granted	Flexible bandwidth	Y	N	Y	Y	User Specified
MM	Unified	Demand service	Y	Y	Y	Y	Location Based
MANO	Simple	Operator based	Y	Y	Y	Y	Advanced better troubleshooting and better capacity communication
SPM	Unified	End-End Services	N	Y	Y	Y	Auto Network Slicing

TABLE 1.4 AI Algorithm Summary

Modules	Sense	Mine	Predict	Reason
Application Support	Compare the network applications on basis of services & events with hybrid sources	Clustering & Classify the Services according to the resources	Do Prediction on the basis of Trend Analysis and Judgement of traffic analysis from hybrid sources	Configure the results and better utility
Proposed Work	LR—Logistic Regression HMM—Hidden Markov Model SVM—Support Vector Machine	GBDT—Gradient bosting decision tree Spectral Clustering SVM Classification RNN-Neural Network	KL—Kalman Filtering ARMA—Auto-Regression-Average-Moving Deep Learning RNN LSTM-Long Short Term Memory Compress Sense	Dynamic Behavior—DB B&B—Bench & Beyond Approach Reinforcement Learning Q-Based Learning Transfer Learning DNN
Review & Analysis	SVM and LR has better accuracy and HMM exhibits large probability of anomalies	The supervised learning approach exhibits quality data services and unsupervised learning exhibits dependency on data accuracy rate	ARMA- KL exhibits better performance in onetime sequences generation. Deep learning, RNN, LSTM are better and provide advance level traffic analysis and mobility patterns	Dynamic behavior generalizes the behavior of Artificial Intelligence, better optimizes solution and better supportive environment with hybrid approach of RL and TL

it also manages the resources in emergency cases. The AI centers integrated with global controller constitute the multitier network support system and strengthen the 5G network.

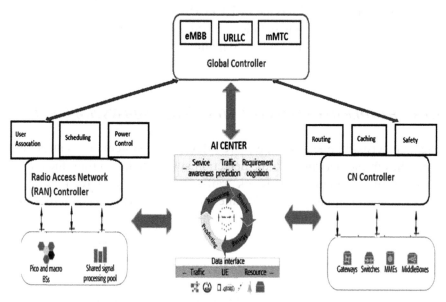

FIGURE 1.2   AI empower intelligent 5G network.

1.4   OPPORTUNITIES IN INTELLIGENT 5G NETWORKS

Emerging of AI with the 5G network supports the following issues in 5G networks.

1.4.1   TRAFFIC MANAGEMENT

The 5G networks visualized the large amount of data and different types of networks. The integration of AI in 5G networking helps to allocate the network resources. It helps in predicting the network traffic and best traffic management practices, mining of relevant data from the abundant data, and providing more appropriate service to configure network. AI helps to generate the reports based on the trained data set and dynamic data to summarize the network users and the relevant network usage policies.

1.4.2   HETEROGENEITY IN 5G NETWORKS

The inclusion of pico cells, micro cells, macro cells, even different network configuration deployed the network in heterogeneity. AI helps in managing the services in terms of service efficient (SE), and energy efficient (EE), and so on. AI generates new policies and rules to configure the pico BSs for larger throughput to the macro BSs to maintain the efficient networking data exchange.

1.4.3   HANDLE UNCERTAINTIES TO SUPPORT SUBSYSTEMS IN 5G

The 5G network operators have well-developed system to manage the anomalies in the network. So the detection system helps to train the AI for detection of the abnormal network traffic patterns. Therefore, it helps in experiencing the unfamiliar traffic patterns and handles the uncertainties. So, here AI helps in shielding the safety threats and also counters the anomalies.

1.4.4   ISSUES IN INTEGRATED RANS AND CNS

Issue relates to isolation of the RAN and CNs that not scaled enough in network. Thus, the AI center grants the controller to manage the wired and wireless resources and resource management and appropriate content distribution and caching server, and also provide the unified protection against the potential network threats.

1.4.5   CHALLENGES IN 5G NETWORKS

The major challenges are to effectively apply the AI in the 5G networks. The data in 5G network is variety of data. The challenges for AI to recognize the large set of patterns analyze it and remember the patterns and then derive the result or take the appropriate decisions. Thus, the challenge in AI is to define the appropriate parameters, time is the major concern in mining the huge set of data, also the significant amount of storage, adequate security, and privacy policies are required. These are the main added computational capabilities of the network entities and the BSS and also manage the cost of the technology.

1.5 CONCLUSION

This chapter creates the vision of the future 5G networks. It provides the details of the future promising technology like edge computing, SDN, virtualization, wireless and wired networks, cloud computing, fog computing, and so on. This aggregates the open challenges—both the technical challenges and the governance policies. Here, we inculcate the benefits of AI to the future generation cellular networks. AI provides the opportunities in 5G networks to analyze and recognize the patterns. This also provides the discussion of the AI with the algorithms for managing the different aspects of the 5G networks, that is, mobility management, load management, general management, service monitoring, and security and privacy aspect as well. Finally, the 5G network has empowered with the intelligence of AI to achieve success in the digitalized world. In future, we will further analyze the various use case for 5G network to provide the maximum benefit of AI and deep learning.

KEYWORDS

- **5G networks**
- **software-defined networking**
- **artificial intelligence**
- **network function virtualization**

REFERENCES

1. Statista. *Internet of Things Connected Devices Installed Base Worldwide from 2015 to 2025.* www.statista.com/statistics/471264/IoT-number-ofconnected-devices-worldwide/
2. Vijay, G., Ji, L., Lee, S., and Han, B., "Network Function Virtualization: Challenges and Opportunities for Innovations". *IEEE Comm. Mag.* Vol. 53, (2015), pp. 90–97.
3. Sasu, T., Jon, C., Aaron, Y. D., and Flinck, H., "Software Defined Networking for Security Enhancement in Wireless Mobile Networks". *J. Comp. Net.* Vol. 66 (2014), pp. 94–101.
4. J. Costa-Requena, Kantola, R., Manner, J., Liu, Y., and Aaron, Y. D., "SD 5G Mobile Backhaul". *Proceeding of 1st International Conference on 5G for Ubiquitous Connectivity*, Levi, Finland, 26th–27th November, 2014.
5. Crowcroft, J., Liu, Y., Sasu, T., Flinck, H., and Ding, A. Y., "Demo: An Open-source Software Defined Platform for Collaborative and Energy-aware WiFi Offloading".

Proceeding of Mobile Communication ACM, (Mobicom 2015), pp. 182–184, September 2015.

6. Aaron, Y. D., Crowcroft, J., Liu, Y., Schulzrinne, H., and Flinck, H., "Vision: Augmenting WiFi Offloading with an Open-source Collaborative Platform". *Proceeding of Mobile Communication ACM*, pp. 44–48, September 2015.

7. Ding, Y., "*Collaborative Traffic offloading for Mobile Systems*". PhD Thesis, University of Helsinki, Finland, 2015.

8. Flores, H., Su, X., Hui, P., Li, Y., et al., "Large-scale offloading in the IoT". *Proceeding of the IEEE* Conf. *on the Pervasive Computing and Communications & Workshops (Per Com)*, March 2017.

9. Zanella, A., Vangelista, L., Bui, N., and Castellani, A., "IoT for Smart Cities". *IEEE IoT J.* Vol. 1, 1 (2014), pp. 22–32.

10. Fettweis, G. P., "The Tactile Internet: Applications and Challenges". *IEEE Vehicular Tech. Mag.*, Vol. 9, 1 (2014), pp. 64–70.

11. Simsek, M., Aijaz, A., and Fattweis, G. P., "5G-E. Tactile Internet". *IEEE J. Sel. Areas in Comm.*, Vol. 34, 3 (2016), pp. 460–473.

12. Shishkov, B., Larsen, J. B., and Warnier, M., "3 Cat. of CAS". *Proceeding of International Symposium on Business Modelling and Software Design*, Vienna, Austria, Springer, July 2–4, 2018.

13. Svein Olens, et al., "Blockchain in Government.: Benefits and Implications of DLT for Information Sharing". *Govt. Inf. Quart.*, Vol. 34, 3 (2017), pp. 355–364.

14. Nakamoto, S., "*Bitcoin: A P2P Electronic Cash System.*" https: //bitcoin.org/bitcoin.pdf.

15. Felten, E., et al., "*Bitcoin and Cryptocurrency Technologies: A Comprehensive Introduction*". Princeton University Press, 2017.

16. Tapscott, D., and Tapscott, A., "The Impact of BC Goes Beyond Financial Services." *H. Buss. Rev.*, 2016. https://hbr.org/2016/05/theimpact-of-the-blockchain-goes-beyond-financial-services

17. Suomaalainen, L., et al., "Demo: Cloud-based Security as a Service for Smart IoT Environment." *Proceeding of Workshop on Wireless of the Student, by the Student and for the Student*, ACM MobiArch Communications, S3, September 2015.

18. Suomalainen, L., et al., "Securebox: Toward Safer and Smarter Internet of Things Networks." *Proceeding of (CAN' 2016) Workshop on Cloud Assisted Networking*, ACM, pp. 55–60, December 2016.

19. Ibbad, H., Ding, A. Y., and Suomaalainen, L., "IoTURVA: Securing D2D Communication in IoT Networking". *Proceeding of 12th Workshop on Challenged Networks, ACM Mobi-Arch Communications*, CHANTS, pp. 1–7, October 2017.

20. Ding, A. Y., Flinck, H., et al, "SDN for Security Enhancement in the Proceeding of WMN." *Comp. Net.*, Vol. 66, 2014, pp. 94–101.

21. Ding, A. Y., et al., "Demo: An Open-source SD Platform for Collaborative and Energy-aware WiFi Offloading". *Proceeding of International Conf. on Mobile Computing and Networking, ACM MobiArch Communications*, pp. 182–184, Paris, France, September 2015.

22. Ding, A. Y., Liu, Y., Tarkoma, S., Schulzrinne, H., Flinck, H., and Crowcroft, J., "Vision: Augmenting WiFi Offloading with An Open-source Collaborative Platform". *Proceeding of International Workshop on Mobile Cloud Computing & Services, ACM MobiArch Communications, MCS*, Paris, France, 2015.

23. Korhonen, J., et al., "Toward Network Controlled IP Traffic Offloading". *IEEE Comm. Mag.*, Vol. 51, 3, 2013, pp. 96–102.

24. Srinivasan, A., et al., "Enabling Energy-Aware Collaborative Mobile Data Offloading for Smartphones". *Proceedings of 10th International Conference of IEEE Communications Society Conf. on Sensor Mesh & Ad-Hoc Comm Networks SECON*, LA, USA, 23–24th June, 2013.

25. Cuervo, E., et al., "MAUI: Making Smartphones Last Longer with Code Offload". *Proceedings* of *ACM MobiArch Mobile Computing Systems*, California, USA, Jun 15th–18th, 2010.

26. Naik, M., et al., "CloneCloud: Elastic Execution between Mobile Device and Cloud". *Proceeding of ACM Euro System*, Salzburg, Austria, pp. 181–194, Apr, 2011.

27. Aucians, A., et al., "ThinkAir: Dynamic Resource. Allocation and Parallel Execution in the Cloud for Mobile Code offloading". *Proceeding of Int. Conf. of Computer-Communications, IEEE INFOCOM*, Orlando, USA, 25th–30th March, 2012.

28. Ding, A. Y., et al., "Managing Internet of Things at the Edge: The Case for BLE Beacons". *In the Proceeding of 3rd Workshop on Exp. With Design & Implementation of Smart Objects, ACM MobiArch Communications, SMART OBJECTS*, 2017.

29. Ott, J., et al., "Demo: iConfig: What I See Is What I Configure". *Proceeding of 12th Workshop on Challenged Networks* (CHANTS), 2017.

30. Moriarty, K., and Morton, A., "*Effects of Pervasive Encyclopedia on Operators, RFC 8404*", 2018.

31. Haus, M., et al., "Security and Privacy in D2D Communications: A Review." *IEEE Communications Surveys & Tutorials*, Vol. 19, 2, 2017, pp. 1054–1079.

32. Jarvine, I., et al., "Effect of Competing TCP Traffic on Interactive Real-time Communication." *Proceeding of 14th International Conference on Passive and Active Measurement*, China, pp. 94–103, March 18th–19th, 2013.

33. Korhenen, J., et al., "Bridging the Gap Between International Standardization and Network Research." *SIG COMM Comp. Comm. Review*, Vol. 44, 1, ACM, 2014, pp. 56–62.

34. Matheus, R., and Janssen, M., "How to Become a Smart City?: Balancing Ambidexterity in Smart Cities". *Proceeding of 10th International Conference on Theory and Practice of Electronic Governance*, pp. 405–413, New Delhi, India, March 2017.

35. Janssen, M., et al., "Big and Open Linked Data to Create Smart Cities and Citizens: Insights from Smart Energy and Mobile Cases." *Proceeding of 14th IFIP International Conference on Electronic Governance*, pp. 79–90, Sweden, August 2015.

36. Imran, A., et al., "Challenges in 5G: How to Empower SON with Big Data for Enabling 5G." *Journal and Magazines, IEEE Network*, Vol. 28, 6, 2014, pp. 27–33.

37. Qadir, J., Imran, M. A., Ni, Q., and Vasilakos, A. V., "Artificial Intelligence Enabled Networking." *Journals and Magazines, IEEE Access*, Vol. 3, 2015, pp. 3079–3082.

38. Li, R., Zhao, Z., et al., "TACT: A Transfer Actor-Critic Learning Framework for Energy Saving in Cell. Radio Access Network." *IEEE Transaction on Wireless Communication*, Vol. 13, 4, 2014, pp. 2000–2011.

39. Vijay, R. K., et al., "Actor-Critic Algos." *SIAM J. Cont. Opt.*, Vol. 42, 4, 2000, pp. 1143–1166.

40. Janssen, M., et al., "Opportunities for the Applications Using 5G Networks. Requirements, Challenges and Outlook." *Proceeding of ICTRS, 7th Internal Conference on Telecomm & Remote Sensing*, Spain, pp. 27–34, October 2018.

CHAPTER 2

Energy Harvesting Implementation for Wireless Sensor Networks

JASPREET KAUR* and SILKI BAGHLA

JCDM College of Engineering, Sirsa, Haryana 125055, India

Corresponding author. E-mail: jaspreet25913@gmail.com

ABSTRACT

Energy harvesting is the demand of present day wireless communication for improving the energy efficiency of a network and a way to green communication as well. Wireless sensor networks (WSNs) suffer from energy depletion of nodes and energy harvesting is a promising solution to enhance the life-time of sensor nodes in the area having lesser human intervention. In this work, different energy harvesting techniques have been presented and electromagnetic-based energy harvester model is deployed with WSN to evaluate its performance. Low energy adaptive clustering hierarchy protocol has been used as a routing protocol for sensor nodes. The performance of the proposed model is evaluated with variation in hardware characteristics of energy harvester and analyzed for sensor characteristics such as the number of dead nodes, alive nodes as well. The energy harvester model and WSN have been implemented on the MATLAB platform.

2.1 INTRODUCTION

Development of wireless communication networks lead to several challenges which need to be resolved. These challenges include low latency, high data rates, energy efficiency, increase traffic handling capability, and network integration. Among these challenges, improving energy efficiency of the whole network is of prime concern. Nowadays, conventional batteries are a source of power in electronics devices. These batteries have a finite life span and need to be charged after some time. In mobile terminals, option of charging is available but the problem becomes tedious in case of wireless sensor networks (WSNs). In WSN, nodes are deployed in an area where human intervention is generally not feasible. In that case, replacement of battery or time to time charging is not possible. Moreover, batteries also place a limitation on the miniaturization of micro electro-mechanical systems. So, energy harvesting techniques have drawn the attention of researchers in the past few years to improve the performance of the network in terms of energy efficiency. It is also suggested as a major technique for improving energy efficiency in the development of the fifth generation of wireless mobile networks [1, 9].

Different energy sources existing in the environment around a system such as solar, wind, tidal energy geothermal energy, and other mechanical vibration can be the options for energy harvesting. Ease of availability, reliability, mobility, lesser cost, and their eco-friendly nature are other important advantages of these sources.

With the improvements in integrated circuits, the size and power consumption of current electronics has dramatically decreased. So, energy harvesting from the ambient natural environment has received great interest and has been investigated by many researchers. Other sources of ambient energies include the flow of liquids or gases, the energy produced by the human body, and also the action of gravitational fields produces ambient energy. These ambient energies are in the form of vibrations. Energy harvesting can be done by converting these vibrations into electrical energy.

The rest of the chapter is organized as follows: Section 2.2 describes various techniques of vibrational energy harvesting. Section 2.3 explains the model of electromagnetic energy harvester used in this work, Section 2.4 provides simulation setup for performance evaluation of the model of energy harvester, Section 2.5 provides results obtained and Section 2.6 concludes the work with future remarks.

2.2 TYPES OF VIBRATIONAL ENERGY HARVESTING TECHNIQUES

Depending on the availability and environment of the vibrational energy, energy harvesting techniques can be categorized as:

- *Electromagnetic energy harvester*: In this type of energy harvesting, electrical energy is produced by using a magnetic field. According to Faraday's law, the rate of change of magnetic flux linkages with a coil results in induced emf in it. So, in electromagnetic energy harvester, a coil wrapped around a mass is allowed to oscillate in a magnetic field which results in the production of voltage across it. The produced voltage is generally very small (~0.1 V) so an amplifier circuit is attached to obtain the desired output voltage. Moreover, the induced voltage can be varied by change in magnetic field strength, number of turns in the coil, mass or diameter of the coil as well. This method of energy harvesting has the advantage that it needs no external voltage source for its operation. Wind vibration and mechanical vibration-based cantilever systems are examples of electro-magnetic energy harvesting methods.

- *Electrostatic (capacitive) energy harvester*: As its name indicates, this type of harvesting is based on changing the capacitance of vibration-dependent variable capacitors. Vibrations from the ambient atmosphere separate the plates of an initially charged variable capacitor (varactor), resulting in a change in its capacitance. Now, for a fixed charge value, a change in capacitance results in a change in induced voltage across it. So, this method requires an external voltage source and converts mechanical energy into electrical energy as both the plates move up and down (mechanical constraints are needed). The produced voltage is relatively high (2–10 V). It can be easily worked with MEMS. The system can be placed in a car near to the shock absorber, where the vibration is maximum.

- *Piezoelectric energy harvester*: Piezoelectric or electromechanical energy harvester, harvests vibrational energy from stress and compression and converts mechanical energy into electrical energy. A piezoelectric material is strained and deformed by applying mechanical energy resulting in equivalent electrical energy (voltage drop) as defined by the phenomenon of piezoelectric effect. In these harvesters, oscillating system is typically a cantilever beam structure with a mass (piezoelectric material) at one end of the lever. Piezoelectric materials are used in systems where it is subjected to stress or compression, producing a voltage of about 2–10 V [2, 10].

Vibration energy harvesting devices can be either electromechanical or piezoelectric. Due to the lack of availability of piezoelectric material, mostly electromagnetic harvester is used.

2.3 ELECTROMAGNETIC ENERGY HARVESTER FOR WSN

Figure 2.1 shows the model of electromagnetic harvester used in this work. It consists of a cantilever beam supported on a fixed support. A permanent magnet with mass "*m*" is mounted on the cantilever beam on which a coil is wrapped around. The vibrations applied to the cantilever beam move the magnet up and down resulting in a change of magnetic flux linked with the coil. Hence the voltage is induced in it which is applied to the load attached with the coil.

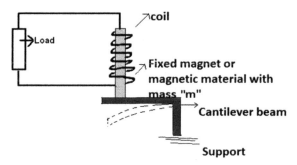

FIGURE 2.1   Cantilever-beam-based energy harvester.

Source: Reprinted from Ref. [8]. Open access.

For a given mass of cantilever, maxim stress "σ_{max}" imposed depends upon its length "*L*," thickness "*t*," and moment of inertia "*I*" as given by

$$\sigma_{max} = \text{Maximum stress} = \frac{FLt}{2I} \qquad (2.1)$$

Here $F = \text{mg N}$.

Maximum allowable deflection of the cantilever beam is given by

$$Y_{max} = \frac{2L^2}{3Et}\sigma_{max} \qquad (2.2)$$

where Y_{max} = maximum allowable deflection,
$\quad L$ = length of cantilever (11 mm)
$\quad E$ = Young's modulus,
$\quad t$ = thickness of cantilever (0.2 mm).

So, the maximum power generated by the cantilever beam-based energy harvester shown in Figure 2.1 is given by [2]

$$P_{Lmax} = \frac{mY^2\omega n^3}{16\varepsilon_p}(\frac{R_{load}}{R_{load} + R_{coil}}) \qquad (2.3)$$

where P_{Lmax} = maximum power generated,

$$m = \text{mass of cantilever beam (mg)},$$

ε_p = damping factor,

Y = maximum allowable deflection,

R_{load} = load resistance,

R_{coil} = coil resistance.

The produced energy being very small is then amplified and applied to WSN as shown in Figure 2.2.

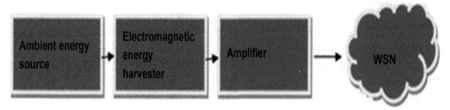

FIGURE 2.2   Electromagnetic energy harvester-based WSN.

2.4   SIMULATION SETUP

The proposed model of electromagnetic energy harvester is implemented on the MATLAB platform. Table 2.1 provides the simulation set up used in this work. Mass of cantilever is varied from 490 to 530 mg. The proposed model is implemented with a fixed value of thickness and width of the cantilever as 0.2 and 0.3 mm, respectively. The performance of the energy harvester model used in this work is evaluated in terms of maximum power generated "P_{Lmax}" with variation in mass and length of the cantilever beam. The generated power is applied as initial energy to WSN consisting of 100 nodes. Low energy adaptive clustering hierarchical routing algorithm has been used for routing in WSN [4].

The performance of WSN is evaluated in terms of the number of alive nodes, dead nodes, and remaining energy.

2.5   RESULTS AND DISCUSSION

Figure 2.3 shows the variation of maximum allowable deflection and natural frequency with variation in the length and mass of the beam. It is observed that the natural frequency tends to decrease with an increase in the length of the beam and mass of the cantilever beam. It is also observed that the maximum allowable deflection of the cantilever beam increases with an increase in length of the beam. Figure 2.4 provides the maximum power generated by the energy harvester model used in this work for variation in mass of the cantilever beam. It can be observed that the output power decreases with an increase in the mass of the beam and maximum power is generated for a mass of 490 mg as 2.408×10^{-8} W.

TABLE 2.1   Simulation set up for energy harvester

Mass of cantilever (mg)	490-530
Thickness of cantilever beam (mm)	0.2
Length of cantilever beam (mm)	4-11
Width of cantilever beam (mm)	0.3
No. of nodes in WSN	200
Area of WSN (m^2)	200 x200
No. of rounds	200
Initial energy of WSN	2.4 J

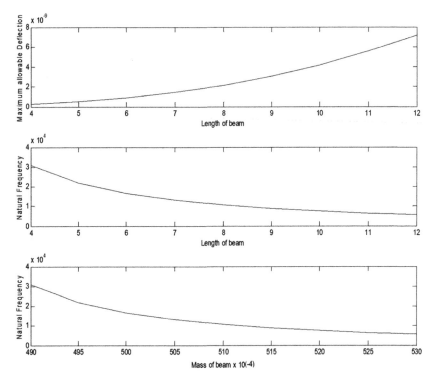

FIGURE 2.3   Maximum allowable deflection and natural frequency for variation in length and mass of the beam.

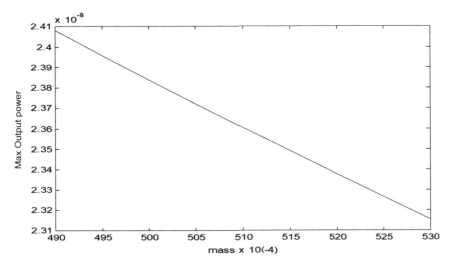

FIGURE 2.4 Maximum power generated for variation in mass of cantilever beam.

The power generated is applied to WSN constructed in an area of 200 × 200 m² having 200 nodes. Figure 2.5 provides node deployment in selected the area of WSN.

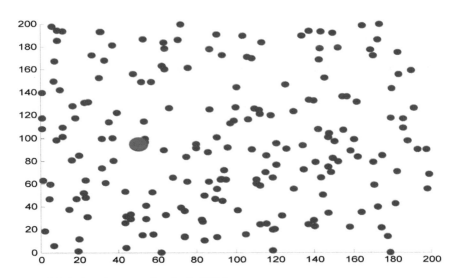

FIGURE 2.5 Deployment of nodes in WSN.

The performance of WSN is evaluated in terms of the number of alive nodes, dead nodes, and remaining energy. Energy of nodes is diminished with an increase in the number of rounds. Once a node is run out of its energy, it is assumed as a dead node. A dead node no longer can send or receive any data. In a network having a fixed number of nodes, the number of dead nodes increases with the number of rounds, and the number of alive nodes decreases accordingly.

It is observed that for the given value of energy harvested from the energy harvester model used in this work, the number of nodes alive for 80 rounds and got dead after that. Similarly, energy of WSN diminished after 80 rounds as shown in Figures 2.6–2.8.

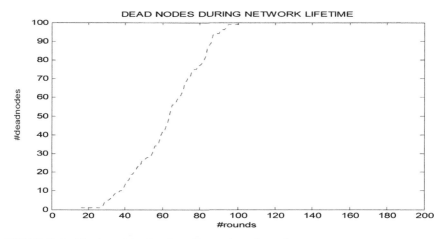

FIGURE 2.6   Number of dead nodes with number of rounds.

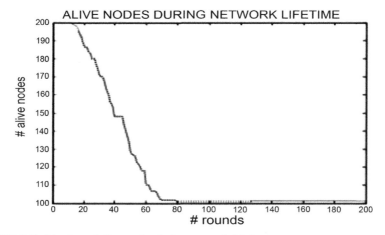

FIGURE 2.7   Number of alive nodes during network lifetime.

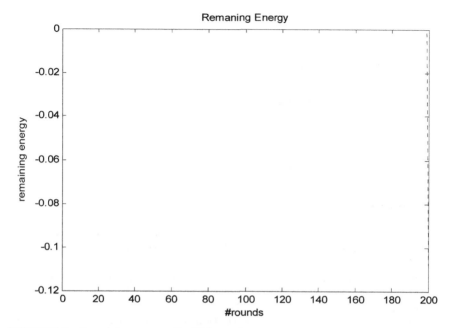

FIGURE 2.8 Remaining energy after 200 rounds.

Figure 2.7 shows the total number of alive nodes in the network during the 200 rounds. The node whose energy is not completely depleted after the simulation or they have enough energy to transmit or receive data are alive nodes.

The remaining energy of the network is defined as the sum of energy of all the alive nodes after each round. Figure 2.8 presents the energy of the network after 200 rounds.

2.6 CONCLUSION

Energy harvesting has gained a lot of attention from researchers in the past few years for different applications. In WSN also, energy efficiency is of main concern. So, this work is an effort to design the energy harvester-based WSN. The performance of the electromagnetic energy harvester has been evaluated for variation in the mass of the cantilever. The energy generated is applied to WSN to estimate the lifetime of nodes. The model can be modified with energy-efficient routing techniques employed with WSN and variation in the design of the energy harvester.

KEYWORDS

- **energy harvesting**
- **energy efficient**
- **green communication**
- **LEACH**
- **WSN**

REFERENCES

1. Hossain, E. and Hasan, M. "5G cellular: key enabling technologies and research challenges," IEEE Instrumentation & Measurement Magazine, Vol. 18, Issue 3, pp. 11–21, June 2015.
2. Jackson, N., O'Keeffe, R., Waldron, F., O'Neill, M., and Mathewson, A. "Evaluation of low-acceleration MEMS piezoelectric energy harvesting devices" Springer-Verlag, Berlin Heidelberg, 25, November 2013.
3. Rahman, T., Sakir, S. R., and Onna, S. D. "Design of an efficient energy harvester from ambient vibration," BSC Thesis, BRAC University, April 2012.
4. Heinzelman, W., Chandrakasan, A., and Balakrishnan, H., "Energy-efficient communication protocols for wireless microsensor networks," Proceedings of the 33rd Hawaaian International Conference on Systems Science (HICSS), January 2000.
5. Fang, L. H., Idris, S., Hassan, S., Abd Rahim, R. B., and Abd Malek, M. F., "A study of vibration energy harvester," ARPN Journal of Engineering and Applied Sciences, ISSN 1819-6608, 2006–2015.
6. Ojo, F. K., Akande, D. O., and Mohd Salleh, M. F. "An overview of RF energy harvesting and information transmission in cooperative communication networks," Springer Science+Business Media, LLC, part of Springer Nature, 2018.
7. Zakaria, J., and Salleh, M. F. M. "Wireless energy harvesting on AF relaying system over outdated channel conditions," 2018 7th International Conference on Computer and Communication Engineering (ICCCE).
8. Rahman, T., Sakir, S.E., Onna, S.D. Design on an Efficient Energy Harvester from Ambient Vibration: A report submitted to Department of Electrical & Electronic Engineering, (EEE) BRAC University in fulfillment of the requirements for thesis work. 2012. http://hdl.handle.net/10361/1832
9. Chandrakant Mallick, Suneeta Satpathy, "Challenges and Design Goals of Wireless Sensor Networks: A Sate-of-the-art Review", International Journal of Computer Applications (0975 – 8887), 2018.
10. Sachi Nandan Mohanty, E.Laxmi Lydia, Mohamed Elhoseny, Majid M. Gethami Al Otabi, K.Shankar, Deep learning with LSTM based distributed data mining model for energy efficient wireless sensor networks, Physical Communication, vol. 40, Issue-4, 101097-102008, (2020). https://doi.org/10.1016/j.phycom.2020.101097.

CHAPTER 3

An Approach to Enhance the Wireless Sensor Network Efficiency Through Coverage and Energy Utilization Technique

KARANDEEP SINGH[1*], and SATNAM SINGH SEKHON[2]

[1]*Department of Electronics and Communication, BFCET, Bathinda, Punjab, India*

[2]*Department of Mechanical Engineering, BFCET, Bathinda, Punjab, India*

Corresponding author. E-mail: Krndeep3@gmail.com.

ABSTRACT

Nowadays, wireless sensors are emerging in the field of industrial as well as in scientific research. These wireless sensor networks are having issues regarding coverage as well as major issue of battery life span, so in this chapter issues are discussed and then algorithms are proposed to enhance the coverage and battery life of the sensor network. The techniques covered in these sections work on time management and optimal sampling rate to extend both the range and life of the network.

3.1 INTRODUCTION

A wireless network of sensors consists of a large number of sensory nodes which ranges from low to high for performing different tasks in numerous fields. As wireless sensor network is emerging these days and covering wider area in different applications like local monitoring to military surveillance. Sensor nodes collect the information from other several nodes after sensing and processing of the data. Sensor network revolves around set of issues like its ranging and power backup.

These several nodes can be setup either by planned or unplanned manner according to the situations where they have to be installed. In inaccessible areas, only unplanned or random deployment of sensor is possible for example, in a battlefield or disaster relief operations, planned deployment is not possible due to risk.

3.2   ISSUES ASSOCIATED WITH WIRELESS SENSOR NETWORK

1. These working life times of sensor are very small as sensors are battery operated and they vanish during monitoring of the targets.
2. *Battery issues*: During communicating information with the other nodes in the network it consumes power and sensor die out. The size and cost factor restrict the battery power extension in the sensors.
3. *Installation issues*: In case of planned deployment, sensors can be installed and modified according to the need of network but in case of unplanned or random field it is too difficult to install the sensor on precise location. Using an aircraft, it can be made possible to deploy sensor in the field but sometimes it is not feasible to use this method in the battlefield zone.
4. *Coverage issues*: In some cases, sensors are deployed randomly in the network and after that, sometimes it is difficult to locate the exact location of node and change the sensor in case of faulty nodes. As a result of this, they impact on coverage performance and information is lost in this case on nodes.
5. *Target motion:* In case of dynamic target, sometimes sensor fails to respond to capture relevant information related to the targets due to its motion. The mobility of the target sometimes remains unrevealed or targeted by sensor which becomes the issue of target motion.

3.3   SOLUTION TO OVERCOME OVER THE PROBLEM FACED IN WIRELESS SENSOR NETWORKS

3.3.1   COVERAGE

These issues can be resolved by using different methods which help to cover the whole network and able to function properly for efficient functioning.

Tracing and serving the cells:

- Divide the cluster area into different cells, which means the whole cluster is segmented into small parts.
- In this way, it is possible to trace the weak and uncovered areas of cells.
- After collecting information of uncovered and weak zone by their respective heads, forward this information to the other cells.
- It will help to save energy and resources as centralized computation is not required because each cell is responsible to cover the divided area.

Movement of redundant node:

It will become the responsibility of the head of the cluster to find the redundant node of the network and plan to move this redundant node to the uncovered area for coverage to the network.

Time management of the node movement:

The relay movement based on the Dijkstra or Floyd algorithm method helps node to find out the intelligent path to serve the destination node to boost the coverage power. This phenomenon helps to cover the uncovered slot by their neighbor node and which is also covered by their last node through this redundant node settling down in the empty slot near to it.

3.3.2 FOR BATTERY LIFE

Wireless sensor network having issues like finite on board battery power which is a major thrust area. So power saving of sensor nodes increases life time of the whole network. There are a number of routing methods that have been introduced to solve the issues of energy conservation in sensor network. These techniques are:

1. *Low energy adaptive clustering hierarchy*: It works on the formation of cluster head and on rotation policy to balance the load.
2. *Power efficient gathering in sensor information*: It works on the principle of creating a chain to cover all the networks and conserve the energy.
3. *Sensor protocol for information via negotiation*: This approach helps to decrease transmission of unnecessary and redundant data and it

also saves energy wastage by transferring meta-data. This helps to conserve more energy.

4. *Greedy perimeter stateless routing*: In this method, routing is done either by forwarding the data toward the closest node or by following right-hand rule which means data is forwarded to the right-neighbor node to forward the data to the destination.

5. *Energy allocation algorithm*: This technique allows sensor node to work efficiently by utilization of proper energy resources based on battery level. In this technique, sensor node does not fall short of power as in this case the current power level is firstly compared with the energy amount required and balance can be assigned. The procedure is followed as:

   • Energy is distributed among all nodes.
   • Main node as well as sensor node becomes power bank.
   • Harvesting energy initialization.
   • Data transmission to all nodes.
   • Optimal energy allocation.

So this technique allows the sensor node to manage its energy use efficiently.

1. *Optimal sampling rate assignment*: This technique firstly sets the passing sampling rate so that its energy is not depleted. This adaptive sampling rate helps to reduces energy loss during its transmission. The sampling rate can be varied according to its requirement of sensor. This allows for data transmission and communication between nodes at the optimal sampling rate assigned to the sensor nodes.

2. *External energy utilization time determination*: This method involves decision-making power regarding the right time external energy harvesting so that improvement is done over time and energy estimation. In this case,

   • Balance energy level is taken into account at each node.
   • The optimal time slot at which energy can be harvested at each node is determined.
   • If the energy reserve at a node is below a certain level, then energy is harvested at the optimal time slot.
   • Nodes can communicate with the help of the supplemented energy at the optimal time.

This technique provides improvization to both the previous algorithm in terms of time determination for energy harvesting.

3.4 CONCLUSION

In this chapter, we have focused on techniques to overcome the problem of coverage and battery-related issues faced in wireless sensor network without violating the performance of the whole network. This method helps to cover more targets as each and every node according to their schedule becomes active to serve the cell, this scheduling helps also to conserve the energy and life of sensor is extended to some extents.

KEYWORDS

- **sensor network**
- **coverage**
- **battery life**

REFERENCES

1. Zhou, Zude, Huang, Zheng, Liu, Quan, Zhou, Ying, A Study on the Coverage Problem in Wireless Sensor Network, ICWMMN2006 Proceedings.
2. Cardei, Mihaela, Du, Ding-Zhu, Improving Wireless Sensor Network Lifetime Through Power Aware Organization, Wireless Networks, Vol. 11, pp. 333–340, 2005.
3. Mitra, Rudranath, Khan, Tauseef, Improving Wireless Sensor Network Lifetime Through Power Aware Clustering Technique, Fifth International Conference on Advances in Recent Technologies in Communication and Computing (ARTCom 2013), 2013.
4. Lindsey, Stephanie, Raghavendra, Cauligi S., PEGASIS: Power-Efficient Gathering in Sensor Information Systems, Computer Systems Research Department.
5. GPSR: Greedy Perimeter Stateless Routing for WirelessNetworks_BradarpHarvard University/ACIRI karp@eecs.harvard.eduH. T. KungHarvard.
6. Vikash et al., "Wireless Sensors Networks: Security Issues, Challenges and Solutions" International Journal of Research in Engineering and Technology, November 2014.
7. Qin et al., "An Advanced Survey on Secure Energy-Efficient Hierarchical Routing Protocols in Wireless Sensor Networks" International Journal of Computer Science Issues, Vol. 10, Issue 1, January 2013.

8. Shukla, Kajal V., "Research on Energy Efficient Routing Protocol LEACH for Wireless Sensor Networks" International Journal of Engineering Research and Technology, March 2013.

9. Singh, Namdeep, Singh, Jasvir, "A Security Framework for Wireless Sensor Networks" Journal of Global Research in Computer Science, 2013.

10. Kaur, Kamaldeep, Kaur, Parneet, Singh, Sharnjeet, "Wireless Sensor Network: Architecture, Design Issues and Applications" International Journal of Scientific Engineering and Research (IJSER), ISSN (online): 2347–3878, Vol. 2, Issue 11, November 2014.

CHAPTER 4

A Modified Track Sector Clustering Scheme for Energy Efficiency in Wireless Sensor Networks

DIVJOT KAUR,* ABHILASHA JAIN, and SWATI JINDAL

PTU GZS Campus, Bathinda, 151001 Punjab, India

Corresponding author. E-mail: divjots93@gmail.com

ABSTRACT

In wireless sensor networks (WSNs), the main issue is energy conservation. The protocols in WSN focus on energy conservation to evaluate the efficiency of networks. In this chapter, existing track sector clustering scheme and our proposed work "A Modified Track Sector Clustering Scheme" is being discussed. A modified track sector clustering scheme follows concentric clustering hierarchical routing protocol approach. Two additional parameters—weight value and relay nodes are used in proposed work. The packet delivery ratio parameter is evaluated to calculate delivery of data packets. On evaluation of results, the efficiency of "A Modified Track Sector Clustering Scheme" is 61%–62% whereas efficiency of existing Track Sector Clustering Scheme is 56% only.

4.1 INTRODUCTION

Wireless sensor networks (WSNs) are groups of sensor nodes deployed in environmental monitoring areas between source and destination (base station [BS]) and the sensor nodes transmit aggregated data to the BS. WSNs are used in various fields like monitoring environmental conditions, health care, surveillance of battle field, power monitoring, and so forth [1]. Resources like bandwidth, computation, memory, power of battery, and so forth are the main parameters of network to evaluate the performance. The main issue discussed in WSN is energy conservation [1–8, 15]. Hence, to balance the energy and long lifetime of the network, routing protocols are to be designed effectively from time to time. The routing protocols in WSN consume less energy and improve network lifespan [3].

4.2   RELATED WORKS

4.2.1   CHAIN-BASED ROUTING PROTOCOLS

There are various chain-based routing protocols designed for WSN communication such as Power Efficient Gathering in Sensor Information Systems (PEGASIS), Low-energy Adaptive Clustering Hierarchy (LEACH), Chain-Cluster Mixed-Routing Protoco (CCM), Chain Routing based on Coordinates-Oriented Cluster (CRBCC), etc. They form chains in the form of single long chain, parallel chains; X and Y coordinate clusters for data transmission [4]. These routing protocols are developed for making WSN more reliable by improving energy efficiency, transmission delay, and so forth. But long chain formation is a big issue in energy conservation and stability of network.

4.2.2   ARCHITECTURE OF WIRELESS SENSOR NETWORKS FOR ENVIRONMENTAL MONITORING

The purpose of this chapter is to understand the environment to design the network [11]. Environment monitoring is sensed on the basis of challenges like scalability, power management, remote communication, usage, and so forth. The architecture for environment monitoring includes layered structure. Service platform layer, sensor network intelligence layer, sensor network abstraction layer, and so forth which provide the way to access, process, and transmit data in the network.

4.2.3   ROUTING TECHNIQUES IN WIRELESS SENSOR NETWORKS: A SURVEY

Protocols are designed to achieve energy efficiency in network. The routing protocols are based on network structure and protocol operation. The network structure protocols are flat hierarchical, and location based. Network structure is negotiation based, multipath based, query based, quality of service based, coherent based [7]. The objective of all these routing protocols is to enhance the lifetime of the network.

4.2.4 ENERGY EFFICIENT CLUSTERING SCHEME

In this chapter, nodes distribution is adopted to control energy dissipation [8]. The results of this work show that the nodes in lower level die early. This is because lower level nodes receive data from higher level nodes as well as from their own level and send the aggregated data to the BS. As the data at lower level nodes increases, it takes more energy to transmit bulky data. So energy consumption increases and cause loss of life of lower level nodes and performance of the network decreases.

4.2.5 A DELAY-CONSTRAINED AND MAXIMUM LIFETIME DATA GATHERING ALGORITHM FOR WIRELESS SENSOR NETWORKS

In this chapter, to improve the delay, the constraint method is approached. The data gathering at each round is researched. The delay constraint is researched at each round. This is called NP-complete problem. DMCL approach is used to resolve delay constraint [13]. The construction of tree reduces the energy consumption and helps in reducing the delay. Hence the results of this paper show how the delay control achieves the prolong network lifetime.

4.2.6 PEGASIS PROTOCOL IN WIRELESS SENSOR NETWORK BASED ON AN IMPROVED ANT COLONY ALGORITHM

In this chapter, ant colony algorithm is used for the nodes to find the routing path. Ant colony method is the method which is based on pheromone. Nodes find path using ant algorithm approach. One cluster head (CH) is chosen on the basis of maximum energy which transmits the aggregated data to BS. This routing protocol was developed to increase the lifetime of the network and energy conservation. But long chain formation may lead to early death of the CH.

4.2.7   THE CONCENTRIC CLUSTERING SCHEME FOR EFFICIENT ENERGY CONSUMPTION IN THE PEGASIS

This clustering scheme uses the concentric hierarchy approach. In this clustering scheme, network is divided into concentric circles. Each concentric circle is assigned levels. The circle nearest to the BS is assigned the lowest number whereas circle farthest from the BS is assigned the highest number [5]. In each layer of circle, nodes form chain and one CH is chosen. CH collects data from each node of its layer and then aggregates the data and transmits it to the next lower level CH and then to BS. This approach is used to improve the long chain formation and energy efficiency. But transmission of large amount of data may take more energy and reduce lifetime of CH.

4.2.8   IMPROVED CONCENTRIC CLUSTERING ROUTING SCHEME ADAPTED TO VARIOUS ENVIRONMENTS OF SENSOR NETWORKS

Following concentric clustering routing approach, CH of the highest level track is selected on the basis of maximum energy and rest CH of inner tracks are selected on the basis of distance [6]. The track is divided virtually into two halves, the nodes at right side transmit data anticlockwise whereas nodes at left side transmit data clockwise and data is aggregated at CH. This criterion is followed to reduce energy consumption. The drawback of this network is that CH of next levels is selected on the basis of distance. Hence there is the chance that CH with minimum energy can be selected. This may cause early death of the CH and effect efficiency of the network.

4.2.9   TRACK-SECTOR CLUSTERING FOR ENERGY EFFICIENT ROUTING IN WIRELESS SENSOR NETWORKS

In this work, concentric clustering scheme is approached [10]. CH selection is done randomly. The node with less energy may be selected as CH which may die early in the network and hence network lifetime may reduce. Due to this, the network may not exist for longer time. Moreover, data transmission gets delayed due to traffic congestion at lower level CH nodes because lower level CH has to aggregate the data coming from higher level CH with their own data. This may result in data traffic and cause loss of data packets during transmission. To transmit this heavy data, higher energy will be consumed. To overcome the shortcomings of this network, modified track sector clustering (TSC) scheme is proposed. The results of proposed work have shown better performance than the existing one. In the next section, the detailed description of proposed work is discussed.

4.3   PROPOSED WORK

The modified TSC scheme is one of the types of hierarchical routing protocol. In this, network is divided into concentric circular tracks and sectors. The working model of modified TSC scheme is described below.

4.3.1   SENSOR NODE DEPLOYMENT AND NETWORK SETUP NODE DEPLOYMENT

The network setup begins with sensor deployment in the monitoring area. The position of nodes remains fixed after their deployment. The BS receives information about node coordinates from all sensor nodes. The sensor node deployment is shown in Figure 4.1.

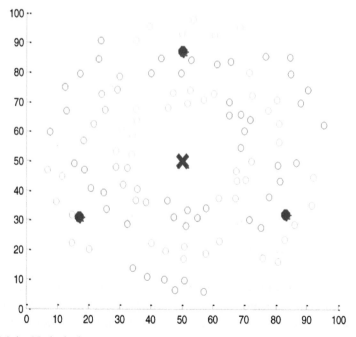

FIGURE 4.1   Node deployment.

4.3.1.1   NETWORK SETUP

The BS senses the nodes in that area and set up a virtual network by covering all the nodes. It virtually constructs the concentric circles around the nodes. The nodes are divided in the tracks in equal numbers. It virtually assigns each track a number. The number increases as the distance from BS increases. The radius of circles is set by BS. The radius R of the network varies from 0 to 50, that is, $0 \leq R \leq 50$.

The inner radii of levels—1, 2, and 3 are set in the value ranges in between the area dimensions. The network setup is shown in Figure 4.2.

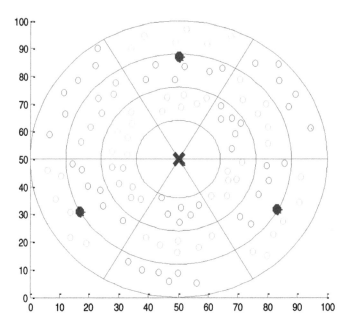

FIGURE 4.2   Network setup.

4.3.2   CHAIN FORMATION AND CLUSTER HEAD SELECTION

4.3.2.1   CHAIN FORMATION

After virtual track setup, sensor nodes deployed in tracks form chains within the tracks to communicate. The chain formation is done by calculating the slope value of X and Y coordinates of nodes. Each level nodes form chains simultaneously. Chain formation is shown in Figure 4.3.

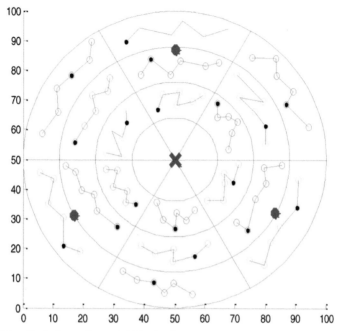

FIGURE 4.3 Chain formation and CH selection.

4.3.2.2   *CLUSTER HEAD SELECTION*

When chain formation is completed, BS assigns CH to each chain. BS set the CH on the basis of weight value. Weigh value concept is discussed in the next section. Communication starts from higher level to lower level CH and to BS at the end.

4.3.2.3   *WEIGHT VALUE*

It is the concept in which CH is selected whose value is directly proportional to energy and inversely proportional to distance from BS. With this, a relevant CH is selected which performs efficient functioning in the network.

4.3.3   *RELAY NODE INSERTION*

When virtual network setup is completed, then relay nodes are deployed in the outer layer of the network. The relay node collects the data from neighbor

CHs and transmits it to BS. Relay nodes set up communication path between inter track CHs and BS.

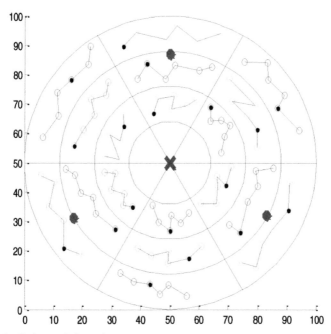

FIGURE 4.4   Relay node insertion.

The insertion of relay nodes is done to enhance fault tolerance in the network. This approach is proved to be effective in making the network stronger. In WSN, the nodes have limited energy power. While working in the network, their energy dissipates after a time period. Relay nodes help the nodes to transmit data directly to sink without any disturbance via multi hop path. The operational working of relay includes three steps. A radio communication section for transmitting/receiving the information, an information recording section for storing the information received from the sensor node, and an information conveying section for determining a destination of the information [9].

4.3.4   ENERGY ANALYSIS OF MODIFIED TSC SCHEME

To compute energy consumption during data transmission between CH, from CH to BS, and from relay nodes to BS, the Equation (4.3) is followed.

The total energy for a transmitter to send a k-bit message over a distance d is given by

$$E_{total}(k, d) = E_{elec}k + \varepsilon_{amp}kd^2 \qquad (4.1)$$

where ε amp is the energy constant for the radio transmission and E_{elec} is the energy per bit [10].

To calculate the energy consumption of our network system, let the number of concentric circles or tracks be NT as shown in Figure 4.2. Then the radio transmission energy consumed to transmit k-bit message over distance $d1$, from head node to the head node in lower level track and finally to the BS over distance $r2$ is calculated as

$$ETx(k,d) = \varepsilon_{amp}k \left[Ns(n''-1) d^2 + \sum_{i=1}^{Ns=1} d_2^{\,2} + r_2^{\,2} \right] \qquad (4.2)$$

where Ns is the number of sectors, n'' is the average number of nodes in a sector, and d_2 is the distance between head nodes in two neighboring clusters in the same sector.

4.3.5 PACKET DELIVERY RATIO

Implementation of relay nodes in the network also improved the quality of network by increasing packet delivery ratio (PDR). PDR is the ratio which gives the net percentage of number of packets received by the BS. To calculate the net PDR the following equation is used:

$$PDR = \frac{\text{Total Packet (received)}}{\text{Total Packet (transmitted)}} 100 \qquad (4.3)$$

4.3.6 EVALUATION OF PERFORMANCE METRICS

The simulation environment used to evaluate the performance metrics of existing as well as modified work is MATLAB. The network area used for simulation result is 100×100 sq m. While comparing various parameters of existing as well as modified work, we came to conclusion that our modified TSC scheme performs better than TSC scheme. To test the performance of networks, we used parameters shown in Table 4.1.

In our network simulation environment, the nodes are deployed in the area of 100×100 m². The number of deployed nodes in our network area is 108. The sectors are divided into 60° angle. The number of tracks is four. We assumed the initial energy of the nodes to be 0.24 J as per the conditions favorable to our software used for evaluation. We used the simulation time to 3000 rounds. Each round calculates the energy of the nodes and after completion the energy of the network is calculated.

TABLE 4.1 Variables used for Numerical Analysis and Network Simulation [10]

Type	Parameter	Value
Transmitter amplifier	$\varepsilon\,amp$	10j
Number of Nodes	N	108
Number of Tracks	NT	4
Number of Sectors	NS	6
Avg number of nodes in track	n'	6
Avg number of nodes in sector	n"	108/6
Avg number of relay nodes	Nr	3

To evaluate and compare the performance of existing and modified TSC scheme, we used three performance metrics—energy efficiency, network lifetime, and PDR.

The simulation results of energy efficiency that came from our evaluation have been proved better. The residual energy of our modified TSC scheme had shown better results than TSC scheme. The energy efficiency of modified TSC scheme is 10–15 J whereas in TSC scheme it is 20–25 J. The results are shown in Figure 4.5.

The second performance metric that we used to evaluate and compare performance of the existing and modified work is network lifetime. The presence of alive nodes shows the stability of the network. More the number of alive nodes available in the network, longer will be the lifetime of the network. Similarly, lesser the dead nodes more will be the stability of network. So, in our simulation results the alive nodes in our modified TSC scheme were 50–60 whereas in TSC scheme they were 10–20 only. The dead nodes in our modified TSC scheme were 50–60 whereas in existing work there were 80–90 dead nodes. The result of alive node count and dead node count is shown in Figures 4.6 and 4.7.

As discussed earlier that stability of the network is evaluated on the basis of the durability of node in network. If the node remains alive for longer time then the lifetime of the network will increase automatically. In this work we calculated the time when the first node as well as half nodes dies in both the networks. The expiry of first node and then half of the nodes is shown in Figures 4.8 and 4.9.

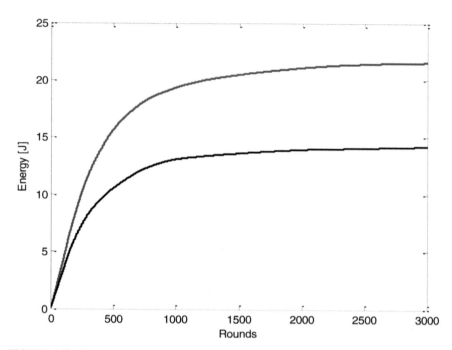

FIGURE 4.5 Energy consumption.

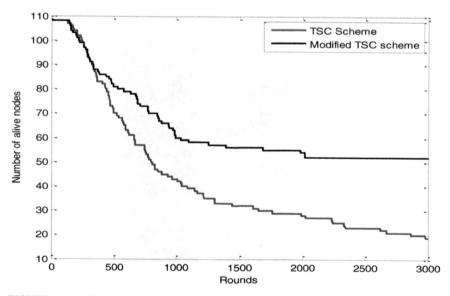

FIGURE 4.6 Alive nodes comparison.

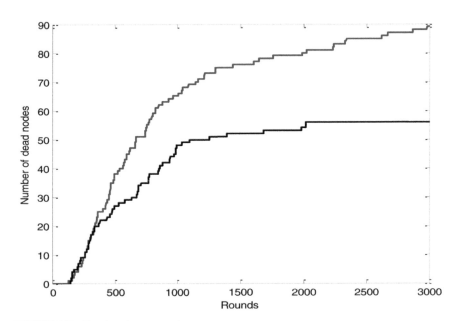

FIGURE 4.7 Dead nodes comparison.

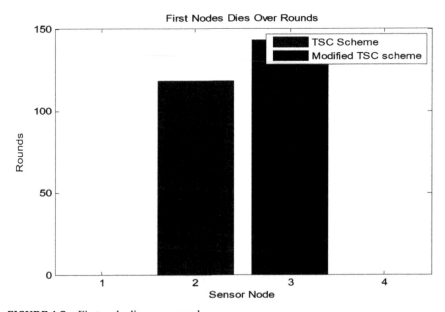

FIGURE 4.8 First node dies over round.

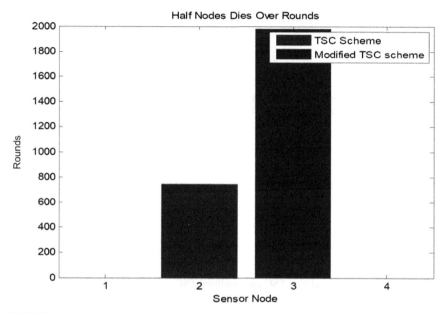

FIGURE 4.9   Half nodes dies over round

The first node in TSC network dies after 110 rounds while in modified TSC first node dies after 140 rounds. The half nodes in TSC die after 700 rounds while in modified TSC half nodes die after 1900 rounds. This has improved lifetime of our modified TSC scheme.

The PDR of existing work is 90% whereas modified TSC is 95%. The results of PDR have shown the better performance of modified TSC scheme. This result has proved that network quality of modified TSC is better than existing TSC scheme. The result comparison of energy efficiency of existing and modified TSC scheme is that our modified TSC scheme is 61%–62% efficient while existing TSC scheme is only 56% efficient. The efficiency comparison graph is shown in Figure 4.11.

4.4   CONCLUSION

In this chapter, we approached concentric clustering routing protocol technique for network setup. The selection of CH on the basis of weight value has improved the operations of CH in network. Insertion of relay nodes in our proposed work has improved the quality of network. Therefore results have proved that our proposed work is better than existing one.

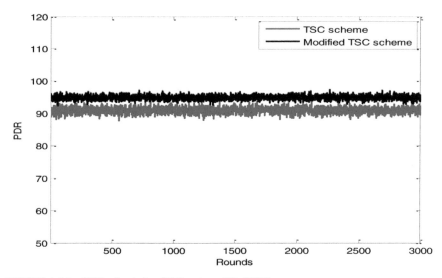

FIGURE 4.10   PDR of existing TSC and modified TSC.

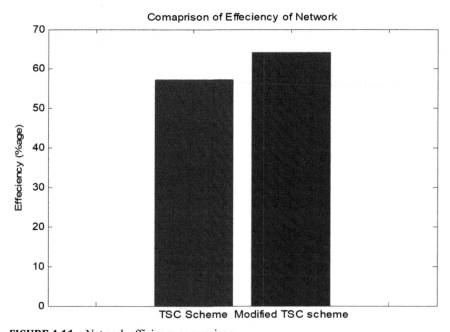

FIGURE 4.11   Network efficiency comparison.

KEYWORDS

- **cluster head**
- **packet delivery ratio**
- **relay nodes**
- **weight value**

REFERENCES

1. Zhang, Shiwei, Zhang, Haitao, "A Review of Wireless Sensor Networks and Its Applications," IEEE, August 2012.
2. Rabiyahanfi, Yogeshrai, "Wireless Sensor Network," IJECS, Vol. 05 Issue 1, pp. 15492–15496, January 2016.
3. Liu, Xuxun, "Atypical Hierarchical Routing Protocols for Wireless Sensor Networks: A Review," IEEE Sensors Journal, Vol. 15, pp. 5372–5383, October 2015.
4. Marhoon, Haydar Abdulameer, Mahmuddin, M., AwangNor, Shahrudin, "Chain-Based Routing Protocols in Wireless Sensor Networks: A Survey," ARPN Journal of Engineering and Applied Sciences, Vol. 10, 1389–1398, February 2015.
5. Jung, Sung-Min, Han, Young-Ju, Chung, Tai-Myoung, "The Concentric Clustering Scheme for Efficient Energy Consumption in the PEGASIS," ISBN February. 12-14, 2007 ICACT 2007.
6. Gupta, Chitiz, Jain, Rahul, Lohia, Ravi, Shankar, Ravi, Tapaswi, Shashikala, "Improved Concentric Clustering Routing Scheme Adapted to Various Environments of Sensor Networks," IEEE, Vol 2, pp. v2630–v2634, 2010.
7. Al-Karaki, J. N. and Kamal, A. E. "Routing Techniques in Wireless Sensor Networks: A Survey," IEEE Wireless Communications, Vol. 11, pp. 6–28, December 2004.
8. Seongsoolang, Kim, Ho-Yeon, Kim, Nam-Uk, Chung, Tai-Myoung, "Energy-Efficient Clustering Scheme with Concentric Hierarchy", IEEE, December 2011.
9. Vallimayil, A., Sarma Dhulipala, V.R., Raghunath, K., Chandrasekaran, R., "Role of Relay Node in Wireless Sensor Network: A Survey," IEEE 2011 3rd International Conference on Electronics Computer Technology.
10. Gautam, Navin, Lee, Won-Il, and Pyun, Jae-Young, "Track-Sector Clustering for Energy Efficient Routing in Wireless Sensor Networks," IEEE Ninth International Conference on Computer and Information Technology.
11. Lan, Shi, Qilong, Miao, Du, Jinglin, "Architecture of Wireless Sensor Networks for Environmental Monitoring," IEEE 2008 International Workshop on Education Technology and Training & 2008 International Workshop on Geoscience and Remote Sensing.
12. Guo, Wenjing, Zhang, Wei, Lu, Gang, "PEGASIS Protocol in Wireless Sensor Network"

13. Based on an Improved Ant Colony Algorithm, "Second International Workshop on Education Technology and Computer Science 2010."
14. Liang, Junbin, Wang, Jianxin, and Chen, Jianer, "A Delay-Constrained and Maximum Lifetime Data Gathering Algorithm for Wireless Sensor Networks," 2009 Fifth International Conference on Mobile Ad-hoc and Sensor Networks.
15. Sachi Nandan Mohanty, E.Laxmi Lydia, Mohamed Elhoseny, Majid M. Gethami AI Otabi, K.Shankar, Deep learning with LSTM based distributed data mining model for energy efficient wireless sensor networks, Physical Communication, vol.40, Issue-4, 101097-102008, (2020). https://doi.org/10.1016/j.phycom.2020.101097.

CHAPTER 5

A Comprehensive Survey of RFID-Based Localization Techniques for Wireless Networks

MANPREET KAUR and SUKHWINDER SINGH SRAN*

Department of Computer Engineering, Punjabi University, Patiala, Punjab, India

Corresponding author. E-mail: SUKHWINDER.SRAN@gmail.com

ABSTRACT

Radio frequency identification (RFID) is a popular wireless technology that uses radio waves to transmit and receive the data for providing automatic identification to various objects such as valuable things and human beings. It relies on RFID tags (transponders) that store a unique identification number and an RFID reader (interrogator) that sends interrogation signals to an RFID tag to be identified. Due to its low price and reliability of the reader, RFID technology is getting popularity nowadays. RFID has been widely used for various applications in manufacturing, warehousing, retailing, agriculture, and so forth for traceability, access control, and logistics from last two decades. An RFID-based system for the localization and tracking of missing objects or human beings who require special care like dementia's patients is the recent research area of IoT (Internet of things) based networks. In this chapter, a comprehensive survey of RFID-based localization techniques for wireless networks is investigated. Moreover, a comparative study of various algorithms along with their pros and cons is presented.

5.1 INTRODUCTION

Radio frequency identification (RFID) is a well-known technology for automatic identification of objects. It controls individual target by using computers or machines through radio waves [1]. Generally, an RFID system is made up of three components: tags (transmitters or transponders), readers (transmitters or receivers), and an antenna. The tag can be chip-based or chipless that stores unique identification information and it is attached to the object being identified. Based on the volatile or nonvolatile nature of information stored in tag, RFID tags can have two types: read-only tags and read/write tags. These tags have a predefined unique ID [4]. An antenna that is embedded with receivers or readers [2, 3] makes the communication possible between a tag and a reader. To read or write data from a tag, an antenna emits radio signals in a distance up to 100 feet or even more. This distance actually depends upon the radio frequency and the power output of the reader.

A reader is a fixed mounted or a handheld device that is mainly used for collecting data. When an RFID tag comes in the electromagnetic zone of an antenna, radio signals activate that tag. The reader decodes the encoded data of tag's integrated circuit and this decoded data can be transferred to any computer system for further processing [5]. The complete communication process of RFID-based system is shown in Figure 5.1.

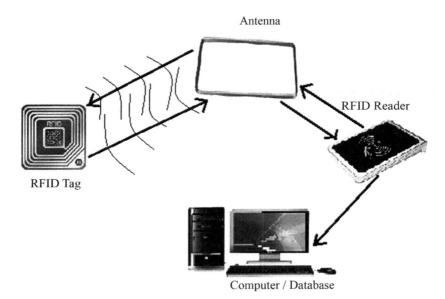

FIGURE 5.1   Communication in an RFID-based system.

Based on different frequencies range used for communication, RFID-based systems can be of three types: low frequency, high frequency, and ultrahigh frequency [6]. Every country and region has different range of frequencies for RFID-based applications which are given in Table 5.1. Low-frequency systems are used for short-distance transmission (approx. from few inches to six feet) and the frequency used for these systems is generally 125 kHz. High-frequency systems can transmit from few inches to several feet and the transmission frequency is typically 13.56 MHz. Finally, ultrahigh-frequency systems can communicate over more than 25 feet on 433 MHz frequency [7, 8].

TABLE 5.1 Country wise RFID based applications frequency range

Frequency Range / System Type	Country Names
125-134 kHz / LF	USA, Canada, Japan, Europe
13.56 MHz /HF	USA, Canada, Japan, Europe
433.05-434.79 MHz / UHF	In most of USA and Europe and under consideration in Japan
865-868 MHz / UHF	Europe
866-869 and 923-925 MHz / UHF	South Korea
902-928 MHz / UHF	USA
952-954 MHz / UHF	Japan (for passive tags after 2005)
2400-2500GHz and 5.725-5.875 GHz / Microwave Frequency	USA, Canada, Japan, Europe

Except these three main systems, microwave RFID systems can also be used which have range more than 30 feet and work on 2.45 GHz. As RFID-based systems have a wide range of applications including access control, inventory management, IT assets and tools tracking, library management, interactive marketing, and many more. But RFID-based localization of various objects and human beings who need special care like the dementia patients and the persons who are suffering from mental illness is one of the active research fields.

In a survey [9], it was observed that in developed countries like USA, Australia, Austria, and so forth, one in 10 persons of age 65 or more is suffering from dementia. Moreover, 60% of these patients are wandering, [10] and of those 60%, up to 50% who are not found in 24 h suffer from serious injuries or even death too. In such cases, RFID technology can be very beneficial to localize (track or detect) them easily.

In many applications like cyber physical systems, e-health [11–14], weather forecasting [15], environment monitoring [16], and office automation [17, 18], and so forth, localization is extensively used. These applications require location-based services [19] such as to monitor the health of any patient, to observe air quality, and so forth. Besides RFID technology, other technologies for the localization are: infrared, bluetooth, GPS (global positioning system), and so forth. GPS is a good solution for these types of localization problems but due to its high cost, poor performance inside the buildings, and high power consumption necessitated the use of other technologies better than this, for instance, RFID passive tags which have low cost and do not require any battery power. Due to these benefits, popularity of RFID-based localization is growing for a wide variety of applications.

There are several RFID-based techniques for localization in the existing literature. This chapter will provide a comprehensive survey of various RFID-based localization techniques. There can be a number of classifications based on different parameters such as type of area for localization (indoor and outdoor), which component is initiating the communication process (reader or tag), whether chip is present in the tag or not that is, being used in localization (chip-based and chipless RFID localization) [20] and so forth. The benefits and limitations of each technique will also be discussed.

The chapter is organized in the following systematic manner. Section 5.2 provides a brief history of RFID technology from its start and its progress till now. Section 5.3 explains the various types of RFID-based localization techniques, their advantages, and disadvantages. Finally, a conclusion of these techniques is presented in Section 5.4.

5.2   A BRIEF HISTORY OF RFID

RFID technology appeared first time in 1945, as a surveillance device for the Soviet Union. In the similar way, the identification friend or foe transponder was used to identify aircraft as friend or foe by the allies in World War II and this transponder was developed in United Kingdom [21]. In 1948, first research finding was given by Harry Stockman in his publication titled "Communication by Means of Reflected Power" [22]. Harrington investigated the electromagnetic theory with RFID in 1964 [23]. In 1960, two companies named Sensormatic and Checkpoint started the use of RFID. In a collaboration of these two companies with another company "Knogo" a new device named electronic article surveillance was developed to overlook the merchandise [24].

During 1973–1975, multinational companies, like RCA and Raytheon developed few electronic identification RFID-based systems. Various universities like Northwestern University, Los Alamos Scientific Laboratory as well as research laboratories, the Los Alamos Scientific Laboratory were actively engaged in the RFID research. In Norway, the first RFID-based commercial application was developed in 1987. Afterward, in 1989, the United States developed the first toll gate named "Dallas North." Various American states, for instance, Kansas and Georgia implemented RFID readers-based traffic management system in the 1990s. In 2001, very small-sized RFID tags were introduced and used in a wide variety of applications such as electronic tolling [24]. These tags were in the form of labels and attached with the objects which were going to be organized and managed.

From the last decade, use of RFID-based systems was started in medical care applications too. Various applications of RFID in medical are pharma-ceutical drugs, medical disposals and other items, sensor-based applications, real-time locating system, and so forth [25]. Moreover, a number of RFID security algorithms were developed to protect our valuable belongings. Nowadays, RFID-based systems are secure enough and hence RFID tags are being used for the localization of human beings too.

5.3 LOCALIZATION TECHNIQUES

Localization of various objects and human beings is an active area of research. A number of techniques are already developed for this purpose. For instance, for the outdoor localization, GPS is there but it requires a line of sight (LOS) with the satellites so it cannot be used for the indoor services. So to enhance the performance of localization, various other techniques are also developed for the same. These techniques further use various algorithms to perform the localization. Generally, localization techniques can be classified based on several parameters in three categories which are shown in Figure 5.2. The comparative study of these techniques along with advantages and disadvantages is presented in Tables 5.2–5.5.

5.3.1 PLACEMENT OF RFID READERS AND TAGS

RFID readers and tags can be placed on different places or objects. RFID tags are usually attached with those objects which are going to be tracked, but it is not mandatory that only RFID tags can be affixed with objects. Based on it that whether an RFID tag or a reader is with the object under tracking, RFID localization systems can be of two types [26]:

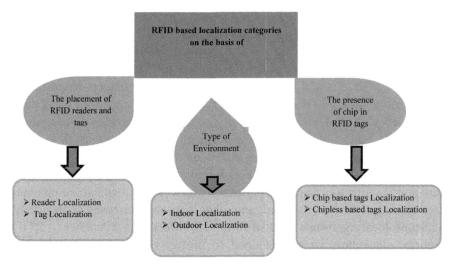

FIGURE 5.2 The RFID-based localization techniques.

5.3.1.1 READER LOCALIZATION

The reader is affixed with tracked entity and tags (active or passive) are present in the hidden area in reader localization. Generally, passive tags are deployed on the floor and active tags are on the ceiling. By using this technique, location of moving object and its displacement information can be recorded. In the literature, many algorithms are implemented based on reader localization. We illustrate the four major algorithms in Table 5.2 along with their pros and cons.

5.3.1.2 TAG LOCALIZATION

Due to low cost of RFID tags, this localization technique is mainly used for various applications. In tag localization, an RFID tag is attached with the object or human being that is to be localized. The application area of this type of localization is from tracking books in the library to locating the patients of various hospitals which especially deal with the patients of dementia and mental illness. The accuracy level of both tag-based localization and reader-based localization is the same. The algorithm based on tag localization can locate both moving and stationary objects. The performance of tag localization is comparatively less than the reader localization in case of moving entity.

TABLE 5.2 Comparative Study of RFID Reader Localization algorithms

System	Technique	Infrastructure	Accuracy/ Precision	Advantages	Disadvantages
Self-localization using SVM [27]	Support Vector Machine (SVM)	0.5x0.5 m²	80%	• Self-localization • No tag pattern required • Optimal number of tags • Propagation environment independent.	• A training set for SVM is required • Need of a reader with signal intensity output. • Lack of orientation information.
Lee & Lee [28]	Weighted average & Hough Transform	Tag interval 0.05m Speed:0.3m/s	0.026m	• Both positional and orientation • Reduce the errors due to the boundary tag of read range.	• Need of a large number of tags to improve the accuracy.
Triangular pattern for tag [29]	Tag arrangement & pre-estimation and compensate position	Tag interval 0.05m and next line shift by 0.025m Speed:0.25m/s	0.016m	• Provide both positional and orientation • It require less no of tags with the same frequency as Lee & Lee • Can obtain the orientation by 1 reader.	• More computation at the server.
Random Sampling Algorithm [30]	Bayesian inference	Tag interval 5m in 40x40 m² room.	1.5m	• Insensitive to NLOS • Fewer sample number.	• Depend on movement probabilistic model.

TABLE 5.3 Investigation of RFID tag localization algorithms

System	Technique	Infrastructure	Accuracy/Precision	Advantages	Disadvantages
SpotON [31]	Ad hoc lateration	cluster at least 3 tags	Depend on cluster size	• 3D localization • Low cost • No fixed infrastructure	• Attenuation less accurate than time of flight • No special tag required
LANDMARK C [32]	K nearest neighboring & weighting	4 readers per room, extra reference tags	50%, 1.09-18m.	• Use off the self-active tags • Accuracy with less reader and low cost.	• Dense configuration of reference tags • Need a reader with signal intensity output.
R-LIM [33]	Data filtering	Whole book shelf	N/A	• Suitable for very large coverage area.	• Reset reading counting • Need item location database to be updated regularly.
Tsai et al. [34]	Field generator graphic coloring theorem	Whole floor	N/A	• Large coverage	• Need field generator.
Jin et al. [35]	K nearest neighboring	4 readers per room, reference tags	N/A	• Use off the self-active tags • Accuracy & low cost. • Less computation	• Require the reader with signal intensity output
Alippi et al. [36]	Bayesian	5x4m² 4 readers	0.6m	• Passive tags, low cost • Insensitive to NLOS (No Line of Sight) signal.	• Depend on layout and the number of readers.

TABLE 5.4   RFID Indoor Localization algorithms and their pros and cons

Algorithm	Accuracy	Advantages	Disadvantages
CoO (cell of Origin) [38]	Medium	• Simple algorithms	• Discrete Positioning • Positioning Accuracy depends upon the size of cells, • A large number of sensors may be needed
Fingerprinting [39]	High	• Environmental effects considered in training phase • Continuous positioning.	• Inaccurate in a dynamic environment due to the RSS variations • Affected by the RSS directional patterns and the errors in the training phase.
Lateration [40]	Medium	• Continuous positioning, • No training phase required.	• Requires at least three receivers. • RSS based distance estimates contains large errors because of environmental effects.

TABLE 5.5 RFID Outdoor Localization algorithms and their pros and cons

System/Year	Accuracy	Advantages	Disadvantages
Scout [41], 2006	Medium	• Independent on other communicational technologies • Cost effective • Improves the higher values of reader density, window-size.	• Depends upon environmental effects • Average Error Distance should be less than 7m.
RFID outdoor locator [42], 2015	High	• Can use in disaster management • Can be used to prevent theft in a specific area.	• Did not apply it in real time systems • Hard to understand.
Localizing missing entities [43], 2018	High	• Less costly, • No special infrastructure and set up required. • No new installation • No extra power supply	• Requires a number of parked vehicles. • Can be performed at a static area.

Various algorithms are used for tag localization in the literature. The earliest location sensing algorithms were usually based on the signal strength analysis. Hightower et al. proposed an algorithm, known as SpotON [31] which uses clusters having at least three tags. A summary of tag localization algorithms which are widely used is provided in Table 5.3. A comparative study of these algorithms based on various parameters, advantages, disadvantages is presented in which technique and infrastructure used by these algorithms for localization, what is their accuracy, and precision level are also shown.

5.3.2   BASED ON THE TYPE OF ENVIRONMENT OF LOCALIZATION

RFID-based localization can be of two types based on the type of environment: indoor and outdoor. In indoor RFID localization, readers and tags are placed in a specific indoor area (a specific building) for the tracking of a particular thing or human being. Although in outdoor localization, the region of interest is generally an open area. Various schemes developed for indoor and outdoor localization are discussed below:

5.3.2.1   INDOOR LOCALIZATION

In this type of localization, RFID tags are attached with the entity or human being and readers are generally in stationary form. RFID-based indoor localization has become an important part of many applications like asset tracking, location-based network access, manufacturing, government, shopping, health care and tour guides, and so forth, but there is no fixed standard for this localization. Indoor localization schemes can be further subdivided as: active localization and passive localization. Moreover, among different methodological advances utilized in active indoor localization includes infrared, ultrasonic, bluetooth, RFID, and so forth. On the other hand, in passive indoor communication device-free passive [35], ultra-wideband, physical contact, and so forth, are used. Table 5.4 demonstrates RFID-based indoor algorithms which are highly used in various applications [37]. This table also shows some advantages and disadvantages of these algorithms.

5.3.2.2   OUTDOOR LOCALIZATION

Recently, outdoor localization techniques are based on GPS and other cellular communication methods. As this is the era of internet and new technologies such as RFID are developing every day. The traditional ways of communication cannot be coped up with the modern technology. For instance, the Internet of things (IoT) includes thousands of small devices which are connected with each other through the internet. So we cannot use GPS and other cellular technologies in case of IoT for localization as these technologies consume high power. There are many applications in which RFID is used for the outdoor environment and shows better performance than the existing non-RFID techniques.

Various RFID-based systems in which RFID is used for the outdoor environment are given in Table 5.5. In addition, with the innovations in cloud computing and IoT, use of RFID-based systems has increased rapidly. Scout [41] was the first RFID-based system used for the outdoor localization. The author claimed that the use of RFID technology in outdoor environment provides better accuracy at low cost. RFID outdoor locator and localizing the missing entities are the recent work published in the RFID-based outdoor localization.

5.3.3   BASED ON THE PRESENCE OF THE CHIP IN RFID TAGS

As discussed earlier, RFID tags store a unique information which is used to identify the object or human being. This information is generally stored on a chip inside the tag [2–5]. But in some RFID-based systems, tags do not have a chip and the information is stored through different ways. Based on the presence of chip inside of RFID tags, RFID localization systems can be of two types: chip-enabled and chipless. These both types are as follows:

5.3.3.1   CHIP-ENABLED RFID TAG LOCALIZATION

Most of the tags that are used in general applications are chip-enabled RFID tags. These tags consist of a microchip and an antenna for communication with the readers. These chip-enabled RFID tags are further subdivided into three types: active, semipassive, and passive RFID tags [44, 45]. The active RFID tags have their own battery as the power source, whereas passive tags do not have their own batteries and activated by the radio waves which are transmitted by the RFID readers. In semipassive RFID systems, a battery is available but communication is done by the RFID reader and sometimes use the concept of duty cycling as in [52, 53]. The chip-enabled RFID tags are expensive as compared to the chipless tags. Although the price of chip-enabled RFID tags are higher but these tags are more secure than the chipless tags.

5.3.3.2   CHIPLESS RFID TAGS LOCALIZATION

It is not a new concept because a device known as surface acoustic wave (SAW) has been utilized as a wireless passive sensor that operates on a time getting technique [46–49]. In this technique, sensed data is separated from the environmental reflection. Process of producing the SAW and to attach it with the antenna is very expensive as compared to the tags made from silicon. Another limitation of these SAW-based tags is their lossy nature. That is why SAW-based tags are not used in any practical application of RFID [50, 51]. But it provides the fundamental idea of chipless tags.

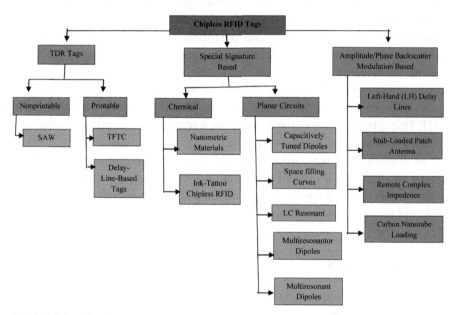

FIGURE 5.3   The chipless RFID tags types [51].

5.4   FINDINGS OF THE SURVEY

It has been observed in the survey that self-localization using SVM [27] has the highest accuracy rate and it does not require any specific tag pattern. In self-localization propagation, environment does not depend upon the reader's position in contrast to the Lee and Lee algorithm [28]. The random sampling algorithm [30] depends upon the movement probabilistic model so the reader can detect all the tags present in its vicinity easily. In case of tag localization, the algorithm proposed by Alippi et al. [36] provides best performance in terms of accuracy/precision by using four readers in an area of 5×4 m^2. The cost of tag localization is very low as it uses passive tags for the tracking purpose in comparison with the reader localization.

The major problem of using the algorithm proposed by Alippi et al. is that its performance depends upon the number of readers to be used and their deployment. Another algorithm named "SpotON" [31] does not use any fixed infrastructure as the number of tags can vary in a given cluster. R-LIM algorithm [33] is more suitable and provides better results when the coverage area of tracking is very large.

Cell of Origin [38] uses a large number of sensors for indoor localization and it is simple to use. The accuracy of this algorithm is comparatively low as it uses discrete positioning instead of continuous positioning. Fingerprinting algorithm [39] uses the continuous positioning to enhance the accuracy of indoor localizations. But due to RSS variations, it may produce inaccurate results in dynamic environment. In outdoor localization policy, missing entities using parked vehicles scheme is best among all other methods because there is no need to create any special infrastructure for localization [43]. This setup has low maintenance, but it requires any nearby parking area to use the network of parked vehicles.

In chip-enabled tags, information to provide a unique identity to each object is stored in a chip. These tags are expensive as compared to the chipless tags (printed tags). These both kinds of tags are extensively used for different modern applications.

5.5   CONCLUSION

This chapter provides a comprehensive review of various RFID-based localization techniques and the algorithms. The comparative study of these techniques and algorithms is also provided based on various parameters. Some alternatives of RFID-based localization are also discussed along with the reasons why RFID systems are better than other techniques. As in indoor areas, GPS is not a good solution because it requires LOS to the satellites. In addition to it, RFID tags perform much better in case of indoor tracking services. In order to improve the performance and quality, chipless tags are widely used. By utilizing a number of technologies, unique information stored in these tags provides identity to various objects and human beings. This information is highly useful to track missing objects.

KEYWORDS

- **localization**
- **passive RFID tags**
- **transponders**
- **readers**

REFERENCES

1. McCarthy, J. F., Nguyen, D. H., Rashid, A. M., and Soroczak, S., "Proactive display & the experience UbiComp project," *Adjunct Proceedings of the Fifth International Conference on Ubiquitous Computing (UbiComp 2003)*, 12–15 October 2003, Seattle, pp. 78–81.
2. Nath, B., Reynolds, F., and Want, R., "RFID technology and applications," IEEE Pervasive Computing, Vol. 1, pp. 22–24, 2006.
3. Jia, X. L., Feng, Q. Y., and Ma, C. Z., "An efficient anti-collision protocol for RFID tag identification," IEEE Communications Letters, Vol. 14, no. 11, pp. 1014–1016, 2010.
4. Smith, B., "An approach to graphs of linear forms (Unpublished work style)," unpublished.
5. Finkenzeller, K., "*RFID Handbook*," 2nd ed. New York: Wiley, 2003.
6. Kraiser, U. and Steinhagen, W., "A low-power transponder IC for high performance identification systems," IEEE Journal of Solid-State Circuits, Vol. 30, no. 3, pp. 306–310, Mar. 1995.
7. Preradovic, S., Karmakar, N., and Balbin, I., "RFID transponders," IEEE Microwave Magazine., Vol. 9, no. 5, pp. 90–103, Oct. 2008.
8. Kraiser, U. and Steinhagen, W., "A low-power transponder IC for high-performance identification systems," IEEE Journal of Solid-State Circuits, Vol. 30, no. 3, pp. 306–310, 1995.
9. Jalaly, I. and Robertson, I. D., "RF bar codes using multiple frequency bands," *Proceedings of IEEE MTT-S International Microwave Symposium Digest 2005*, Long Beach, pp. 4–7, June 2005.
10. Qiu, C., Kivipelto, M., and von Strauss, E. "Epidemiology of Alzheimer's disease: occurrence, determinants, and strategies towards intervention," Dialogues in Clinical Neuroscience, Vol. 11, no. 2, pp. 111–128, 2009.
11. Alzheimer's Association, 2018, "Alzheimer's disease facts and figures," Alzheimer's & Dementia, Vol. 14, no. 3, pp. 367–429, 2018.
12. Mangini, L. and Wick, J. Y., "Wandering: unearthing new tracking devices," The Consultant Pharmacist®, Vol. 32, no. 6, pp. 324–331, 2017.

13. Konstantas, D., The Mobihealth Project. IST Project, Technical Report, IST-20 01-360 06, European Commission: Deliverable 2.6, http://www.mobihealth.org, 2004.
14. Maurer, U., Rowe, A., Smailagic, A., and Siewiorek, D. P., "ewatch: a wearable sensorand notification platform," *International Workshop on Wearable and Implantable Body Sensor Networks*, 2006.
15. Kulkarniand, P., Öztürk, Y. "Requirements and design spaces of mobile medical care," ACM SIGMOBILE Mobile Computing and Communications Review, Vol. 11, no. 3, pp. 12–30, 2007.
16. Ramesh, M. V., "Wireless sensor network for disaster monitoring," Wireless Sensor Network, 2010, pp. 51–70.
17. Huang, G. T., "Casting the wireless sensor network technology review," 2003, [Online]. Available: http://www.technologyreview.com/Infotech/ 13235.
18. Lee, H., Wu, C., Aghajan, H., "Vision-based user-centric light control for smart environments," Pervasive Mobile Computing, Vol. 7, no. 2 pp. 223–240, 2011.
19. Bangali, J., Shaligram, A., "Energy efficient smart home based on wireless sensor network using lab view," American Journal of Engineering Research (AJER), Vol. 2, no. 12, pp. 409–413, 2013.
20. Wang, X., Liu, Y., Yang, Z., Lu, K., Luo, J., "Robust component-based localization in sparse networks," IEEE Transactions on Parallel and Distributed Systems, Vol. 25, no. 5, pp. 1317–1327, 2014.
21. Natarajan, S., "A 32 nm logic technology featuring 2nd-generation high-k + metal-gate transistors, enhanced channel strain and 0.171 μm^2 SRAM cell size in a 291Mb array," in *Proceedings of IEEE International Electron Devices Meeting 2008 (IEDM '08)*, San Francisco, pp. 1–3, Dec. 15–17, 2008.
22. Dittmer, K., "Blue force tracking—a subset of combat identification," Military Review, Sep/Oct 2004 <http://usacac.leavenworth.army.mil/CAC/milreview/download/English/SepOct04/ditt.pdf/
23. Stockman, H., "Communication by means of reflected power," in *Proceedings of the IRE*, pp. 1196–1204, October 1948.
24. Harrington, R. F., "Theory of loaded scatterers," in *Proceedings of the IEE*, Vol. 111, no. 4, pp. 617–623, 1964.
25. Landt, J., "The history of RFID," IEEE Potentials, Vol. 24, no. 4, pp. 8–11, 2005.
26. Song, J., Haas, C. T., Caldas, C., Ergen, E., and Akinci, B., "Automating the task of tracking the delivery and receipt of fabricated pipe spools in industrial projects," Elsevier: Automation in Construction, Vol. 2, pp. 166–177, March 2005.
27. Sanpechuda, T., and Kovavisaruch, L., "A review of RFID localization: Applications and techniques," *5th International Conference on Electrical Engineering/Electronics, Computer, Telecommunications and Information Technology, 2008, ECTI-CON 2008*, Vol. 2, pp. 769–772, IEEE, 2008.
28. Yamano, K., Tanaka, K., Hirayama, M., Kondo, E., Kimura, Y., and Matsumoto, M., "Self-localization of mobile robots with RFID system by using support vector machine," in *Proceedings of IEEE International Conference on Intelligent Robotics and System*, pp. 3756–3761, September 2004.
29. Lee, H. J. and Lee, M. C., "Localization of mobile robot based on radio frequency identification devices," in *SICE-ICASE, International Joint Conference,* pp. 5934–5939, October 2006.

30. Han, S. S., Lim, H. S., and Lee, J. M., "An efficient localization scheme for a differential-driving mobile robot based on RFID system," IEEE Transactions on Industrial Electronics, Vol. 54, pp. 3362–3369, December 2007.
31. Xu, B. and Gang, W., "Random sampling algorithm in RFID indoor location system," in *IEEE International Workshop on Electronic Design, Test and Applications (DELTA'06)*, 2006.
32. Hightower, J., Wantand, R., and Borriello, G., "SpotON: an indoor 3D location sensing technology based on RF signal strength," *Technical Report UW-CSE*, University of Washington, Department of Computer Science and Engineering, Seattle WA, 2000.
33. Ni, L. M., Liu, Y., Lau, Y. C., and Patil, A. P., "LANDMARC: indoor location sensing using active RFID," *IEEE International Conference on Pervasive Computing and Communication*, pp. 407–415, March 2003.
34. Choi, W. and Oh, D. I., "R-LIM: an Affordable Library Search System Based on RFID," *International Conference on Hybrid Information Technology*, 2006.
35. Tsei, M. H., Huang, C. L., Chung, P. C., Yang, Y. K., Hsu, Y. C., and S.L Hsiao, "A psychiatric patients tracking system," IEEE International Symposium on Circuits and Systems, pp 4050–4053, May 2006.
36. Jin, G. Y., Lu, X. Y., and Park, M. S., "An indoor localization mechanism using active RFID tag," *IEEE International Conference on Sensor Networks, (SUTC'06)*, 2006.
37. Alippi, C., Cogliati, D., and Vanini, G., "A statistic approach to localize passive RFIDs," *IEEE Int. Conf* ISCAS 2006.
38. Bai, Y. B., Wu, S., Wu, H. R., and Zhang, K., "Overview of RFID-based indoor positioning technology," in *GSR*, 2012.
39. Álvarez, C. N. and Cintas, C. C., "Accuracy evaluation of probabilistic location methods in UWB-RFID systems," Aalborg University 2010.
40. Koyuncu, H., and Yang, S. H., "A survey of indoor positioning and object locating systems," International Journal of Computer Science and Network Security, Vol. 10, pp. 121–128, 2010.
41. Kefalakis, N., Soldatos, J., Mertikas, E., and Prasad, N. R., "Generating business events in an RFID network," in *IEEE International Conference on Paper Presented to RFID-Technologies and Applications (RFID-TA), 2011*, 15–16, September 2011.
42. Montz, A. B., Mosberger, D., O'Mally, S. W., Peterson, L. L., and Proebsting, T. A., "Scout: a communications-oriented operating system," in *Proceedings Fifth Workshop on Hot Topics in Operating Systems, 1995, (HotOS-V)*, pp. 58–61, IEEE, 1995.
43. Lukas, V., Neruda, M., Skapa, J., Novotny, J., Bortel, R., and Korinek, T., "Design of RFID outdoor localization system: RFID locator for disaster management," in *5th International Conference on the Internet of Things (IOT), 2015*, pp. 4–11, IEEE, 2015.
44. Griggs, W. M., Verago, R., Naoum-Sawaya, J., Ordóñez-Hurtado, R. H., Gilmore, R., and Shorten, R. N., "Localizing missing entities using parked vehicles: an RFID-based system," IEEE Internet of Things Journal, Vol. 5, no. 5, pp. 4018–4030, 2018.
45. Konstantinos, D., Kumar, B., and Anumba, C., "Radio-frequency identification (RFID) applications: a brief introduction." Advanced Engineering Informatics, Vol. 21, no. 4, pp. 350–355, 2007.
46. Choudhury, T. J. S., Elkin, C., Devabhaktuni, V., Rawat, D. B., and Oluoch, J. "Advances on localization techniques for wireless sensor networks: a survey," Computer Networks, Vol. 110, pp. 284–305, 2016.

47. Harma, S., Plessky, V. P., Hartmann, C. S., and Steichen, W., "SAWRFID tag with reduced size," in *Proceedings of IEEE Ultrasonics Symposium 2006*, Vancouver, Canada, pp. 2389–2392, Oct. 2006.

48. Chen, Y. Y., Wu, T. T., and Chang, K. T., "A COM analysis of SAW tags operating at harmonic frequencies," in *Proceedings of IEEE Ultrasonics Symposium 2007*, New York, pp. 2347–2350, Oct. 2007.

49. Harma, S., Plessky, V. P., and Li, X., "Feasibility of ultra-wideband SAW tags," in *Proceedings of IEEE Ultrasonics Symposium 2008*, Beijing, China, pp. 1944–1947, November 2008.

50. Plessky, V. P., Kondratiev, S. N., Stierlin, R., and Nyffeler, F., "Sawtags: new ideas," in *Proceedings of IEEE Ultrasonics Symposium 1995*, Cannes, France, Vol. 1, pp. 117–120, Nov. 1995.

51. Han, T., Wang, W., Wu, H., and Shui, Y., "Reflection and scattering characteristics of reflectors in SAW tags," IEEE Transactions on Ultrasonics, Ferroelectrics and Frequency Control, Vol. 55, no. 6, pp. 1387–1390, June 2008.

52. Anee, R. E. A. and Karmakar, N. C., "Chipless RFID tag localization." IEEE Transactions on Microwave Theory and Techniques, Vol. 61, no. 11, pp. 4008–4017, 2013.

53. Sran, S. S., Singh, J., and Kaur, L., "Aggregation aware early event notification technique for delay sensitive applications in wireless sensor networks," International Journal of Sensor Networks, Vol. 28, no. 1, pp. 11–21, 2018.

54. Sran, S. S., Singh, J., and Kaur, L., "Structure free aggregation in duty cycle sensor networks for delay sensitive applications," IEEE Transactions on Green Communications and Networking, Vol. 2, no. 4, pp. 1140–1149, 2018.

CHAPTER 6

Mitigating collision in Multihop Wireless Networks – A Survey

R. RADHA[1], K. VINUTHNA REDDY[2], and K. KATHIRAVAN[3]

[1]*Associate Professor, School of Computer Science Engineering, Vellore Institute of Technology, Chennai.*

[2]*Department of Computer Science and Engineering, Koneru Lakshmaiah Education Foundation, Hyderabad, India*

[3]*Department of Computer Science and Engineering, Easwari Engineering College, Chennai, India*

ABSTRACT

The presence of hidden terminals and the broadcast nature of wireless transmission diminish the performance of upper-layer protocols to a great extent over multi-hop wireless networks. Instability in transmission control protocol (TCP) congestion control causes severe link-layer contentions heading to collision drops and rerouting. Numerous algorithms have been implemented at diverse layers of the TCP/IP protocol suite that openly or in an alternate way mitigate the collision drops through congestion and contention control. This chapter focuses on the overview of the specified proposals and their key ideas.

6.1 INTRODUCTION

Mobile ad hoc network (MANET) is pervasively conveyed in different situations wherein instantaneous connectivity becomes essential. It plays a vital role in emergency operations like flood relief activities, disastrous evacuation, and military correspondence. MANET can likewise be utilized for snappy correspondence among a gathering of individuals in a video meeting/conference or get-together introductions. Advances in wireless technology and consumer electronics have pushed the application of MANET outside the military domain. Multihop ad hoc networks are all around utilized in segments like vehicular ad hoc networks; wireless sensor networks, wireless mesh networks, and home networking [110]. Multihop ad hoc networks will be the key component in the fifth-generation wireless communications [1, 103–108].

6.2 MULTIHOP AD HOC NETWORKS

Ad hoc network is an assortment of dynamic, self-designed, and radio-equipped wireless nodes with no infrastructure. Source and destination nodes are placed at different locations from each other in multihop and ad hoc networks, which require each intermediate node to act as a router in receiving and sending the data toward the destination node. The shared and broadcast nature of wireless transmission imposes noteworthy issues in the design of higher layers [103–107].

Wireless node furnished with an omnidirectional antenna propagates the signal in all the possible directions. Signal proliferation has certain extents as rendered in Figure 6.1 [2,103–108]. At the point when a sender node 0 engenders a signal, the nodes which are in the transmission extend named as neighbors (hub 1) will have the option to receive and decode the signal effectively. Nodes that are in the detection or carrier sensing range are able to detect and differentiate the received signal from background noise but are unable to decode the signal in an effective manner due to the high error rate. Nodes in the impedance range (node 2) will be meddled by node 0's transmission and the signal will be received as background noise by them. As rendered in Figure 6.1, Node 3 is out of the signal propagation range of node 0, which implies that node 3 will not be interfered with by node 0 but by node 1.

In order to make the data transferred from node 0 to node 1 in an effective manner nodes situated in the transmission, detection, and interference ranges of node 0 and node 1 ought not to be engaged with the transmission. For the most part, the medium access control (MAC) convention running at every node is made liable for selective medium access to that node. IEEE 802.11 carrier sense multiple access with collision avoidance (CSMA/

CA) has been a predominant MAC protocol for multihop wireless ad hoc networks [107].

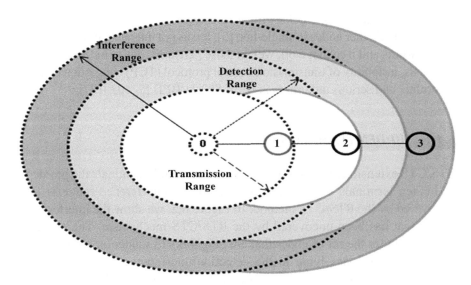

FIGURE 6.1   Signal propagation ranges for node 0 and node 1.

6.3   CA USING IEEE 802.11

IEEE 802.11 uses Binary Exponential back (BEB) off algorithm for CA. To minimize the collisions among hidden nodes (i.e., nodes which cannot directly hear each other but have the potential of interfering with each other), RTS/CTS extension was introduced in CSMA/CA. After waiting for DIFS plus random back off period, the node transmits a request to send (RTS) control packet to the receiver that includes the time duration required for data transmission. Neighbors of the sender overhear the RTS and set their network allocation vector (NAV) timer [107]. Receiver node responds with a clear to send (CTS) control packet if it senses the medium to be free. Receiver node too specifies the time duration for data reception in CTS packet. Neighbors of the receiver overhear CTS set their own NAV accordingly. The use of NAV empowers virtual carrier detecting and limits physical carrier detecting by making the node sleep for the indicated term thereby saving the power. Along these lines, RTS/CTS exchange maintains a strategic distance from superfluous crashes with hidden data and acknowledgement (ACK) transmissions follow RTS/CTS exchange [107].

6.4   PROBLEMS IN IEEE 802.11 OVER MULTIHOP AD HOC NETWORKS

IEEE 802.11 is a good technology for ad hoc networks where each node will be able to hear all other nodes in single-hop [5]. It was not intended for multihop ad hoc networks and it cannot work well in those networks, due to hidden/exposed terminals, instability of transmission control protocol (TCP) congestion control algorithm, and serious unfairness in IEEE 802.11 BEB [5, 103–107].

6.4.1   HIDDEN TERMINALS

RTS/CTS extension of IEEE 802.11 cannot completely eliminate the problem of hidden terminals [4]. A large portion of the interference range is left uncovered by the RTS/CTS method. In Figure 6.2, we show the interference region that has been uncovered by the RTS/CTS mechanism. The covered region includes the set of nodes that are neighbors to sender or/and receiver. The remaining nodes lying in the detection/interference range of sender/ receiver will not be able to decode the RTS/CTS messages thereby missing out on the opportunity of virtual carrier sensing. Physical carrier sensing at transmitters cannot help much in detecting unless a very large carrier sensing range is adopted [4, 103–107]. In this manner, the uncovered region leads to potential interference in multihop ad hoc networks.

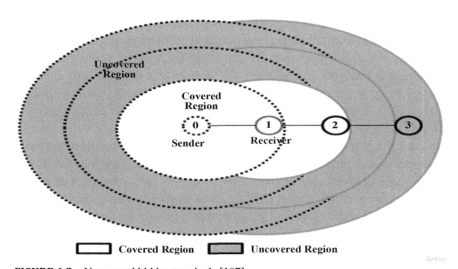

FIGURE 6.2   Uncovered hidden terminals [107].

6.4.2 INSTABILITY OF TCP CONGESTION CONTROL ALGORITHM

TCP is a predominant transport layer protocol for data transmission over the Internet. Hence, IEEE 802.11 MAC must support TCP as a transport layer protocol in multihop ad hoc networks [106, 107]. TCP being touted as the "protocol that saved the internet" due to its widely acclaimed congestion control algorithm has started choking with the advent of challenges faced in the decentralized multihop wireless ad hoc networks [106, 107].

TCP utilizes ACK timing component and is used to increase the congestion window size directly and may begin delivering a couple of packets together which starts overburdening of the system [7, 107]. TCP doesn't monitor the time at which the last packet was sent and whether the present arrangement of packets will prompt any impedance among them. Routing protocols like ad hoc on demand distance vector (AODV), DSR, and destination sequenced distance vector (DSDV) dole out a similar course to the back and forth ways of DATA-ACK packets related to a TCP connection. ACK that competes with the data packets for medium access in an inverted way further signifies the dispute levels [103–107]. Different TCP associations make the situation even terrible. The impact of overwhelming connection layer conflicts is delineated in Figure 6.3. It shows the effect at each layer which prompts a decrease in throughput [103–107].

This is a typical instance of a misinterpreted route failure that occurs many times during transmissions [6]. All this adds up to the cost of overheads and reduces the throughput undesirably. These types of MAC retry and retransmission occurs at many points all over the forward and reverse path while transmitting TCP-DATA and TCP-ACK packets. It also causes frequent timeouts followed by retransmissions at TCP source [8, 103–107]. Unnecessary retransmissions due to lost ACK will again lead to increased interferences.

IEEE 802.11 uses RTS/CTS system to hold the channel for information transmission. Increased contention leads to dispute prompts extreme impacts because of hidden terminals in the revealed area. At the point when the RTS retry check surpasses the breaking points, it drops the information parcel and reports connect inability to the system layer which superfluously starts the route discovery. This is a regular occasion of a misinterpreted route failure that happens numerous times during transmissions [6, 103–107]. This means the expense of overheads and decreases the throughput, unfortunately. These sorts of MAC retry and retransmission happens at numerous focuses everywhere throughout the forward and invert way while transmitting TCP-DATA

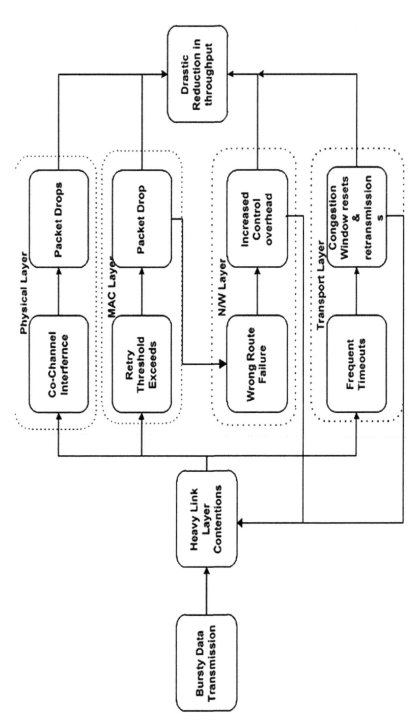

FIGURE 6.3   Effect of interference over multihop ad hoc network [107].

and TCP-ACK packets [103-107]. It likewise causes visit breaks followed by retransmissions at TCP source [8]. Superfluous retransmissions because of lost ACK will again prompt expanded obstructions [107].

Controlling the substantial disputes can limit the interference. Two kinds of interferences can be drawn from the TCP perspective: (1) interflow interference and (2) intraflow interference. Interflow interference happens between the nodes when they transmit packets having a place with adjoining or close by TCP streams. Whereas intrastream interference occurs between the packets of the same TCP connection. It is comprehended that the burst conveyance of window-based transmission of TCP isn't appropriate for ad hoc networks [4, 108]. Burst transmission of TCP prompts interference explicitly intraflow interference. Rate-based transmission at the transport layer spreads the traffic in uniform way with certain postponement between progressive packets. Throughput investigation of window-based and rate-based transmission demonstrates that rate-based transmission performs superior to anything window-based transmission [9, 107]. Being the controller of all the traffic, the transport layer can assume the liability of controlling the intraflow interference by utilizing rate-based transmission [103-107].

The next section highlights the research works implemented at various layers of TCP/IP protocol architecture to control collision drops and improve the performance of ad hoc networks. Transport layer proposals concentrate on controlling the congestion over end to end path thereby mitigating the contention. The proposals which have been implemented at the network layer strive to improve the routing instability caused by severe collisions. MAC layer strategies have the objective of controlling the contentions to improve the efficiency over ad hoc networks. These proposals are implemented either using layered architecture or using cross-layer design. We also outline the cross-layer approaches and the information used by them to implement cross-layer design [107].

IEEE 802.11 uses RTS/CTS component to save the channel for data transmission. Expanded contention prompts severe collisions because of hidden terminals in uncovered areas. RTS retry check surpasses the breaking point and drops the information packet and reports link failure to the network layer which pointlessly initiates the route discovery. This is an ordinary case of a misconstrued course disappointment that happens numerous multiple times during transmissions [6, 107]. This means the expense of overheads and diminishes the throughput, unfortunately. These sorts of MAC retry and retransmission happens at numerous focuses everywhere throughout the forward and invert way while transmitting TCP-DATA and TCP-ACK packets. It additionally causes frequent timeouts followed by retransmissions at TCP source [8, 107]. Unnecessary retransmissions because of lost ACK will again prompt expanded interferences [103–105].

Controlling the substantial disputes can limit the interference. Two kinds of interferences can be drawn from the TCP perspective: (1) interflow interference and (2) intraflow interference. Interflow interference happens between the nodes when they transmit bundles having a place with adjoining or close by TCP streams whereas intraflow interference occurs between the parcels of the same TCP association [103–107].

It is understood that the burst delivery of window-based transmission of TCP is not suitable for ad hoc networks [4, 107]. Burst transmission of TCP leads to interference specifically intraflow interference. Rate-based transmission at the transport layer spreads the traffic in uniform manner with a certain delay between successive packets. Throughput analysis of window-based and rate-based transmission proves that rate-based transmission performs better than window-based transmission [9, 109]. Being the controller of end-to-end traffic, the transport layer can take the responsibility of controlling the intraflow interference by using the rate-based transmission.

The next section highlights the research works implemented at various layers of TCP/IP protocol architecture to control collision drops and improve the performance of ad hoc networks. Transport layer proposals concentrate on controlling the congestion over the end-to-end path thereby mitigating the contention. The proposals which have been implemented at the network layer strive to improve the routing instability caused by severe collisions. MAC layer strategies have the objective of controlling the contentions to improve the efficiency over ad hoc networks. These proposals are implemented either using layered architecture or using cross-layer design. We also outline the cross-layer approaches and the information used by them to implement cross-layer design [103-107].

6.5   TRANSPORT LAYER PROPOSALS

Transport layer proposals try to improve the performance by controlling burst data transmission thereby alleviating the congestion over ad hoc networks or by balancing the contention between the data and ACK packets according to the network congestion. Toward these objectives, algorithms implemented at the transport layer are classified into two divisions, as shown in Figure 6.4 [103–107].

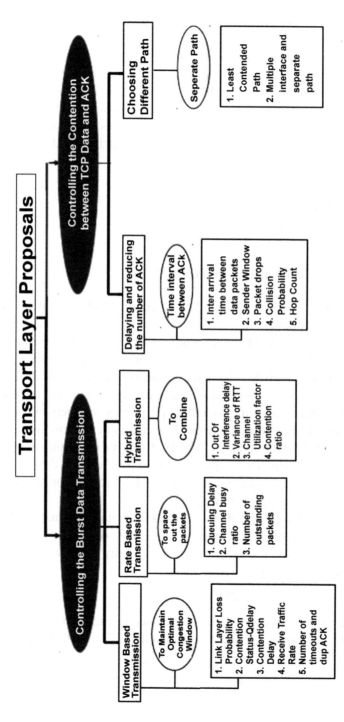

FIGURE 6.4 Classification of transport layer proposals [104].

6.5.1 CONGESTION CONTROL APPROACHES

To control the packet losses that occur due to heavy traffic, congestion control algorithms should ensure that the remaining data in the network pipe will not exceed the capacity of the entire network [11]. Bandwidth delay product (BDP) is used as the primary factor for measuring the capacity of the network pipe [12]. Congestion control algorithms are divided into three major types based on the method or mode in which they deliver out the packets [103–107]. They are as follows:

1. Window-based transmission
2. Rate-based transmission
3. Hybrid transmission.

6.5.1.1 WINDOW-BASED TRANSMISSION

TCP is the most widely used window-based protocol. TCP window size represents the maximum number of packets that could be sent without overloading the network. Many algorithms have been designed with the aim of tuning the TCP congestion window size over multihop networks.

IMPMHOP-CL analyzed the main reason for packet drops in multihop MANET and found that contention is the primary factor for most of the packet losses rather than buffer overflow [13]. For every network topology in a multihop ad hoc network, there exists an optimum window size in which TCP achieves the best throughput [107]. TCP does not maintain this optimum window size but increases it widely which results in reduced throughput and maximum losses. They maintain the optimal TCP congestion window size based on link-layer loss probability [103–107].

The authors showed that there is an upper bound on bandwidth delay product (BDP-UB) over multihop ad hoc network. They have derived BDP-UB in terms of hop count and round trip delay as shown in equations (6.1) and (6.2), respectively.

$$BDP\ UB = k \times N \qquad (6.1)$$

where k is a reduction factor due to interference in multihop ad hoc network whose value is $1/4 \leq k \leq 1/8$ and N is the number of round trip hops.

$$BDP - UB = \frac{\sum_{i=0}^{i=m} d_i + \sum_{j=0}^{j=n} d'_j}{4 \times d_{max}} \qquad (6.2)$$

where d_i and d_j are per-hop transmission delay along with the forward and reverse path, respectively, and d_{max} represents the maximum per-hop transmission delay in the round trip path. They dynamically updated congestion window size based on BDP-UB and achieved better throughput than TCP.

CWADAPT-CL proposed a solution that adapts the congestion window size based on the contention status received from the network [14, 107]. The contention round trip time (RTT) is measured using queuing delay from the intermediate nodes which is a metric for reflecting contention. Variance in contention RTT per hop is calculated and compared against a threshold to find the contention status [103–107]. This algorithm does not provide any guideline for fixing up the threshold.

The rate control algorithm (TRATE-CL) controls congestion window size by the factors, namely, channel utilization and contention ratio [15, 107]. These values are measured by intermediate nodes using its transmit/ receive time and waiting time [103–107].

Steady-state behavior of TCP throughput over multihop ad hoc networks based on well-known TCP friendly rate control (TFRC) equation and finds that TCP is aggressive over such networks [7, 103–107]. They propose a congestion preventive solution (CLTCP-CL) that fractionally increments the window size based on packet loss rate and then they provide a routing layer solution that suppresses the overreactions caused by TCP. They improve the overall TCP throughput results through simulations.

In [17], the authors proposed a slow congestion avoidance algorithm where the increase in congestion window size is <1 segment per RTT. It increases congestion window size by 1 after receiving many successive ACKs. Their aim is to inject less number of packets to avoid congestion.

In [18], CC-CL collected the bandwidth and delay information from the link-layer of every intermediate node in the forward and reverse path. They measure the BDP by multiplying the minimum bandwidth in the forward direction by round trip delay excluding queuing delay. They dynamically adjust the congestion window size to the calculated BDP.

Based on the observation that the throughput of user datagram protocol (UDP) is better than TCP with the exception of packet loss rate, the authors proposed an approach named application controlled transport protocol (ATP) [19, 97]. ATP can be assumed to be UDP with packet delivery status report or ACK. But, ACK is sent to the application layer which can decide whether to retransmit the packet or not. ATP reduces the number of retransmissions thereby reducing the congestion. But, it does not implement any new mechanism for congestion control.

A contention control approach (TCPCC-CL) was propounded wherein the TCP receiver monitors contention delay and achieved throughput periodically and is used to measure the traffic rate and feedback to the sender [20, 107]. Contention control algorithm running at the receiver also measures the sending rate to achieve maximum throughput and minimum contention [107].

WXCP-CL (wireless explicit congestion protocol) is the extension XCP and was developed for multihop ad hoc networks. WXCP adjusts its congestion window based on the aggregate feedback received from intermediate nodes [21, 105]. Aggregate feedback is a function calculated using local bandwidth, interface queue length, and the number of link-layer retransmissions. WXCP performs fairness and congestion control separately. It adapts pacing into rate-based ideas when the number of allowed sent-out packets exceeds the threshold.

A variant of TCP called intelligent TCP (iTCP) that uses neural networks to find out the congestion window size was proposed [22, 105]. iTCP applies the number of duplicate ACKs, number of consecutive timeouts, and current congestion window as inputs to a multilevel neural network that consists of three layers of neurons and obtains the next congestion window size as the output. Every neuron finds out the output using the weights of its inputs and the activation function which is then applied to the next layer. They do not take into account the RTT or its deviation into the algorithm. They show better throughput than TCP.

The sole purpose of the above-mentioned approaches is to strive for the control of the burst window size. They are not intended to spread the data uniformly so as to avoid the interference that may happen between its own packets.

6.5.1.2   RATE-BASED TRANSMISSION

Throughput analysis of window-based and rate-based transmission proves that throughput of rate-based protocols is inversely proportional to the square root of the propagation delay of the link whereas throughput of window-based transmission is inversely proportional to propagation delay [9, 97]. It reveals that rate-based protocols perform better than window-based protocols over high delay links. Moreover, rate-based algorithms ensure that the packets are delivered and spread uniformly over the network [23, 105].

TCP friendly rate control (TFRC-CL) is the rate-based protocol developed for the wired network [24]. Equation-based congestion control of TFRC uses TCP response function to measure steady sending rate in response to loss events [25, 104]. They intend to halve the sending rate in response to a successive loss of packets in an RTT. Loss events are calculated by the destination and are fed through the ACK. However, TFRC does not perform well in a multihop ad hoc network due to MAC layer contentions. TFRC overloads the network that leads to inaccurate RTT calculation, increased loss rate, and reduction in throughput [26, 107]. ETFRC-CL enhanced the rate estimation algorithm of TFRC by introducing a model for RTT in terms of MAC layer back off delay and service delay. They showed substantial throughput improvement over TFRC.

In EXACT-CL, every intermediate node keeps a dedicated state variable for each flow running through it [27, 107]. The intermediate node measures the bandwidth that can be shared with each flow. An explicit minimum data rate is inserted into the packets traveling through the intermediate nodes. Based on the received bottleneck data rate, the sender can decide whether or not to increase the rate. The limitation of EXACT is that every node has to maintain a separate state variable for each flow running through it. The authors proposed a well-known rate-based protocol called ATP-CL [28, 97] for ad hoc networks. It transmits the data packets at a specific interval. The time interval between the packets is found by collecting cross-layer feedback from the intermediate nodes. Every node in the end-to-end path should maintain average queuing delay and average transmission delay. It then stamps these current delays in the incoming packet if the stamped delay in the packet is smaller than the current delay. The destination node copies this delay information into the ACK forwarded to the source. The source node finds out the exponential average of received delay and adapts to the new rate. ATP protocol spreads the traffic uniformly but it does not consider the spatial reuse of the multihop network.

A rate-based congestion control algorithm was proposed using fuzzy logic (FARCC-CL) [29]. Fuzzy logic algorithm running at the destination calculates congestion level as the fuzzy output (low, medium, and high) based on the inputs collected from intermediate nodes through data packet. The input parameters are maximum queuing delay, channel busy ratio from intermediate nodes, and current input rate from the source node. The congestion level is fed to the source node through ACK. The source node finds out the new rate by performing multiplicative increase or additive increase or multiplicative decrease according to the congestion level (low, medium, high) [97].

Mostly, the rate-based algorithms are intended to spread the traffic uniformly based on the congestion/contention status of the network. A rate control algorithm that considers the spatial reuse of the multihop network and the dynamic out of interference delay that reflects the interference happening between the packets in order to calculate the interpacket delay among the successive packets was proposed [30, 105].

6.5.1.3   HYBRID TRANSMISSION

Hybrid transmission combines window-based and rate-based transmissions. It maintains the congestion window size to decide the maximum number of outstanding packets in the network pipe but it follows rate-based transmission to schedule packet transmission. In [31], the authors proposed a rate-based end-to-end congestion control algorithm (RBCC-CL). It adds a sublayer below TCP that acts as a leaky bucket for controlling the data delivery rate. The channel busyness ratio collected from the intermediate nodes reflects the congestion status and network utilization and this ratio plays a major role in controlling the data rate. Through extensive simulations, they prove that RBCC outperforms TCP in terms of channel utilization, delay, and fairness.

Authors found a hybrid approach that performs adaptive pacing to control congestion over multihop wireless ad hoc networks [32, 107]. Updating the congestion window size is similar to TCP. But, the time interval between successive packets is calculated using out of interference delay and variance of recently measured RTTs. This algorithm uses end to end approach and does not receive any cross-layer feedback. Out of interference delay is assumed to be four hop propagation delay and it is calculated using RTT. However, this algorithm assumes that the queuing delay is the same for both forward and reverse paths and it works on the upper bound of TCP congestion window size [107].

6.5.2   CONTENTION CONTROL BETWEEN DATA AND ACK

Reliability at the transport layer is achieved with the overhead of ACK packets. Every TCP data packet receives an ACK from TCP destination. ACK is transmitted like a data packet in the reverse path. It also needs to compete for medium access for every hop. This contention leads to interference losses. Many transport layer algorithms have been developed to control the contention among data and ACK packets by delaying ACK.

Delaying ACK improves the TCP performance over multihop ad hoc network. As per RFC1122, a delayed ACK can be sent for every two packets ($d = 2$). In [33], authors dynamically increase d from 1 to 4 according to the sequence numbers. Delaying ACK is initiated after the slow start phase. They show that delayed ACK works better when the window size becomes larger. They set three different increasing thresholds on sequence numbers. When the sequence number of the packet reaches each threshold, they increase the value of d by 1. They achieved a better result. However, they tested the algorithm on a single flow [107].

The authors changed the number of packets d for delayed ACK from 1 to 20, and they proved that a large value of d is beneficial for short-range network and not for the long-range network [34].

Delaying the ACK during the slow start phase deteriorates the TCP performance. They propose a mechanism that speeds up the data rate during a slow start and the receiver delays ACK after the slow start is over. However, the scheme requires signaling from sender to receiver to intimate about completion of slow start [35].

Delaying the ACK based on packet loss event is done by TCP-DAA [36]. The delay window limit is £4. Whenever there is no packet loss, they start increasing the delay window. They decrease the value of d to 2 during out of order packet delivery.

Authors dynamically selected delay window size based on the hop count of the end to end path (TCPDEL-CL) [37]. They argue that there exists an optimal delay window that achieves the best throughput ACK- delay timeout period is used to delay the ACK [38]. ACK is sent out only when a timeout occurs. TCP sender adds an additional field called congestion window size to every packet. When the number of unacknowledged packets exceeds the congestion window size before the occurrence of delay timeout, the receiver delivers out the ACK without waiting for a timeout. This method achieves a larger delay window size and improves the throughput significantly.

In TCP-MDA-CL, Armaghani et al. [39] use the collision probability collected from the intermediate nodes over the forward path to decide the number of packets for delaying ACK. The collision probability is calculated by the MAC layer at every intermediate and stamped through the data packet to the TCP receiver. Whenever the channel condition is bad, that is, when the collision probability exceeds a threshold, the receiver generates more ACKs to avoid unnecessary retransmissions at the source due to a timeout event. If the channel condition is good, it increases the delay window up to 4. TCP-MDA outperforms CP-DDA. It works well over a static multihop network. The performance has to be tested on mobility.

In TCP-ADW-CL, the receiver adjusts the delay window dynamically based on learning the network condition [40]. The input parameters are sender congestion window size, interarrival time between the packets, path length, and packet loss event. At every instant, delay window increases or decreases based on these input parameters. Extensive simulations prove that TCP-ADW outperforms TCP in terms of throughput.

The above methods of delaying ACK can reduce the contention between data and ACK significantly. However, delayed ACK leads to incorrect calculation of RTT that will degrade the function of TCP and its enhancements over multihop ad hoc networks.

6.6   NETWORK LAYER PROPOSALS

Many research works are carried out to address the problem of rerouting. Network layer proposals are classified into two types based on their goals, as shown in Figure 6.5. They are as follows:

1. To build routing table based on congestion in the network—congestion aware routing.
2. To use alternate path on route failure—multipath routing.
3. To choose multiple parallel paths to mitigate contention—path diversification.

6.6.1   CONGESTION AWARE ROUTING

Congestion-aware routing protocols construct and maintain the route based on the congestion status of the network which will improve the TCP performance significantly over multihop ad hoc networks.

Dynamic load aware routing protocol (DLAR-CL) selects the route based on the load of the nodes in the network [41]. During route discovery, every node appends its interface queue length along with the route request (RREQ) packet. Upon receiving RREQ from multiple paths, the destination node is responsible for selecting the route based on the load of the path. The intermediate nodes piggyback its interface queue length along with every data packet. During heavy load, the destination node looks for an alternate path by route rediscovery.

Congestion aware distance vector routing (CADV-CL) considers the hop count as well as the average delay for selecting the next-hop node [42]. Average delay is calculated using the waiting time of packets transmitted over a short period of time. CADR improves the packet delivery ratio over AODV.

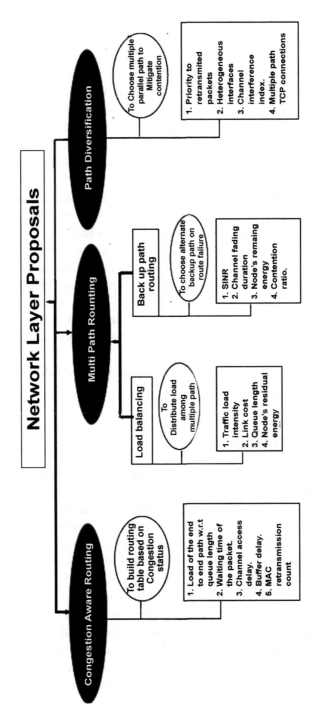

FIGURE 6.5 Classification of network layer proposals.

Congestion aware routing protocol (CARP-CL) mitigates congestion by constructing the routes based on data rate, channel access delay, and buffer delay and retransmission count of the intermediate nodes [43]. CARP introduces a metric weighted channel delay (WCD) that is expressed in terms of channel access delay, buffer delay, and retransmission count. WCD is calculated by every node at the MAC layer. They also employ a route effective data rate category scheme that selects a data rate from multiple heterogeneous data rates of the path considering channel access delay. CARP mitigates congestion over multirate multihop ad hoc networks.

The authors proposed a congestion adaptive routing (CRP-CL) that minimizes the congestion while constructing the route and adapts to it when it occurs during transmission [44]. When there is a tendency of congestion, every congested node (red node) has to warn its previous-hop node to bypass the next green node. The green node is the node without congestion. Congestion status can be measured using any of the following say the average queue length, the percentage of all packets discarded for lack of buffer space, the average packet delay, the number of packets timed out and retransmitted, and the standard deviation of packet delay. Congestion probability is used to select the next bypass node.

Mostly the congestion aware routing protocols do not address the effect of interference due to hidden terminals.

6.6.2   MULTIPATH ROUTING

Multipath routing protocols build up numerous ways between a source and destination. The setup ways can be hub disjoint or interface disjoint. Node disjoint ways don't share any nodes practically aside from the source and goal and have no links in common. Whereas disjoint paths have no links in common; however, they may have common nodes among them. Multiple paths can accomplish load adjusting by disseminating the information packets over various disjoint paths. In [45], the authors use load balancing to surpass congestion in addition to frequent link failures. Traffic among multiple paths are dependent on the load condition of the system (NMLBR-CL) [46]. Venkatasubramanian et al. [47] performed load adjusting and give QOS support. Load balanced congestion adaptive routing (LBCAR-CL) proposes multiway steering that decides different ways dependent on traffic load force and connection cost [48]. Traffic load force is determined at each hub dependent on its line length over an inspecting period. Connection cost is estimated utilizing the hub's vitality and lingering vitality. LBCAR discovers the way with the least traffic load force and most extreme lifetime.

Nonetheless, these conventions experience the ill effects of out of request conveyance of TCP bundles at TCP goal which is misconstrued as clog misfortune by TCP source that prompts decreased throughput [49].

Among the different ways, numerous conventions utilize one way as essential and staying as optional (reinforcement ways). The reinforcement ways are helpful when essential way comes up short. These conventions give better adaptation to noncritical failure by performing quicker and productive recuperation from course disappointment. Mahesh et al. [50] proposed a convention that finds accessible connection disjoint circle freeways among source and goal. In MPSINR-CL, Jiwon et al. [51] discovered the numerous ways dependent on SINR during course revelation. In CAR-CL, Xiaoqin et al. [52] discovered the following jump dependent on divert blurring term in. In DREAOMDV-CL, Tekaya et al. find the ways dependent on most extreme nodal remaining vitality [53, 54] discovered courses dependent on the congestion information.

Authors analyzed the performance of TCP over multipath routing and specify that usage of multiple parallel paths may actually degrade the TCP performance comparing backup path routing due to the out of order delivery of TCP packets and inaccurate calculation of RTT [55]. They have proposed two methods for selecting the paths. In the first method, the minimum hop path is chosen to be primary and minimum delay path is secondary. In the second approach, minimum delay path is selected as primary and maximum disjoint path with respect to primary path has been chosen as secondary. Through extensive simulations, they proved that back up routing improves the performance of TCP over multihop ad hoc network.

Authors estimate the available bandwidth of the path and perform load balancing [56]. They apprehend and avoid intraflow and interflow interferences using factors like link quality, link availability, and loss rate. They demonstrate the ability to choose routes with high throughput and limited delay.

Many multipath routing protocols are compared and specified that long TCP connection gets benefited from multipath routing to a certain extent while short TCP connections suffer from performance degradation [57]. They also proved that spatial reuse of multiple paths for simultaneous transmission is very limited.

6.6.3   PATH DIVERSIFICATION

In COPAS-CL, path asymmetry is used to avoid contention between data and ACK [58]. They use disjoint forward and reverse path for transmitting DATA and ACK packets, respectively. They employ a contention balancing algorithm that measures the MAC layer contention to dynamically change the forward and reverse path. They achieved good performance in terms of throughput and routing overhead.

A smart traffic split scheme called multipath retransmission is used to avoid contention between the data packets and retransmitted data packets by transmitting them through different paths [59]. Retransmitted packets are given priority and passed via the least contended path. This method eliminates the out-of-order delivery issue.

In REMW-CL, the authors proposed a scheme that embeds two heterogeneous interfaces in each node [60]. Primary interface runs IEEE 802.11a, reactive routing protocol DSR, and secondary interface runs IEEE 802.11b, proactive routing protocol DSDV. During the normal condition, TCP data packets are transmitted through the primary path that has a high data rate and TCP-ACK packets are sent through secondary interface. During route failure, data packets follow the secondary path through secondary interface until the failed route recovers. The limitation of this scheme is that every node has to equip with two interfaces, which is not cost-effective. [61] Proposed a similar scheme J-CAR-CL that uses multiple interfaces on each node. One of the interface acts as a control interface and others are used for transmitting data. It dynamically selects the least interfered path for data transmission based on the channel interference index.

The authors proposed an approach where a single TCP connection is divided into multiple TCP flows [62]. Multipath routing assigns a path to every flow individually. It makes a simultaneous transmission of data in all the paths. Packet reordering is done at the TCP destination. It eliminates TCP degradation due to out of order delivery. However, it increases the overhead and processing delay.

Even though path diversification enables simultaneous transmission through multiple paths between the source and destination, it leads to the problem of route coupling, that is, it causes interference between the simultaneous paths. Even node disjoint paths are not sufficient to eliminate route coupling instead zone disjoint paths can be effective. Two paths are said to be zone disjoint if the transmission in one path does not interfere with the other path. When the nodes are embedded with Omni antenna, it is difficult to have zone disjoint paths in a multihop ad hoc network [63]

6.7   MAC LAYER PROPOSALS

MAC layer has the responsibility of controlling or scheduling the medium access to the competing nodes without any collision among them. It is a challenging task in multihop ad hoc networks due to the distributive nature of nodes and broadcast property of wireless transmission. IEEE 802.11 has been widely used as a MAC protocol for multihop ad hoc networks. But it does not perform well over multihop network as discussed above. Several proposals have addressed those issues. In this section, we are going to study the research articles addressing the problem of contention control. We classify MAC layer approaches based on the following objectives, as shown in Figure 6.6.

1.   Enhancing the back off algorithm for contention control.
2.   Assigning multiple channels to reduce contention.
3.   To reduce the number of transmissions to mitigate contention through network coding.

6.7.1   ENHANCING THE BACK OFF ALGORITHM

Random BEB algorithm of IEEE 802.11 failed to improve the throughput over heavily congested multihop ad hoc networks. Many algorithms have been developed to tune the contention window (CW) according to the congestion status. The algorithms proposed in the literature can be put under two categories based on the way of devising input information. They are overhearing-based and nonoverhearing-based solutions.

Irregular BEB calculation of IEEE 802.11 was neglected to improve the throughput over vigorously clogged multibounce impromptu systems. Numerous calculations have been created to tune the conflict window (CW) as indicated by the clog status. The calculations proposed in the writing can be put under two classifications dependent on the method for formulating input data. They are catching-based and noncatching-based arrangements.

6.7.1.1   OVERHEARING-BASED SOLUTIONS

Overhearing-based solutions generally gather input information, like data rate, channel utilization and buffer status, and so on, from neighbors and adjust to the new CW as indicated by some approach. Overhearing by a node specifies that the packet is intended for some other node; however,

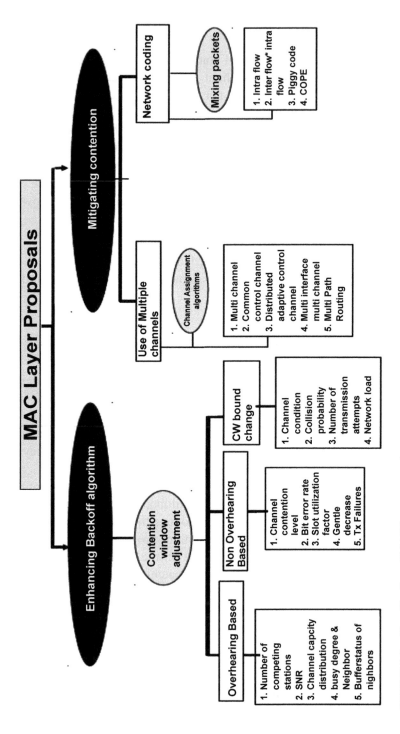

FIGURE 6.6   Classification of MAC layer proposals.

the node is in the transmission wrath of the sender and can interpret the parcel effectively.

P-tenacious MAC directs that a node to detect the medium and access it with the likelihood of P [64]. The authors determined a scientific model to discover the ideal P-value that arrives at the hypothetical throughput limit for P-constant IEEE 802.11 convention. To carry out this, every node has to know the number of stations in the system and it relies upon criticism data from neighbors. In view of P, they logically infer the normal dispute window size that accomplishes hypothetical throughput limit. They likewise demonstrate that improving the back off calculation can accomplish the hypothetical throughput farthest point of IEEE 802.11.

6.7.1.2 NONOVERHEARING-BASED SOLUTIONS

Nonoverhearing put together arrangements don't depend with respect to neighbors. Rather, they utilize their very own nearby data to quantify the channel dispute and improve the back off calculation. It enormously diminishes the overhead. Be that as it may, the accuracy of the nearby data about the channel which is being impacted by neighbors ought to be carefully assessed.

Authors utilize direct programming calculation to upgrade the base conflict window size that is dependent on the channel condition and number of contending stations [65]. They pick the access mode and CWmin with an explanatory way to optimize the throughput. They rely upon arrange input to gather the channel condition status. Virtual back off calculation (VBA) was created utilizing sequencing procedure to decrease the quantity of collisions and improving the throughput [66]. Be that as it may, VBA functions admirably just in relentless state where the quantity of nodes is fixed. VBA experiences impacts in a unique situation.

Asymptotically optimal back off algorithm powerfully adjusts the back off window size to the channel conflict level and accomplishes ideal channel use [67]. Channel contention level is estimated by every hub utilizing its own opening usage and normal size of the transmitted casings. Opening usage is characterized as the proportion of number of occupied spaces to the quantity of accessible spaces. Every hub ascertains the likelihood of transmission utilizing its space usage factor and number of endeavors made to transmit the present frame.

Back off window is powerfully balanced dependent on channel conflict status and bit error rate [68]. Channel conflict status is powerfully refreshed for each hub dependent on number of transmission disappointments out of the quantity of endeavors. They estimate the quantity of dynamic stations and conflict window utilizing transmission likelihood and bit blunder rate. They determine a systematic model to examine the hypothetical throughput breaking point of p-relentless CSMA.

CW size is logically inferred dependent on opening use and improved the throughput in both saturated and nonsaturated conditions [69]. It uses just nearby data like occupied openings and free spaces and doesn't require assessing the quantity of dynamic stations. Authors propose an algorithm GDCF wherein they perform delicate decline of dispute window to lessen impact probability [70]. They don't reset the conflict window size after each effective transmission. Rather, they find ideal counter c and the dispute window is divided after c back-to-back effective transmission. This technique decreases the impact when the quantity of nodes is huge. Hubs need to know the quantity of nodes in the system to discover the ideal estimation of c. Authors improve both decency and throughput utilizing this algorithm.

A control theoretic methodology is confined to tune CW dependent on the locally accessible data [71]. By looking at the normal number of continuous idle slots between two transmissions against the ideal set point, this strategy tunes CW and accomplishes ideal throughput and reasonableness. This strategy utilizes nearby data; however, it additionally relies upon the quantity of dynamic stations.

Authors accomplish decency and weighted reasonableness among nodes utilizing proposed increment with the synchronized multiplicative decline that supports background transmission [72]. Channel limit is distributed among contending nodes through overhearing [73, 107]. This aids in improving the decency among nodes. MadMAC convention accomplishes both decency and throughput utilizing restricted neighborhood data like number of experienced collisions and carrier sensing data [74]. Authors utilize fuzzy logic to tune the conflict window dependent on the fuzzy parameters, for example, occupied level of the medium and number of neighbor hubs [75, 107]. This methodology diminishes collisions probability and improves throughput and furthermore decency. Improved back off calculation (SBA) utilizes just neighborhood data like an achievement, impact probability to tune CW [76, 107]. There are just two potential sizes for CW called CWmin (31) and CWmax (1023). CW is doled out to CWmin and CWmax during light load and overwhelming burden, individually. Creators guarantee to improve decency and throughput. In any case, this calculation builds the deferral because of the huge CW.

6.7.1.3   CW BOUND ADJUSTMENT

All of the above algorithms concentrate on tuning CW according to the congestion level of the medium and they finally select the back off interval randomly between [0, CW].

In [77], authors change the lower bound and upper bound of the back off interval based on the number of one-hop neighbors and number of transmission attempts. They prove that their algorithm reduces the number of collisions. In [78], the authors enabled the nodes to change the upper and lower bounds based on the current network load and history. In [79, 107], authors introduce different subranges for back off interval with respect to different network contention levels. Although these methods change their lower and upper bounds, the final selection is done randomly within the new bound.

The entirety of the above calculations focus on tuning conflict window as indicated by the blockage level of the medium and they at long last select the back off interim arbitrarily between [0,CW]. In [77], creators change the lower bound and upper bound of the back off interim dependent on the quantity of one jump neighbors and number of transmission endeavors. They demonstrate that their calculation lessens the quantity of crashes. In [78], creators empower the hubs to change the upper and lower limits dependent on the present system load and previous history. In [79], creators present distinctive subranges for back off interim as for various system conflict levels. Despite the fact that these strategies change their lower and upper limits, last determination is done arbitrarily inside the new bound.

6.7.2   MULTICHANNEL ASSIGNMENT

Unlicensed ISM band of IEEE 802.11a and IEEE 802.11b supports 12 and 3 nonoverlapping channels, respectively [80]. Allowing nodes to use multiple nonoverlapping channels facilitates concurrent transmissions and also mitigates congestion thereby improving the overall throughput of the network. Substantial research has been done on designing multichannel MAC protocols. The protocols are classified into single rendezvous (SR-MCMAC) and multirendezvous multichannel MAC (MR-MCMAC). In SR-MCMAC, handshake between a transmitter–receiver pair happens through only one channel at a time whereas handshake between different transmitter–receiver pairs in MR-MCMAC happens through multiple channels at a time.

Designing a multichannel, MAC is a highly challenging task than single-channel MAC due to channel allocation to the distributive nodes and missing receiver problems [81, 103–105].

A kind of the SR-MCMAC protocols [83, 84] use the common hopping pattern and hop between channels. They are called common hopping protocols. All nodes in the network follow the common hopping sequence at a regular time interval. When two nodes want to communicate with each other, they will retain the current channel and other nodes jump to the next channel in the sequence. After transmission, the two nodes will join the other nodes in hopping. Here all channels are used for data transmission. However, accurate global clock synchronization is required among the nodes and this type of MCMAC does not address the problem of a missing receiver where the sender node transmits the packet to the receiver without knowing its busy status [82, 103–107].

Another set of SR-MCMAC protocols [85–89, 103–107] called dedicated control channel SR-MCMAC uses a dedicated channel for transmitting control information and all other channels for data. The control channel is used as the default channel. When a node wants to transmit, it should send a request message to the receiver through control channel. Upon receiving the reply, both the nodes switch to the accepted channel for data transmission and then return back to the control channel. However, congestion on the control channel becomes the overhead [82-89].

A channel usage list is maintained by every node to select the free channel for sender and receiver [87]. In this approach, exposed nodes will not be able to maintain the updated channel list which leads to multichannel exposed node problem [86–89]. It reduces this problem by making the nodes to reserve the channel in advance and then compete for channel access.

The third set of SR-MCMAC protocols [90, 91] divides the time into a sequence of control and data time slots. During control time slots, the nodes compete on the primary channel to reserve the channel. During the data time slot, the node that has won the medium switches to the corresponding channel. In MR-MCMAC, SSCH has many hopping sequences as there are many rendezvous and multiple channels [92]. Each node will follow many sequences where each sequence is uniquely identified by the seed of a random number generator. When a node wants to transmit to a receiver, it has to wait until the receiver is on the same channel. If the sender frequently talks with the receiver, it can follow one or more sequences of the receiver. In McMAC, every node uses its seed to generate a unique sequence [93, 107]. Every node sends its seed along with its packet. Every other node hearing the packet can learn the sender sequence to communicate with it. MR-MCMAC reduces the congestion that happens in the common channel of SR-MCMAC.

6.7.3   NETWORK CODING APPROACHES

Various research works have been carried out with regard to TCP performance in a wireless scenario. At the same time, a lot of interest has been shown in the field of network coding which has stemmed out of the field of information coding theory. It was the seminal paperwork by [94, 103] which brought light to the concept of network coding. The following section summarizes the numerous network coding schemes, the impact of intraflow contention, and why it needs to be addressed.

The authors proposed the network coding technique that acted like the traditional routing approach by making the intermediate network nodes combine the received incoming packets and create a new packet [95]. This leads to substantial reduction in the number of transmissions across the medium.

In I2MIX-CL, Chuan et al. [96] have given us a first-of-a-kind proposal to integrate both inter- and intra-flow wireless network coding. The special thing about this work is that the packets belonging to the same flow, that is, intraflow as well as the packets belonging to a different flow, that is, interflow, are involved in the network coding process to reduce the number of transmissions. However, this work when reproduced in a TCP environment has major fallbacks with a very high control overhead.

Combo-coding is a recent technique [97] that is rooted in the concept of pipeline coding [98], wherein a coded packet is constituted by a linear combination of multiple packets and encoding and decoding happen progressively. This is in sharp contrast to batch coding, where the destination either decodes all of the data packets in a batch or none of them. Combo-coding as the name suggests is a combination of interflow and intraflow network coding that was developed to address both random loss and interference problems. Combo-coding is done at the network layer and is transparent to the other layers of the protocol stack. In addition, combo-coding makes the use of a timer to encode packets. Data packets are made to wait for a suitable ACK packet to be EXOR-ed with, till the timer expires. Combo-coding also partially backs up on PiggyCoding [10] technique to reduce the interference between DATA-ACK belonging to the same TCP flow. Hence, Combo-coding is another example of clubbing the intraflow and interflow coding.

The essential thought of PiggyCode is like COPE [99] (which will be portrayed later in this segment), in that the two plans entrepreneurially code bundles together. "PiggyCode" has its root from the term piggybacking where the TCP-ACK parcels are sent alongside TCP-DATA bundles. PiggyCode is structured explicitly here for a unique sort of bidirectional traffic. It is realized that in remote multibounce situations, the TCP-DATA stream and ACK stream may make an obstruction with one another, which diminishes throughput. The principal objective of PiggyCode is to improve TCP execution by entrepreneurially XORing TCP-DATA and ACK parcels in middle of the road hubs. After accepting a TCP-ACK, the halfway hub checks its MAC layer support for a TCP-DATA parcel. On the off chance that such a bundle exists, the MAC layer plays out an XOR of the two parcels with extra proper ID and transmits this recently made "PiggyCoded" parcel; generally, the ACK is conveyed without encoding. To oblige this procedure, all parcels are cradled before being conveyed. After getting a PiggyCoded bundle, the two recipients play out another XOR activity with the cradled parcels to recoup the first bundles.

The primary advantage of PiggyCode is that it requires no TCP change. The significant test here is that a PiggyCoded parcel is theoretically a "dual-cast" packet in the connection layer, which means there are two planned collectors that ought to get the parcel effectively. Because of the absence of double ACK support in 802.11, PiggyCode throughput gain is seen to be constrained. Likewise, PiggyCoding requires the middle nodes to keep up a MAC level cushion of unbounded limit, all together that packets are decoded effectively, which ends up being an extra overhead as far as memory necessities.

COPE proposed by [99] is a network coding approach to bridge theory and practice, remarkably the first of its kind. COPE has been incorporated into the network coding stack and deployed on a 20-node wireless environment. COPE inserts a coding layer in between the IP layer and MAC layer which opportunistically EXORS multiple packets together and forwards them in a single transmission.

A characteristic feature of COPE design is opportunistic listening. This technique enables nodes to exploit the intrinsic broadcast nature of the wireless medium to overhear packets destined for other nodes. COPE sets the nodes in promiscuous mode, makes them snoop on all communications over the wireless medium, and store the overheard packets for a limited time period. Additionally, nodes periodically exchange reception reports to announce to the neighbors what packets have been stored.

On the flip side though, COPE's nodes need to store the overheard packets for future decoding thereby making the storage requirement higher. Opportunistic listening also increases nodes' power consumption.

MORE is another practical test-bed implementation of a network coding technique, which relieves the nodes from the coordination effort in order to perform encoding and decoding of packets [100]. This work proposes a new opportunistic routing protocol that avoids node coordination. Routers code packets going to the same destination and forward the coded versions. The destination decodes and deciphers the original packets.

There are a few works that induce changes in the TCP layer with the idea of going for a network coding scheme. Sundararajan et al. [101] have proposed one such mechanism that involves changes in the TCP stack with the objective of congestion control in the network and better throughput. Their work allows the source to transmit a linear combination of all packets in the congestion window. They employ network coding only at the end-hosts and define a new kind of interpretation of ACKs. The receiver acknowledges every new unit of information, that is, the degree of freedom rather than the original packets. The potential of encoding packets even in the relay nodes has not been unleashed, which could further improve the performance of network coding. Moreover, the overheads are quite noticeable with respect to the choice of a large field size for random linear coding involved.

6.8   CROSS-LAYER APPROACHES

Broadcast nature of the wireless networks imposes greater challenges to the design of protocols for such networks. The traditional approach of strict layering with the OSI model may not be optimal [8]. In order to optimize the performance, it becomes necessary to utilize the information available across the layers of the network nodes.

Vivek et al. [102] observing the loss of TCP throughput stability suggested that "TCP should be modified for use in wireless networks, and that a cross-layer redesign of wireless TCP and MAC is needed to explicitly account for the effects of the wireless nature of interference." Many TCP improvement algorithms make use of cross-layer information and enhance the performance. In the literature, many cross-layer algorithms have been implemented. Moreover, most of the algorithms discussed in the previous section make use of cross-layer design. We classified the cross-layer algorithms in

Table 6.1 based on the layer at which it is implemented and the layer from which it received cross-layer feedback.

TABLE 6.1   Cross-layer Approaches

Implemented	Approach	Cross-layer Information	Cross-layer Feedback
Transport layer	IMPMHOP-CL	Link layer loss probability	MAC
	CWADAPT-CL	Contention RTT, queuing delay	MAC
	TRATE-CL	Channel utilization, contention ratio	MAC
	CLTCP-CL	Packet loss rate	MAC
	CC-CL	Min bandwidth	Physical
	TCPCC-CL	Contention delay	MAC
	WXCP-CL	Local rate, queue length, link layer retransmissions	MAC, link
	ETFRC-CL	MAC layer back off delay and service delay	MAC
	EXACT-CL	Explicit minimum data rate	MAC
	ATP-CL	Average queuing delay and average transmission delay	MAC
	FARCC-CL	Maximum queuing delay, channel busy ratio	MAC
	RBCC-CL	Channel busyness ratio	MAC
	tcpdel-cl	Hop count	N/W
	TCP-MDA-CL	Collision probability	MAC
	TCP-ADW-CL	Path length	N/W
Network layer	DLAR-CL	Queue length	Link layer
	CADV-CL	Waiting time	MAC
	CARP-CL	Data rate, channel access delay, buffer delay, and retransmission count of the intermediate nodes	MAC
	CRP-CL	Average queue length, the percentage of all packets discarded for lack of buffer space, the average packet delay, the number of packets timed out and retransmitted, and the standard deviation of packet delay	MAC

TABLE 6.1 *(Continued)*

Implemented	Approach	Cross-layer Information	Cross-layer Feedback
	LBCAR-CL	Traffic load intensity and link cost, queue length and node's energy, and residual energy	Physical & MAC
	NMLBR-CL	Load state	MAC
	MPSINR-CL	SINR	Physical
	CAR-CL	Fading duration	Physical
	DREAOMDV-CL	Maximum nodal remaining energy	MAC
	COPAS-CL	Contention	MAC
	REMW-CL	Data rate	MAC
	JCAR-CL	Channel interference index	MAC

6.9 CONCLUSION

CA over multihop ad hoc networks is still an open research problem. Numerous transport layer algorithms have been proposed to control the congestion thereby collision. Contention and collision control from the MAC layer has also been the active area of research. However, CA has not been well studied from the view of the transport layer and can be used in the future work.

KEYWORDS

- **collision**
- **multihop**
- **broadcast**
- **ad hoc network**

REFERENCES

1. Osseiran, A., Boccardi, F., Braun, V., Kusume, K., Marsch, P., Maternia, M., Queseth, O., Schellmann, M., Schotten, H., Taoka, H., Tullberg, H., Uusitalo, A. M., Timus, B., Fallgren, M., 2014, Scenarios for 5G mobile and wireless communications: the vision of the METIS project. IEEE Communications Magazine, 52(5): 26–35.
2. Schiller, H. J., 2000, Mobile Communications, Addison-Wesley: Boston, MA, USA.
3. Johnson, B. D., Maltz, A. D., Hu, C. Y., 2003, The dynamic source routing protocol for mobile ad hoc networks (DSR), IETF Draft, work in progress.
4. Kaixin, X., Gerla, M., Bae, S., 2002, How effective is the IEEE 802.11 RTS/CTS handshake in ad hoc networks. IEEE Global Telecommunications Conference, 72–76.
5. Basagni, S., Conti, M., Giordano, S., Stojmenovic, I., 2004, IEEE 802.11 AD HOC networks: protocols, performance, and open issues. Mobile Ad Hoc Networking, Wiley-IEEE Press, Hoboken, NJ, USA, 69–116.
6. Ng, C. P., Liew, C. S., 2004, Re-routing Instability in IEEE 802.11 multi-hop ad-hoc networks. 29th Annual IEEE International Conference on Local Computer Networks, IEEE Computer Society, Washington, DC, 602–609.
7. Nahm, K., Helmy, A., Kuo, C.-J. C., 2008, Cross-layer interaction of TCP and ad hoc routing protocols in multihop IEEE 802.11 Networks, IEEE Transactions on Mobile Computing, 7(4): 458–469.
8. Gavin, H., Nitin, V., 1999, Analysis of TCP performance over mobile ad hoc networks, ACM/IEEE International Conference on Mobile Computing and Networking, 219–230.

9. Özgür A. B., 2004, On the throughput analysis of rate-based and window-based congestion control schemes. The International Journal of Computer and Telecommunications Networking, 44(5): 701–711.

10. Scalia, L., Soldo, F., Gerla, M., 2007, PiggyCode: a MAC layer network coding scheme to improve TCP performance over wireless networks, IEEE Global Telecommunications Conference, Washington, DC.

11. Chen, K., Xue, Y., Shah, S., Nahrstedt, K., 2004, Understanding bandwidth-delay product in mobile ad hoc networks. Computer Communications, 27: 923–934.

12. Peterson, L. L., Davie, S. B., 2000, Computer Networks. Morgan Kaufmann: San Francisco, CA.

13. Fu, Z., Zerfos, P., Luo, H., Lu, S., Zhang, L., Gerla, M., 2003, The impact of multi hop wireless channel on TCP throughput and loss. Twenty-second Annual Joint Conference of the IEEE Computer and Communications Societies, 1744–1753.

14. Xin, Z. M., Wen, Z. B., Na, L. N., Dan, S. K., 2010, TCP congestion window adaptation through contention detection in ad hoc networks. IEEE Transactions on Vehicular Technology, 59(9): 4578–4588.

15. Xinming, Z., Nana, L., Wenbo, Z., Dan, S., 2009, TCP transmission rate control mechanism based on channel utilization and contention ratio in Ad hoc networks. IEEE Communications Letters, 13(4): 280–282.

16. Nahm, K., Helmy, A., Kuo, C., 2008, Cross-layer interaction of TCP and ad hoc routing protocols in multihop IEEE 802.11 networks. IEEE Transactions on Mobile Computing, 7(4): 458–469.

17. Papanastasiou, S., Ould-Khaoua, M., 2004, TCP congestion window evolution and spatial reuse in MANETs. Journal of Wireless Communications and Mobile Computing, 4(6): 669–682.

18. Kliazovich, D., Granelli, F., 2006, Cross-layer congestion control in ad hoc wireless networks. Ad Hoc Networks, 1(4): 687–708.

19. Liu, J., Singh, S., 1999, ATP: application controlled transport protocol for mobile ad hoc networks. IEEE Wireless Communications and Networking Conference, 3: 1318–1322.

20. Ehsan, H., Veselin, R., 2007, TCP contention control: a cross layer approach to improve TCP performance in multihop ad hoc networks. 5th International Conference on Wired/Wireless Internet Communications, Springer-Verlag, Berlin, 1–16.

21. Yang, S., Thomas, G., 2005, WXCP: explicit congestion control for wireless multi-hop networks, Thomas Gross Quality of Service—International Workshop on Quality of Service, Lecture Notes in Computer Science, 3552: 313–326.

22. Alim Al Islam, B. A., Raghunathan, V., 2015, iTCP: an intelligent TCP with neural network based end-to-end congestion control for ad-hoc multi-hop wireless mesh networks. Wireless Networks, 21(2): 581–610.

23. Lochert, C., Scheuermann, B., Mauve, M., 2007, A survey on congestion control for mobile ad hoc networks. Wireless Communications and Mobile Computing, 7: 655–676.

24. Sally, F., Mark, H., Jitendra, P., Jorg, W., 2000, Equation-based congestion control for unicast applications. ACM SIGCOMM Conference, Stockholm, 43–56.

25. Padhye, J., Firoiu, V., Towsley, D., Kurose, J., 1998, Modeling TCP throughput: a simple model and its empirical validation. SIGCOMM Symposium on Communications Architectures and Protocols.

26. Mingzhe, L., Choong-Soo, L., Emmanuel, A., Mark, C., Robert, K., 2004, Performance enhancement of TFRC in wireless ad hoc networks, 10th International Conference on Distributed Multimedia Systems (DMS) Hotel Sofitel, San Francisco, CA, 8–10.

27. Chen, K., Nahrstedt, K., Vaidya, N., 2004, The utility of explicit rate-based flow control in mobile ad hoc networks, IEEE Wireless Communications and Networking Conference, 3: 1921–1926.
28. Sundaresan, K., Anantharaman, V., Hung-Yun, H., Sivakumar, R. A., 2005, ATP: a reliable transport protocol for ad hoc networks, IEEE Transactions on Mobile Computing, 4: 588–603.
29. Hamideh, Z., Fazlollah, A., Vali, D., 2013, A rate based congestion control mechanism using fuzzy controller in MANETs. International Journal of Computers, Communications & Control, 8(3): 486–491.
30. Radha, N., Kathiravan, K., 2016, Mitigating intra flow interference over multi hop wireless ad hoc networks. Journal of Information Science and Engineering, 32: 763–781.
31. Liu, J., Singh, S., 1999, ATP: application controlled transport protocol for mobile ad hoc networks. IEEE Wireless Communications and Networking Conference, 3: 1318–1322.
32. ElRakabawy, M. S., Lindemann, C., 2011, A practical adaptive pacing scheme for TCP in multihop wireless networks. IEEE/ACM Transactions on Networking, 19: 975–988.
33. Altman, E., Jiménez, T., 2003, Novel delayed ack techniques for improving TCP performance in multihop wireless networks. Personal Wireless Communications Theory, 237–250.
34. Johnson, R. S., 1995, Increasing TCP throughput by using an extended acknowledgment interval. Master's Thesis, Ohio University, Athens, OH.
35. Allman, M., 1998, On the generation and use of TCP acknowledgments, SIGCOMM Computer Communication Review, 28: 4–21.
36. Oliveira, R., Braun, T., 2005, A dynamic adaptive acknowledgment strategy for TCP over multihop wireless networks. IEEE Computer and Communications Societies, 3: 1863–1874.
37. Chen, J., Gerla, M., Lee, Y., Sanadidi, M., 2008, TCP with delayed ack for wireless networks. Ad Hoc Networks, 6(7): 1098–1116.
38. Al-Jubari, M. A., Othman, M., Ali, M. B., Hamid, N. A. W. A., 2013, An adaptive delayed acknowledgment strategy to improve TCP performance in multi-hop wireless networks. Wireless Personal Communications, 69(1): 307–333.
39. Armaghani, R. F., Jamuar, S. S., Khatun, S., Rasid, M. F. A., 2008, An adaptive TCP delayed acknowledgment strategy in interaction with MAC layer over multi-hop ad hoc networks. IEEE Computer Society, Washington, DC, 137–142.
40. Al-Jubari, M. A., Othman, M., 2010, A new delayed ACK strategy for TCP in multi-hop wireless networks. International Symposium, 2(15-17): 946–951.
41. Lee, J. S., Gerla, M., 2001, Dynamic load-aware routing in ad-hoc networks. IEEE International Conference on Communications, 3206–3210.
42. Lu, Y., Wang, W., Zhong, W., Bhargava, W., 2003, Study of distance vector routing protocols for mobile ad-hoc networks. IEEE International Conference Pervasive Computing and Communications, 187–194.
43. Xiaoqin, C., Jones, M. H., Jayalath, A. D. S., 2005, Congestion-aware routing protocol for mobile ad hoc networks. IEEE 66th Conference on Vehicle Technology, 21–25.
44. Raghavendra, H., Tran, A. D., 2006, Congestion adaptive routing in ad hoc networks. IEEE Transactions on Parallel and Distributed Systems, 17(11).
45. Murakami, T., Sasase, I., Bandai, M., 2005, SMR-LB: split multi-path routing protocol with load balancing policy to improve TCP performance in mobile ad hoc networks. International Symposium on Personal, Indoor and Mobile Radio Communications, 3(14): 1424–1428.

46. Lu, X., Xu, C., Wu, M., Zhen, Y., Wu, D., 2009, Design and realization of a novel multi-path load-balancing routing protocol in ad hoc network. International Conference on Information Engineering, 247–250.

47. Venkatasubramanian, S., Gopalan, P. N., 2009, A QoS-based robust multipath routing protocol for mobile ad hoc networks. International Conference on Internet, 1–7.

48. Jung-Yoon, K., Geetam, T. S., Laxmi, S., Sarita, B. S., Won-Hyoung, L., 2014, Load balanced congestion adaptive routing for mobile ad hoc networks, International Journal of Distributed Sensor Networks, 2014(10): 532043.

49. Gavin, H., Nitin, V., 2002, Analysis of TCP performance over mobile ad hoc networks. Kluwer Academic Publishers Wireless Networks, 8: 275–288.

50. Mahesh, M. K., Samir, D. R., 2006, Ad hoc on-demand multipath distance vector routing. Wireless Communications & Mobile Computing, 6(7): 969–988.

51. Jiwon, P., Sangman, M., Ilyong, C., 2008, A multipath AODV routing protocol in mobile ad hoc networks with SINR-based route selection. IEEE International Symposium on Wireless Communication Systems, 682–686.

52. Xiaoqin, C., Haley, J. M., Dhammika, J., 2011, Channel-aware routing in MANETs with route handoff. IEEE Transactions on Mobile Computing, 10(1): 108–121.

53. Tekaya, M., Tabbane, N., Tabbane, S., 2011, DRE-AOMDV: delay remaining energy for AOMDV protocol. International Conference on Wireless Communications, Networking and Mobile Computing, 23–25.

54. Wannawilai, P., Sathitwiriyawong, C., 2010, AOMDV with sufficient bandwidth aware. International Conference on Computer and Information Technology, 305–312.

55. Haejung, L., Kaixin, X., Gerla, M., 2003, TCP Performance over multipath routing in mobile ad hoc networks. IEEE International Conference on Communications, 2: 1064–1068.

56. Chiraz, H., Hanen, I., Adrien, V. D. B., Leila, S. A., Thierry, V., 2017, Inter-flow and intra-flow interference mitigation routing in wireless mesh networks. Computer Networks, 120:141–156,

57. Krishnamurthy, V. S., Tripathi, K. S., 2004, Effects of multipath routing on TCP performance in ad hoc networks. Global Telecommunications Conference, 60: 4125–4131.

58. Carlos, D. M. C., Samir, D. R., Dharma A. P., 2002, COPAS: dynamic contention-balancing to enhance the performance of TCP over multi-hop wireless networks. 10th International Conference on Computer Communications and Networks, 382–387.

59. Xiaoyuan, G., Jiangchuan, L., Shiguo, L., 2011, Real-time video streaming over multipath in multi-hop wireless networks. Multimedia System, 17(4): 287–297.

60. Yoon, W., Vaidya, N., 2010, Routing exploiting multiple heterogeneous wireless interfaces: a TCP performance study, Computer Communications, 33(1): 23–34 .

61. Hon, C. S., Yeung, L. K., King-Shan, L., 2009, J-CAR: an efficient joint channel assignment and routing protocol for IEEE 802.11-based multi-channel multi interface mobile Ad Hoc networks. IEEE Transactions on Wireless Communications, 8: 1706–1715.

62. Nagaraja, T., Anand, K., Ravi, P., 2006, TCP-M: multiflow transmission control protocol for ad hoc networks. EURASIP Journal on Wireless Communications and Networking, 1–16.

63. Siuli, R., Somprakash, B., Tetsuro, U., Kazuo, H., 2002, Multipath routing in ad hoc wireless networks with omni directional and directional antenna: a comparative study. Distributed Computing of the series Lecture Notes in Computer Science, 2571: 184–191.

64. Cali, F., Conti, M., Gregori, E., 2000, Dynamic tuning of the IEEE 802.11 protocol to achieve a theoretical throughput limit. IEEE/ACM Trans. on Networking, 8(6):785–799.

65. Chang, Y. S., Wu, C. H., 2009, Novel adaptive DCF protocol using the computationally-efficient optimization with the feedback network information for wireless local-area networks. IEEE Transactions on Wireless Communications, 8(6): 2827–2830.

66. Krishna, V. P., Misra, S., Obaidat, S. M., Saritha, V., 2010, Virtual backoff algorithm: an enhancement to 802.11 medium-access control to improve the performance of wireless networks. IEEE Transactions on Vehicular Technology, 59(3): 1068–1075.

67. Gregori, E., 2000, Design and performance evaluation of an asymptotically optimal backoff algorithm for IEEE 802.11 Wireless LANs. Proceedings of the 33rd Annual Hawaii International Conference on System Sciences, 4–7.

68. Deng, D.-J., Ke, H. C., Chen, H. H., Huang, Y.-M., 2008, Contention window optimization for IEEE 802.11 DCF access control. IEEE Transactions on Wireless Communications, 7(12): 5129–5135.

69. Hong, K., Lee, K. S., Kim, K., Kim, H. Y., 2012, Channel condition based contention window adaptation in IEEE 802.11 WLANs. IEEE Transactions on Communications, 60(2): 469–478.

70. Wang, C., Li, B., Li, L., 2004, A new collision resolution mechanism to enhance the performance of IEEE 802.11 DCF. IEEE Transactions on Vehicular Technology, 53(4): 1235–1246.

71. Xia, Q., Hamdi, M., 2006, Contention window adjustment for IEEE 802.11 WLANs: a control-theoretic approach. IEEE International Conference on Communications, 3923–3928.

72. Jian, Y., Chen, S., 2008, Can CSMA/CA networks be made fair? 14th Annual International Conference on Mobile Computing and Networking, ACM, San Francisco, CA, 235–246.

73. Shigang, C., Zhan, Z., 2006, Localized algorithm for aggregate fairness in wireless sensor networks. 12th Annual International Conference on Mobile Computing and Networking, New York, NY, 274–285.

74. Razafindralambo, T., Guerin-Lassous, L., 2008, Increasing fairness and efficiency using the Mac protocol in ad hoc networks. Ad Hoc Networks, 6(3): 408–423.

75. Chen, J., Wu, W., 2004, Dynamic contention window selection scheme to achieve a theoretical throughput limit in wireless networks: a fuzzy reasoning approach. IEEE Vehicular Technology Conference, 5: 3196–3200.

76. Razafindralambo, T., Lassous, G. I., 2009, SBA: a simple backoff algorithm for wireless ad hoc networks. International IFIP-TC Networking Conference, Aachen, 5550: 416–428.

77. Gannoune, M., Robert, S., 2004, Dynamic tuning of the contention window minimum (CWMIN) for enhanced service differentiation in IEEE 802.11 wireless ad-hoc networks. IEEE 15th International Symposium on Personal, Indoor and Mobile Radio Communications, 311–317.

78. Balador, A., Movaghar, A., Jabbehdari, S., Kanellopoulos, D., 2012, A novel contention window control scheme for IEEE 802.11 WLANs. IETE Technical Review, 29(3): 202–212.

79. Ksentini, A., Nafaa, A., Gueroui, A., Naimi, M., 2005, Determinist contention window algorithm for IEEE 802.11. IEEE 16th International Symposium on Personal, Indoor and Mobile Radio Communications, 4: 2712–2716.

80. Kyasanur, P., Vaidya, N., 2005, Routing and interface assignment in multi-channel multi-interface wireless networks. IEEE Wireless Communications and Networking Conference, 4: 2051–2056.

81. Chih-Min, C., Hsien-Chen, T., 2014, A channel-hopping multichannel MAC protocol for mobile ad hoc networks. IEEE Transactions on Vehicular Technology, 63(9): 4464–4475.

82. Mo, J., So, S. H., Walrand, J., 2008, Comparison of multichannel MAC protocols. IEEE Transactions on Mobile Computing, 7(1): 50–65.

83. Tzamaloukas, A., Garcia-Luna-Aceves, J., 2000, Channel-hopping multiple access. IEEE International Conference on Communications, 1: 415–419.

84. Yang, Z., Garcia-Luna-Aceves, J., 1999, Hop-reservation multiple access (HRMA) for ad-hoc networks. International Conference on Computer Communications and Networks, 1: 194–201.

85. Wu, L. S., Tseng, C. Y., Lin, Y. C., Pheu, J., 2002, A multi-channel MAC protocol with power control for multi-hop mobile ad hoc networks. The Computer Journal, 45(1): 101–110.

86. Almotairi, H. K., Shen, X., 2013, Distributed power control over multiple channels for ad hoc wireless networks. Wiley Journal of Wireless Communications and Mobile Computing, 13(18): 490–516.

87. Wu, S.-L., Lin, C.-Y., Tseng, Y.-C., Sheu, J.-L., 2000, A new multi-channel MAC protocol with on-demand channel assignment for multi-hop mobile ad hoc networks, International Symposium Parallel Architectures, Algorithms and Networks, 232–237.

88. Han, C., Dianati, M., Tafazolli, R., Liu, X., Shen, X., 2012, A novel distributed asynchronous multichannel mac scheme for large-scale vehicular ad hoc networks. IEEE Transactions on Vehicular Technology, 61(7): 3125–3138.

89. Almotairi, H. K., Shen, X., 2013, Multichannel medium access control for ad hoc wireless networks. Wireless Communications and Mobile Computing, 13(11): 1047–1059.

90. Chen, J., Sheu, S., Yang, C., 2003, A new multichannel access protocol for IEEE 802.11 ad hoc wireless LANs. Proceedings on Personal, Indoor and Mobile Radio Communications, 3: 2291–2296.

91. Jungmin, S., Nitin, V., 2004, Multi-channel MAC for ad hoc networks: handling multi-channel hidden terminals using a single transceiver. ACM International Symposium on Mobile Ad Hoc Networking and Computing, 222–233.

92. Bahl, P., Chandra, R., Dunagan, J., 2004, SSCH: slotted seeded channel hopping for capacity improvement in IEEE 802.11 ad-hoc wireless networks. International Conference on Mobile Computing and Networking, 216–230.

93. So, W. H., Walrand, J., 2005, McMAC: a multi-channel MAC proposal for ad-hoc wireless networks. Technical Report, University of California, Berkeley.

94. Ahlswede, R., Ning, C., Shuo-Yen, L. R., Yeung, W. R., 2000, Network information flow. IEEE Transactions on Information Theory, 46(4): 1204–1216.

95. Sprintson, A., 2010, Network coding and its applications in communication networks. Algorithms for Next Generation Networks, 343–372.

96. Chuan, Q., Yi, X., Chase, G., Naveen, S., Srihari, N., 2008, I²MIX: integration of intra-flow and inter-flow wireless network coding. IEEE Annual Communications Society Conference on Sensor, Mesh and Ad Hoc Communications and Networks Workshops, 1–6.

97. Chien-Chia, C., Clifford, C., Soon, O. Y., Mario, G., Sanadidi, Y. M., 2011, ComboCoding: combined intra/inter-flow network coding for TCP over disruptive MANETs. Journal of Advanced Research, 2(3): 241–252.

98. Chien, C., Soon, O. Y., Phillip, T., Mario, G., Sanadidi, Y. M., 2010, Pipeline network coding for multicast streams. 5th International Conference on Mobile Computing and Ubiquitous Networking, Seattle.

99. Katti, S., Rahul, H., Wenjun, Hu., Katabi, D., Medard, M., Crowcroft, J., 2008, XORs in the air: practical wireless network coding. IEEE/ACM Transactions on Networking, 16(3): 497–510.

100. Chachulski, S., Jennings, M., Katti, S., Katabi, D., 2006, MORE: a network coding approach to opportunistic routing. Technical Report MIT-CSAIL-TR-2006-049.

101. Sundararajan, K. J., Shah, D., Medard, M., Mitzenmacher, M., Barros, J., 2009, Network coding meets TCP. International Conference on Computer Communications (INFOCOM), 280–288.

102. Vivek, R., Kumar, R. P., 2007, A counterexample in congestion control of wireless networks. Performance Evaluation, 64(5): 399–418.

103. Radha, R., Kathiravan, K., "Enhancing the selection of backoff interval using fuzzy logic over wireless ad hoc networks. The Scientific World Journal, 2015, 680681.

104. Kathiravan, K., Radha, R., 2012, An opportunistic cross layer multi path routing protocol to improve TCP performance over mobile ad hoc networks. International Conference on Recent Trends in Information Technology, Chennai.

105. Radha, R., Kathiravan, K., Bhuvaneswari, S., 2018, Adaptive ARX rate controller for multi hop MANET. International Journal of Engineering & Technology, 7: 235.

106. Radha, R., Kathiravan, K., A cross layer rate based transport solution to control intra flow contention in multi hop MANET. 2013 7th IEEE GCC Conference and Exhibition, Doha.

107. Ammar, A. M.-J., Mohamed, O., Borhanuddin, A. M., Nor, A. W. A. H., 2012, An adaptive delayed acknowledgment strategy to improve TCP performance in multi-hop wireless networks. Wireless Personal Communications, 69, 307–333.

108. Giri, P. K., "A Survey on Soft Computing Techniques for Multi-Constrained QoS Routing in MANET", International Journal of Computer and information Technology (IJCIT), Research and Publication Unit, University of Asia Pacific, Vol. 03, Issue. 2, 2012.

109. Chandrakant Mallick, Suneeta Satpathy, "Challenges and Design Goals of Wireless Sensor Networks: A Sate-of-the-art Review", International Journal of Computer Applications (0975–8887), 2018.

110. Sachi Nandan Mohanty, E.Laxmi Lydia, Mohamed Elhoseny, Majid M. Gethami Al Otabi, K.Shankar, Deep learning with LSTM based distributed data mining model for energy efficient wireless sensor networks, Physical Communication, vol.40, Issue-4, 101097-102008, (2020). https://doi.org/10.1016/j.phycom.2020.101097.

PART II

Smart Monitoring and Control System with the Internet of Things

CHAPTER 7

Internet of Things and Smart Homes: A Review

RAJAT VERMA, PRASHANT KUMAR MISHRA, VISHAL NAGAR, and SATYASUNDARA MAHAPATRA[*]

Pranveer Singh Institute of Technology, Kanpur, Uttar Pradesh, India

[*]Corresponding author. E-mail: satyasundara123@gmail.com

ABSTRACT

In today's digital era, Internet of Things (IoT) is an amalgamation of various systems that incorporate conventional embedded systems, compact wireless sensors, and self-operating controlling mechanisms. The evolution of small and powerful hardware, high-speed Internet, and wireless communication has led to the increasing use of IoT-based applications in various application domains. Famous term "smart home" is a modern automated setup that makes use of Internet connected devices for the management of electronic devices, smart lighting solutions, and other home appliances. IoT-based smart-home-enabled devices can also work in combination with the other home devices and transfer information to other connected smart devices. Various smart-home application solutions empower the homeowners to remotely manage portions of the home often via a mobile app. Homeowners can configure time schedules for energy-efficient use of smart devices while providing additional convenience and time savings. While the emerging smart-home market still has plenty of potential for growth, smart-home devices based on IoT currently available in the market include Internet-enabled and controlled refrigerators and televisions, smart lights with light occupancy sensors, smart thermostats, smart door locks, and security systems. Let us explore the present and future of IoT-based smart-home applications and services in this chapter.

7.1   INTRODUCTION

In the initial days of the Internet (early 1990s), a paradigm shift is witnessed from the "Internet of Computers" to the "Internet of People" [1]. The major reason behind this evolution is social networking, which uses diverse platforms such as WhatsApp, Facebook, Twitter, and Snapchat, and so forth, to connect billions of people together. The devices made in the initial stages were bigger and bulky but gradually their size has become minimalistic. According to Cisco Systems, there is a postulation as "Internet of Everything" that brings the four entities that is, people, process, data, and things together that result in a pertinent and beneficial networked connection. One thing is for sure that the notion of Internet of Things (IoT) is not restricted to a certain dimension but it is an extensive approach. Gubbi et al. [2] explained that there are three subdivisions in the IoT element categories that are hardware, software, and interface. As an important remark, the IoT can be defined as a combination of the quick-thinking devices capable of communicating with the other devices, objects, technical environment and thus producing an enormous amount of data. The IoT is basically an extension of a real-time data analytical program known as supervisory control and acquisition of data [3].

As far as the concept of smart home is concerned, the home appliances become automated and all their controls are readily available at your fingertips, generally via mobile app. Suppose you are at a geographic location that is very far from your home and your guests have arrived at your home. The color of the lighting and air conditioner's temperature needs to be changed. So, this can be done right from your Android, iOS, or Windows device. This is one of the many IoT-based applications and services in smart homes.

This chapter focuses on the IoT-based smart homes. One of the most significant features of IoT-based smart-home technology is connectivity. Nowadays, the cloud plays a key role as complete setup of a smart home can be unified with powerful third-party tools, substantial processing power, and storage.

In this chapter, Section 7.1 outlines the overview, features, and application architecture of IoT. In Section 7.2, overview, evolution, and components of smart homes and commercial devices and services for smart homes are reviewed along with the recent developments in smart-home automation. In the last section, the future of smart homes is projected followed by the conclusion of the chapter.

7.2   AN OVERVIEW OF THE IOT

The IoT is visualized as expanding the limits of the Internet beyond computers and smartphones to an entire range of other processes, devices, and surroundings [2]. IoT is one of the building blocks of advanced smart-home architecture [4]. IoT is an environment of interconnected devices that are reachable with the help of the Internet [5]. The "thing" in IoT could be a person with a smartphone with built-in-sensors or a temperature monitor that is, objects with an assigned IP address. These connected devices and networking components have the power to gather and transmit the data over a network without any manual operation. IoT is a broad network of people and connected things [6]. The dimension of IoT has evolved due to recent technologies such as embedded systems, automation, and control systems, and so forth.

7.2.1   FEATURES OF IOT

The IoT has some notable features that improve the performance of devices. These features are highlighted below:

- *Intelligence:* The combination of algorithmic rules, hardware components, software components, computations, precise user-friendly interface makes the IoT smart.
- *Connectivity:* The day-to-day objects are brought in contact that recognizes the connectivity and thus empowers IoT.
- *Dynamic Nature*: The ever-changing states of IoT device contribute to this feature. Its example can be on/off status of a device or connected/disconnected status of the connected device.
- *Enormous Scale:* The devices communicating with each other need to be controlled and managed. The number of devices connected to Internet is growing with a rapid pace.
- *Sensing:* The concept of IoT is incomplete without sensors. The sensors have the capability to measure any updation in the network and are capable enough to create the record of the same updation.
- *Heterogeneity:* The platforms as well as networks used by diverse IoT devices are based on different technologies.
- *Security:* Since the concept of IoT is completely transparent, the security of IoT is a major concern.

Various measures used for security are listed below:

- Public key infrastructure (PKI) [X.509 certificate]
- Digital signature
- Application programming interface (API) security
- Hardware and network security
- Network monitoring
- Network access control
- Software updates
- Security gateways
- Security awareness to consumers.

7.2.2   APPLICATION ARCHITECTURE OF IOT

In general, the application architecture of the IoT comprises of seven layers. The application architecture of IoT is shown in Figure 7.1.

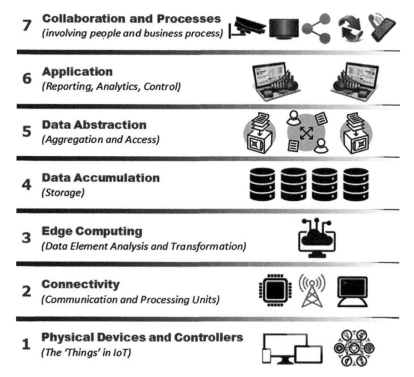

FIGURE 7.1   Application Architecture of IoT.

First layer of the architecture comprises of physical devices and controllers commonly known as the "things" in IoT. This includes sensors, devices, machines, and edge nodes of all types. S*econd layer* is related to connectivity and comprises of communication and processing units. *Third layer* is of edge computing where data element analysis and transformation take place. Above that, there is *fourth layer* of data accumulation where the work of storage is done. *Fifth layer* of data abstraction aggregates and accesses the data. *Sixth layer* is the application section where the work of reporting, analytics, as well as control is done. The last layer is of collaboration and process that involves people and business processes.

7.3   AN OVERVIEW OF THE SMART HOME

A smart home is often referred to as the residential extension of a building [7]. It provides homeowners convenience, security, and comfort by allowing them to control the smart devices, often by a smartphone, time schedule, or other networked IoT devices [8]. The popularity of smart home has enhanced the daily lives of the people and made it better and simpler. With the increasing number of connected devices in smart home, the facilities for the people will be increased at a tremendous pace [9].

Generally, IoT and smart homes work together by communicating and sharing the data to automate the activities based on the homeowner's choice and selection.

The concept of smart home has transformed the manner in which people live. Some of the examples are the switching on the air conditioner or heater before the user could actually come inside a room or playing news updates using a voice-based virtual assistant like Alexa. In general, the smart-home concept is the future of a convenient life style at home.

7.3.1   EVOLUTION OF SMART HOME

The journey of smart homes began in the year 1975 with the release of home automation's communication protocol X10 [10]. This communication protocol (X10) uses 120 kHz radio frequency bursts of digital data onto a home's electricity circuit via programmable switches. These radio frequency signals carry commands to specific home appliances, monitoring how and when the appliances operate.

However, as electrical wiring is not intended to be mostly free from radio band "noise," X10 was not continuously reliable and acted as a one-way technology, so the smart devices cannot send and receive the data at the same time. After some time, more costly and enhanced variant of X10 devices based on two-way technology became available as shown in Figure 7.2.

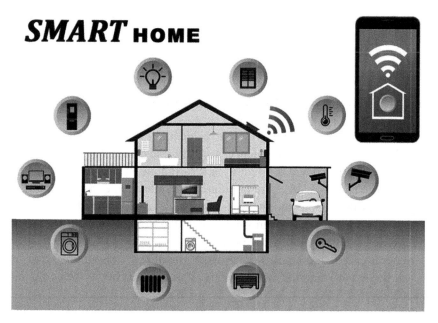

FIGURE 7.2   Smart home environment [31].

In 2005, the home automation company "Insteon" presented a technology that combined wireless signals and electric wiring. Since then, some other protocols like Z-Wave and Zigbee have been developed to solve the issues prone to X10 [11].

In the year 2010, Nest Labs was established. Next year, that is, in 2011, company released the "Nest Learning Thermostat" (Figure 7.3) with other products such as security cameras, smart smoke/carbon monoxide detectors, and so forth. Three years later in January 2014, Google acquired Nest Labs.

More recently, companies including Amazon, Apple, and Google have released their own smart-home products and domotics platforms, including Amazon Echo, Apple HomeKit, and Google Home.

FIGURE 7.3   Nest thermostat [32].

7.3.2   COMPONENTS OF SMART HOME

Smart home paradigm is illustrated in Figure 7.4. Main components of typical smart home setup are as follows:

- *Sensors*: Sensors are responsible for measuring the home conditions by capturing data from the internal and external sources. The sensors are connected to the devices present in the homes [12]. They are not IoT sensors. Their data is transferred continuously to the smart-home server with the local network available.
- *Processors*: Processors are used for performing integrated and local actions. For providing extra resources for applications, it can connect to cloud architecture. The data obtained from the sensors is then processed by the local servers available.
- *Database*: Database is a collection of inter-related records. It is used to store the information generated by the sensors. Use of database also provides some diverse features such as visualization, data analysis, and presentation, and so forth. This filtered information is stored in the allotted database for future use.
- *Actuators*: Actuators execute the command in the connected devices or on the server. They are also responsible for the launch of commands to the allotted device processors.

- *API*: Application programming interface allows the external applications to execute it, and follow a predefined parameter format. API can process the sensor's data or control necessary actions.

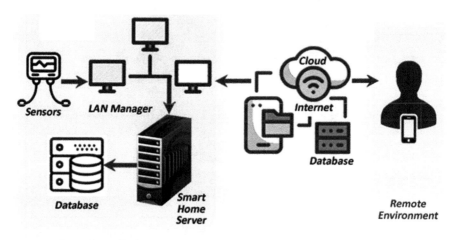

FIGURE 7.4   Smart home paradigm.

7.3.3 EXAMPLES OF SMART-HOME IMPLEMENTATIONS

The technology has entered almost every aspect of our lives. Some of the major household implementations are highlighted below:

- Efficient and controlled thermostats such as Nest, comes with integrated wireless-fidelity technology, allows the user to monitor, schedule, and control home temperatures remotely. These are well efficient in learning the behavior of a homeowner and can modify the settings accordingly to suit the comfort for all residents in a house. These thermostats can also provide notifications to change filters, energy use, and other things.
- Apart from being remotely controlled, smart lighting solutions such as "Hue" from Philips (Figure 7.5) are capable of detecting occupants in a room and can adjust the lightings as required.
- On-demand access to music and videos is possible through the applications installed on a smart TV (Figure 7.6) connected to the Internet. Smart TV also utilizes voice and gesture recognition features.

FIGURE 7.5 Philips Hue smart light kit [33].

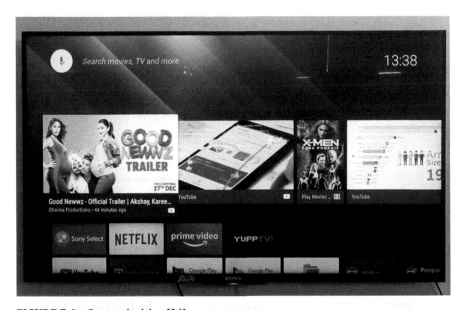

FIGURE 7.6 Smart television [34].

- Smart security cameras such as the August Doorbell camera allow the people to monitor who is coming in or going out of the house remotely [13]. They have the capability to differentiate among visitors, burglars, pets, and obviously residents. These smart security cameras also provide notifications to the residents on their smart phones if the camera detects any suspicious activity.

- Smart doorbell camera (Figure 7.7) such as August's doorbell camera is an IoT enabled device that allows the user to monitor the real-time activities happening in front of the door by capturing the motions. The best part is that it lets the user monitor all the activities right on his smartphone. Previous video recording feature is also available. Affordable subscriptions are available which user can select and pay only for the services purchased.

FIGURE 7.7   Doorbell camera [35].

- With the efficient door openers and smart locks (Figure 7.8), the people can deny or grant access to visitors. Smart locks can also automatically sense the presence of a resident and unlock the doors for them when required.

FIGURE 7.8   Smart lock [36]

- Connected feeders are used to feed the pets in home automatically [14].
- Connected timers automate the watering of plants and lawns in home.
- Monitoring of household appliances is possible as the water failure, freezing of pipes, or electric surge can be sensed and the action can be taken accordingly.
- Smart kitchen [15] appliances are capable of doing wonders. As the smart coffee maker can make a cup of coffee within the time allotted, the refrigerators are capable enough to make shopping lists or creating recipes based on the food left out in the fridge or the tracking of expiry dates of the packaged material. Some other home appliances such as dryers, washing machines, cookers, and toasters can be more effective than before with the integration of the smart-home technology.
- By using, voice-based intelligent personal assistants [16] such as Google Home (Figure 7.9), the user can control the lights, audio (Google Play Music, iHeart Radio, Spotify, and so forth), photos and videos (Google Photos, YouTube, Netflix, and so forth), tasks (Google Keep and Google Calendar, and so forth), and News Updates.

In general, there are many products available in the home automation markets that are making the lives of users easy. There are also many devices available that are not connected to Internet. Yet by using motion, light, and other sensors, efficient use of various home appliances is possible. For example, lights in a room can detect the presence of a person, or light and can be switched on/off as per requirement.

Google Home with Home Hub and Home Mini   Amazon Echo Dot

FIGURE 7.9   Smart speaker and display devices using intelligent personal assistant (IPA) [37,38]

7.4   RECENT DEVELOPMENTS IN SMART-HOME AUTOMATION

Smart Homes have become a mainstream concept worldwide. Technological innovations are continuously growing up in this area. Traditional systems were designed to work with limited connectivity. But with increased penetration of high-speed Internet among home users worldwide, the smart-home residents are now moving seamlessly ahead.

Some of the significant and innovative trends in the smart-home industry are highlighted below:

- *Contact-Less Control*: Technology has vanished the idea of using multiple remotes for different home appliances. Nowadays, IoT-based home appliances can be controlled with just a touch through user's smart phone or touch-based control system [17].
- *System Suiting the Interior*: Nowadays, the smart devices that are being made are of pleasing designs that suit really well with the interior of the house. The products are really trendy that can suit any decor.
- *Automated Door Lock*: Automated door lock is a really hassle-free device that allows the user to operate the lock from anywhere. The user can monitor each and every person that comes in or goes out from the

house. Many a time, when the user is in a hurry and forgets to lock his house, then it provides the notification as well as locks the door [18].

- *High-End Security Systems*: With IoT, the user can keep track of the people coming in and going out of the house. Filters can be applied to protect the homes from unauthorized access. Alarms can be customized for different situations.

7.5   FUTURE OF SMART HOME

The forecasted data predicted that by 2020, the global market of smart homes will reach 58 billion dollars (approx.) [19]. More variety of smart-home devices will be available for making our lives easier and more comfortable. It ranges from household products to diverse security systems. Examples of the former can be smart kettles, dryers, air conditioners, and refrigerators while the latter can be circuit security cameras and advanced alarm systems. A lot of operations can be effectively managed with the distinct characteristics of smart homes. Advanced features will result in reduced energy, costs, and time.

Still, a big point of concern is the higher cost of new generation smart-home devices. Some of the devices are a bit costly at first but will be highly efficient in saving energy and money in the future. Upcoming years will be beneficial for the smart-home industry.

Future of smart-home industry is supposed to be benefitted from the use of following next generation technologies, techniques, and services:

- *The Upgraded Role for Artificial Intelligence (AI)*: Nowadays, people use electronic surveillance for keeping an eye on their property [21]. AI, if integrated with electronic surveillance properly, then the surveillance process can be enhanced to the next level with high efficiency as the user will be able to get the threat alerts automatically.
- *Data Sharing*: Sharing data with businesses and digital users will be the next big thing in the smart-home industry [21]. The data collected from users will act as a feedback for the diverse IoT companies to build user-friendly products and services. For example, it will be great if the food can be ordered automatically from the kind of items remaining in the refrigerator.
- *Test-Phase Products Alternatives*: The smart homes can be made simpler and efficient with the three major parameters that are technology, automation, and innovation [22]. In the upcoming future, people will

observe the increment in the IoT devices. The alternatives will continue to develop in the future.

- *Key Focus Areas*: There are two key focusing areas that are surveillance and applications. The user feels really excited when he/she gets to know that he/she can control home appliances in an interactive manner. Similarly, surveillance has become really important in this era. With the IoT smart homes, applications and surveillance are possible.

- *Increased Control, Customization, and Efficiency*: With the help of AI, increased, efficient, and customized control of a smart home will be possible [23].

- *Standards of Higher Cross-Compatibility*: Making progress in any project is certainly important and for that, working on enhancement of standards plays a key role. As the smart-home concept is in the developing phase, the final picture is still not clear but one thing is for sure that the market for the smart-home industry is really positive and promising. There is a great possibility that in the near future, cross vendor-compatible standards and solutions will be developed and made available at an affordable price. Cross vendor solution means that smart devices should be compatible with all technology platforms by Google, Amazon, Microsoft, or Apple, and so forth [24].

- *Excellent Customer Service*: As there are diverse IoT-enabled smart-home devices present in the market, the smart-home companies are supposed to focus on developing excellent customer service. Since the technology is new for everyone, people will certainly face a number of consequences. It may range from data privacy to troubleshooting. The notable point is that the companies that are offering excellent customer services will be certainly far ahead [25].

- *Increased Integration of Voice Control*: Scientists have predicted that use of integrated technologies will affect our lives. Car dashboard, TV, cellphones, home audio systems will be controlled just by the voice of the user. Our daily lives are certainly transformed by this integration [26].

- *Outdoor Smart Spaces*: As smart-home technology is the latest in town, its cost is really high. But, slowly and gradually, increased use of smart-home devices will make them more affordable. In future, the commercial aspect of smart homes will rise to adapt and build mobile workplaces.

- *Efficient Kitchen Appliances*: Intelligent personal assistants like Amazon's Alexa can work with the kitchen appliances to make the food in a more automated and faster way with the control command from user's smart phone [27].
- *Changing Lives through IoT Smart-Home Automation*: It is believed that the solutions provided by diverse IoT smart-home appliances are capable enough to change how we live our lives.

So, impact of IoT-based home automation on a person's life can be summarized as follows:

- *Improving the Quality of Life:* With IoT-enabled smart-home devices, people will be able to live a comfortable quality life [28].
- *Saving Money:* IoT smart homes allow the user to get the benefit of smart-grid integration technology so that the user can efficiently use various electrical home appliances and save money in electricity bills [29].
- *Saving Time:* The aim of making IoT-based smart-home devices is saving the time. When people are getting more time due to the automation of devices, they can enjoy their vacant time by spending quality time with their family or by doing some other productive work [30].

7.6 CONCLUSION

In this chapter, implementation of IoT in smart-home automation is discussed. The IoT and smart home are revolutionizing the world. The overview, features, and IoT application architecture are explained to understand the basic terminology and working of IoT. The smart-home solutions discussed are enhancing and enriching the lives of the common people. The evolution and recent development of technologies in smart homes are highlighted to present a glimpse of recent developments in the home automation industry. Impact of smart home devices on three parameters namely time, money, and quality of life is also illustrated. Future direction of the smart home industry is forecasted after analyzing the integration of latest and advanced technologies like AI into home automation products and services. So, application of IoT in smart-home devices and services enhances improved user-friendly features, security, energy efficiency, remote access, and control to make life more convenient at home.

KEYWORDS

- **Internet of Things (IoT)**
- **smart home**
- **supervisory control and acquisition of data**
- **automation**
- **wireless sensor networks**

REFERENCES

1. Nayak, P. (2017). Internet of Things Services, Applications, Issues, and Challenges. In *Handbook of Research on Advanced Wireless Sensor Network Applications, Protocols, and Architectures* (pp. 353–368). IGI Global.
2. Gubbi, J., Buyya, R., Marusic, S., and Palaniswami, M. (2013). Internet of things (IoT): A vision, architectural elements, and future directions. *Future Generation Computer Systems, 29*(7), 1645–1660.
3. Sajid, A., Abbas, H., and Saleem, K. (2016). Cloud-assisted IoT-based SCADA systems security: A review of the state of the art and future challenges. *IEEE Access, 4*, 1375–1384.
4. Piyare, R. (2013). Internet of things: Ubiquitous home control and monitoring system using android based smart phone. *International Journal of Internet of Things, 2*(1), 5–11.
5. Al-Fuqaha, A., Guizani, M., Mohammadi, M., Aledhari, M., and Ayyash, M. (2015). Internet of things: A survey on enabling technologies, protocols, and applications. *IEEE Communications Surveys & Tutorials, 17*(4), 2347–2376.
6. Perera, C. (2017). *Sensing as a service for Internet of things: A roadmap.* Lulu. com.
7. Domb, M. (2019). Smart Home Systems Based on Internet of Things. In *IoT and Smart Home Automation.* IntechOpen.
8. Ho, G., Leung, D., Mishra, P., Hosseini, A., Song, D., and Wagner, D. (2016). Smart locks: Lessons for securing commodity Internet of things devices. In *Proceedings of the 11th ACM on Asia Conference on Computer and Communications Security* (pp. 461–472). ACM.
9. Aldrich, F. K. (2003). Smart Homes: Past, Present and Future. In *Inside the Smart Home* (pp. 17–39). Springer, London.
10. Dietrich, D., Bruckner, D., Zucker, G., and Palensky, P. (2010). Communication and computation in buildings: A short introduction and overview. *IEEE Transactions on Industrial Electronics, 57*(11), 3577–3584.
11. Gungor, V. C., Sahin, D., Kocak, T., Ergut, S., Buccella, C., Cecati, C., and Hancke, G. P. (2011). Smart grid technologies: Communication technologies and standards. *IEEE Transactions on Industrial Informatics, 7*(4), 529–539.
12. Ricquebourg, V., Menga, D., Durand, D., Marhic, B., Delahoche, L., and Loge, C. (2006). The smart home concept: Our immediate future. In *2006 1st IEEE International Conference on e-Learning in Industrial Electronics* (pp. 23–28). IEEE.

13. Sivanathan, A., Gharakheili, H. H., Loi, F., Radford, A., Wijenayake, C., Vishwanath, A., and Sivaraman, V. (2018). Classifying IoT devices in smart environments using network traffic characteristics. *IEEE Transactions on Mobile Computing, 18,* 1745–1749.
14. Possis, Z. C. (1989). *U.S. Patent No. 4,889,077.* Washington, DC: U.S. Patent and Trademark Office.
15. Desai, H., Guruvayurappan, D., Merchant, M., Somaiya, S., and Mundra, H. (2017). IoT based grocery monitoring system. In *2017 Fourteenth International Conference on Wireless and Optical Communications Networks (WOCN)* (pp. 1–4). IEEE.
16. Hoy, M. B. (2018). Alexa, Siri, Cortana, and more: An introduction to voice assistants. *Medical Reference Services Quarterly, 37*(1), 81–88.
17. Tomičić, I., Grd, P., and Bača, M. (2018). A review of soft biometrics for IoT. In *2018 41st International Convention on Information and Communication Technology, Electronics and Microelectronics (MIPRO)* (pp. 1115–1120). IEEE.
18. Ha, I. (2015). Security and usability improvement on a digital door lock system based on Internet of things. *International Journal of Security and Its Applications, 9*(8), 45–54.
19. Majumder, S., Aghayi, E., Noferesti, M., Memarzadeh-Tehran, H., Mondal, T., Pang, Z., and Deen, M. J. (2017). Smart homes for elderly healthcare—Recent advances and research challenges. *Sensors, 17*(11), 2496.
20. Lyon, D. (1994). *The Electronic Eye: The Rise of Surveillance Society.* University of Minnesota Press.
21. Lee, I., and Lee, K. (2015). The Internet of things (IoT): Applications, investments, and challenges for enterprises. *Business Horizons, 58*(4), 431–440.
22. Breivold, H. P., and Sandström, K. (2015). Internet of things for industrial automation--challenges and technical solutions. In *2015 IEEE International Conference on Data Science and Data Intensive Systems* (pp. 532–539). IEEE.
23. Ramchurn, S., Vytelingum, P., Rogers, A., and Jennings, N. R. (2012). Putting the "smarts" into the smart grid: A grand challenge for artificial intelligence. *Communications of the ACM, 55*(4), 86–97.
24. Khan, M., Silva, B. N., and Han, K. (2016). Internet of things based energy aware smart home control system. *IEEE Access, 4,* 7556–7566.
25. Witkowski, K. (2017). Internet of things, big data, industry 4.0–innovative solutions in logistics and supply chains management. *Procedia Engineering, 182,* 763–769.
26. Meng, Y., Wang, Z., Zhang, W., Wu, P., Zhu, H., Liang, X., and Liu, Y. (2018). Wivo: Enhancing the security of voice control system via wireless signal in IoT environment. In *Proceedings of the Eighteenth ACM International Symposium on Mobile Ad Hoc Networking and Computing* (pp. 81–90). ACM.
27. Cui, X. (2016). The Internet of things. In *Ethical Ripples of Creativity and Innovation* (pp. 61–68). Palgrave Macmillan, London.
28. Basatneh, R., Najafi, B., and Armstrong, D. G. (2018). Health sensors, smart home devices, and the Internet of medical things: An opportunity for dramatic improvement in care for the lower extremity complications of diabetes. *Journal of Diabetes Science and Technology, 12*(3), 577–586.
29. Lobaccaro, G., Carlucci, S., and Löfström, E. (2016). A review of systems and technologies for smart homes and smart grids. *Energies, 9*(5), 348.
30. Shah, S. H., and Yaqoob, I. (2016). A survey: Internet of Things (IOT) technologies, applications and challenges. In *2016 IEEE Smart Energy Grid Engineering (SEGE)* (pp. 381–385). IEEE.

31. https://pixabay.com/illustrations/smart-home-house-technology-2005993/
32. https://en.wikipedia.org/wiki/File:Nest_front_official.png
33. https://commons.wikimedia.org/wiki/File:Philips_Hue_hub_and_2_bulbs.jpg
34. https://upload.wikimedia.org/wikipedia/commons/9/94/Sony_Bravia_Android_TV.jpg
35. https://commons.wikimedia.org/wiki/File:Ring_video_doorbell.jpg
36. https://upload.wikimedia.org/wikipedia/commons/4/4e/August_2nd-gen_smart_lock.jpg
37. https://en.wikipedia.org/wiki/Google_Home
38. https://commons.wikimedia.org/wiki/File:Amazon_Echo_Dot_(black)_on_a_wood_surface.jpg

CHAPTER 8

Employment of the IoT Toward Energy Efficient Home Automation: State of the Art

MONIKA MANGLA[1*], RAJESHRI ANEESH[2], and ARCHANA ARUDKAR[2]

[1]Department of Computer Engineering, LTCoE, Navi Mumbai, Maharashtra 400709, India

[2]Department of Computer Engineering, Faculty, PHCET, Navi Mumbai 400705, India

*Corresponding author. E-mail: manglamona@gmail.com

ABSTRACT

Internet of Things (IoT) has significantly dominated the lifestyle over the past few decades. There remains hardly any sector unaffected by IoT. During the past decade, the IoT is being intensively employed in the automation of homes and buildings thus developing smart homes and smart buildings. In principle, technology in smart homes focuses on providing utmost satisfaction to its occupant with the help of connection and integration of various intelligent and sensing devices. In smart homes, various kinds of devices are deployed to collect and process the data. The authors in this chapter present a summarized review for smart homes with respect to IoT. The chapter also presents the various constraints and challenges for widespread employment of home automation.

8.1 INTRODUCTION

IoT has been a buzzword during the past few decades. There are numerous definitions available for Internet of Things (IoT) in literature. Most of these definitions define IoT as the interconnection of sensing nodes and other processing devices to provide an automated and desirous environment. Over the past few decades, field of IoT has been completely revolutionized and has substantially transformed each sector of human life. Examples of sectors, that are influenced by IoT, include weather monitoring system, traffic management, agriculture automation, etc. Additionally, IoT has also been prominently accepted for automation of homes, that is, smart homes. The key advantages of smart homes are its convenience, comfort, and security [1]. Subscribers are capable to remotely monitor and manage various home appliances with the help of smart devices and thus eradicating the constraint of physical distance. Smart home (home automation) can also be defined as an application where the home environment is managed for providing context-aware services and providing remote home control. But most importantly, smart homes aim to provide the desired comfort to its occupants in an energy efficient manner. Therefore, the automation of homes also minimizes carbon emission and thus provides an eco-friendly solution.

Resultantly, home automation can be considered to be an upcoming and promising technology. Consequently, exhaustive research is being carried out in this field. This chapter is attempting to present a state of the art in the field of smart homes and IoT. Additionally, it presents the concept of energy efficiency. The chapter has been organized as follows. Section 8.1 focuses on the introduction while motivation has been discussed in Section 8.2. The current state of the art has been presented in Section 8.3. Thereafter, Section 8.4 discusses the concept of energy efficiency and associated challenges and constraints. Finally, Section 8.5 concludes the chapter and presents possible avenues for research in the domain.

Automation of homes (smart home) was incepted 80 years ago [2]. Since then, it has evolved significantly and has touched exemplary heights. Consequently, home automation has observed its real-life application during the past few decades [3–5]. Since its inception has been continuously evolving to achieve new benchmarks. This real-life application and escalation in home automation are achieved owing to growth and development in the area of broadband internet connectivity and wireless technology. Wireless technology enables various devices to communicate with each other and thus share information without concerning about the portability aspect [6, 25, 26]. The smart home also requires various devices to be integrated and interconnected for providing desired services to the occupants inside and outside the house. The basic model of a smart home is represented in Figure 8.1. Hence, smart home is an indispensable application of IoT and also has become part of IoT.

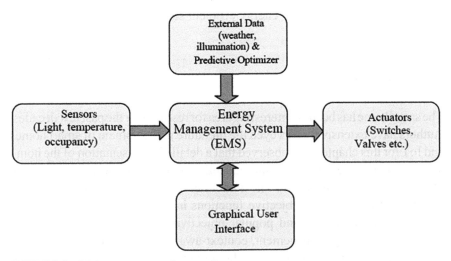

FIGURE 8.1   Major components in smart home.

The authors in this chapter provide an overview of the research in home automation and associated technologies. Various sensors, multimedia devices, and protocols used for implementing smart homes are also discussed. Authors also present various solutions given by researchers to achieve energy efficient home automation. Few constraints and challenges associated with home automation are also discussed. Finally, the chapter presents some concrete guidelines for upcoming researchers in order to develop a practical and sustainable smart home.

8.2 MOTIVATION

The massive deployment of IoT in the field of home automation is the key factor for undertaking this topic for research. Smart homes focus on providing comfort to its occupants in an energy efficient manner thus providing an eco-friendly solution. The lifestyle of people these days has further motivated the authors to choose this topic for research. Additionally, it has been observed in reports from various sources that the energy usage at homes and offices majorly contributes toward environmental emission. These reports persuade the authors to comprehend the existing smart home approaches. Understanding the existing approaches further helps to uncover any scope for improvement and thus providing energy efficient solution. Thus, the authors aim to understand the rudimentary of home automation which will help to devise an energy efficient solution while maintaining the comfort of its occupants.

8.3 RELATED WORK

The smart home has been an interesting area for research for the past few decades. Authors have extensively surveyed the literature in the domain of smart homes and IoT for this chapter. It is observed that a detailed representation of the home structure is required which is subsequently followed by the interconnection of various subsystems within. The authors in this chapter present the state of the art related to various objective functions in the implementation of smart homes. Some promising and popular objective functions are, namely, real-time system, energy management, context-aware automation, etc. Authors in the chapter classify the research in home automation on the basis of these objective functions. The following subsections provide the state of the art for various objective functions in home automation.

8.3.1 ENERGY MANAGEMENT

Management of energy in smart homes is the most crucial objective function in smart homes. Consequently, there exist ample papers focusing on energy management in smart homes. Saad Al-Sumaiti et al. [7] presented goals of smart home and associated energy management system. Factors that affect the customer's electricity bill are mentioned. Associated challenges and possible solutions are also discussed in this paper [7]. Here, the authors focused on energy management and thus reducing environmental emissions.

Gul and Patidar [8] claimed that nearly 19% of the total CO_2 is produced from commercial buildings. The authors further state that observing energy consumption for a nonresidential building is complex as it involves inconsistency in the number of occupants and their behavior. This inconsistency results in unpredictable patterns of energy consumption which subsequently necessitates understanding the energy demand of individual buildings. Here, a study was conducted to understand the relationship between the activities of users and demand profile of electrical energy for a university building. Various methods, like questionnaire, interview, are used to have a better understanding of the building usage. This study revealed that change in occupancy levels does not significantly affect energy consumption rather major electrical consumption occurs in preset heating/cooling systems.

Various approaches have been proposed by different authors that mainly emphasize energy management. All research papers have a common objective of optimizing the average energy consumption without compromising the ease of occupants. Missaoui et al. [1] proposed a global model based anticipative building energy management system (BEMS) that optimally trades off user comfort and energy cost considering occupant expectations and physical constraints. The proposed model is based on both reactive and anticipative global algorithms thus introducing a real-time energy management-decision model. In this model, two scenarios are considered: comfort-preferred solution (focus is given to comfort) and cost-preferred solution (focus is given on the cost). The proposed model is also validated using MATLAB/Simulink. Further smart grids are approved as an effective measure to improve energy efficiency where managers are motivated to real-time scenarios and weather conditions [9]. But unfortunately, most of the systems rely on conventional BEMS having static parameters. Authors in [9] investigate the performance of real-time decision making in comparison to a conventional energy management system. Authors are successful in proving that smart BEMS significantly reduces energy consumption than its counterpart.

As already discussed that 40% of global energy is consumed in nonresidential buildings. These buildings also produce 30% of the total CO_2 in the environment. These figures act as the driving force behind taking some conscious decisions to maintain stability of the environment. Consequently, some authors suggest the installation of energy meters and sensors to track energy usage and environmental conditions within buildings. Authors in [10] present a comprehensive review for integrating meters and sensors in the BEMS.

Furthermore, it is also mentioned that energy consumption is primarily influenced by occupant behavior [11]. But unfortunately, the understanding of occupant behavior for building design and its operation is insufficient. This insufficiency for understanding occupant behavior results in simplified modeling. The authors in [11] attempt to evaluate the impact of occupant behavior on energy usage within the building.

Authors in [2] designed a house model to demonstrate the simulation of reduced energy consumption for lighting and temperature maintenance. The model uses wireless communication through antennas. Usage of antennas causes degradation in the quality of communication and dwindling signal strengths due to obstructions along the antenna path. Here, antennas are also suggested to be employed in smart LEDs, which enhance the efficiency of the smart home.

The urgency of devising energy efficient approaches for home automation can be understood by the fact that [12] the manufacturing industries for ICT technologies are continuously progressing and has been striving for innovative methods, which proves to be revolutionary, known as smart manufacturing. This smart manufacturing is a future growth engine and still has a broad scope for innovation. Understanding the urgency of devising energy efficient solutions in home automation, researchers have suggested context-aware automation where energy usage depends on its context. The recent research in context-aware automation has been discussed in the subsequent subsection.

8.3.2   CONTEXT-AWARE AUTOMATION

In context-aware automation, optimization of energy usage in smart homes is learnt based on the learning from movement and device usage patterns of its occupants [13]. While optimizing energy usage, it is ensured that occupants do not experience any deficiency in their stay and experience. In order to have the widespread implementation of home automation, context knowledge needs to be exploited in full. The context has been classified into user context and physical context which can be obtained using various kinds of sensors. Here physical context refers to the temperature, time, and other environmental factors while user context focuses on the preferences of the user, for example, age, gender, habits, etc.

Furthermore, context-based automation has been classified into active context and passive context. In an active context, appliances themselves change their behavior in accordance with the context of the environment. On the contrary, in a passive context, the system is responsible to modify the mode of operation in response to context, for example, occupancy level. Figure 8.2 represents the basic model of context-aware automation. Das et al. [14] have proposed such a model where context is sensed using numerous sensors. This context is communicated to the recommendation system that further controls various actuators in the system. Zhang et al. [15] have proposed a generic layered model for context-aware automation. The proposed model [15] has mainly five layers, namely, context acquisition layer, context representation layer, context aggregation layer, context interpretation layer, and context utilization layer. In context-aware automation, the future activities and movements of the occupant is estimated and devices are regulated accordingly. This prediction of occupant activity enhances the comfort of occupants in addition to optimizing energy efficiency. Thus, context-aware automation aims to eliminate any energy leakage occurring in heating, ventilation, and air conditioning (HVAC). Lu et al. [16] have also proposed a Hidden Markov Model for context-aware automation.

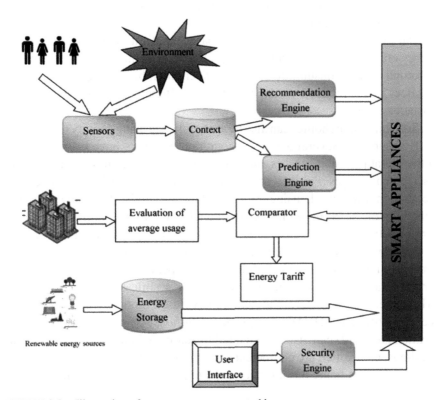

FIGURE 8.2   Illustration of context-aware automated home.

Apart from energy efficiency, there exists an objective function of real time-system that aims to provide service in the minimum possible time even at the cost of higher energy consumption. Real-time automation mainly observes its implementation in the industrial domain as industrial applications can't afford to have service delay even at the cost of energy efficiency. The research for real-time system has been presented in the subsequent subsection.

8.3.3   REAL-TIME SYSTEM

Employment of real-time response results in smart homes that are capable of recognizing occupants' activities and responding accordingly. In the literature, it is noticed that despite rigorous research in the area of smart homes and IoT, usage of real-time information still has a wide scope for exploration. Although till date most companies are able to observe energy consumption but still lack real-time response. This subsection presents the implementation of real-time systems in smart homes.

Tan et al. [17] introduced an IoT-based application that monitors the energy efficiency of manufacturing industries in real-time. It suggests finding abnormal energy consumption patterns. Thereafter, best energy management practices are embedded to improve energy efficiency by avoiding energy wastages.

Real-time smart homes can also be accomplished using activity recognition of its occupants. Several activity recognition solutions have been proposed in the literature using sensors and smart devices but it still poses interesting research challenges. Perumal et al. [18] have proposed an IoT-based activity recognition framework using multiple devices within the home network. Validation of the proposed framework concluded that it can robustly identify various activities with high accuracy and thus can be reliably deployed.

Salman et al. [2] have analyzed real-time model of a house to demonstrate simulation studies for lighting and temperature control. The authors further examined signal integrity to ensure seamless communication of IoT-enabled devices. Here, the authors have used motion sensors for home security system and HVAC. The proposed *In-house Smart Wireless Communication model* [2] can also be extended to automate home parts, commercial buildings, etc., which are competent to response activities of its occupants in real time. Smart home has a broad scope to pursue research in the real-time automation.

Although there has been rigorous research in the field of home automation and automation of cities, it lacks its widespread employment in real-life. Several people are still resistant to incorporating automation into their daily routine. Resultantly, there has been a lack of the widespread employment of automation despite rigorous research in the field. The associated constraints and challenges have been presented in the following section.

8.4   CONSTRAINTS AND CHALLENGES FOR HOME AUTOMATION

The widespread application and implementation of home automation faces several challenges and constraints. The major challenges that have been observed in research are human behavior and technological constraints as follows.

8.4.1   HUMAN BEHAVIOR

Although the whole world is thinking about devising energy efficient solution but in reality people have a callous attitude about energy conservation. Therefore, there remains a hidden challenge to modulate customer's attitude toward energy saving. There exists a gap in the understanding of consumers' behavior and integrating this understanding during the implementation of smart home technology [19]. In [19], the authors focus on an understanding of Singapore households and its usage to save energy by undertaking three case studies.

The first case study is to analyze the attitude of consumers for energy saving in Chongqing, China. Here, 246 consumers are analyzed through questionnaire via face to face. The basis for conducting this survey is that energy conservation has doubled in China from 2000 to 2008. As a result, the government of China is also taking proactive steps in the direction of manufacturing energy efficient appliances. This causes a positive influence on energy consumption but unfortunately, people used the saved money to purchase other energy-consuming appliances. Thus, the major challenge is the lack of knowledge and attitude of consumers. This survey concluded that consumers are willing to save energy without compromising their comfort.

Another case study is performed to analyze consumers' perspective on the employment of smart meters. The case study is performed in Sweden. It is observed that although the appliances have become energy efficient but number of appliances per home is rapidly increasing, thus resulting in escalated energy consumption. The smart meter can collect energy consumption data thus informing consumer well in advance to control the energy usage. Smart meters also displays dynamic tariff of energy during peak-load hours thus suggesting consumers to adjust their energy usage accordingly. The survey revealed that smart homes having smart meters recorded higher energy efficiency. The survey also unveiled the need to educate consumers about appliance energy consumption. One more case study is also done to understand the impact of smart meter and in-home display on consumers' behavior in China. This study revealed that homes with in-home displays saved a significant amount of energy. Moreover, this also helped in reducing the energy requirement during peak-load hours. Thus, there was a positive impact of smart meters and in-home displays on consumers' behavior.

Moreno et al. [20] have also discussed the higher and complex requirements of the users. At the international level, energy efficiency has been recognized as a prioritized requirement among various requirements to boost the energy sustainability of the planet. Numerous solutions have been suggested to address the requirement of energy efficiency, for example, context-based energy consumption. Moreno et al. [20] have considered three different contexts using reference smart buildings for each context. Authors have also carried experiments to demonstrate the effect of parameters in energy consumption. Authors claimed 23% energy saving using context-aware model therefore aligning with the global aim of minimizing environmental emissions. Even countries like Europe are also in infancy for energy management systems in homes and offices.

8.4.2 TECHNOLOGICAL CONSTRAINTS

Any IoT network consists of various devices including sensors. These sensors are powered using battery that cannot be charged or changed [21]. It is not impossible to replace the battery after deployment, but it is nearly impossible as sensors may be generally deployed beyond human reach and undesirable locations. For instance, sensors are attached to wild animals in order to track them or sensors may also be deployed in mines to monitor the various parameters. Resultantly, the key constraint faced by any IoT device is its power limitation as a battery replacement for sensing devices creates a major hurdle and causes a significant increase in the incurred cost. On the contrary, an exponential increase in the number of IoT devices results in enhanced energy consumption. According to a report by CiSCO, the number of IoT devices surpassed the number of humans during 2008/2009. This number of IoT devices is still evolving rapidly. Thus, significant research needs to take place to minimize the energy consumption of IoT devices for large scale deployment of IoT networks [22, 23]

Basically, a sensor node consists (1) sensing subsystem (2) processing subsystem (3) communication subsystem (4) power source. All these subsystems require energy; however, the energy consumption for the communication subsystem is highest. It is worth mentioning that IoT devices results in a reduction in energy consumption (electricity usage). For the same, the energy used by IoT devices should be minimized. Hence, energy efficiency for IoT devices the major challenge.

A mechanism should be devised that provides the longest lifespan to the battery of IoT devices. This can be achieved by combining several principles like managing energy supply mechanism and further effective consumption of supplied energy. The principle of energy supply management can be achieved by energy harvesting that aims to scavenge ambient energy (solar, wind, hydropower) into a useable form. The principle of energy conservation focuses on reduced energy consumption of IoT devices. The energy can be conserved using various schemes like data reduction, duty cycling, etc.

For energy harvesting, the methodology should be implemented to buffer the energy (solar, wind, etc.) during its abundance as these external energy sources do not have consistent behavior during lifecycle of the system. Resultantly, energy buffering is strongly advocated and advisable for IoT systems. For energy conservation, various researchers have recommended several methodologies. Few popular schemes are broadly classified as follows:

1) sleep/wake-up,
2) data driven,
3) mobility based, and
4) data aggregation and transmission.

8.4.2.1 SLEEP/WAKE-UP SCHEME

Sensor node does not receive or send data every time during its lifespan. There exist some slots when these sensors and idle do not communicate. These idle states also consume some energy. It is observed that energy consumed during idle states is higher than the energy consumption during active states. Moreover, idle listening of wireless transceiver requires an equal amount of energy. Thus, the focus should be laid to minimize energy consumption during idle states. Energy can be conserved by putting the node at sleep mode during idle time (also known as low energy consumption mode). It reduces the unnecessary consumption of energy. Switching between the sleep and wake-up states is the main concept of sleep/wake-up schemes. The node is switched from idle/sleep state to wake-up mode when it needs to communicate and put back to sleep mode immediately after communication is over.

8.4.2.2 DATA-DRIVEN SCHEME

Sleep/wake-up techniques discussed above are typically unaware of data to be sampled by the nodes. The energy consumed by a node varies with the amount of data to be transmitted and/or received by a node. According to data-driven schemes, it further enhances the energy efficiency. This approach aims at data reduction prior to its communication in order to minimize the energy requirement.

Energy consumption of a node escalates for redundant sampling while communicating temporal and/or spatial correlation at regular intervals. So, data-driven approach is used to control the sensing tasks and unwanted sampling as data acquisition and transmission turns expensive in terms of energy consumption. This approach mainly emphasizes reducing the amount of data to be sampled while considering sensing accuracy.

8.4.2.3   MOBILITY-BASED SCHEME

In general, each approach assumes that sensing nodes in the network are static. However, the mobility of node has been recently considered for energy efficient data gathering in sensor networks. Mobility of node is feasible and it can be achieved in various ways. For example, a mobilizer can be equipped with the sensor to change its location, but mobilizers are expensive in terms of energy consumption. Hence, it is not advisable but confining the mobility to a limited range can be beneficial. On the contrary, sensors can also be deployed into mobile elements like car, animals, bus, etc. In such case, there is no extra energy consumption but the mobility pattern of mobile element needs to be considered. Mobile nodes can be part of the network or it can be part of the environment. When a mobile node is part of a network, it can be controlled completely. In another case, when a node is part of the environment, it might not be possible to control it. Node mobility is quite useful for decreasing energy consumption. Packets from source to sink traverse network following multihop path. When the nodes are static, some nodes on a particular path are more loaded than the others according to the network topology used. Specially nodes in the neighborhood of the sink node consume more energy because they have to receive and forward each packet directed toward the sink node. Therefore, these nodes will have energy deficiency. Thus, mobile nodes are necessary to prolong the network lifetime.

8.4.2.4   DATA AGGREGATION AND TRANSMISSION PROCESS

It is evident that data transmission consumes more energy in comparison to data processing. Hence, it is advisable to merge/aggregate the data coming from various sources [24]. Here, sources of data refer to IoT devices. As per this policy, the data coming from various sources are consolidated into a single packet which subsequently minimizes the data transmission. During the process of consolidation, redundancy is eliminated. Data transmission significantly utilizes this aggregation and thus controlling the energy consumption. Optimization algorithms can be used in order to eliminate redundancy and consolidation as an aid to minimize energy consumption [24].

Now it is evident that it becomes absolutely mandatory to overcome these constraints and challenges before the widespread application of home automation. In order to address the issue of human behavior, occupants must be trained and motivated to understand the need for energy saving. For the same, there could be some provision to appreciate the conscious and motivated smart home occupant. Alongside, technological constraints can be overcome by advancement in technology. Hence, in order to have the utmost benefit of home automation, human and technology need to go hand in hand to provide the most energy efficient solution.

8.5   CONCLUSION AND FUTURE SCOPE

IoT has substantially influenced the lifestyle of people these days. Each aspect of the human life has been affected by the advancement in IoT technology in a way or other. IoT has completely dominated automation of homes and offices thus moving toward smart homes and smart offices. Here, authors review various papers discussing technologies for the implementation of smart homes and associated energy management. This helps us to identify the research gap and thus finding possible avenues for research. During the study, it is realized that widespread employment of IoT networks (for home and city automation) faces few constraints and challenges. We need to address these constraints and challenges to garner the full-fledged employment of IoT in our daily life.

During this survey, we notice that IoT results in integration and interconnection of various things in the network thus sharing sensitive information. This information sharing requires reliable secured communication and thus future research is required for privacy research in smart homes. Moreover, pervasive research is required for energy conservation. There is a very bright chance to carry out research for using renewable sources of energy in smart homes as energy conservation is the most compelling problem at the international level.

KEYWORDS

- **IoT**
- **smart homes**
- **energy efficiency**
- **context-aware automation**
- **HVAC**

REFERENCES

1. Missaoui, R., Joumaa, H., Ploix, S., Bacha, S. (2014). Managing energy smart homes according to energy prices: analysis of a building energy management system. *Energy and Buildings* 71, 155–167.
2. Salman, L., Salman, S., Jahangirian, S., Abraham, M., German, F., Blair, C., & Krenz, P. (2016, December). Energy Efficient IoT-based Smart Home (pp. 526–529), IEEE.
3. Vinay, S. K. N., Kusuma, S. M. (2015). Home automation using Internet of Things. *Int. Res. J. Eng. Technol.* 2(3), 1965–70.
4. El-Basioni, B. M. M., El-Kader, S. M. A., Abdelmonim, M. (2013). Smart home design using wireless sensor network and biometric technologies. *Inform. Technol.*, 1(2), 413–429.
5. Chan, M., Campo, E., Estève, D., Fourniols, J.-Y. (2009). Smart homes—current features and future perspectives. *Maturitas* 64(2), 90–97.
6. Sriskanthan, N., Tan, F., Karande, A. (2002). Bluetooth based home automation system. *Microprocess. Microsyst.* 26(6), 281–89.
7. Saad Al-Sumaiti, A., Ahmed, M. H., Salama, M. M. A. (2014). Smart home activities: a literature review. *Electr. Pow. Compo. Sys.* 42, 294–305.
8. Gul, M. S., Patidar, S. (2015). Understanding the energy consumption and occupancy of a multi-purpose academic building. *Energy Build.* 87, 155–165.
9. Rocha, P., Siddiqui, A., Stadler, M. (2015). Improving energy efficiency via smart building energy management systems: a comparison with policy measures. *Energy Build.* 88, 203–213.
10. Ahmad, M. W. et al. (2016). Building energy metering and environmental monitoring a state-of-the-art review and directions for future research. *Energy Build.* 120, 85–102.
11. Hong, T. et al. (2016). Advances in research and applications of energy-related occupant behavior in buildings. *Energy Build.* 116, 694–702.
12. Kang, H. S. et al. (2016). Smart manufacturing: past research, present findings, and future directions. *Int. J. Precis. Eng. Manuf. Green Technol.* 3, 111–128.
13. Mangla, M., Akhare, R., Ambarkar, S. (2019). Context-aware automation based energy conservation techniques for IoT ecosystem. In: Energy Conservation for IoT Devices (pp. 129–153). Springer: Singapore.

14. Das, S. K., Cook, D. J., Battacharya, A., Heierman, E. O., Lin, T.-Y. (2002). The role of prediction algorithms in the MavHome smart home architecture. *IEEE Wirel. Commun.* 9(6), 77–84.

15. Zhang, D., Gu, T., Wang, X. (2005). Enabling context-aware smart home with semantic web technologies. *Int. J. Human-Friendly Welf. Robot. Syst.* 6(4), 12–20.

16. Lu, J. et al. (2010) The smart thermostat: using occupancy sensors to save energy in homes. In: *Proceedings of the 8th ACM Conference on Embedded Networked Sensor Systems*, pp. 211–224.

17. Tan, Y. S., Ng, Y. T., Low, J. S. C. (2017). Internet-of-Things enabled real-time monitoring of energy efficiency on manufacturing shop floors. *Procedia CIRP* 61, 376–381.

18. Perumal, T., Chui, Y. L., Bin Ahmadon, M. A., Yamaguchi, S. (2017). IoT based activity recognition among smart home residents. In: *2017 IEEE 6th Global Conference on Consumer Electronics*, pp. 1–2.

19. Bhati, A., Hansen, M., Man Chan, C. (2017). Energy conservation through smart homes in a smart city: a lesson for singapore households. *Energy Policy* 104, 230–239.

20. Moreno, M. V., Úbeda, B., Skarmeta, A. F., Zamora, M. A. (2014). How can we tackle energy efficiency in IOT based smart buildings? *Sensors* 14, 9582–9614. www.mdpi.com/journal/sensorsArticle.

21. Mittal, M., Pandey, S.C. (2019). The rudiments of energy conservation and IoT. In: Energy Conservation for IoT Devices (pp. 1–17). Springer: Singapore.

22. Sethi, P., Sarangi, R. S. (2017). Internet of things: architectures, protocols, and applications. *Int. J. Electr. Comput. Eng.* 2017, 1–25. https://www.hindawi.com/journals/jece/2017/9324035/cta/

23. Benazzouz, Y., Munilla, C., Gnalp, O., Gallissot, M., Grgen, L. (2014). Sharing user IoT devices in the cloud. In: *2014 IEEE World Forum on Internet of Things*, p. 373. https://doi.org/10.1109/WF-IoT.2014.6803193

24. Kumar, C., Paulus, R. (2014). A prospective towards M2M communication. *J. Converg. Inf. Technol.* 9, 102–114.

25. Sachi Nandan Mohanty, E.Laxmi Lydia, Mohamed Elhoseny, Majid M. Gethami AI Otabi, K.Shankar, Deep learning with LSTM based distributed data mining model for energy efficient wireless sensor networks, Physical Communication, vol.40, Issue-4, 101097-102008, (2020). https://doi.org/10.1016/j.phycom.2020.101097.

26. Chandrakant Mallick, Suneeta Satpathy, "Challenges and Design Goals of Wireless Sensor Networks: A Sate-of-the-art Review", International Journal of Computer Applications (0975–8887), 2018.

CHAPTER 9

IoT-Based Home Electronic Appliances Control System with Voice Control

PULKIT JAIN[1*], AMAN GUPTA[2], MAYANK VERMA[2], and
VIVEK CHAUHAN[2]

[1]*Department of ECE, Chandigarh University, Mohali, Punjab, India*

[2]*Department of Mechatronics Engineering, Chandigarh University,
Mohali, Punjab, India*

Corresponding author. E-mail: pulkitjaindav@gmail.com.

ABSTRACT

The continuous growth in automation and various related technologies has led to home automation using Internet of things (IoT) where every appliance can be converted into a smart appliance by integrating wireless control with the help of Internet using network protocol (TCP/IP). This book chapter discusses about IoT-based home electronic appliance control system which has been designed with the help of ESP8266-based NodeMCU IoT development board. The mentioned system can control the basic tasks like switching that is, ON and OFF state of any home appliance to much complex tasks over the Internet from anywhere in the world with the help of an Android or iOS mobile application known as Blynk, which provides a user interface for a system. Moreover, the system is also voice-controlled which can be commanded over Google Assistant.

9.1 INTRODUCTION

The Internet of things (IoT) is a network of interconnected and uniquely identifiable computing devices embedded in everyday artifacts [1]. IoT architecture may vary from system to system depending on its application.

A generalized architecture of IoT is shown in Figure 9.1. There is not necessarily always a two-way communication between all the components of an IoT system, it may also be one way or may vary from system to system.

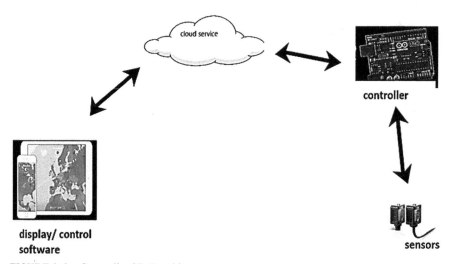

FIGURE 9.1　Generalized IoT architecture.

IoT has progressed toward becoming the way of life of an individual with extraordinary potential [2]. It is even targeting various undertakings that are prerequisites of human intelligence. In the present scenario, IoT has the potential to encompass all the necessities of human dealings in their day-to-day life. It has already been introduced in our day-to-day life which includes our smart refrigerators, smart washing machines, and many other appliances [3]. It includes connecting our physical devices to the Internet and then accessing them from a distant location through a web interface.

This chapter aims toward developing a hardware design which can control our home electronic appliances such as fans, lights, AC, door alarms, electronic door locks, and television over the Internet with the help of two controls for a single system. For demonstration purpose, an eight-channel relay system has been designed which is capable of switching AC or DC appliances and is controlled by an ESP8266 system-on-chip-based micro-controller named as NodeMCU [4]. User interfacing devices such as mobile or laptop send the data to the cloud/server and then this data through server is transferred to the controller which further performs an appropriate action in response to the command received from the cloud/server. Lastly, the voice control system is built over an If This Then That (IFTTT) platform using Google Assistant and Blynk.

Arrangement of the chapter is as follows: introduction to IoT and a brief idea of this chapter's work is covered in Section 9.1. In Section 9.2, the already existing approaches for the said objective have been discussed, Section 9.3 describes about the hardware and software schematics of the proposed system, Section 9.4 provides an insight into the working of the system while Section 9.5 contains the prospective advantages that this system holds over other existing systems followed by conclusion at the end.

9.2 RELATED WORKS

Despite the fact that the idea of smart homes is new in India, extensive measure of work has been completed in different nations, where smart homes are now set up. Kang et al. [5] discussed about procurement and investigation of sensor information which will be utilized crosswise over smart homes. They proposed a design for separating relevant data by investigating the information procured from different sensors and provide context aware services. JeyaPadmini and Kashwan [6] talked about reducing power dissipation and methods to conserve energy in smart homes utilizing IoT. It utilizes cameras for perceiving human exercises through picture-handling methods. The need for common standards and protocols with the aim to achieve sustainable IoT-based applications has been discussed by Kamilaris and Pitsillides [7] focusing particularly on smart homes. Gaikwad et al. [8] discussed about difficulties and issues that arise in IoT-based smart-home systems by conducting a survey and have also provided possible solutions. Though similar works are carried out elsewhere, but authors in this book chapter have integrated Google Assistant with the existing systems in order to make it voice controllable.

9.3 PROPOSED SYSTEM DESIGN

The complete system may be divided into two segments: system hardware and system software. The hardware and software components of the proposed system in the form of block diagram are shown in Figure 9.2.

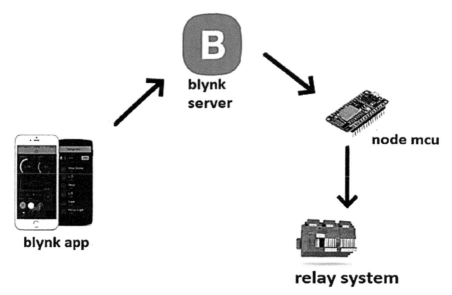

FIGURE 9.2   Block diagram of the proposed system.

9.3.1 HARDWARE DESIGN

The system hardware comprises of eight relays, 12 V constant power supply source, NodeMCU board, 7805 voltage regulator, heat sink, ULN2803 IC, PC817 Opto-coupler IC, and IN4007 diodes (for reverse current protection).

NodeMCU: NodeMCU is an IoT development board consisting of ESP8266, system on chip integrating a 32-bit microcontroller. It has 16 General Purpose Input Output (GPIOs) and a processing unit which is operating at a clock frequency of 80–160 kHz. NodeMCU is Lua Script-based programmable device and it can also be programmed by using Arduino IDE. The pin diagram of NodeMCU is depicted in Figure 9.3.

PC817: PC817 is a four pin Opto-coupler IC. The purpose of this IC is to isolate the development board from the external circuitry in order to avoid loading effect on it.

ULN2803: Uln2803 is an 18 pin IC and it has eight Darlington pairs in it having eight inputs and eight outputs. The purpose of using this IC in the system is to meet the current requirements of relays. It is each output provides a maximum current of 500 mA.

Relays: Relays serve the purpose of switching element in the system. Appliances are connected to Common and Normally Open terminals of relay.

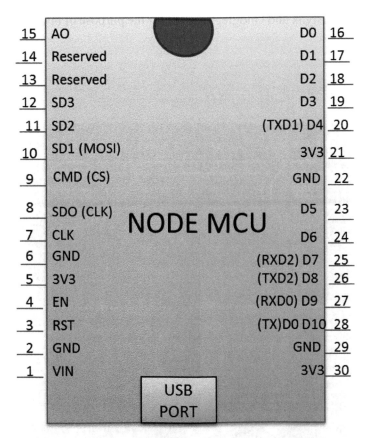

15	AO		DO	16
14	Reserved		D1	17
13	Reserved		D2	18
12	SD3		D3	19
11	SD2		(TXD1) D4	20
10	SD1 (MOSI)		3V3	21
9	CMD (CS)		GND	22
8	SDO (CLK)	NODE MCU	D5	23
7	CLK		D6	24
6	GND		(RXD2) D7	25
5	3V3		(TXD2) D8	26
4	EN		(RXD0) D9	27
3	RST		(TX)D0 D10	28
2	GND		GND	29
1	VIN		3V3	30
		USB PORT		

FIGURE 9.3 Pin configuration of NodeMCU with respect to Arduino.

9.3.2 SYSTEM SOFTWARE

The software used for the system are Blynk interface and Google Assistant, where Google Assistant provides a voice controlling ability to the system.

Blynk: Blynk is an IoT platform which has applications for both Android and iOS which facilitate the building of a graphical interface as shown in Figure 9.4, for controlling the system simply by dragging and dropping widgets such as buttons, sliders, maps, and so forth. Blynk server is on different IP addresses for different countries, for India, IP address of Blynk server is 188.166.177.186.

IFTTT: IFTTT basically provides a platform to synchronize or inter-link two or more softwares in order to perform a specific task. We have synchronized Blynk and Google Assistant for the purpose of building a voice control system.

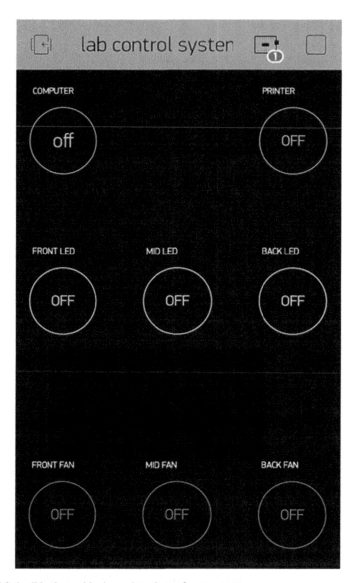

FIGURE 9.4 Blynk graphical user interface of our system.

Google Assistant: Google Assistant voice control system is a Google account secured system. It is only operable on the specific Google account on which it is configured. This voice control system is build using IFTTT platform and its interface is depicted in Figure 9.5. We have used IFTTT to synchronize Blynk server and Google Assistant. In IFTTT, one has to decide that how and by which means we want to trigger the system and what action has to be performed associated with that trigger. This combination of trigger and action is called recipe.

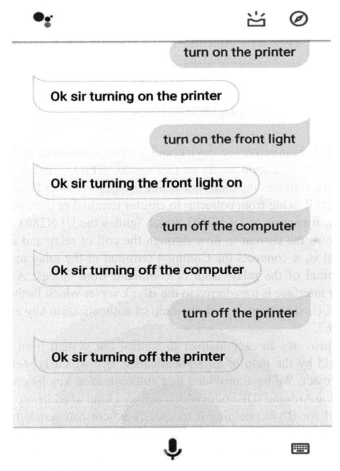

FIGURE 9.5   Google Assistant interface of system.

9.4   WORKING OF THE SYSTEM

Figure 9.6 depicts the simple working of the designed system.

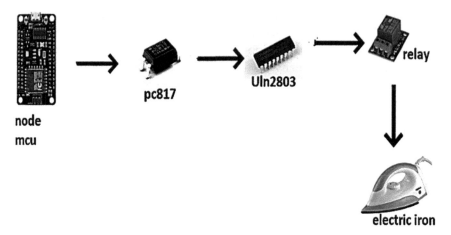

FIGURE 9.6   Functional block diagram of the system.

NodeMCU is an active low device, and it is programmed in such a manner that whenever the button sends an ON signal, GPIO switches to ground which in turn activates the transistor inside the Opto-coupler IC. As a result, current starts flowing from collector to emitter terminal of the transistor and via emitter, it reaches to ULN2803 which ignites the ULN2803 IC, which further allows the current to flow through the coil of relay and activates a switch, that is, it connects the Common terminal of the relay to Normally Open terminal of the relay. Data or command from Google Assistant or Blynk user interface is transferred to the Blynk server which further sends it to NodeMCU, specifying it with the help of authentication key as depicted in Figure 9.7.

Blynk provides an easy manner to control our system from anywhere in the world by the help of an authentication key which is specific for a specific project. We have provided that authentication key by creating our project in the Arduino IDE code, which acts as a kind of address of development board for Blynk, helping it to specify where commands have to be sent. For our system, a specific phrase is set for a specific relay allowing Google Assistant to control it. When a specific phrase is sent to Google Assistant by either typing or sending a voice command, Google Assistant responds and gets triggered in accordance with the sent phrase. It further sends a command to the Blynk server by sending a web request through the Webhooks in IFFT using the following URL: http://ip(blynk)/authtoken/update/pin.

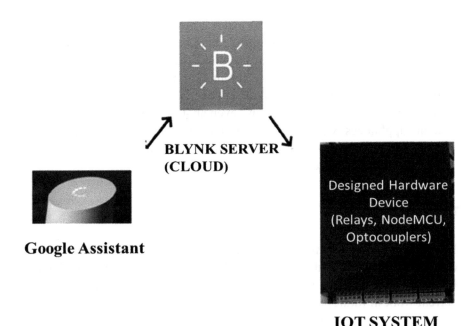

IOT SYSTEM

FIGURE 9.7 Directional flow of data between the software and the designed hardware IoT system.

9.5 ADVANTAGES OF THE PROPOSED SYSTEM

The proposed system may be configured with custom-designed controllers for handicapped people. The voice commands are fully reconfigurable for blind people. The best advantage is that the entire system is secured by Google, wherein a system is operated via a single Google account, making it secure. Moreover, the given system may be modified as a security system, wherein alerts and actions can be taken by the system without intervention of the user.

9.6 CONCLUSION

Many existing IoT systems provide only a single type of interface for home-automation applications, but in this book chapter Google Assistant has been integrated with the existing systems in order to make it voice controllable. Moreover, the presented system eliminates the need to install any extra software in user's mobile phone to make it voice controllable, as Google Assistant is one of the inbuilt/preinstalled application in the Android smart phones. From the literature, it can be found that most of the applications developed for the purpose of home automation are Android based, thereby restricting the iOS mobile users for controlling the systems. The Blynk application used in this chapter allows even an iOS user to control switching of home appliances with the Blynk interface. Even an iOS user can control the appliances using voice commands by simply installing Google Assistant application in his/her phone.

9.7   FUTURE SCOPE

Further a house-sitting mode may be added in the proposed system, which can control the state of the lights at predefined intervals to indicate that the house isn't empty, when in fact it is. This may be considered as the scope of current work in future.

KEYWORDS

- **Blynk**
- **Google Assistant**
- **IFTTT**
- **IoT**
- **Lua**
- **NodeMCU**
- **SoC**

REFERENCES

1. Aldossari, M. Q. and Sidorova, A., "Consumer acceptance of Internet of things (IoT): smart home context," *Journal of Computer Information Systems*, 60(6), pp. 507–517 (**2020**).
2. Durani, H., Sheth, M., Vaghasia, M., and Kotech, S., "Smart automated home application using IoT with Blynk app," 2nd *International Conference on Inventive Communication and Computational Technology (ICICCT)*, Coimbatore, pp. 393–397 (**2018**). Available:

https://www.semanticscholar.org/paper/Smart-Automated-Home-Application-using-IoT-with-App-Durani-Sheth/dbd7b513f21a064a15437aa880cbb37b9e9bfa24#citing-papers.

3. Pavithra, D. and Balakrishnan, R., "IoT based monitoring and control system for home automation," *Global Conference on Communication Technologies (GCCT),* Thuckalay, Tamil Nadu, pp. 169–173 (**2015**).

4. Nodemcu, http://www.nodemcu.com/, Nodemcu, 2017. [Online]. Available: http://www.nodemcu.com/.

5. Kang, B., Park, S., Lee, T., and Park, S., "IOT based monitoring system using tri-level context making model for smart home services," *IEEE International Conference on Consumer Electronics (ICCE),* pp. 198–199 (**2015**).

6. JeyaPadmini, J. and Kashwan, K. R., "Effective power utilization and conservation in smart homes using IoT," *International Conference on Computation of Power, Energy, Information and Communication (ICCPEIC),* pp. 0195–0199 (**2015**).

7. Kamilaris, A. and Pitsillides, A., "Towards interoperable and sustainable smart homes," *IST-Africa Conference & Exhibition,* Nairobi, pp. 1–11 (**2013**).

8. Gaikwad, P. P., Gabhane, J. P., and Golait, S. S., "A survey based on smart homes system using Internet-of-things," *International Conference on Computation of Power, Energy, Information and Communication (ICCPEIC),* Chennai, pp. 0330–0335 (**2015**).

CHAPTER 10

Real-Time Data Communication with IoT Sensors and ThingSpeak Cloud

AMIT SUNDAS* and SURYA NARAYAN PANDA

School of Engineering, Ajeenkya DY Patil University Pune, India 412105, Chitkara University Institute of Engineering and Technology, Patiala, Punjab, India

Corresponding author. E-mail: amitsundas1992@gmail.com.

ABSTRACT

This chapter proposed the implementation of detecting various sensor data in real time and sending those data to the cloud. Based on the popularity of Internet of things (IoT), this chapter inspired to deal with various sensor data. Each result was fetched by Wi-Fi module using a computer software named Arduino integrated development environment. After plotting sensor data, the data was sent to the cloud with the help of an open-source platform named ThingSpeak. The experiment is completely based on IoT and cloud. This report will briefly describe the complete process of how the execution was done to plot the sensor data and sent to the cloud. The results will be explained by the end of this chapter.

10.1 INTRODUCTION

Internet of things (IoT) is the massive system that consists of electronic devices such as home electronic appliances, vehicles, mobile phones, and many more smart objects. IoT has grabbed a reputed position in the field of technology. These days, IoT is being used for almost every field that could be related to the research area, health science, security system, or manufacturing of any devices. In short, IoT has made daily life easier and more reliable to live [1, 2]. The major features of IoT are storing sensor data in real time, sending real-time data to the cloud, accessing those data from anywhere [3, 18]. The real-time data of sensor is stored by using any Wi-Fi module like NodeMCU or bluetooth modules like HC-05. By this generation of technology, sensors have become the most important object [4]. Sensors are small in size but highly perfect for the features of sensing motion, pressure, and human touch, even the atmosphere temperature. The size and light weight make the best advantages of sensors that help to design a device. The fetched data of sensors are processed with the help of an open and free source platform software named Arduino integrated development environment (IDE) [2, 5]. Arduino IDE is a free and open-source computer software [6]. ThingSpeak is a cloud-based platform and is used to keep the sensor data in MATLAB-based cloud where ThingSpeak is also a free and open source website platform based on cloud [4,5].

This chapter motivates the implementation of fetching real-time data of various sensors and storing those data in cloud-based platform. Various sensors such as ultrasonic, humid sensor DHT 22, accelerometer were used for this experiment. Before sending any data to the cloud, first, the data in real time needs to be fetched. The outputs of fetched data in real time were shown in Arduino Software IDE. By the end of the chapter, experimental results are also explained briefly.

The chapter starts with introduction in Section 10.1. Section 10.2 will cover literature review, then, Section 10.3 will elaborate about what resources were used to implement this experiment. Section 10.4, related work will explain about the complete process of the experiment. Section 10.5 covers how the data were sent to cloud and followed by Section 10.6 which discusses the conclusion part by the end of the chapter.

10.2   LITERATURE REVIEW

The aims of reviewing the literature are to gather the latest literature available in the field of IoT and its application by evaluating outcomes as per the study approaches. The authors have focused the duration of studies between 2012 and 2018 on literature.

The application challenges of wireless sensor networks (WSNs) to monitor the environment as well as those challenges faced by approaches and opportunities [39,40]. This chapter elaborated with the help of SDN how approaches and opportunities can be released on the applications of WSNs (Modieginyane, 2018). An investigation on the scientific plan of a sensor where cloud dependent on properties of the virtualization. Granting to the outcomes, creators pronounced that sensor and its lifetime expanded by only 3.25% and vitality utilization diminished with 36.68% (Misra, 2017). Additional examination identified with savvy urban areas just as condition, observing in four explicit applications, the scientists looked at the utilization energy of media access control (MACs) address conventions. The scientists used the traffic of a multiclass model to analyze the vitality utilization of MACs convention at a low information rate (AlSkaif, 2017). A framework depends on the start to finish body territory detecting name KNOWME coordinated with Nokia mobile of model N95. The motivation behind writing this chapter was to cover and assess four significant difficulties of physical activities (Mitra, 2012). The improvement of constant information securing module of sensors such as humid and temperature utilizing DHT22/11 and NodeMCU. The sensor information is conveyed into detecting the structure space, agreeing and saving the information of hotness, stickiness or the air quality, considered by the analyst (Miqdad, 2017). An examination concentrated on the ongoing advancements of wearable sensor and its applications which incorporate well-being and health, security for the human body, early discovery of confusion (Patel, 2012). A paper depicted how the multioperator arrangement of the plant based on electricity can be sieved out powerfully in the network of critical thinking dependent on it. The analysts have investigated the checking and how it would be taxi is controlled (Chandra, 2017). A research paper centered on giving a steering instrument of vitality effective with snags from the WSNs by accepting the mobile data collector as a low rate to bring information on or after static sensors (Xie, 2017). To screen pH dependent on the incorporated cloud with a paper presented a model of WSNs which additionally gives an answer for breakdown of oxygen parameter from squander water. The model delivers a stage name that is, Telerivet, informing which will not exclusively identify of water contamination even sends warning by means of SMS (Zakaria, 2017). The creators discovered Common Offer Acceptance Portal convention as the best possibility for elevated standard among inserted frameworks and cloud (Peniak, 2016). To obtain and screen the constant information in the field of agriculture and natural parameters help with the assistance of WSNs, Wi-Fi, Android web-based apps (Ajao, 2017). Acquainted a venture that pointed with making an incredible and dependable stage comprises of without wire types sensor which can be further used in media players (Yetgin, 2017). Different creators inspected of improvements of WSNs, utilizations of WSNs, structure limitations which include lifetime estimation model. They additionally presented the methods of network lifetime boost with plan rules (Torresen, 2013). The word picture of certain calculations that how to create valuable machines in a simple manner which diminishes human endeavors. As suggested by the creators, the idea of brilliant home improves the standard method to live at home (Poojari, 2017). The specialists talked about the correspondence of data acquisition system known as DAS to 52° North SOS. The creators acquainted a methodology with making a minimal effort programmed data acquisition system that will get urban destination information on temperature and damp. For the methodology, creators gave the total foundation to information perception in the real context of enormous information and depend on it (Sim, 2016). The paper coordinated with two methodologies, one is harmed confinement strategy dependent on adaptability that permits exchange-off between a few sensors and goals. Another single is about adaptability-based vitality effectiveness, engineering of staggered processing structured. The authors clarified an examination of recreated bracket structure just as a genuine full-scale structure that shows the productivity of framework in vitality effectiveness and harm confinement (Hackmann, 2014). The specialists studied about it as an incorporated stage for implanted frameworks. The report gives an issue related to customary hierarchal correspondence.

10.3   RESOURCES

This experiment implies many components such as sensors, Wi-Fi modules, Arduino IDE, cloud based on an open source platform. Short descriptions of all the requirements are explained below.

10.3.1   WI-FI MODULE

Among many Wi-Fi modules, NodeMCU ESP8266 is used for this experiment. NodeMCU is small in size and has much functionality but here the purpose of using this component is sending sensor data to the cloud. One of the great features of the Wi-Fi module is that it makes a wireless internet connection. NodeMCU is an IoT-based electronic device, and is having open source license platform with SOC Espressif system in ESP8266 Wi-Fi [7,8,21].

10.3.2   SENSOR

This experiment includes various sensors such as ultrasonic, DHT 22, and accelerometer. Ultrasonic sensor is used to detect the distance of any object.

DHT 22 is a humid sensor that is used to detect the temperature and humidity of the environment. Accelerometer is used to sense the acceleration in all the three axes that is, X-axis, Y-axis, and Z-axis [9].

10.3.3 ARDUINO IDE

This is an open-source user friendly computer-based software where users are allowed to perform for free of cost. All the real-time numbers of various sensors are fetched in Arduino IDE using computer programming [5, 16].

10.3.4 THINGSPEAK

This platform is a cloud-based open source platform. In this platform, real-time data of any object can be sent and stored as the representation of a graph. To send and store data in this platform require any Wi-Fi modules or bluetooth modules [10,11]. According to the requirement, NodeMCU was chosen as a Wi-Fi module to implement this experiment [15, 18].

10.4 RELATED WORK

This implementation was done using three sensors (ultrasonic, DHT 22, and accelerometer) in two different steps. The first step was to perform individual connectivity of all sensors one by one with their individual outputs. The second step is to make one connection with all of the three sensors to get one output with different sensors in one sheet. The real-time data is fetched by NodeMCU ESP8266 and stored in ThingSpeak [20]. The author studied about all the resources and technology before starting with the implementation. Figure 10.1 shows the architecture of all the components how connections are made. All the steps of this experiment are explained with their results.

10.4.1 ULTRASONIC

The experiment was beginning with ultrasonic and followed by two other sensors that is, DHT 22 and accelerometer. The use of ultrasonic is to measure the distance of any object. For this implementation ultrasonic is used to measure the distance and fetch the data in real time, then the output is shown in Arduino IDE. Figures 10.2 and 10.3 show the connection of ultrasonic with Wi-Fi module and the output in Arduino IDE, respectively [12].

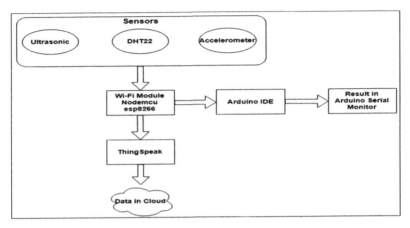

FIGURE 10.1   The overall system architecture.

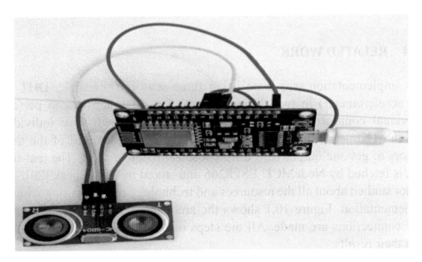

FIGURE 10.2   The connection of ultrasonic with NodeMCU ESP 8266.

10.4.2   DHT22

A humid sensor named DHT 11 and DHT 22 is based on sensing both temperature and humidity. DHT 22 was found suitable for implementing this experiment of sensing the temperature and humidity. The real-time data of temperature and humidity was fetched by connecting DHT 22 with NodeMCU ESP8266. Figures 10.4 and 10.5 show how DHT 22 was connected with Wi-Fi module and fetched data as output in Arduino IDE [13,17,19].

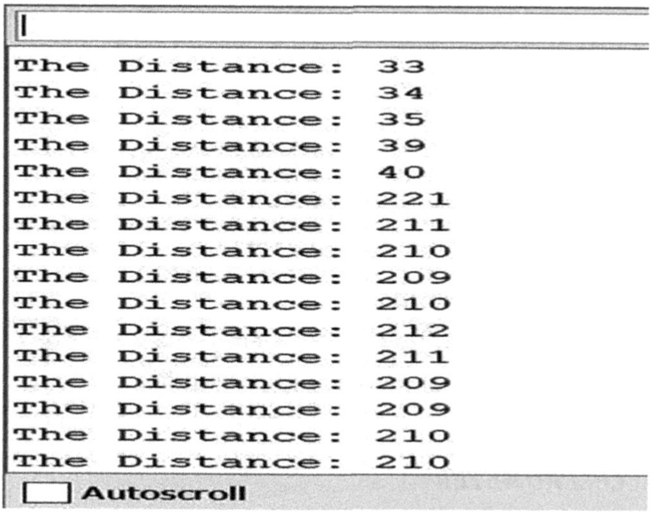

```
I
The  Distance:  33
The  Distance:  34
The  Distance:  35
The  Distance:  39
The  Distance:  40
The  Distance:  221
The  Distance:  211
The  Distance:  210
The  Distance:  209
The  Distance:  210
The  Distance:  212
The  Distance:  211
The  Distance:  209
The  Distance:  209
The  Distance:  210
The  Distance:  210
   Autoscroll
```

FIGURE 10.3   The result of ultrasonic sensor data in Arduino IDE.

FIGURE 10.4   The connection of humid sensor with NodeMCU ESP 8266.

```
Humidity: 50.70 %, Temp: 21.30 Celsius
Humidity: 50.80 %, Temp: 21.30 Celsius
Humidity: 50.80 %, Temp: 21.20 Celsius
Humidity: 50.80 %, Temp: 21.10 Celsius
Humidity: 50.90 %, Temp: 21.10 Celsius
Humidity: 51.00 %, Temp: 21.10 Celsius
Humidity: 51.00 %, Temp: 21.00 Celsius
Humidity: 51.00 %, Temp: 21.00 Celsius
Humidity: 51.10 %, Temp: 21.00 Celsius
Humidity: 51.10 %, Temp: 20.90 Celsius
Humidity: 51.20 %, Temp: 20.90 Celsius
Humidity: 51.30 %, Temp: 20.90 Celsius
Humidity: 51.40 %, Temp: 20.90 Celsius
Humidity: 51.40 %, Temp: 20.80 Celsius
Humidity: 51.40 %, Temp: 20.80 Celsius
```

☑ Autoscroll   No line ending ∨

FIGURE 10.5   The result of humid sensor data in Arduino IDE.

10.4.3   ACCELEROMETER

To get the data of acceleration here the author used an accelerometer sensor. This sensor can fetch acceleration in all the three axes that is, *X*-axis, *Y*-axis, and *Z*-axis. Figures 10.6 and 10.7 show the connection of accelerometer with Wi-Fi module and the output in Arduino IDE [14].

10.4.4   COMBINED

After completing the first step, this part includes the process of fetching all the three sensors data in one connection with NodeMCU ESP8266 and showing their outputs in Arduino IDE. Figure 10.8 shows how the connection was done and the output of this connectivity is in Figure 10.9.

10.5   THINGSPEAKS

This part will briefly elaborate how the sensor's data were sent to the cloud using the platform named ThingSpeak. However, after receiving the data from all the three sensors, then the major process is to send the data to the cloud [10,18]. NodeMCU ESP8266 was found suitable for this experiment due to it being easy to work with [14]. Figure 10.8 shows the connection of all the three sensors with NodeMCU. Figure 10.10 shows the result of ultrasonic sensor which was sent to cloud using ThingSpeak in representation of a graph. Figure 10.11(a) and (b) shows the output of humid sensor DHT22 where (a) has the output of humidity and (b) has the output of temperature. Figure 10.12(a)–(c) has the output of accelerometer where (a) represents the data of X-axis, similarly (b) and (c) represent the in Y-axis and Z-axis, respectively.

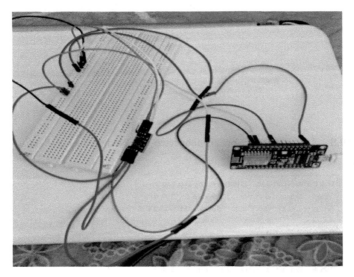

FIGURE 10.6   The connection of accelerometer sensor with NodeMCU ESP 8266.

```
x-axis= 303      y-axis= 304      z-axis= 302
x-axis= 303      y-axis= 304      z-axis= 302
x-axis= 303      y-axis= 303      z-axis= 301
x-axis= 303      y-axis= 303      z-axis= 301
x-axis= 303      y-axis= 304      z-axis= 302
x-axis= 304      y-axis= 304      z-axis= 302
x-axis= 303      y-axis= 304      z-axis= 302
x-axis= 303      y-axis= 304      z-axis= 302
x-axis= 302      y-axis= 302      z-axis= 300
x-axis= 300      y-axis= 300      z-axis= 299
x-axis= 299      y-axis= 299      z-axis= 298
x-axis= 299      y-axis= 300      z-axis= 298
x-axis= 300      y-axis= 300      z-axis= 298
x-axis= 300      y-axis= 300      z-axis= 298
x-axis= 300      y-axis= 300      z-axis= 298
x-axis= 300      y-axis= 300      z-axis= 298
☐ Autoscroll
```

FIGURE 10.7   The result of accelerometer sensor data in Arduino IDE.

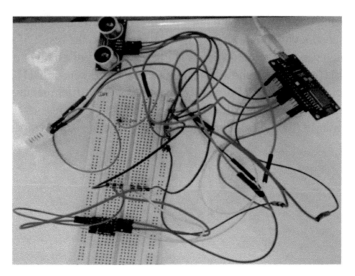

FIGURE 10.8   All the three sensors are connected with NodeMCU ESP 8266.

```
UltraSonic Sensor Data:
The Distance in cm: 144
Accelerometer Sensor Data
469x      436y       414z
 DHT22 Sensor Data
Humidity: 54.70 %, Temp: 19.60 Celsius
UltraSonic Sensor Data:
The Distance in cm: 143
Accelerometer Sensor Data
388x      387y       389z
 DHT22 Sensor Data
Humidity: 54.70 %, Temp: 19.60 Celsius
UltraSonic Sensor Data:
The Distance in cm: 142
Accelerometer Sensor Data
374x      377y       379z
☐ Autoscroll
```

FIGURE 10.9   The real-time results of all three sensors in Arduino IDE.

ThingSpeak stores data in a representation of graph. The user needs to create an account in ThingSpeak, and then ThingSpeak will provide the cloud services. Figures 10.10–10.12 are the final results of this execution which were sent to the cloud [14, 22]. Figure 10.10 has the result of distance fetched by the ultrasonic sensor which was sent to the cloud through ThingSpeak in a representation of a graph. Figures 10.11(a) and (b) have the results of humidity and temperature fetched by humid sensor DHT 22, respectively, those data were sent to the cloud through ThingSpeak. Similarly, Figure 10.12(a)–(c) has the results of *X*-axis, *Y*-axis, and *Z*-axis fetched by accelerometer sensor, respectively and data were sent to MATLAB-based cloud platform using ThingSpeak in a representation of a graph. In Arduino IDE, different programming codes were used to get the results from each sensor by connecting with NodeMCU ESP8266. Moreover, NodeMCU makes wireless internet connection, by which sending data to the cloud was possible via ThingSpeak. As wireless network mobile hotspot was used for Internet connection in this experiment.

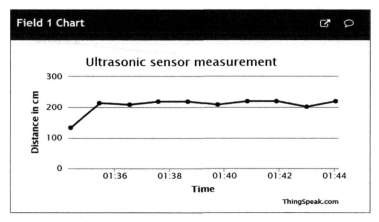

FIGURE 10.10   Data of ultrasonic sent in ThingSpeak.

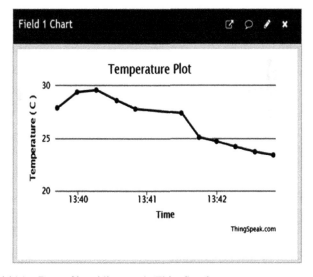

FIGURE 10.11(a)   Data of humidity sent in ThingSpeak.

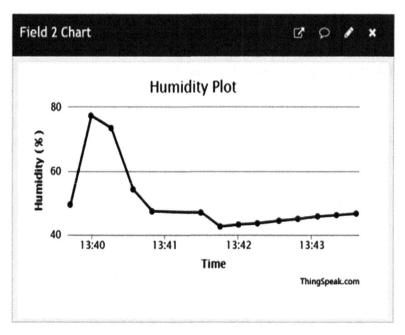

FIGURE 10.11(b)　Data of temperature sent in ThingSpeak.

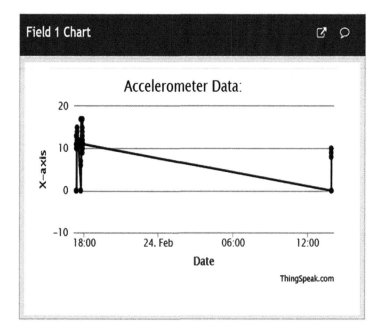

FIGURE 10.12(a)　Data of accelerometer of *X*-axis sent in ThingSpeak.

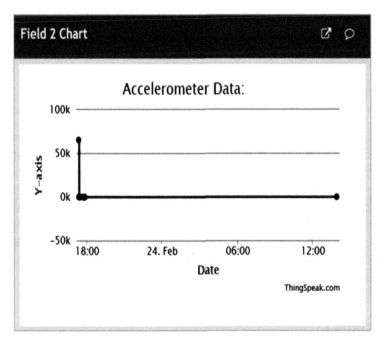

FIGURE 10.12(b)   Data of accelerometer of *Y-* axis sent in ThingSpeak.

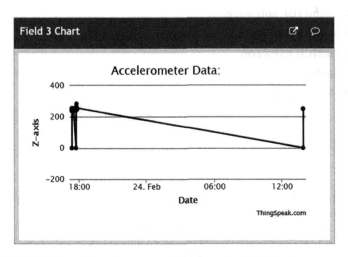

FIGURE 10.12(c)   Data of accelerometer of Z-axis sent in ThingSpeak.

This technology can be used for car parking. Ultrasonic sensor can be used for distance measurement. This sensor can provide signals with an alarm system if some objects are nearby the car while parking. Clearly, accelerometer can be used for checking acceleration of the car. Similarly, purpose of using DHT 22 can be regular checking of the temperature and humidity of car engine by which it can maintain the temperature if required.

10.6   CONCLUSION

The inspiration of working with Internet of things is plotting the real-time data and sending the data to the cloud. After completing the experiment, final results are stored in ThingSpeak as a representation of a graph and the data sent to cloud. However, this technique was found easier and more reliable for sending real-time data to cloud with the help of ThingSpeak. With the assistance of NodeMCU ESP-8266 Wi-Fi module and Arduino IDE, it is possible to send the data in real-time information directly within the cloud via ThingSpeak while not exploiting wires, which probably will be known as IoT-based wireless communication system.

KEYWORDS

- **Arduino IDE software**
- **Internet of things (IoT)**
- **NodeMCU ESP8266**
- **ThingSpeak**
- **Wi-Fi modules**

REFERENCES

1. Aksu, H., Babu, L., Cont, M., G. Tolomei, and Uluagac, A. S., "Advertising in the IoT Era: Vision and Challenges," pp. 1–7, 2018.
2. Kell, S. D. T., Suryadevara, N. K., and Mukhopadhyay, S. C., "Towards the Implementation of IoT for Environmental Condition Monitoring in Homes," IEEE Sensors Journal, Vol. 13, Issue 10, pp. 3846–3853, 2013.
3. Lahane, V., Band, P., and Valunjkar, S. T., "Wireless Sensor Network (WSN) Implementation in IOT Based Smart City," pp. 703–706, 2018.
4. Ejofodomi, O. and Ofualagba, G., "Exploring the Feasibility of Robotic Pipeline Surveillance for Detecting Crude Oil Spills in the Niger Delta. New Brunswick, Canada," IJUSEng, Vol. 5, Issue 3, pp. 38–52, 2017.

5. Georgitzikis, V., Akribopoulos, O., and Chatzigiannakis, I., "Controlling Physical Objects via the Internet using the Arduino Platform over 802. 15. 4 Networks," IEEE Latin America Transactions, Vol. 10, Issue 3, pp. 1686–1689, 2012.
6. Roca, D., Milito, R., Nemirovsky, M., and Valero, M., "Tackling IoT Ultra Large Scale Systems: Fog Behaviors," In: Rahmani A., Liljeberg P., Preden JS., Jantsch A. (eds). Fog Computing in the Internet of Things. Springer, Cham. pp. 33–48, 2018.
7. Vikram, N., Harish, K. S., Nihaal, M. S., Umes, R., Aashik, S., and Kuma, A., "A Low Cost Home Automation System Using Wi-Fi Based Wireless Sensor Network Incorporating Internet of Things (IoT)," 2017 IEEE 7th International Advance Computing Conference.
8. Das, S., Salehi, H., Shi, Y., Chakrabartty, S., Burgueno, R., and Biswas, S. "Towards Packet-Less Ultrasonic Sensor Networks for Energy-Harvesting Structures," Computer Communications, Vol. 101, pp. 94–105, 2017.
9. Sing, C., Joseph, J., Singh, Y. N., and Tripathi, K. K., "A Review of Indoor Optical Wireless Systems," IETE Technical Review, Vol. 19, Issue 1–2, pp. 3–17, 2002.
10. Nisio, A. Di, Noia, T. Di, Carducci, C. G. C., and Spadavecchia, M., "Design of a Low Cost Multipurose Wireless Sensor Network," in IEEE International Workshop on Measurements & Networking (M&N), 2015.
11. Nageswararao, G. K. M. J. "Wireless Weather Monitor Using Internet," i-manager's Journal on Embedded Systems, Vol. 6, Issue 1, pp. 2017, 2018.
12. Kazi, S. S., Bajantri, G., and Thite, T. "Remote Heart Rate Monitoring System Using IoT," pp. 2956–2963, 2018.
13. Vikram, N., Harish, K. S., Nihaal, M. S., Umesh, R., Shetty, A., and Kumar, A., "A Low Cost Home Automation System Using Wi-Fi Based Wireless Sensor Network Incorporating Internet of Things (IoT)," in 2017 IEEE 7th International Advance Computing Conference (IACC), pp. 174–178, 2017.
14. ThingSpeak official website. https://thingspeak.com.
15. Magar, S., Saste, V., Lahane, A., Konde, S., and Madne, S., "Smart Home Automation by GSM Using Android Application," International Conference on Information Communication and Embedded Systems (ICICES 2017).
16. Bisio, I., Delfino, A., Lavagetto, F., and Sciarrone, A., "Enabling IoT for in-Home Rehabilitation: Accelerometer Signals Classification Methods for Activity and Movement Recognition," IEEE Internet of Things Journal, Vol. 4, Issue 1, pp. 135–146, 2017.
17. Jaladi, A. R., Khitkani, K., Pawar, P., Malvi, K., and Sahoo, G., "Environmental Monitoring Using Wireless Sensor Networks (WSN) Based on IoT," International Research Journal of Engineering and Technology, Vol. 4, Issue 1, pp. 1371–1378, 2017.
18. Lin, K., Poslad, S., Wang, W., Li, X., Zhang, Y., and Wang, C. "A Public Transport Bus as a Flexible Mobile Smart Environment Sensing Platform for IoT," in 12th International Conference on Intelligent Environments (IE), 2016, pp. 1–8, IEEE, 2016.
19. Kaushik, S., Chouhan, Y. S., Sharma, N., Singh, S., and P. Suganya, "Automatic Fan Speed Control Using Temperature and Humidity Sensor and Arduino," International Journal of Advance Research, Ideas and Innovations in Technology, Vol. 4, Issue 2, pp. 453–457, 2018.
20. Mercer, C. and Dónal Leech, "Cost-Effective Wireless Microcontroller for Internet Connectivity of Open-Source Chemical Devices," Journal of Chemical Education, Vol. 95, Issue 7, pp. 1221–1225, 2018.

21. Nettikadan, D. and Subodh, R. M. S. "IoT Based Smart Community Monitoring Platform for Custom Designed Smart Homes," in 2018 International Conference on Current Trends Towards Converging Technologies (ICCTCT), pp. 1–6, IEEE, 2018.

22. Cooper, J. and A. James, "Challenges for Database Management in the Internet of Things," IETE Technical Review, Vol. 26, Issue 5, pp. 320–329, 2009.

23. Modieginyane, K. M., Letswamotse, B. B., Malekian, R., and Abu-Mahfouz, A. M. (2018). Software defined wireless sensor networks application opportunities for efficient network management: A survey. Computers & Electrical Engineering, Vol. 66, pp. 274–287.

24. Bera, S., Misra, S., and Vasilakos, A. V. (2017). Software-defined networking for internet of things: A survey. IEEE Internet of Things Journal, Vol. 4, Issue 6, pp. 1994–2008.

25. AlSkaif, T., Bellalta, B., Zapata, M. G., and Ordinas, J. M. B. (2017). Energy efficiency of MAC protocols in low data rate wireless multimedia sensor networks: A comparative study. Ad Hoc Networks, Vol. 56, pp. 141–157.

26. Yerramalli, S., Jain, R., and Mitra, U. (2012, October). Characterization of equilibria for the degraded Gaussian broadcast and sum power MAC channels. In 2012 50th Annual Aller-ton Conference on Communication, Control, and Computing (Allerton) (pp. 1206–1212). IEEE.

27. Miqdad, A., Kadir, K., and Ahmed, S. F. (2017, November). Development of data acquisi-tion system for temperature and humidity monitoring scheme. In 2017 IEEE 4th International Conference on Smart Instrumentation, Measurement and Application (ICSIMA) (pp. 1–4). IEEE.

28. Patel, S., Park, H., Bonato, P., Chan, L., and Rodgers, M. (2012). A review of wearable sen-sors and systems with application in rehabilitation. Journal of Neuroengineering and rehabilitation, Vol. 9, Issue 1, pp. 1–17.

29. Chandra, A. A., Jannif, N. I., Prakash, S., and Padiachy, V. (2017, August). Cloud based re-al-time monitoring and control of diesel generator using the IoT technology. In 2017 20th International Conference on Electrical Machines and Systems (ICEMS) (pp. 1–5). IEEE.

30. Xie, G., Ota, K., Dong, M., Pan, F., and Liu, A. (2017). Energy-efficient routing for mobile data collectors in wireless sensor networks with obstacles. Peer-to-Peer Networking and Applications, Vol. 10, Issue 3, pp. 472–483.

31. Zakaria, Y., and Michael, K. (2017). An integrated cloud-based wireless sensor network for monitoring industrial wastewater discharged into water sources.

32. Peniak, P., and Franekova, M. (2016, September). Model of integration of embedded sys-tems via CoAP protocol of Internet of Things. In 2016 International Conference on Ap-plied Electronics (AE) (pp. 201–204). IEEE.

33. Lukman, Ajao. (2017). "Wireless Sensor Networks Based-Internet of Thing For Agro-Climatic Parameters...".

34. Yetgin, H., Cheung, K. T. K., El-Hajjar, M., and Hanzo, L. H. (2017). A survey of network lifetime maximization techniques in wireless sensor networks. IEEE Communications Surveys & Tutorials, Vol. 19, Issue 2, pp. 828–854.

35. Torresen, J., Hafting, Y., and Nymoen, K. (2013, May). A New Wi-Fi based Platform for Wireless Sensor Data Collection. In NIME (pp. 337–340).

36. Joshi, S.A., Poojari, S., Chougale, T., Shetty, S., and Sandeep, M.K.: Home automation sys-tem using wireless network. In: IEEE, 2nd International Conference on Communi-cation and Electronics Systems (ICCES) (pp. 803–807) (2017, October).

37. Simoes, N. A., and de Souza, G. B. (2016). A low cost automated data acquisition system for urban sites temperature and humidity monitoring based in Internet of Things. In 2016 1st International Symposium on Instrumentation Systems, Circuits and Transducers (INSCIT) (pp. 107–112). IEEE.
38. Hackmann, G., Guo, W., Yan, G., Sun, Z., Lu, C., and Dyke, S. (2013). Cyber-physical codesign of distributed structural health monitoring with wireless sensor networks. IEEE Transactions on Parallel and Distributed Systems, Vol. 25, Issue 1, pp. 63–72.
39. Sachi Nandan Mohanty, E.Laxmi Lydia, Mohamed Elhoseny, Majid M. Gethami AI Otabi, K.Shankar, Deep learning with LSTM based distributed data mining model for energy efficient wireless sensor networks, Physical Communication, vol.40, Issue-4, 101097-102008, (2020). https://doi.org/10.1016/j.phycom.2020.101097.
40. Chandrakant Mallick, Suneeta Satpathy, "Challenges and Design Goals of Wireless Sensor Networks: A Sate-of-the-art Review", International Journal of Computer Applications (0975–8887), 2018.

CHAPTER 11

Value Creation Model for Waste Management in Smart Cities Ecosystems

PANKAJ DEEP KAUR,[1*] VARINDER KAUR ATTRI,[1] and
SHIVANI CHAUDHARY[2]

[1]Department of Computer Science & Engineering,
Guru Nanak Dev University Regional Campus, Jalandhar, Punjab

[2]Department of Computer Science & Engineering, CT Group of Institutes,
Jalandhar, Punjab

*Corresponding author. E-mail: pankajdeep.csejal@gndu.ac.in

ABSTRACT

Introduction of an adamant problem for the environment is a waste product that causes inconsistency, shakiness, and agitation to the ecosystem. Waste disposed of by the citizens leads to hazards and becomes a cause of diseases and epidemics. In this chapter, a model is created for generating the value for waste pick up in the waste management system by prioritizing different types of trash cans or dustbins on the basis of different domains and weight. This is basically an optimization model to reduce the cost of waste collection. The radio frequency identification technology is used for the storage of accurate information regarding dustbin's weight and other domains. Three different types of dustbins are introduced in this chapter that is being used for collecting different types of waste. The model introduced in this chapter works using three stages. The first stage gives the shape to the waste collected in bins for value creation. The second stage analyses the value generated. The last stage explains the impact of the values on society.

11.1 INTRODUCTION

Our society is facing the major challenges related to waste generation, waste management, and inadequate disposal of waste. Nowadays the affirmation of cleaning and a healthy globe is one of the necessary priorities of smart cities ecosystem. Everyday waste gets disposed of in heavy amount per citizen. This waste leads to various hazards like bad odor and ugliness. The World Bank has predicted that the volume of solid waste by 2025 will reach 2.2 billion tonnes [1], which would be difficult to manage for the lower income countries. Smart cities' ecosystem is becoming a perceptible factor in this scenario. Estimation of waste production in European Union countries says that 457 kg of waste is generated by each citizen of these countries annually [2]. Reuse and recycling of the waste in recent years is a positive improvement in the waste management system. The rate of recycling of household waste has reached 45% from 2014 to 2015 [3]. Every region and the country have different economic factors. Similarly, waste management and recycling programs would be also different. Socioeconomic condition of India is changing rapidly. DEFRA gives the cost-beneficial public policy interventions that are used in a cost-effective way [6]. Being an efficient city service, the waste collection should be in an organized way. It is inefficient to only focus on emptying the containers of waste [7]. Characterization of municipal solid waste (MSW) is the challenge for waste management [12]. It is important to organize the waste in different categories for the optimized collection of waste. In this chapter, waste material is categorized with the help of three types of trashcans or bins with an ultrasonic sensor mounted on them for regular monitoring. In traditional approaches, there were no proper monitoring and maintenance of the garbage. It is very necessary to improve the waste management. Economically, it is affecting the region and country. The garbage management model has been introduced as a group of services like garbage collection, garbage transportation for special space, preparation for reuse of services [17]. Table 11.1 gives a comparison of different types of the waste disposal system. Here, we are calculating the value which will be used for the dumping and reuse of the waste.

Waste material is categorized with the help of three types of trashcans or bins with an ultrasonic sensor mounted on them. Three dustbins are as follows: first is GREENBIN, which is used for collecting food and garden waste, the second is BLUEBIN which is used for collecting mixed dry recycling like cans, cardboard, paper, glass, etc., and third is REDBIN, which is used for collecting nonrecyclable waste like nappies, etc. The monitoring of waste is based on the priority value generated on the basis of different domains like technical, economic, environmental, and social. So this chapter proposed an optimization model in which there is value generation on basis of different parameters like the weight of bin, reusability degree, and degree of hazardousness. The output of the calculation of value generation will give the indication to collectors to pick the prioritized bin. This will help them to collect the waste in an organized and optimized way. The model introduced in this chapter works using three stages. The first stage gives the shape to the waste collected in bins for the value creation. The second stage analyses the value generated through the mobile application. The last stage explains how this value impacts on society.

TABLE 11.1 Comparison of different Garbage Collection System

Types	Pros	Cons
Plastic bags	i. The convenience of having a bag that is ready forcheckout.	i. Single use of plastic bags is not biodegradable.
	ii. Disposable plastic bags are durable.	ii. Damaging to the ecosystem and posea major threat toanimals.
Chips –Stickers	i. Remedies for weaknessesof plastic.	i. Measurement of inaccuracy bags.
	ii. A number of different charge commissioning methods.	ii. Inopportune dustbin management.
RFID based garbage management system	i. Data accuracy in measurementand calculation.	i. Data concentration serveroverload.
	ii. Reduce manual work.	ii. Lowadaptability.
		iii. The high cost of RFID tags.

11.2 LITERATURE REVIEW

The concept of smart waste management and smart trashcans has been discussing for a long time. There are different categories of waste management practices, these are ranging from collection and segregation to the recovery of waste. There are assorted technologies that are used to develop this smart system for the smart city has also developed gradually, that is, from wireless sensor network (WSN) to radio frequency identification (RFID) to now the most popular Internet of Things (IoT). All ideas seem to be similar but are slightly different at their core and our proposed work has no exception from the same. Pune city's current waste [10] collection logistic is carried out by emptying containers according to predefined schedules and routes that are repeated at a set frequency. On the hardware side, there is a smart bin with a sensor and RFID tag, which is used for the unique identification of dustbins. Pranjal Lokhande and Pawar in their paper "Garbage Collection Management System" proposed a system in which there is a different type of garbage is thrown into the sensor-based dustbin. When the dustbin is full or overflowed then the ultrasonic sensor is detected the level of garbage in the dustbin or some wet garbage, that is thrown into the dustbin, is detected by the moisture sensor or some unpleasant smell, as well as toxic gases are generated when the gas sensor gives the information [20]. Bohma gives the cost estimation function for both MSW collection, disposal services, and curbs side recycling programs. This paper's result suggests the waste collection cost and disposal exceed the costs of recycling [5]. Hassan et al. proposed a system with a novel prototype of a solid waste bin monitoring system that uses WSNs [21]. Kumar et al. proposed a system in his article "IOT Based Smart Garbage alert system using Arduino UNO," which averts the irregular cleaning of the dustbins by sending alerts to the concerned individual at regular intervals [18]. It also additionally endorses the system with the status of cleaning and measure the performance of the team. In this system, all the alert notifications are displayed on the android application and it also helps the residents to lodge the complaint in case of any discrepancies. Hong and Park proposed an IoT-based smart garbage system (SGS) for replacing existing RFID-based garbage collection systems. To provide differentiation from passive collection bins and other types of RFID-based food garbage collection systems, they also proposed components required in external and public environments and designed the SGS based on these components [19]. The literature on vehicle routing will help us to find the research gaps in the waste collection problem. There are numerous heuristic and nonheuristic models for transportation have been developed. Reed et al. [4] proposed a dynamic solution for the vehicle routing issues. Jose M. Gutierrez and Michael Jensenb in their interesting journal article "Smart Waste Collection System Based on Location Intelligence" proposed an idea for an intelligent waste collection of practical Smart City. It also includes the idea of waste collection cyber-physical system. The system is based on an IoT sensing prototype that measures the waste level of trashcans and sends these data over the internet to a server for storage and processing [24]. On the basis of these data, the creation of the optimum collection routes given by an optimization process, and these routes are readdressed to workers. Shah et al. in his paper presents the model for waste collection and recovery of waste value [23]. This paper is working on the minimization of transportation cost but this model is using two types of trucks to collect the waste that needs more budget. Likotiko et al. has worked on municipal solid waste management. This paper proposed architecture of IoT for real-time monitoring and collection of the waste, it also improves and optimizes solid waste collection in a city. In this paper, Netlogo Multiagent platform has been used to simulate real-time monitoring and smart decisions on waste management. In this system, citizens are also involved in paying for the waste collection services. It works on WSNs [28].

11.3   SYSTEM DESCRIPTION

Some of the phases of the smart city are repeatedly emphasized and some phases are sustainable smart city and sensor-based smart city. Smart waste management covers both phases. Cities with adequate resources and proper infrastructure are called smart cities [9] that are widely defined, but it still remains an obscure concept. Day by day, the smart city is becoming a global trend [10, 11]. The key issue in the waste management system is the segregation and collection of the waste. The well-organized waste material will be helpful for the collectors to collect the waste in an easy way. A smart city is divided into a number of sectors. In each sector, bins have been installed in a common area. In this chapter, we have used three types of dustbins to collect different types of waste material. The bins are smart, equipped with IoT components like sensor, RFID, actuator, and GPS system. The value is measured on the basis of different factors like technical, economic, environmental, and social. When the value is calculated then this value generates on a mobile application server and it will display on the graphical user interface of the android application. That value can be used for reusability and recovery of the waste. This chapter propounds an idea of the smart waste management system. So there is a comparison between several garbage disposable systems. Traditional approaches do not work properly or in favor of the environment. In this garbage management system, we have proposed three types of dustbins to collect several types of garbage. Following are the three types of dustbins:

1.   GREENBIN (food waste, garden waste).
2.   BLUEBIN (plastic waste, mixed dry recycling, food cans, cardboard boxes).
3.   REDBIN (nonrecyclable, disposable nappies, broken crockery).

Figure 11.1 shows the symbolic representation of a smart city with different waste bins and collection trucks.

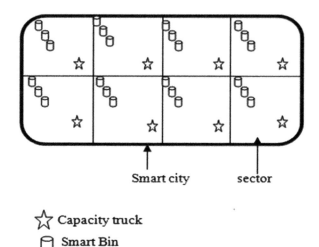

FIGURE 11.1   Smart city divided into sectors.

11.4   MODEL FOR VALUE GENERATION IN SMART GARBAGE

In this model, trucks are allocated to each sector by using an allocation algorithm [26]. This model as shown in Figure 11.2 constitutes the different stages, from the accession of data to its proceedings for the creation of services. It also includes an analysis of the impacts. In Figure 11.2, the first stage is a characterization of the waste based on the weight and domains and generates value, which will be the input to the next stage. The second stage focuses on the use of value. The third stage analyzes the impacts of the use of value on society and the economy.

FIGURE 11.2   Model for value generation.

11.4.1   *STAGE 1: ACQUISITION OF DATA AND CALCULATION*

The first step is based on the acquisition of data by RFID and the generation of the value. The data are the weight and other information on the garbage bin or trash can. Data are in the form of weight and prioritized domains of the different waste are stored in RFID tag and then this information transmitted over the server for the value calculation.

System demonstrated in Figure 11.1 has mathematical representation as follows:

Sectors X: 1,2,3.........x
Waste Bin B: 3x
Capacity truck C:1,2,3.......c Cb bin capacity.

$$Gavg = \frac{G1+G2+G3}{3}$$

$$Bavg = \frac{B1+B2+B3}{3}$$

$$Ravg = \frac{R1+R2+R3}{3}$$

$$MRDEV = max(Gavg, Bavg, Ravg)$$

$$MGDEV = max(37.3333333, 48.3333333, 45) = 48.333333.$$

Other approaches lacked in data accessibility methods, which are based on comparing the information from real data. To overcome this problem, a metric is introduced which is named as a metric for garbage data evaluation (MGDEV) in Figure 11.3. It is designed to quantify the degree of management. In [22], an extensive review of metrics for data quality is carried out. The main feature of this metric is to be easy-to-use because it assesses limited dimensions. The first dimension of a metric is GREENBIN referring to the green waste, having weight. The second dimension of metric is BLUEBIN referring to the plastic waste having weight. The third dimension of metric is REDBIN referring to the nonrecyclable waste having weight. RFID technology can deliver a rich knowledge base. It has the potential to raise the weight that is considered as a domain of value creation. This value is calculated on the basis of the following.

11.4.1.1 FILLED WEIGHT

It means when bin is filled and RFID stores its weight. The dustbin which would have more weight will have priority of analysis of the weight is the main task for RFID tag. Weight is dynamic that analyzed weight, which is then sent to the server for value generation. G1, B1, and R1 are denoting the weight of GREENBIN, BLUEBIN, and REDBIN bins, respectively. Weight of bin W_b: 1, 2, 3..., w kg.

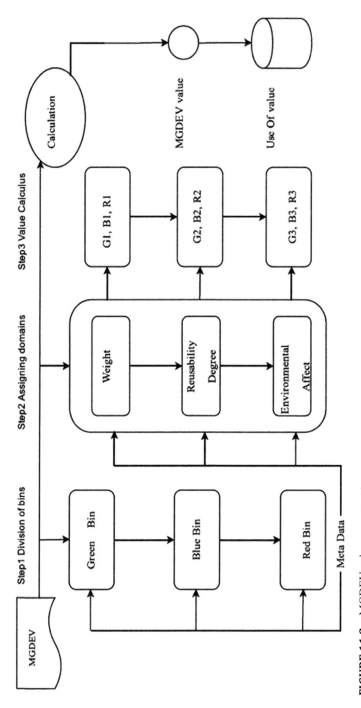

FIGURE 11.3 MGDEV value assessment.

11.4.1.2 REUSABILITY DEGREE

It refers to the reusability of the waste collected in the dustbins. The reusability degree plays a key role to determine what factors and conditions can motive data reuse. Some wastes like food waste and plastic can be reused by some operational processes. Reusability degree varies with different wastes. G2, B2, and R2 are denoting the reusability degree of green, blue, and red trash can, respectively. Reusability degree R_d: 1,2,3...,r%.

11.4.1.3 ENVIRONMENTAL EFFECT

In this aspect, this is basically related to the environmental effect of collected waste. This degree of hazardousness is analyzed and then used as a parameter for estimating the value. For value generation average of these three aspects is measured as prioritizing the pickup value of the different waste. This MGDEV metrics works in three steps. The first step is the division of the dustbins. The second step is assigning of the dataset metadata domains to the dustbins. The third step is about the calculus of the value by applying the formula on parameters. G3, B3, and R3 are denoting the environmental effect of GREENBIN, BLUEBIN, and REDBIN bins, respectively. Degree of hazardousness H_d: 1,2,3...,h%.

In Table 11.2, average is calculated by using some static values of parameters. After that MGDEV value is calculated.

TABLE 11.2   Static average value calculation

Wastebin	Weight Wb in kg.	Reusability Degree Rd in %	Degree of Hazardousness in %	Average Value
Greenbin	42	30	40	37,33333333
Bluebin	35	20	90	48,33333333
Redbin	40	75	20	45

11.4.2   STAGE 2: VALUE ANALYSIS

In the second stage, the generated value is analyzed after the calculation. These stage studies are the legal use of the value. This stage is about the integrity plausibility of the value. Analyzed value is a filtered value to be used for further processing of management of waste. Analysis of this value is based on the following three factors.

11.4.2.1   TECHNICAL

Technical analysis may seem complex on the surface but it encapsulates and analysis of demand in the surrounding. Optimization of the expected function of the calculated value of the different wastes depends upon the ameliorate control and flourished removal/installation of devices (RFID tags, sensors on the bin) at the right location [13]. It can be done by using the right hardware if the data accessibility will be accurate than value calculation will also be accurate.

11.4.2.2   ECONOMIC

The generated value is analyzed for the economic factor. Garbage waste is a derivate of yield and consumption by industry, households. Once the waste is produced, it needs management [14]. The value generated for management can be used as input to further reuse of the waste. Analyzed value passes through the decision of use in the economic phase.

11.4.2.3   ENVIRONMENTAL

Value is analyzed from the environmental point of view. Waste disposal has huge environmental impacts and can cause serious problems. Blue bin garbage waste releases the toxic gasses that have a bad effect on the environment. The waste management value is further used for one purpose among two, whether for reuse or dumping.

11.4.3   STAGE 3: SOCIAL VALUE

This last stage focuses on the social impact of the value. Awareness of the public regarding waste management is necessary. Based on a review of previous studies, social and economic values are inherently linked. The additional factor is that society is the phase that more previously affected due to the waste generation whether it is economically or technically [15]. Analyzed value is working as an input to the social value. This stag is about the impact of the generated value on society. Garbage is generated by the society but it reversely affects society. This effect is bad which is converted to the diseases and epidemics. The generated value can be used for the minimization of the waste. With average analysis of the different waste generated which has a high value that will be minimized. The value is used for the services and applications implementation to the society.

11.5 CONCLUSION

A smart waste management system has the potential to enhance our everyday life in many different aspects. In this chapter, we explored the use of different dustbins by partitioning with different colors. This partitioning is based on the different types of the waste disposed of by the society. The waste is collected in different colored dustbins. The model that we proposed in this paper gives the acquisition of data used in value calculation to social impacts. The value generated from the calculations is used as a priority of the waste pickup. That value is used by haulers for the quick action on the management of the waste. That value reduces the time consumption of waste collection and management. So this is an optimized way of collection of waste. There is no need for waste separation unit because waste is already disposed separately. It reduces the need for extra trucks. The implementation of this IoT-based garbage collection system reassures the cleaning of trash cans as early as possible. This system also gives the optimal way to collect the waste by segregation of waste. This reduces the need for low capacity truck and high capacity truck that means reduces the cost of overall system implementation. This model can be further used for the real value analysis of waste generation and can be used for recovery value analysis.

KEYWORDS

- **smart city**
- **waste management**
- **IoT-enabled waste collection**
- **segregation of waste**

REFERENCES

1. Hoornweg, D., and Bhada-Tata, P. "What a waste: a global review of solid waste management", Urban development series; knowledge papers no. 15, 87–88, 2012, World Bank, Washington, DC. © World Bank. https://openknowledge.worldbank.org/handle/10986/17388 License: CC BY 3.0 IGO.
2. Hauser, H.-E., and Blumenthal, K. "Each person in the EU generated 475 kg of municipal waste in 2014, *Eurostat Press*, 56/2016.
3. Environment Agency. "Regulating the waste industry," Environment Agency, Bristol, 2016.
4. Reed, M., Yiannakou, A., and Evering, R. "An ant colony algorithm for the multi-compartment vehicle routing problem", *Journal of Applied Soft Computing*, 15, pp. 169–176, 2014.
5. Robert, A. B., David, H. F., Thomas, C. K., and Podolskyd, M. J. "The costs of municipal waste and recycling programs", *Resources, Conservation and Recycling*, 54, pp. 864–871, 2010.
6. "The economics of waste and waste policy waste economics team environment and growth economics", Department for Environment, Food and Rural Affairs Nobel House, 17 Smith Square, London SW1P 3JR, Website: www.defra.gov.uk 2011.
7. Jung, C. "IoT and smart city trends boost smart waste collection market", 2017. *Arabian Journal for Science and Engineering*, 45, pp. 10185–10198, 2020.
8. Bolic, M., Rostamian, M., and Djuric, P. M. "Proximity detection with RFID step toward the Internet of Things", *IEEE Pervasive Computing*, 14, pp. 70–76, 2015.
9. Rudolf, G., Christian, F., Hans, K., Robert, K., Natasa, P., and Evert, M. "Smart cities: ranking of European medium-sized cities", Centre of Regional Science (SRF), Vienna University of Technology, Vienna.
10. Vanolo, A. "Smartmentality: the smart city as disciplinary strategy", *SAGE Journals*, 51, pp. 883–898, 2013.
11. Hajduk, S. "The concept of a smart city in urban management", *Business, Management and Education,* 14, pp. 34–49, 2016.
12. Joshi, R., and Ahmed, S. "Status and challenges of municipal solid waste management in India: a review", *Cogent Environmental Science*, 2(1), pp. 1139434, 2016.
13. Cheng, M.-Y., and Chang, N.-W. "Radio frequency identification (RFID) integrated with building information model (BIM) for open- building life cycle information management", *28th International Symposium on Automation and Robotics in Construction and Mining*, pp. 485–490, 2011.
14. Finnveden, G., Bjorklund, A., Moberg, A., Ekwall, T., and Moberg, A. "Environmental and economic assessment methods for waste management decision support: possibilities and limitations", *International Solid Waste Association*, 25, pp. 263–269, 2007.
15. Schindler, H. R., Schmalbein, N., Steltenkamp, V., Cave, J., Wens, B., and Anhalt, A. In: Commission (Ed.), "SMART TRASH: study on RFID tags and the recycling industry", RAND Corporation, Santa Monica, CA, 2012.
16. Vetrò, A., Canova, L., Torchiano, M., Orozco Minotas, C., Iemma, R., and Morando, F. "Open data quality measurement framework: definition and application to open government data", *Government Information Quarterly*, 33, pp. 325–337, 2016.
17. Anagnostopoulos, T., Zaslavsky, A., Kolomvatsos, K., Medvedev, A., Amirian, P., Morley, J., and Hadjieftymiades, S. "Challenges and opportunities of waste management

in IoT-enabled smart cities: a survey", *IEEE Transactions on Sustainable Computing*, 2, pp. 275–289, 2017.

18. Satish Kumar, N., Vijay Lakshami, B., Jenifer Prarthana, R., and Shankar, A. "IOT based smart garbage alert system using Arduino UNO", IEEE Region 10 International Conference TENCON, IEEE Part Number: CFP16TEN-USB ISBN: 978-1-5090-2596-1.

19. Hong, I., Park, S., Lee, B., Lee, J., Jeong, D., and Park, S. "IoT-based smart garbage system for efficient food waste management", *Scientific World Journal*, 2014, 2014.

20. Lokhande, P., and Pawar, M. D. "Garbage collection management system", *International Journal of Engineering and Computer Science*, 5(11), pp. 18800–18805, 2016, ISSN: 2319-7242.

21. Abdulla Al Mamun, M., Hannan, M. A., Hussain, A., and Basri, H. "Wireless sensor network prototype for solid waste bin monitoring with energy efficient sensing algorithm", *16th International Conference on Computational Science and Engineering*, 2014.

22. Abella, A., Ortiz-de-Urbina-Criado, M., and De-Pablos-Heredero, C. "A model for the analysis of data-driven innovation and value generation in smart cities' ecosystems", *Cities*, 64, pp. 47–53, 2017.

23. Jatinkumar Shah, P., Anagnostopoulos, T., Zaslavsky, A., and Behdad, S. "A stochastic optimization framework for planning of waste collection and value recovery operations in smart and sustainable cities", *Journal of Waste Management*, Vol. 78, pp. 104–114, 2018.

24. Gutierreza, J. M., Jensen, M., Henius, M., and Riazc, T.. "Smart waste collection system based on location intelligence", *Conference Organized by Missouri University of Science and Technology, San Jose, 2015*, pp. 120 127.

25. David Likotiko, E., Nyambo, D., and Mwangoka, J. "Multi-agent based IoT smart waste monitoring and collection architecture", *International Journal of Computer Science, Engineering and Information Technology*, 7, pp. 1–14, 2017.

26. Anagnostopoulos, T. T., Zaslavsky, A., and Medvedev, A. "Robust waste collection exploiting cost efficiency of IoT potentiality in smart cities", *IEEE 1st International Conference on Recent Advances in Internet of Things*, Singapore, 2015.

CHAPTER 12

Safeguarding Location Privacy in the Internet of Things

JASHANPREET KAUR* and JYOTSNA SENGUPTA

Punjabi University, Patiala

*Corresponding author. E-mail: jashn00042@gmail.com

ABSTRACT

The visualization of ubiquitous approach to intelligence, anyplace and anytime, is flattering into a truth, permitted by promptly evolving wireless broadcastings with an analysis that varies from a few inches to many miles. In near future, the world will be completely intertwined and the quantity of smart gadgets will explode to an extensive number; the estimate is 10 times the human populace. Internet of Things (IoT) shall bring plethora of advantages and ease in our habitual life. But what about all the data including personal information, location monitoring, daily routine, etc., be shared and stored over Internet. It is vital to maintain the accuracy and extensiveness of biometrics for the authorization of an individual. So, there is a need for highly reliable methodologies. Nevertheless, with the evolution of the IoT applications, the communication transfer will have tremendous growth, both in terms of ease and privacy issues. We have studied many privacy issues and have proposed a methodology keeping in mind location privacy. A secure system will build trust and, thus, will make the client more secure and private while moving from one place to another.

12.1 INTRODUCTION

The term "Internet of Things" (IoT) was coined 18 years prior by the originators of the first MIT Auto-ID Center, with unique reference to Kevin Ashton in 1999 and David L. Brock in 2001. The expression "Auto-ID" signifies to any wide class of identification tools utilized in productions to mechanize, diminish mistakes, and boost competence. IoT is a model where everything is equipped/outfitted with distinctive IP address for identification, a sensor for sensing capabilities, Internet connection for communication, and a processor for processing function that will assist the objects to interchange data and information over Internet to accomplish the required tasks. To be precise, IoT will make the world a brilliant place to live in with an assumed procedure of anything, anyplace, anytime. Figure 12.1 defines the scope of IoT as any object, anyone, any network, anywhere.

FIGURE 12.1   IoT concept depicting anything, anytime, and anywhere.

IoT devices predominantly drive the worldwide connection progression—both on the user side (e.g., smart home) as well as on the enterprise/B2B side (e.g., linked equipment). By 2020, the total number of IoT devices that will be active is expected to be 10 billion and 22 billion by 2025 [1]. Figure 12.2 shows the detailed facts about the growth of IoT nowadays and in near future. The graphs depict that the total number of B2B connection will approximately double the number from 2018 to 2020. Nowadays, nearly 3 billion B2B IoT connections are available which will be more than 6 billion by 2020.

In this chapter, we review various challenges and issues in the fields of IoT and present various contributions done. We also propose a methodology to prevent the intruder from attacking the node. The remainder of this paper is structured as follows. In Sections 12.2 and 12.3, we present various challenges in IoT following the contributions done by various researchers. Section 12.4 describes the proposed method and results obtained. We conclude the chapter with a conclusion drawn and some scopes for further research (Section 12.5).

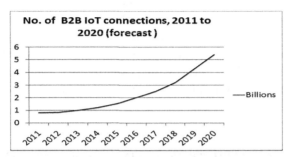

No. of B2B IoT connections, 2011 to 2020 (forecast)

—Billions

FIGURE 12.2   A line graph representing the progressive growth of IoT connections by 2020.

12.2   PRIVACY CHALLENGES AND CONTRIBUTIONS BY RESEARCHERS

In IoT, the concerns about security and privacy have increased as the knowledge about the devices or even the information about the presence of a particular thing and their documentation is very often exchanged and shared over a network. IoT is thriving consistently in all significant jobs, it can be in the homes, hospitals, industries, textiles, education, etc. As developing quantities of gadgets are added to the web, it offers various opportunities as well as difficulties, from scaling applications and administrations of trillions of associated gadgets, many challenges which need to be worked on are privacy, security, location privacy participatory identifying, traffic controlling, and device identification, data accommodation, and proficient energy consumption in the associated procedures.

12.2.1   CONTINUITY AND ACCESSIBILITY IN THE PROVISION OF IOT-BASED SERVICES

One of the major challenges is to guarantee continuous accessibility in the arrangement of IoT administrations and to evade any operational disappointments and interferences. For instance, considering smart networks/meters, an intruder can modify the meters remotely, this could cause real power outages and it might be exceptionally troublesome or difficult to continue the power supply to the home, which implies that a few capacities may affect the accessibility of the framework as well.

12.2.2   DESIGN CONCERNS FOR IOT TECHNOLOGIES

Intelligence safety, confidentiality, and security must methodically be tackled at the design phase. It may also restrain the efficiency of the communication safety and confidentiality methods and is less effective in ways of the expenditure to implement them. Moreover, the IoT items do not continually have sufficient processing power to instrument all the applicable safety levels/functionalities, the heterogeneity of things turns out to be very challenging.

12.2.3   RECOGNIZABILITY/PROFILING/UNLAWFUL HANDLING

The expanded collection of information may raise issues of confirmation and trust in many applications. The major issue about privacy is that after utilizing data gathered about and from different items identified with a solitary individual, that individual may turn out to be all the more effectively recognizable and better known, thus losing the individual's secrecy.

12.2.4   LOSS OF CLIENT CONTROL/TROUBLE IN DECIDING/LOSS/ VIOLATION OF INDIVIDUALS' PRIVACY AND DATA PROTECTION

Certainly, mechanized choices will make an impression of loss of control, however, may prompt real loss of control, since one of the principle objectives of the IoT is to give some self-rule to the items and to permit automatic selections. The IoT condition is the frequency of gadgets, sensors, readers, and applications, which can possibly gather a variety of information kinds of people as they travel through such situations [3]. The data gathered depends on question identifiers, sensor information, and the association capacities of IoT frameworks, which in a way to uncover data on people, their propensities, and other individual data, thus loss of rights of an individual on its personal data.

12.2.5   CONTROLLED ACCESS MECHANISM

Access mechanism is an essential component of IoT as every step involves access to users' data, location, daily routines, etc. An individual is permissible to take access only if one occupies the preferred attributes. The mechanism is well developed for the omnipresent applications. Also, the device before-hand does not know the one who wishes to use it. But in case, the customer needs to show his individuality to get access to the device, a serious privacy drawback could follow [9] (Table 12.1).

TABLE 12.1   Challenges in IoT & their brief description

Challenges	Description
Standarization	The various standardization protocols and methodology needs to be designed due to the heterogeneity of devices, various security and privacy issues.
Naming	The IoT will incorporate a staggeringly high number of hubs, every one of which will create content that ought to be retrievable by any approved client paying little heed to her/his position. This requires viable tending to arrangements.
Security	The real issues identified with security concern confirmation and information respectability. Verification is troublesome, as it for the most part requires proper confirmation foundations and servers that accomplish their objective through the trading of fitting messages with different hubs.
Privacy	Individual's worries about protection are without a doubt very much defended. Truth be told, the manners by which information gathering, mining, and provisioning will be practiced in the IoT.
	A) The tracing framework does not gather data about the position and developments of individual clients however just thinks about total clients (position and developments of individuals ought not be linkable to their characters);
	B) Individuals are educated of the extension and the manner by which their developments are followed by the framework (taking individuals educated about conceivable breaks of their security is basic and required by generally enactments);
	C) Information gathered by the following framework ought to be handled for the reasons for controlling the lighting and warming and after that erased by the capacity framework.
Data Integrity	This is normally guaranteed by securing information with passwords. In any case, the secret key lengths upheld by IoT innovations are as a rule too short to give solid dimensions of insurance
QoS and Data Characterization	The data traffic with patterns will be created by the IoT, which will also be entirely different from the one created by the internet. Thus a new Quality of Service schemes and other support methodologies will be required.
Mobility	There are a few recommendations for protest tending to however none for versatility bolster in the IoT situation, where versatility and flexibility to heterogeneous advancements speak to essential issues

12.3 LOCATION PRIVACY, ROUTING, AND VARIOUS CONTRIBUTIONS

Keeping in mind location privacy, we present the flow of knowledgeable data, starting from the initial phase of sensing and to include all other interaction that comes in the flow. The various levels of information flow and connected privacy regulators are described below.

Sensing detection of a particular thing/processing maybe obstructed by any ways that counteract signal communication. This may be the various blocking tag that can be used in radio frequency identification devices or fabricated tags. Several laws prohibit the use of sensitive devices such as cameras and cell phones at border customs stations, locker rooms, and other sensitive sites.

Identification has been considered an important factor in the field of IoT and achieved a large amount of attention. Communal standards habitually authorize and on occurrence boost unrecognizability in letterings to papers and placements to accessible chat mediums. Lawful implementation of anonymity is approximately entirely projected and imposed in certain situations for instance voting canvass casting [8].

The confidentiality for space is permitted across numerous procedural approaches, considering purely not delivering a space skill and encryption of stockpiled data. The Snapchat facility remained publicized as a transient method of shot sharing, nevertheless was speedily and effortlessly beaten [2].

Processing stage methodical confidentiality includes a sum of design principles that also apply to other phases [3] and various anonymizing and privacy-enhancing and privacy-preserving technologies [2]. Official lawful measures contain preventions or restraints on database similarity and distributing of acquaintance amongst commercial things.

Restricting the communications channels available, for example, not implementing or turning off facilities such as Bluetooth and Wi-Fi may technically implement privacy. Societal agencies are principally the responsibility of clients to control request circumstances and track suggested rules for suitable allotment. Authorized controllers for distribution have lately acknowledged substantial thought—for instance the US Federal Trade Commission has just acclaimed that Congress give customers extra power over the facts brokerage business [5] and European courts have needed that exploration machines instrument a "right to be forgotten" [4].

Multirouting random walk methodology was proposed by Zhou et al. [7] and has to accomplish location confidentiality in sensor networks. It is basically focusing on protecting the sensor's location by creating the suitable alterations to sensor routing in-order to make it tough for an intruder to regulate the genuine location. The major benefit of this strategy was that the eavesdropping of the packets was reduced successfully.

In one of the routing called phantom routing, the information from the position of a panda to the destination is transmitted in order to conserve its privacy of the place. The message is transmitted for a few steps from the source but later it is being transferred by flooding technique or a single path routing technique to the base station [10].

When data about the position is shared, an individual's privacy should not be exposed to the communicating system. The problem of issue id is described in the work of Hoh et al. [1]. The algorithm confuses the intruder by going through the path in which at least two customers will meet. Different paths are used for all the possible meetings and, thus, modifying the location values according to the solution, which is optimized. Thus, the intruder can offer an upsurge to faults and source erroneous routes being estimated. However, the location information is not contained directly in this scheme.

X Star was developed by Wang et al. [11] on various privacy schemes. To keep users' location privacy, the methodology divides the total area into a number of sectors-based upper on the selection of users for clocking stars. A random sampling of users' location data was done and further enlarging other locations. Though this method has restraints in real-time managing schemes, as location data processing is too long.

In order to hide an individual's identity, Mokbel projected a scheme called New Casper, which used the grid pattern for the purpose [9]. The user specifies different secrecy requisites and on these bases, the scheme had the ability to set many different cloaked spatial regions and thus hiding the client's identification at any location. The disadvantage of this scheme is that it can only be applicable under the supposition that the identity of the user should not be revealed. The scheme aids in shielding the location data but it cannot be used practically use in real-time processing systems, as the identity of the user cannot be known in this scheme

Oh et al. proposed a point transformation scheme for location data privacy. This scheme has a symmetric movement by making a choice based on a previous location route [6] so that the novel location of data can be preserved and protected. The benefit is the fast transformation of location data of different parts. The author performed three different simulations which included many attacks like tailored attack, general attack, etc., to perform the comparison between various transformation schemes, such as highly sensitive data (HSD), error-based transformation (ERB), and HSD*. The results proved that the PTS works the same way as traditional schemes and provides similar security services. In addition, PTS proved to be beneficial for various applications, which make the use of location attributes in real life.

12.4   METHODOLOGY AND RESULTS

To preserve the location confidentiality, we have used the multirandom routing path for the packets so that one cannot track the route of the packets delivered. Here, we have 50 numbers of nodes and the path is selected on the basis of the location distance from the source node to another. The packets are forwarded from one node to another until it reaches its desired destination. The packet is forwarded without any defined path to avoid the detection of the location of a particular packet. The parameters used to decide the performance of the routing methodology are throughput, packet delivery ratio, energy consumption, and the effects of distortion. The basic network criteria followed to carry out the research methodology are explained in Table12.2.

TABLE 12. 2   The Network Criteria used

Network Criteria for Methodology	
Number of Nodes	50
Number of Packets	1000
Coverage Area	1000*1000m
Number of Iterations	10
Routing Used	AODV

The flow of methodology goes as the following flowchart in Figure 12.3.

The coverage limit taken for the execution of the method is 1000 × 1000 m in the network. We define the source and destination to check our routing technique under the effects of distortion. The nodes start to pass the message from source to destination. The routing method is used to select the best nodes for sending the message from the source node to the destination node. The description is shown in Figure 12.4.

The routing scheme checks for the various nodes, which fall in the category of the communication system. The nodes, which fall in the near coverage limit, are used for forwarding the packets automatically. To avoid the intrusion from the attacker, the packet forwarding is done randomly. Figure 12.5 shows the source node processing various nearby nodes. Every packet has also been given a time to live keeping in mind the security and performance aspects.

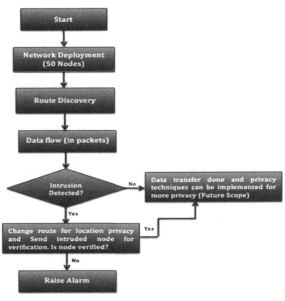

FIGURE 12.3 Flowchart of research technique used.

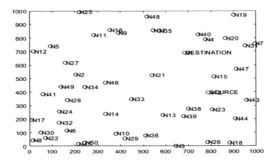

FIGURE 12.4 The creation of source and destination nodes with the coverage limit as 1000 × 1000 m.

In Figure 12.6, it is shown how a source node has identified numerous neighboring nodes. These neighboring nodes act as communicating way depending on which node is selected by the source node to forward the packet. Forwarding the packet randomly from one node to another and finally reaching the destination.

We introduced the intruder to study affect, while the routing of packets is going on. This analysis is done to know if the intruder from outside can know about the node. As our routing proves to be efficient, the attacker fails to know about the location. Thus, giving better results, as shown in Figure 12.7.

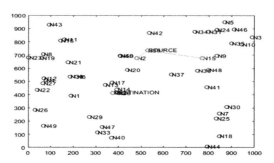

FIGURE 12.5   Source node checking the nearby communicating nodes in its coverage limit.

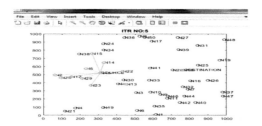

FIGURE 12.6   Various routes from the source to the neighboring nodes.

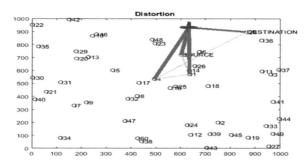

FIGURE 12.7   Red lines mark distortion in the network.

For each iteration, we have clearly observed the results for packet delivery ratio and energy consumption. Figure 12.8 shows the packet delivery ratio (PDR) of our designed methodology. For every simulation, we reinitialize the parameters for iterations to show the evaluation properly. The result shows the reduced distortion and there was no leakage of location when the intruder tried.

Figures 12.9 and 12.10 show the varying results of energy consumption and throughput, respectively. The energy consumption is measured in megajoules and throughput in terms of packets in a total time frame. Both the parameters show significant results and distortion effects are observed to be very minor on a particular node.

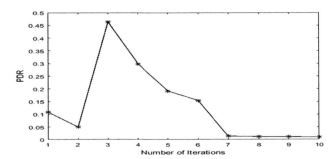

FIGURE 12.8 Packet delivery ratio of different iterations.

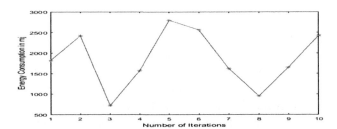

FIGURE 12.9 Energy consumption of all iterations.

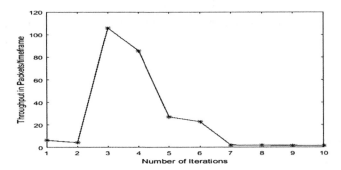

FIGURE 12.10 Throughput of iterations.

Table 12.3 describes simulation rounds and further detailing the energy used and the throughput rate of every iteration.

TABLE 12.3   Energy consumption and throughput values of different iterations

Iteration	Energy Consumption (Mega joule)	Throughput (Data Packets per timeframe)
1	1818.73	6.34
2	2420.84	4.34
3	721.57	105.80
4	1572.95	85.69
5	2796.79	27.00
6	2563.24	22.76
7	1624.52	2.08
8	952.73	1.84
9	1657.89	1.71
10	2429.75	1.55

12.5   CONCLUSION

In this chapter, we have studied various privacy issues and research contributions done to different problems. We have used routing in the wireless sensor network to check the location of a commuting node and have added distortion to check if one can affect the performance of a particular node and know the location and also check the node for verification. In case the node is verified, we transfer data and keep the implementation of privacy techniques as future works. Another side, if the node is not verified, an alarm will be raised and the route for sending packets will be changed randomly. For future work, we have proposed three-tier privacy and anonymization mechanism to hide the identity of a node located at a particular position and sends the data more securely.

KEYWORDS

- privacy
- Web of Things
- RFID
- nanotechnology
- routing
- location privacy

REFERENCES

1. Hoh, B., and Gruteser, M. Protecting location privacy through path confusion, in First International Conference on Security and Privacy for Emerging Areas in Communications Networks, 2005, 194–205.
2. Chow, C.-Y., Mokbel, M. F., and Aref, W. G., Casper*: query processing for location services without compromising privacy, ACM Transactions on Database Systems, 2009, 34, 4, 763–774.
3. Gray, D., and Citron, D., The right to quantitative privacy, Minnesota Law Review, 2013, 98, 2013–2023.
4. Streitfeld, D., European court lets users erase records on web, The New York Times, 2014.
5. FTC Recommends Congress Require the Data Broker Industry to be More Transparent and Give Consumers Greater Control Over Their Personal Information. http://www.ftc.gov/news-events/press-releases/2014/05/ftc-recommends-congress-require-data-broker-industry-be-more (accessed June 14, 2014).
6. Oh, K., Lee, K., and Lim, J., Point transformation scheme to protect location data changing in real time, in 2016 IEEE Military Communications Conference, 2016.
7. Zhou, L., Wen, Q., and Zhang, H., Preserving sensor location privacy in Internet of Things, in Proceedings of IEEE at Fourth International Conference on Computational and Information Sciences, 2012, 856–859.
8. Hutchinson, L., iOS 8 to stymie trackers and marketers with MAC address randomizationk Ars Technica, 2014. http://arstechnica.com/apple/2014/06/ios8-tostymie-trackers-and-marketers-with-mac-addressrandomization/, June 2014, accessed May, 2015.
9. Mokbel, M. F., Chow, C.-Y., and Aref, W. G., The new casper: query processing for location services without compromising privacy, in Proceedings of the 32nd international conference on Very large databases, 2006, 763–774.
10. Kamat, P., Zhang, Y., Trappe, W., and Ozturk, C., Enhancing source-location privacy in sensor network routing, in Proceedings of the 25th IEEE International Conference on Distributed Computing Systems, 2005, 599–608.
11. Wang, T., and Ling, L., Privacy-aware mobile services over road networks, Proceedings of the VLDB Endowment, 2009, 2, 1, 1042–1053.

CHAPTER 13

IoT-RFID Sensing System for Monitoring Corrosion

MANINDER PAL[1*] and TARUN GULATI[2]

[1]*Liverpool John Moores University, United Kingdom*

[2]*MMEC, MM (Deemed to be University), Mullana, Ambala, Haryana, India*

Corresponding author. E-mail: mpal001@dundee.ac.uk, drmaninderpal@gmail.com

ABSTRACT

This chapter presents a low-frequency radio-frequency identification (LF-RFID) sensing system integrated with Internet of things (IoTs) to detect and characterize corrosion. The LF-RFID sensing system comprises of a tag and reader inductively linked with each other. Tag interacts with corroded metal through eddy currents and measure changes in corroded surface conductivity and permeability. Sensitivity and impedance of LF-RFID sensor varies with distance between the tag and the reader which is adjusted to find the optimum working range. The static and transient feature of the LF-RFID sensor signal is used to characterize corrosion at a low computational rate. The size of commercial low frequency tags is very small as compared to the structures in practice. So, IoTs are used to make a wireless sensor network of the proposed sensing system. Results showed an enhancement in sensitivity to corrosion characterization at the optimum distance between the tag and the reader. Using IoTs, several sensors are cascaded to make wireless sensor network and enable monitoring a wide structural area.

13.1 INTRODUCTION

Metals corrode due to their reaction with the surrounding environment [1]. Paint coatings of various chemicals are normally used to prevent its occurrence.

However, this is not a permanent solution and the paint coated metallic structures can corrode with age. Several research studies and equipments have been developed and/or are in progress for its early detection and estimation. For example, electrochemical impedance spectroscopy [2] and electromagnetic nondestructive testing (NDT) and evaluation methods such as eddy current (EC) and pulsed eddy current (PEC) techniques [3,4]. These techniques are conceptually based on measuring the reduction in conductivity and permeability of the corroded area [5, 6]. Their measured signals are normally analyzed through feature extraction techniques to detect and characterize corrosion [7, 8]. The existing nondestructive testing and evaluation techniques have wide applications; however, these are still associated with several shortcomings [9]. For example, the sensitivity of EC and PEC techniques decreases significantly with increasing lift-off distance between their probe and the sample surface under investigation. In addition, the majority of existing techniques are limited to use for real-time monitoring of metal surfaces because of their size, operational complexity, and the cost of instrumentation. Moreover, the existing technologies can only monitor the size of corroded surface equal to the size of the sensor. However in practice, the corroded surface area can be comparatively very large. So, existing techniques need to be repetitively used to cover the corroded area and are thus expensive in both time and cost. Therefore, this paper exploited a combination of low-frequency radio-frequency identification (RFID) tags and IoTs for detecting and characterizing corrosion. This is because these are cheap, passive, and can be permanently embedded into structures for long-term monitoring [9, 10]. To extend the monitoring area, a series of LF-RFID sensors are connected using the FRDM-K64F IoT kit to develop a wireless sensor network for monitoring a large area at one time. In the proposed IoT-LF-RFID system, the tags are placed on the metallic surface to be tested. The response of these tags is measured at the reader sequentially, and its monotonic features are extracted and used to detect and characterize corrosion [10,11]. The principle of LF-RFID sensing system is detailed below.

13.2   MODELING LF-RFID-BASED CORROSION SENSING SYSTEM

The proposed IoT-LF-RFID corrosion sensing system is shown in Figure 13.1. The sensor part consists of two hardware components: reader and tag. The reader primarily consists of RF circuitry to transmit and receive 125 kHz (low-frequency RFID) RF energy to power and communicate with tag. The tag is passive and placed on the metal surface to be investigated. The reader transmits 125 kHz RF signal to power the tag. In return, the tag backscatters

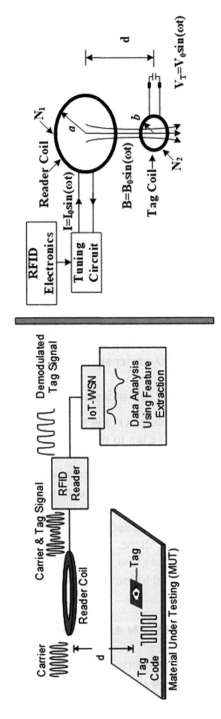

FIGURE 13.1 Functional block diagram of LF-RFID corrosion sensing system.

the code stored in its memory to the reader. This response signal is measured at the reader and its monotonic features are extracted and used to detect and characterize corrosion [10, 11]. The concept of EC models interaction between the tag and corroded metal, whereas, inductive coupling establishes a communication link between tag and reader.

The electrical equivalent model of the developed LF-RFID sensing system is presented in Figure 13.2. The tag and reader are represented by LCR circuit. The metal is conductive in nature, so it is represented as LR circuit. The metal near or in contact with the tag is modeled as an additional parallel inductor with self-inductance (L_M) and resistance (R_M). In the absence of metal (Figure 13.1), the voltage (V_T) induced in the tag is governed by magnetic field passing through the entire surface (S) of tag coil, as

$$V_T = \frac{\pi \mu_0 If N_1 N_2 Sa^2 \sqrt{L_T}}{R_T \sqrt{C_T (a^2 + d^2)^3}} \cos(\alpha) \tag{13.1}$$

where d = coaxial distance between reader and tag coils,

μ_0 = permeability of free space and is $4\pi \times 10^{-7}$ H/m,

N_1 and N_2 = number of turns in reader coil and tag coil, respectively,

a and b = radius of reader and tag coil, respectively;

f = frequency of the RFID carrier signal;

S = area (m^2) of tag coil,

R_T and L_T = resistance and self-inductance of tag coil, respectively.

From (13.1), the induced voltage (V_T) in tag depends upon the angle (α) between B and S, and the relative tag to reader distance. Therefore, the two coils (reader and tag coil) are placed in parallel $(\alpha = 0)$ to each other to pass maximum magnetic flux. Equation (13.1) also indicates that the voltage (V_T) induced in tag coil depends on the coil physical (e.g., number of turn and area) and electrical parameters, and the relative position of tag with respect to the reader coil. This chapter exploited commercial RFID tags, so tag coil parameters (such as dimension, shape, and number of turns) were limited to change. Therefore, from (13.1), the relative tag to reader distance was adjusted to match impedance and to improve sensitivity.

13.2.1   *LF-RFID SENSING SYSTEM AND CORROSION*

To model the effect of metal and corrosion, the voltage (V_R) across reader coil with inductance (L_R) and in the absence of metal is computed using Figure 13.2 as

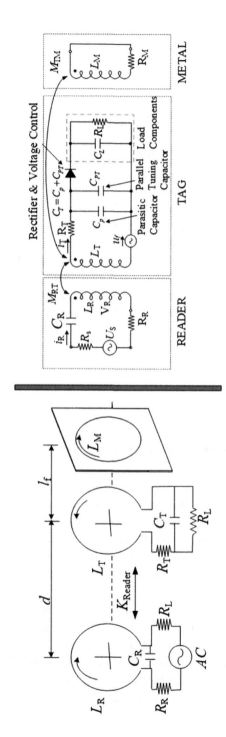

FIGURE 13.2 Electrical equivalent model of the proposed LF-RFID corrosion sensing system showing inductive coupling between reader, tag, and metal.

$$V_R = L_R \frac{di_R}{dt} \pm M_{RT} \frac{di_T}{dt} \tag{13.2}$$

where i_R and i_T represent the current flowing in the reader and tag coils, respectively. M_{RT} is the mutual inductance between reader and tag. Similarly, the tag voltage (V_T) across load can be expressed as

$$V_T = L_T \frac{di_R}{dt} \pm M_{RT} \frac{di_T}{dt} + i_T R_T \tag{13.3}$$

where L_T and R_T represent the respective inductance and resistance of tag coil. In Figure 13.2, the presence of metal as an additional parallel inductor will reduce tag's overall inductance, and thus impedance and sensitivity. This will change current (i_T) and readercoil voltage (V_R), as governed by (13.2) and can be measured through feature extraction. To model the effect of corrosion, it is considered that the resistance (R_M) and inductance (L_M) of metal depend upon its physical properties, for example, dimensions, conductance, and permeability. These properties changes as the corrosion progresses with time. Variation in parameters (L_M and R_M) changes the impedance of LF-RFID sensing system, which can be measured as a monotonic change (increase or decrease) in features of LF-RFID signals. Next section will explain various features of measured signal of LF-RFID sensing system and their sensitivity to corrosion characterization.

13.3 FEATURE EXTRACTION AND SELECTION TO CHARACTERIZE CORROSION

In the absence of any metallic structure, the response of the LF-RFID sensing system should be ideally in the form of square wave pulses, given by (13.1). However, its shape changes when the tag is placed in the proximity of a metal. This phenomenon is due to ECs and impedance mismatch. An example of its shape when tag was placed on a metal is shown in Figure 13.3.

In Figure 13.3, the response is not a perfect square wave and has variations in both top and transient sides. These variations carry information about corrosion and crack on metal surface. This information can be characterized through feature extraction, similar to PEC NDT technique. It is because the wave shape in Figure 13.3 is similar to PEC NDT technique; which has been widely used to characterize defects on metals through feature extraction [6, 7].

Some already studied features include amplitude, duty cycle, zero crossing, and rising edge [6, 7]. In this chapter, two time-domain static and transient features of LF-RFID sensor signal have been explored. These features are selected as these are already proven to be robust and give repeatable results to integrate the LF-RFID system with IoT kit. The static and transient features are shown in Figure 13.3.

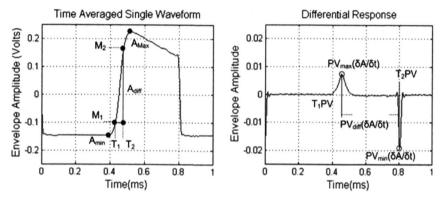

FIGURE 13.3 An example of the measured response of LF-RFID sensing system and its differential showing the transient features. The tag was placed on the noncorroded metallic surface.

To explain features, the measured signal is denoted as A in Figure 13.3. The first static feature (A_{max}) represents the maximum value of pulse A and characterizes the permeability variation. The other static features used for comparison are: A_{diff} and A_{edge}. Feature A_{diff} represents the difference between maximum and minimum of pulse A. Feature A_{edge} represents the rising edge of pulse and is defined by the upper (M_2) and lower (M_1) threshold of rising edge. Transient features were computed by taking the first derivative ($\delta A/\delta t$) of signal (A), as shown in Figure 13.3. The transient feature of interest is $PV_{max}(\delta A/\delta t)$, which represents the maximum peak value of $\delta A/\delta t$. It reflects the variation (reduction) in conductivity of corroded metal with increase in thickness of corrosion layer. Other transient features used for evaluation and comparison include $PV_{min}(\delta A/\delta t)$ and $PV_{diff}(\delta A/\delta t)$. Feature $PV_{min}(\delta A/\delta t)$ represents the minimum peak of $\delta A/\delta t$. Finally, the feature $PV_{diff}(\delta A/\delta t)$ represents the difference between maximum and minimum of differential signal peak. These features are experimentally evaluated in the next section.

13.4   SAMPLE DESIGN AND EXPERIMENTAL SETUP

The progress of the corrosion layer in a metal varies nonuniformly with time. It is due to variations in proportion of its constituents (iron oxides and hydroxides) with the time and atmosphere surrounding the metal. This chapter focuses on early stage corrosion, when the thickness of corrosion increases with time. However, in long-term corrosion, it tends to decrease due to metal loss. For this study, the samples used are shown in Figure 13.4.

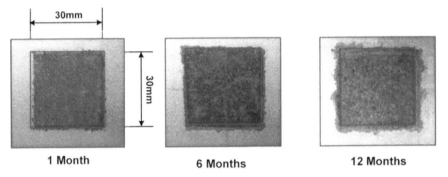

FIGURE 13.4   Images of corrosion patches on the samples.

The corrosion samples are made up of several mild steel plates of various sizes. For example, the plates in Figure 13.4 have dimensions of $200 \times 80 \times 5$ mm (length × width × thickness). To prepare the corrosion samples, a rectangular patch (e.g., 30 mm × 30 mm in Figure 13.4) on plate was left exposed to corrode. The rest of the plate was covered with a plastic tape to keep the steel clean and dry. The atmospheric exposure duration was of 1, 6, and 12 months to develop different levels of corrosion. An example of developed corrosion patches is shown in Figure 13.4. For larger corroded area patches, 16 sensors are connected in a matrix of 4 × 4. For these multiple connected sensors using IoTs, the multiple signals are obtained sequentially and are assessed individually. The developed LF-RFID-based sensor, IoT kit, and the developed algorithms to integrate a sequence of 16 LF-RFID sensors to IoT kit in order to locally preprocess information and then transmitting the processed information to the base station is shown in Figure 13.5.

In the test setup shown in Figure 13.5, the tag used was programmed with code consisting of all "1s" at a data bit rate of 125 kHz/32 = 3.906 kHz with 50% duty cycles. The selection of all "1s" was made because it resulted into a uniform stream of square pulses and thus its averaging can be easily performed at the IoT node. Each tag was placed on the corrosion patch to be monitored. The relative position and alignment of the reader coil, tag, and corrosion patch was maintained throughout the experiments. Readings were taken for a reader tag relative spacing of 0, 10, 20, and 30 mm. The reader circuit was designed for reading the signals, as shown in Figure 13.1. In the reader, the measured signal was firstly demodulated and filtered to remove the 125 kHz carrier and noise. This was done by a diode-based envelope detector followed by an op-amp based filter and buffer. The filtered output signal was then digitized using FRDM-K64F IoT base module. The reader coil in Figure 13.5 was designed of circular shape with 35 mm in diameter, so that most of the RF energy produced by the reader coil spreads over space limited to the area of the tag. The reader coil had a resistance R = 11.35 Ω and inductance L = 738 µH. For these parameters, the reader and tag had a theoretical resonant frequency of 125 kHz in free space. The system was calibrated for this frequency by adjusting the distance between tag and the reader. The experimental outcomes are discussed below.

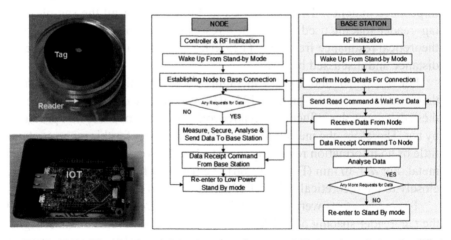

FIGURE 13.5 The developed LF-RFID based sensor, IoT board, and the simplified representation of the developed IoT-\LF RFID node to base interaction algorithm.

13.5 RESULTS AND DISCUSSION

To evaluate the developed IoT-LF-RFID sensing system, two stages of experiments (impedance matching and corrosion characterization) were carried out. The tests were carried out for stand-off distances of 0, 10, 20, and 30 mm between the tag and reader. The measurements were repeatedly taken 10 times for each sample and a relative tag reader distance of 0, 10, 20, and 30 mm. The outcomes are discussed below.

13.5.1 IMPEDANCE VS DISTANCE

In the proposed LF-RFID corrosion sensing system, the impedance was matched by adjusting the distance between tag and reader coils. For this purpose, the frequency of the RFID carrier signal was changed from 116 to 132 kHz. This was repeated for each corroded sample and tag–reader spacing of d = 0, 10, 20, and 30 mm. The LF-RFID sensor signal was measured at the reader for each carrier frequency, sample, and spacing, and is shown in Figure 13.6. The amplitude of measured signals was found to vary with the distance between tag and reader, due to change in impedance. Therefore, for each sample and spacing, the maximum amplitude of measured signal and its corresponding carrier frequency was computed. This carrier frequency gives the resonant frequency of system at which impedance matches. This is reported in Table 13.1 for all the samples and tag–reader spacing used. The highest resonant frequency measured close to theoretical resonance frequency (125 kHz) is marked in Table 13.1 for each distance and discussed below.

For d = 0, 10, and 20 mm in Figure 13.6, a significant variation from theoretical resonant frequency (125 kHz) was obtained. This is because for these distances, the influence of reader coil dominated over the flux produced by tag. Therefore, the measured signal from the reader for this range contains little or no information regarding the interface between the tag and corroded metal. For d = 30 mm (Figure 13.6d), the resonant frequency matched more closely to the theoretical value of 125 kHz for each sample.

To confirm, tests were repeated for the carrier frequency of 125 kHz and the tag–reader spacing of 0, 10, 20, and 30 mm. The LF-RFID sensor signal was measured and its static (A_{max}) and transient feature (PV_{max}) were extracted and shown in Figure 13.7. For d = 0, 10, and 20 mm, the monotonic trend was found not progressively increasing in accordance with the corrosion exposure duration from 0 to 12 months. It is because the signal amplitude obtained at 125 kHz resonant frequency was not found increasing in accordance with the age of corrosion. However, for d = 30 mm, a monotonically increasing response can be seen in Figure 13.7. It is because for this distance (d = 30 mm), the impedance is matched in the presence of a noncorroded metal. This is discussed in the next section through more detailed results obtained at resonant frequency.

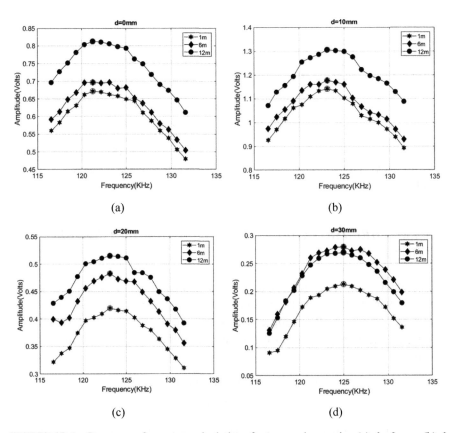

FIGURE 13.6 Resonance frequency calculations for tag–reader spacing (a) $d = 0$ mm, (b) $d = 10$ mm, (c) $d = 20$ mm, and (d) d = 30 mm. The signals were measured for corroded samples with corrosion exposure duration of 1, 6, and 12 months.

TABLE 13.1 Resonant Frequencies Obtained for Different Tag Reader Spacings

Corrosion Sample	Relative Tag Reader Spacing (mm)			
	0	**10**	**20**	**30**
1	123.1250	121.2500	123.1250	124.9850
6	123.1250	121.2500	123.1250	125.0000
12	123.1250	121.2500	123.1250	124.9850

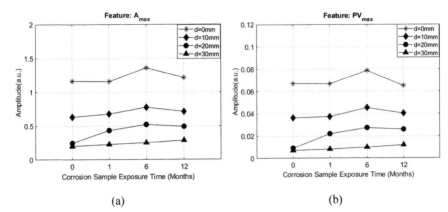

(a)   (b)

FIGURE 13.7   Features (a) A_{max} and (b) PV_{max} variation for corroded metal samples of 1, 6, and 12 months and tag reader relative spacing of 0, 10, 20, and 30 mm.

13.5.2   *CORROSION CHARACTERIZATION THROUGH FEATURE EXTRACTION*

The selection of the most sensitive and robust feature is done using the relative variation (ε), which refers to the percentage difference relative to the same feature of the sample with less corrosion exposure duration. For example, the relative variation for sample 6 and sample 1 is calculated as follows:

$$\varepsilon = \frac{\text{feature of sample6} - \text{same feature of sample1}}{\text{value of feature of sample1}} \times 100 \qquad (13.4)$$

The results for relative variation are compared in Table 13.2 for the six features. For simplicity, an example of samples 1 and 6 is given in Table 13.2. Other samples were also analyzed similarly. The computed six features are divided in two groups: static and transient features, and are shown in Figure 13.8. The relative tag reader spacing was set to $d = 30$ mm (resonant) and carrier frequency to 125 kHz. The selection of $d = 30$ mm was made from the results obtained in previous section; where, the impedance of sensing system was found to be matched at this position.

From the theoretical discussions made above, the proposed LF-RFID corrosion sensing system should show a monotonic change in features with exposure duration, provided the impedance is matched. The same can be seen in Figure 13.8; where, the measured features show a monotonically increasing trend with the exposure time. The error bars are very low showing lower uncertainty of data and an increased accuracy and robustness. However, this monotonic response increased nonuniformly with time. It is because the corrosion grows nonuniformly with time and so does its properties. The performance of features is evaluated using the relative variation mentioned in Table 13.2. The static feature (A_{max}) characterizes the permeability change; whereas, transient feature ($PV_{max}(\delta A/\delta t)$) characterizes the conductivity variation. The transient feature ($PV_{max}(\delta A/\delta t)$) shows higher sensitivity than the static features. Other features also vary in the same monotonic pattern as can be seen in Figure 13.8, and thus prove the robustness of system and may be useful in future for other applications.

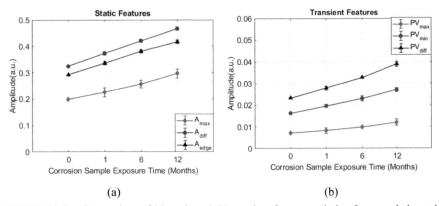

(a)   (b)

FIGURE 13.8 Comparison of (a) static and (b) transient feature variation for corroded metal samples of 1, 6, and 12 months and tag to reader relative spacing of 30 mm.

TABLE 13.2 Features Evaluation for 6 Months and 1-Month Corroded Sample

Static Feature	Sample 6	Sample 1	$\in$(%)	Transient Feature	Sample 6	Sample 1	$\in$(%)
A_{max}	0.2568	0.2255	13.8827	$PV_{max}(\delta A/\delta t)$	0.0118	0.0082	43.9024
A_{diff}	0.4206	0.3730	12.7614	$PV_{min}(\delta A/\delta t)$	0.0270	0.0196	37.7551
A_{edge}	0.3809	0.3357	13.4644	$PV_{diff}(\delta A/\delta t)$	0.0318	0.0278	14.3885

13.6 CONCLUSION AND FUTURE WORK

This chapter presented and evaluated an IoT-LF-RFID corrosion sensing system. The system is flexible, as the distance between the tag and reader can be adjusted to match the impedance and thus attain the optimum working range. However, this working range may vary with the type of tag. For the tag used, a 30 mm separation distance between tag and reader is found to be the closest optimum distance to match impedance, when tag is placed on the mild steel sample. At this distance, the sensitivity and accuracy of the LF-RFID sensing system was found to be significantly increased. This is because at lower stand-off distances ($d \leq 20$ mm), the influence of reader coil dominated the tag and the monotonic change in features was not obtained. However, at higher stand-off distances (d > 30 mm), the tag coil do not receive enough power from the reader coil; thus, reducing its sensitivity to corrosion.

To characterize corrosion, six features of LF-RFID sensor output were extracted and compared. Among these features, two features: static (A_{max}) and transient ($PV_{max}(\delta A/\delta t)$) were selected to, respectively, determine permeability and conductivity changes with corrosion exposure. From selected features, transient responses have proven to be significantly more sensitive and robust with corrosion progression compared to conventional static features. In nutshell, the IoT-LF-RFID sensing system is capable of detecting and characterizing corrosion through feature extraction. Future work will focus on designing miniaturized system suitable for industrial applications.

KEYWORDS

- **LF RFID**
- **feature extraction**
- **feature selection**
- **corrosion characterization**
- **nondestructive testing and evaluation (NDT&E)**

REFERENCES

1. Schweitzer, P. A. (2003, June, 26). *Metallic Materials: Physical, Mechanical, and Corrosion Properties.* Marcel Dekker, New York.
2. Hattori, M., Nishikata, A., and Tsuru, T. (June, 2010). EIS study on degradation of polymer-coated steel under ultraviolet radiation. *Corrosion Science. 52(6).* pp. 2080–2087.
3. Tian, G. Y., Sophian, A., Taylor, D., and Rudlin, J. (Feb., 2005). Multiple sensors on pulsed eddy-current detection for 3-D subsurface crack assessment. *IEEE Sensors Journal.* 5(1). pp. 90–96.

4. Davoust, M. E., Le Brusquet, L., and Fleury, G. (September 2010). Robust estimation of hidden corrosion parameters using an eddy current technique. *Journal of Nondestructive Evaluation.* 29 (3). pp. 155–167.

5. He, Y., Luo, F., and Pan, M. (November, 2010). Defect characterisation based on pulsed eddy current imaging technique. *Sensors and Actuators A: Physical. 164 (1–2).* pp. 1–7.

6. Tian, G. Y., and Sophian, A. (January, 2005). Defect classification using a new feature for pulsed eddy current sensors. *NDT & E International. 38 (1).* pp. 77–82.

7. Chen, T., Tian, G. Y., Sophian, A., and Que, P. W. (September 2008). Feature extraction and selection for defect classification of pulsed eddy current NDT. *NDT & E International.* 41 (6). pp. 467–476.

8. Smith, R. A., and Hugo, G. R. (January, 2001). Transient eddy current NDE for ageing aircraft capabilities and limitations. *Insight-Non-Destructive Testing and Condition Monitoring.* 43(1). pp. 14–25.

9. Fuente, D., Diaz, I., Simancas, J., Chico, B., and Morcillo, M. (February, 2011). Long-term atmospheric corrosion of mild steel. *Corrosion Science.* 53 (2). pp. 604–617.

10. Alamin, M., Tian, G. Y., Andrews, A., and Jackson, P. (February, 2012). Corrosion detection using low-frequency RFID technology. *Insight Non-Destructive Testing and Condition Monitoring.* 54 (2). pp. 72–75.

11. Sunny, A. I., Tian, G. Y., Zhang, J., and Pal, M. (April, 2016). Low frequency (LF) RFID sensors and selective transient feature extraction for corrosion characterisation. *Sensors and Actuators A: Physical.* 241. pp. 34–43.

CHAPTER 14

Blockchain in the IoT: Use-Case and Challenges

ABHINAV BHANDARI[1*], PARMPREET SINGH[1], and GURPREET SINGH[2]

[1]Department of Computer Science and Engineering, Punjabi University, Patiala, Punjab, India

[2]Department of Computer Science and Engineering, PIT, MRSPTU, Rajpura, Punjab, India

*Corresponding author. E-mail: bhandarinitj@gmail.com

ABSTRACT

The Internet of things (IoT) is still moving to its full bloom and making itself a part of the Internet of future. One huge challenge is the ability to tackle billions of IoT devices. A number of technologies exist for managing IoT devices using a centralized control model but each has some kind of technical limitations to handle the abundance of IoT devices. The research motive is to understand blockchain technology and whether or not it can be integrated with IoT. A literature review is conducted on the blockchain technology to understand the fundamental working of blockchain and to document its key features. Some recent researches in the usage of blockchain in IoT are reviewed in the chapter and a generalized architecture for blockchain are described. The chapter also focuses on issues and challenges associated with the integration of blockchain with IoT. Moreover, we provided a few recommendations for future work considering the above-mentioned issues.

14.1 INTRODUCTION

There is an immense hike in the Internet of things (IoT) devices. IoT devices are expected to grow to 26 billion by 2020, spread over to a variety of application areas. In order to tackle this gigantic growth of IoT devices, it is necessary to come up with new architecture or design for hassle-free IoT services [1]. Recent solutions for IoT are mainly dependent on a centralized model [2]. Some other recent technologies like software-defined networking [3], fog computing [4], edge computing [5] also come up for the effective performance of IoT services. Software-defined networking (SDN) and fog computing is going to play a major role in IoT services. SDN increases the network management capability and fog computing combines the cloud and IoT by moving the computing from cloud to IoT edge. Some work has been done in this context but if we consider the objectives of IoT network in future, a peer-to-peer decentralized cloud storage is one of the major requirements. Recently, more focus of researchers is on blockchain in the wide range of industries which was initially restricted to cryptocurrencies only.

Blockchain technology is moving toward many different areas as blockchain works in a distributed manner without a trusted intermediary unlike in centralized systems. Things can be done in a decentralized way without the help of central authorities. We can say blockchain establishes a trustless network as two persons even transact when they do not trust each other. The smart contract in blockchain is the self-executing scripts that reside on blockchain to make more distributed and automated workflow between entities [6]. This advancement makes researchers focus on the usage of blockchain in IoT.

The motive of the work is to provide a detailed description of the background of blockchain and identify how blockchain can be used in the IoT. With this, the reader will be able to understand how and where blockchain can be used with IoT which would further help them to apply blockchain in their desired work. The contributions of this paper are as follows:

- Describe the working of blockchain and its types.
- Discuss the blockchain in the area of IoT and identify the use of blockchain in this area.
- Open challenges and design issues.
- Conclusion and future directions.

The rest of the chapter is organized as follows: in Section 14.2, background of blockchain and its types are explained. In Section 14.3, current usage of blockchain in the IoT area is discussed. Section 14.4 discusses open challenges and design issues and last but not least, inference and future scope are discussed in Section 14.5.

14.2 BLOCKCHAIN BACKGROUND

A blockchain is a ceaselessly growing list of records called blocks. Blocks are coupled and secured with the help of cryptography. Initially, blockchain was built for Bitcoin a cryptocurrency. It was proposed in 2008 and implemented in 2009 [7]. Individual blocks of the blockchain contain records of some kind of transaction data that are stored in individual blocks and individual components of these blocks. These individual blocks are linked together using cryptography.

We can say in the blockchain blocks are time stamped which are linked by cryptographic hashes as shown in Figure 14.1 [8]. However, the blockchain technology was meant for the cryptocurrency but can be used to build other decentralized applications [9]. The blockchain is a linked database handled by systems of the peer-to-peer network. If you want to use blockchain, the first thing required is to build peer-to-peer networks with all nodes which are interested to use a blockchain. It is a new digital concept of storing data. The data is stored in blocks. Data stored in the blockchain is immutable after the block is added to the chain.

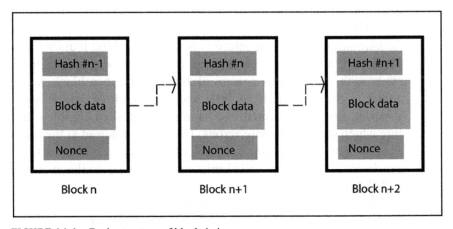

FIGURE 14.1 Basic structure of blockchain.

For a better understanding of basic working of the blockchain, we are considering Bitcoin blockchain as an example. The basic steps of Bitcoin blockchain are shown in Figure 14.2. Following are the main operations in building the blockchain.

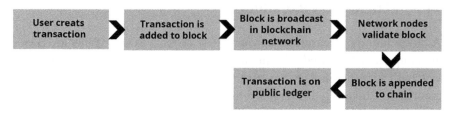

FIGURE 14.2   Basic working steps of Bitcoin blockchain.

- *Data in block.* We are taking the instance of Bitcoin blockchain, thus there is solely transactional information different data could also be present if the other style of blockchain is there. In Bitcoin blockchain, block size is 1 MB. There might be over one transaction.
- *Linking the blocks.* These blocks are now being joined along. Each block incorporates a signature that correlates to data in the block. If something in data changes, then we get a new signature.
- *Creation of hash.* Signature is created with the help of a cryptographical hash function. A cryptographical hash function may be a really difficult code that takes any string as input and change it into a unique output string. Bitcoin blockchain uses SHA-256 hashing algorithm.
- *Validation of block.* A signature is not the only thing required for a block to be added to the blockchain. If its digital signature of block starts with a consecutive range of zeroes only, then block can be added to the blockchain. A little specific chunk of data is added which is modified repeatedly so as to get the desired eligible signature which starts with some zeroes. This can be referred as the nonce value of a block. Changing the value of nonce again and again to get the desired signature is called mining. Those who do this work are called miners.
- *Immutable blockchain.* If a block is altered in the blockchain, all rest of the blocks would be affected, so all the chained blocks have to be validated and chained again. It would be terribly tough seems not possible.
- *Blockchain governance and rules [10].* The public blockchain works on the democracy model and so, in order to update anything the majority of users must agree on the same. In blockchain, longest blockchain is considered to be true because it considers that the longest chain is delineated by the majority.

14.2.1 TYPES OF BLOCKCHAINS

Blockchain is categorized into three types based on access permissions that is, public blockchain, consortium blockchain, and private blockchain [11, 12].

Public blockchain: In public blockchain, every node can read, add transactions, and conjointly engage within the consensus process. A public blockchain is totally transparent and decentralized. Bitcoin or Ethereum are examples of public blockchains.

Consortium blockchain: In consortium blockchain, just some preselected nodes participate within the consensus process. Only specific nodes can read. Blockchain can also be public or restricted, thus we are able to say it's partially decentralized. Hyperledger is the example of consortium blockchain.

Private blockchain: In private blockchain, one central node is having to write permission and read permission are often public or restricted. Most of the private companies are using private blockchain for their desired purpose.

14.2.2 CHARACTERISTICS OF BLOCKCHAIN

With some analysis efforts [11, 13, 14] we are able to describe some basic characteristics of blockchain as described below:

- *Distributed:* Blockchain is designed to be distributed and synchronic across point-to-point networks, which makes it ideal for multiorganizational business networks like supply chains or financial consortia. Each user within the network needs to validate transactions and has a uniform copy of the ledger. After that, encrypted transactions can be added. If any change takes place in a ledger, that would mirror all its copies in a very short time.
- *Immutability:* Once all nodes united on a transaction and recorded it, it will never be modified. You will later record another transaction about that asset to alter its state; however, you will not be able to hide the original transaction. You can trace any asset throughout its life. So, all the valid transactions are practically changeless because of the necessity for verification by all different nodes within the network.
- *Consensus:* An agreement is required to validate the block or transactions. If all the members of blockchain are agreed, only then block or transaction is accepted. All the members should conform to follow the same agreement. A transaction that does not follow the same agreement won't be accepted.

- *Irreversible:* Blockchain is irreversible as hashing is used, so it would be complicated and it's not possible to reverse it. It is not possible to drive a private key from the public key. Even one modification within the input could lead to a totally different hash.

14.3 BLOCKCHAIN IN IOT

The hasty increment in IoT devices with diversity has created problems with scalability, security, efficiency, and accessibility. Even though IoT is still humming along, however it is facing problems in deployment. The two rising technologies SDN and blockchain will play the main role in solving deployment problems with IoT networks. In this chapter, the main focus is on blockchain technology and how it is going to inherit its role in IoT services. Blockchain architecture is characterized by cryptography, immutability, distributed ledger, and consensus. This might strengthen IoT architecture with additional accurate resource utilization with enhanced security. Following are the main benefits of blockchain for IoT [11, 15–17]:

- *Trust:* The distributed, transparent, and decentralized features create a significant role in building trust between participants and devices. This reduces the chance of tampering and collusion.
- *Reduce Cost:* By eliminating the intermediaries, we tend to reduce the cost of the transaction by direct peer-to-peer dealing.
- *Accelerate and automate transactions:* It would facilitate to reduce the settlement time from days to near real-time with the help of smart contracts.
- *Software updates:* Blockchain has the potential to broadcast software updates on the blockchain network, in conjunction with the cryptographic validation by blockchain-connected IoT devices.

Some analysis work has been done within the IoT sector with blockchain that includes: Zhang et al. [18] projected the e-business IoT model supported blockchain and smart contracts. The distributed autonomous corporation is implemented in this model coins and sensor information exchange can be obtained by trading Decentralized Autonomous Corporation (DAC) without a third party. Security and privacy have a significant concern with IoT. Blockchain plays a major role in improving in these areas. Hardjono and Smith [19] describe the privacy-preserving methodology for IoT devices with cloud ecosystem. To register device anonymously without a third party to prove its manufacturing provenance was proposed in Hardjono and Smith [19]. Whereas security concerns a DistBlockNet: a distributed blockchain-based secure SDN architecture [20] was proposed which mixes the advantages of SDN and blockchain technologies. In this, blockchain is employed to update the flow rule table. Then they further extended their work by moving blockchain in fog as well as cloud by proposing software-based fog node-based distributed blockchain cloud architecture [21] in this blockchain is formed also at the edge of IoT devices which improves efficiency and availability.

Even though IoT is still humming along, but facing problems in deployment. The two emerging technologies SDN and blockchain can play a major role in solving deployment issues of IoT networks. In this paper, our focus is on blockchain technology how it may come into the role of IoT services.

Figure 14.3. shows generalized blockchain and IoT collaboration infrastructure when we are embedding the blockchain in IoT where the interaction would take place. We can generalize this interaction at three layers: the device layer, the fog layer, and the cloud layer. If we implement blockchain at the device layer, it could be the fastest. While implementing only IoT, data can be stored in blockchain and interaction with other devices may be done without blockchain. This approach lowers the latency. We can also implement blockchain at the fog layer as all IoT devices interacting with fog nodes for processing. Blockchain can be implemented on these distributed fog nodes and in the same way blockchain can be implemented at the cloud level. A good way is a hybrid approach in which blockchain can be implemented at any level according to the requirement. Real-time IoT interactions are possible with this approach. Fog computing and cloud computing can be used to overcome the limitations of blockchain in IoT.

14.4 CHALLENGES IN THE BLOCKCHAIN-IOT INTEGRATION

Below are some of the design issues and challenges in the IoT area with blockchain integration:

Storage: IoT devices generate massive volumes of data in real-time, thus if we are considering blockchain in IoT. It might be the key challenge to tackle such a massive volume of data because blockchain is initially not created for storing a large volume of data. Implementation of blockchain in IoT would need to think about this challenge.

Place of blockchain end nodes: In a blockchain, we are considering end nodes to those nodes that are a part of the network, can generate new blocks through mining process, and additionally can do verification of transactions. The key problem is to search out the most effective appropriate place to deploy endpoints. They can be deployed at any level according to the requirements.

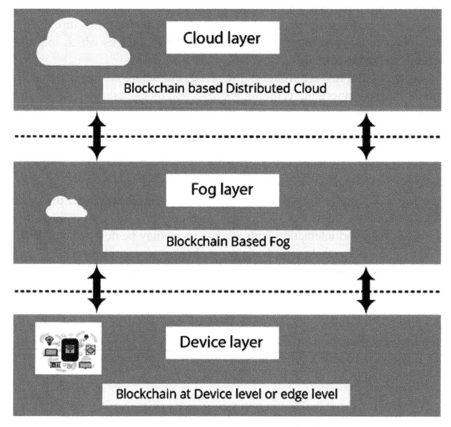

FIGURE 14.3   Generalized blockchain–IoT interaction model.

Consensus and smart contract: Consensus and smart contracts are two major elements of the blockchain [22]. IoT devices are very limited with the recourses, however, consensus algorithms needed more processing power, it might be tough for the IoT devices to take part in consensus and smart contracts [23].

Legal issues: The lack of regulation poses a serious downside for IoT manufacturers and services suppliers. This challenge alone can intimidate several businesses from using the blockchain technology.

14.5 CONCLUSION AND FUTURE DIRECTIONS

Blockchain technology has attracted researchers in truly distributed peer-to-peer systems. It has some distinctive features that make blockchain a totally different approach in storing, updating, and sharing data with additional security. It will have a significant contribution to future internet technologies. Blockchain technology and identified key features of blockchain-like decentralized, immutability, and irreversible are reviewed. The review of previous work in a combination of blockchain and IoT reveals that this combination will be very useful in future. Smart contracts make this technology more appropriate by automating complicated processes. We are able to conclude that integration of blockchain in the IoT area can have an excellent impact in the future however, a great deal of labor is required for blockchain integration with IoT. Some of the challenges like storage, processing power, and smart contract are described. In future, further work can be done to tackle these major challenges.

KEYWORDS

- **IoT**
- **blockchain**
- **consensus fog computing**
- **smart contracts**
- **SDN**

REFERENCES

1. Madakam, S., Ramaswamy, R., and Tripathi, S. (2015) Internet of Things (IoT): A Literature Review. J Comput Commun 3:164–173.
2. Wortmann, F., and Flüchter, K. (2015) Internet of Things: Technology and Value Added. Bus Inf Syst Eng 57:221–224. https://doi.org/10.1007/s12599-015-0383-3.
3. Krishnan, P., Najeem, J. S., and Achuthan, K. (2018) SDN Framework for Securing IoT Networks. Lect Notes Inst Comput Sci Soc Telecommun Eng LNICST 218:116–129. https://doi.org/10.1007/978-3-319-73423-1_11.
4. Oteafy, S. M. A., and Hassanein, H. S. (2018) IoT in the Fog: A Roadmap for Data-Centric IoT Development. IEEE Commun Mag 56:157–163. https://doi.org/10.1109/MCOM.2018.1700299.

5. El-Sayed, H., Sankar, S., Prasad, M., et al (2017) Edge of Things: The Big Picture on the Integration of Edge, IoT and the Cloud in a Distributed Computing Environment. IEEE Access 6:1706–1717. https://doi.org/10.1109/ACCESS.2017.2780087.
6. Christidis, K., and Devetsikiotis, M. (2016) Blockchains and Smart Contracts for the Internet of Things. IEEE Access 4:2292–2303. https://doi.org/10.1109/ACCESS.2016.2566339.
7. Zheng, Z., Xie, S., Dai, H. N., Chen, X., and Wang, H. (2017) Blockchain Challenges and Opportunities : A Survey. 14:1–25. https://doi.org/10.1504/IJWGS.2018.095647.
8. Fernández-Caramés, T. M., and Fraga-Lamas, P. (2018) A Review on the Use of Blockchain for the Internet of Things. IEEE Access 6:32979–33001. https://doi.org/10.1109/ACCESS.2018.2842685.
9. Buterin, B. V. (2009) OffsetMapping. 1–36. https://doi.org/10.5663/aps.v1i1.10138.
10. Atzori, M. (2016) Blockchain Technology and Decentralized Governance: Is the State Still Necessary? SSRN 1–37. https://doi.org/10.2139/ssrn.2709713.
11. Portmann, E. (2018) Rezension Blockchain: Blueprint for a New Economy.
12. Rennock, M. J. W., Cohn, A., and Butcher, J. R. (2018) Blockchain Technology and Regulatory Investigations. Journal: 34–44.
13. Underwood, S. (2016) Blockchain Beyond Bitcoin. Commun ACM 59:15–17. https://doi.org/10.1145/2994581.
14. Pilkington, M. Blockchain Technology: Principles and Applications. Research Handbook on Digital Transformations. Edward Elgar Publishing, 2016.
15. Reyna, A., Martín, C., Chen, J., et al (2018) On Blockchain and its Integration With IoT. Challenges and Opportunities. Futur Gener Comput Syst 88:173–190. https://doi.org/10.1016/j.future.2018.05.046.
16. Cognoscenti, M., Vetro, A., and De Martin, J. C. (2017) Blockchain for the Internet of Things: A Systematic Literature Review. Proc IEEE/ACS Int Conf Comput Syst Appl AICCSA. https://doi.org/10.1109/AICCSA.2016.7945805.
17. Liao, C. F., Bao, S. W., Cheng, C. J., and Chen, K. (2017) On Design Issues and Architectural Styles for Blockchain-driven IoT Services. 2017 IEEE Int Conf Consum Electron, Taiwan, ICCE-TW 2017 351–352. https://doi.org/10.1109/ICCE-China.2017.7991140.
18. Zhang, Y., and Wen, J. (2017) The IoT Electric Business Model: Using Blockchain Technology for the Internet of Things. Peer-to-Peer Netw Appl 10:983–994. https://doi.org/10.1007/s12083-016-0456-1.
19. Hardjono, T., and Smith, N. (2016) Cloud-Based Commissioning of Constrained Devices using Permissioned Blockchains. Proc 2nd ACM Int Work IoT Privacy, Trust Secure IoTPTS '16 29–36. https://doi.org/10.1145/2899007.2899012
20. Sharma, P. K., Singh, S., Jeong, Y. S., and Park, J. H. (2017) DistBlockNet: A Distributed Blockchains-Based Secure SDN Architecture for IoT Networks. IEEE Commun Mag 55:78–85. https://doi.org/10.1109/MCOM.2017.1700041.
21. Sharma, P. K., Chen, M. Y., and Park, J. H. (2018) A Software Defined Fog Node Based Distributed Blockchain Cloud Architecture for IoT. IEEE Access 6:115–124. https://doi.org/10.1109/ACCESS.2017.2757955.
22. Feng, Q., He, D., Zeadally. S., et al(2019) A Survey on Privacy Protection in Blockchain System. J Netw Comput Appl 126:45–58. https://doi.org/10.1016/j.jnca.2018.10.020.
23. Huang, J., Kong, L., Chen, G., et al (2019) Towards Secure Industrial IoT: Blockchain System With Credit-Based Consensus Mechanism. IEEE Trans Ind Informatics 15:3680–3689. https://doi.org/10.1109/TII.2019.2903342.

CHAPTER 15

Participation of 5G with Wireless Sensor Networks in the Internet of Things (IoT) Application

ARUN KUMAR* and SHARAD SHARMA

Maharishi Markandeshwar (Deemed to be University), Mullana, Ambala, Haryana

*Corresponding author. E-mail: ranaarun1.ece@piet.co.in

ABSTRACT

In the coming decades, wireless sensor network turns out to be a noteworthy piece of our day-by-day experience 5G organize is anticipated to help the enormous measure of information traffic and a gigantic number of remote associations. Various information traffic has a diverse quality of service prerequisites. 5G versatile system expects to address the impediments of past cell measures (i.e., 2G/3G/4G) and be an imminent key empowering agent for future Internet of Things (IoT). As the IoT is picking up prominence, there is a necessity for an innovation that can bolster a lot of information transmission proficiently and at extremely high transfer speed. Sooner rather than later, for example, cutting edge IoT gadgets, a portion of the prime targets or requests that should be tended to are expanded limit, improved information rate, and diminished inertness. The improvement of cutting edge remotes versatile correspondence innovation to be specific, 5G vows to satisfy the requirements of complex IoT designs. This section centers around the necessities that can be satisfied by 5G and illuminates engineering, benefits, and negative marks of 5G organize. A point-by-point study on 5G empowered IoT gadgets, the examination on this sort of system have been led in different puts the world over.

15.1   INTRODUCTION

Significant application in different fields like condition and natural surroundings checking, building robotization, fiasco and waste the executives, framework observing, and so forth. Today sensors are all over. Because of the monstrous information traded among enormous quantities of associated gadgets to frame the Internet of Things (IoT), the need to give expanded limit, high information rate, and high availability is expanded. In this way, 5G remote systems considered a key driver for IoT. Fulfilling the expanded prerequisites of IoT drives a few sorts of systems to contend to give the availability for IoT applications. Along these lines, this review intends to feature how the 5G can influence the IoT empowering advances by giving a concise examination over the current remote systems that are considered as alternatives for IoT to give high availability, for example, cell systems, low power wide area networks, and short-range systems The expanded portable network will change society, empowering changes in the manner in which we live and work together, through new uses of remote innovation, for example, fifth generation (5G) versatile innovation; the IoT, otherwise called M2M interchanges; and wearable gadgets. The GSMA has delivered this distribution to deliver addresses identified with introduction to radiofrequency (RF) signals utilized by these systems and gadgets.

FIGURE 15.1   5G with IoT.

Remote systems and gadgets trade data (e.g., voice or information) by means of RF signals a type of electromagnetic vitality, likewise called electromagnetic fields. RF signals are a piece of regular day to day existence, radiated both by common sources like the sun and the Earth and by counterfeit sources, for example, remote systems, TV, and communicate radio. New applications, for example, 5G, remote IoT, and wearable gadgets, are intended to agree to exist introduction limits. The universal presentation rules have been created because of crafted by analysts for a long time. The rules are not innovation explicit and are intermittently investigated. The agreement of surveys by autonomous general wellbeing specialists, master gatherings, and the World Health Organization is that these rules give assurance to all individuals (counting kids) against all settled wellbeing risks.

15.2 BACKGROUND OVERVIEW

The advancement of the 5G remote innovation guarantees the data transfer capacity rate. It is giving a huge telecom limit up to Gigabit which supporting right around 65,000 associations one after another. It is likewise very verifying than 4G and progresses bidirectional transmission capacity modeling. 5G portable framework model is an all-IP-based model that guarantees remote and versatile systems interoperability. The possibility of the IoT is to associate the regular physical items, for example, microwaving, entryways, lightings, etc. The specialized idea of the IoT is to empower these distinctive physical articles to detect data utilizing sensors and sends these data to a server. This server investigates these data to increase some learning and makes an interpretation of them to specific practices or activities. These activities group insightful conditions, for example, savvy homes. The advancement of the IoT empowers billion of associated gadgets to interface with the Internet, which effect in transit individuals live. As expressed beforehand, the quantity of associated gadgets is relied upon to surpass 50 billion gadgets by 2020s. Furthermore, IoT can be generally separated into two classes as proposed by cloud IoT (cIoT) and industry IoT (iIoT). The possibility of cIoT is to improve the manner in which individuals live by setting aside their time and cash. Instances of the associated articles in the cIoT incorporate a microwave, lightings, portable, and any items that have a place with a specific client. The cIoT demonstrates the machine-to-client correspondences. On different hands, the possibility of iIoT is to coordinate different advancements to improve business benefits in various areas. It certainly shows the conduct of machine-to-machine correspondences. Each of cIoT and iIoT as administration areas has its own correspondence necessities that are estimated distinctively in both, for example, unwavering quality, quality of service, and protection. By the by, they share some normal correspondence wireless systems that have improved their highlights as endeavors to stay aware of the development of advances. The different remote cell arranges ages that have been structured until the appearance of 5G cell systems. The 3G and 4G are extensively used for IoT anyway not totally streamlined for IoT applications [1]. The 4G has generally improved the capacities of cell masterminds that can give IoT devices usable Internet get to. Since 2012, the "long stretch advancement" (LTE) to 4G organize, transformed into the snappiest and most unsurprising variety of 4G stood out from battling developments, for instance, BLE [2], WiMaxb [3], ZigBee [4], SigFox [5], LoRa [6], etc. As the front line sorts out, the 5G frameworks and standards are required to handle troubles that looking by 4G frameworks, for instance, progressively snared particular, device computational limits, knowledge, etc., to arrange the necessities in keen conditions, industry 4.0, etc. Figure 15.2 shows the headway of the cell frameworks from 3G to the accompanying 5G engaged IoT. The progression of 5G will be established on the foundation made by 4G LTE, which will give the customer's voice, data, Internet. The 5G will inside and out extend the breaking point and speed to give reliable and fast accessibility to the future IoT [10, 11].

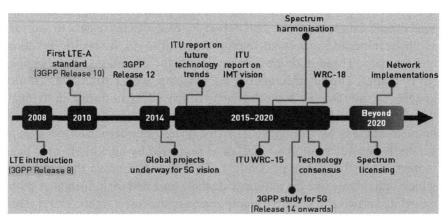

FIGURE 15.2   Timeline toward 5G.

Various research endeavors concentrated on cutting edge inquire about in different parts of IoT and 5G frameworks from scholastics and industry perspectives [7–9]. The point is to offer a setting on the on-going advances in principle, application, institutionalization, and usage of 5G advances in IoT situations. In the previous barely any years, glorious takes a shot at 5G-IoT have been done [7]. The CISCO, Intel, and Verizon have mutually built up a remote research venture on 5G to uncover a novel arrangement of "neuroscience-based calculations" that versatile video quality to the requests of the human eye, implying that highlights remote systems would have worked in human insight [8].

15.3 CHARACTERISTICS OF IOT

15.3.1 INTERCONNECTIVITY

In the IoT, everything can be associated including any virtual or physical articles [11]. The interconnectivity is represented by the association between these various items and the correspondence framework.

15.3.2 THINGS-RELATED ADMINISTRATIONS

The idea of this trademark is to give benefits that can be applied to a few associated things dependent on the limitations of these things [12]. For example, protection assurance as help can be applied to very similar things with their imperatives.

15.3.3 HETEROGENEITY

The heterogeneity highlight of the IoT originates from associating in an unexpected way gadgets that are manufactured utilizing distinctive equipment and run over various stages [14].

15.3.4 DYNAMIC CHANGES

IoT can deal with dynamic changes that are required by included unique objects [15, 16] from [11–16]. A few powerful changes could happen as far as to state changes, for example, inert, associated, and detached, or regarding setting changes, for example, evolving areas.

15.4   SPECTRUM CONSIDERATIONS

Normally, 5G get to systems for certain administrations will require wide bordering transporter data transfer capacities (e.g.,, many MHz up to a few GHz) to be given at an extremely high in general framework limit. To help the prerequisites for wide touching transfer speeds, higher transporter frequencies over 6 GHz should be considered. The thought of any new groups for such administrations will require cautious appraisal and acknowledgment of different administrations utilizing, or wanting to utilize, these groups. Keeping up a steady and unsurprising administrative and range the executives' condition is basic for long haul speculations. Research on this range needs to consider long haul ventures with the goal that they can be safeguarded. The elite portable authorized range task strategies will stay significant regardless of whether new methods might be conceived to improve range use under certain conditions. Driven specifically by video applications and the regularly expanding utilization of cell phones, tablets, and machine correspondence, versatile information traffic is relied upon to become significantly as indicated by a few reports, for example, Analysis Mason5 and Cisco6. These show around 50%–60% yearly development over the multiyear time span 2013–2018, a pattern that may well proceed past 2020. It is likewise expected that 5G get to systems for certain administrations will require wide touching transporter data transfer capacity (e.g., several MHz up to a couple of GHz) to be given at an exceptionally high generally speaking framework limit. These should be bolstered by properly scaled backhaul joins that themselves will require sufficient range assets.

15.4.1   KEY TECHNOLOGICAL COMPONENTS

5G remote will bolster a heterogeneous arrangement of incorporated air interfaces from developments of current access plans to fresh out of the box new innovations. 5G systems will envelop cell and satellite arrangements. Consistent handover between heterogeneous remote access advances will be a local element of 5G, just as the utilization of synchronous radio access advances to expand unwavering quality and accessibility. The sending of ultra-thick systems with various little cells will require new impedance moderation, backhauling, and establishment strategies. 5G will be driven by programming. System capacities are relied upon to run over a brought together working framework for various purposes of the essence, particularly at the edge of the system for meeting execution targets. Therefore, it will vigorously depend on rising advancements. 5G will simplicity and enhance organize the executives' activities. The improvement of intellectual highlights just as the propelled computerization of activity through appropriate calculations will permit enhancing complex business targets, for example, start to finish vitality utilization. Furthermore, the misuse of data analytics and big data systems will prepare to screen the client's quality of experience through new measurements joining the system and social information while ensuring protection. The epic 5G engineering is likewise expected to incorporate both front take and backhaul into a typical vehicle organize. The advances, which have been now distinguished range from fiber optics with programming characterized optical transmission to novel CPRI-over-bundle advances, likewise considering remote connections, for example, millimeter wave. Over them, a general preparing plane is required to do mass tasks in shared transmission media and give bearer grade benefits as far as configurability, vitality proficiency, and multioccupant activities. Besides, to accomplish the normal limit, inclusion, unwavering quality, dormancy, and enhancements in vitality utilization, the 5G design is relied upon to (1) run over a met optical-remote satellite foundation for arrange get to, backhauling, and front pulling with the plausibility of transmitting advanced and balanced flag over the physical associations; (2) influence adaptable intraframework range use; (3) make ideal use of the particular qualities of the diverse fundamental frameworks (for example, influence multicast for satellite or adaptable range for optical).

15.4.2 EFFICIENCY AND SECURITY WILL BE OF PARAMOUNT IMPORTANCE

Vitality effectiveness is likewise in-circuit plan, for example, control intensifiers and simple front-finishes in microwave and millimeter recurrence ranges, DSP-empowered optical handsets forget to and backhaul systems, and ultra-low power remote sensors collecting surrounding vitality, for example, sun based, warm, vibration, and electromagnetic vitality. Furthermore, remote power move innovations and advancement of rest mode exchanging present another energizing option in contrast to battery-less sensor activity for M2M and D2D interchanges. It is, obviously, expected that such an insurgency in the system framework cannot occur without parallel advancement of the associated items (terminals, machines, robots, rambles, etc.) regarding the remote network, computational power, memory limit, battery lifetime, and cost.

In 5G, security issues are drastically intensified by the normal augmentation of the two kinds of partners and quantities of inhabitants. To determine the conceivably expanded multifaceted nature inside the framework related to this, it will get important to work under various settings and to consistently think about security domains. It will require new access control models, as we have seen them rise in the area of online informal organizations and, for the most part, online administrations. Past secrecy, respectability, accessibility, cyber-physical system security, and new security ideas around the need to address the reliability of data, the uprightness of remote stages, logical rightness, evidence of ownership, and comparative subjects. The presence of and support for exceptionally restricted gadgets, for example, sensors will require probabilistic security components sent in parallel to the high-security arrangements referenced previously. Likewise, custom-fitted security at the administration and gadget level ought to be imagined: 5G should seriously mull over unique control and information plane help for various security framework launches to have the option to give separated security benefits on demand. The dynamic creation of the 5G foundation needs security ensures inside the framework: past the common verification and secure correspondence channel foundation, we should dive into subjects of framework/framework honesty and operational security affirmation. The key here is to go past the present winning operational security models like avoidance and insurance, which will in general cut-off degrees of opportunity. On the off chance that the framework elements are vital to accomplish the readiness of partners (as on-going NFV and SDN activities recommend), at that point the survivability must be progressively comprehended as the major operational security model.

15.4.3   5G IOT USE CASES

15.4.3.1   VEHICLE TELEMATICS

Car and Transport (A&T) is relied upon to be the number 1 division for the reception of 5G innovations in IoT applications. A&T is as of now one of the most "IoT" develop portions that as of now has a large number of associated autos utilizing telematics applications, for example, vehicle diagnostics, area following, and client-based protection. These applications, for the most part, include the transmission of little volumes of noncontinuous

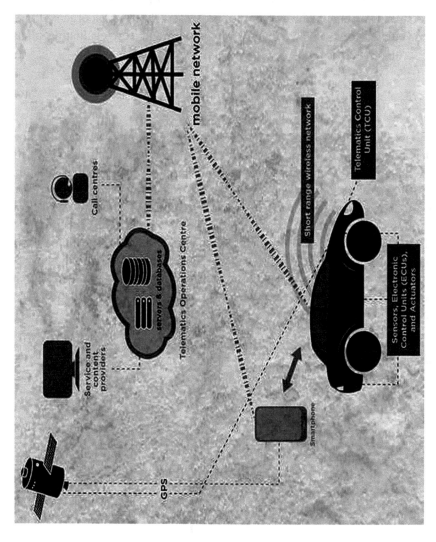

FIGURE 15.3 OEM vehicle telematics architecture.

information gathered from the vehicles and today they are for the most part sent over conventional cell (2G/3G/4G) innovations, that all in all give a good exhibition to deal with their present correspondence needs. In any case, the dispatch of 5G offers the probability to accumulate logically granular data ceaselessly about the prosperity and execution of the vehicle and the drivers' lead and enable the transport of progressively complex organizations (e.g., vehicle OEMs and vehicle organizations) and new evaluating plans (e.g., protection offices).

15.4.3.2   IN-VEHICLE INFOTAINMENT

In-vehicle infotainment is another moderately developed A&T application that is relied upon to profit a ton from 5G availability. Contrasted with its LTE, 5G availability offers the capacity to upgrade these applications and empower new ones, for example, in-vehicle retail and promoting or even AR/VR-based route frameworks and excitement administrations. While for the following couple of years, vehicle infotainment on 5G is relied upon to be for the most part by means of fastened associations (e.g., utilizing a 5G cell phone for the vehicle network), the rise of double mode 4G/5G answers for associated autos throughout the following barely any years, as featured in the past passage, will make ready for increasingly modern in-vehicle infotainment applications.

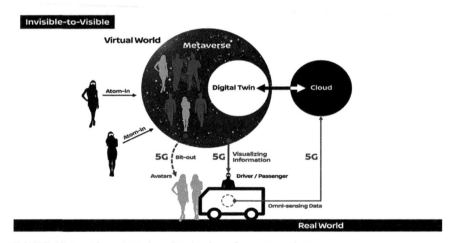

FIGURE 15.4   5G- and AR-based technology for connected cars.

15.4.3.3 SMART GRID AUTOMATION

In the vitality and utility area, 5Gs upgraded abilities make the innovation especially fit to the on-going administration and robotization of the shrewd power network.

These arrangements are planned for enhancing activities and upkeep by rapidly identifying and reacting to flaws along the lattice, yet additionally fulfilling the undeniably stringent need on their network, driven by patterns, for example, the mix of distributed energy resources (DER) like renewables into the power matrix, more tightly guidelines, and advancing cybersecurity dangers. Specifically, the combination of these DER "smaller-scale lattices" to the power organize is very testing because of the high changeability of their vitality creation and requires constant control and mechanization of the feeder line frameworks (i.e., what deals with the bolstering of the produced vitality into the network) to stay away from over-burden and guarantee framework unwavering quality, yet in addition broad message motioning between all the miniaturized scale matrices components. These convert into severe prerequisites as far as correspondence dormancy and system unwavering quality that today can be completely fulfilled just by means of wired correspondence innovations. Truly, most utilities today as of now have a power lattice checking framework setup, ordinarily dependent on wired correspondence arranges over electrical cables (PLC), optical fiber, or copper, while remote interchanges are restricted to the less strategic applications. 5G is relied upon to be a great extent received because of its higher arrangement adaptability and lower cost contrasted with wired other options while offering a comparative degree of execution.

15.4.3.4 MOBILE AND COLLABORATIVE ROBOTS

In the mechanical division, 5G is commonly significant aimed at partner current robots with several grades of adaptability, from static network robots to totally compact robots, for instance, automated guided vehicles (AGVs). These robots have various sensors for situational care while inventive advances are making them logically shrewd and prepared to self-overseeing perform various assignments, for instance, moving a product or doing fixes. As needs are, they ought to have the choice to process a growing proportion of data. Regardless, obliging enough getting ready capacities into these robots can be incredibly trying and expensive, especially for humbler robots.

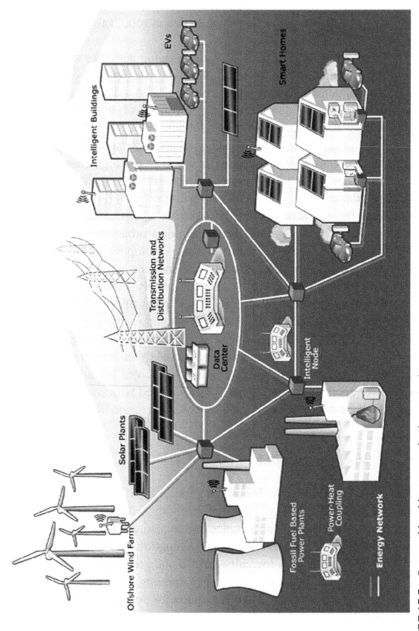

FIGURE 15.5   Smart grid and its communication network.

FIGURE 15.6 A 5G-connected AGV demo from Bosch Rexroth during Hannover Messe 2019.

15.4.3.5 VIDEO SURVEILLANCE

In the mechanical division, there is a general accord that 5G is commonly significant for partner present-day robots with various degrees of adaptability, from static network robots to totally compact robots, for instance, independent guided vehicles (AGVs). These robots have various sensors for situational care while imaginative advances are making them continuously sharp and prepared to self-administering perform various assignments, for instance, moving a product or doing fixes. As needs are, they ought to have the alternative to process a growing proportion of data. Regardless, obliging enough planning capacities into these robots can be uncommonly trying and expensive, especially for more diminutive robots. 5G would assistance be able to understand these issues and appreciation to its low torpidity and high steadfast quality.

15.4.3.6 COOPERATIVE INTELLIGENT MOBILITY

On the mid-long stretch, the greatest impact that 5G is required to have in the A&T portion is to enable the sharing of persistent information about traffic and road conditions among vehicles and other road customers. This new accommodating flexibility and driver help organizations are for both private and open transportation (addressed by two one of a kind air pockets in Exhibit 1, separately by pleasant movability for private and sharp urban adaptability for the open vehicle). This requires the advancement of a 5G-based V2X (Vehicle-to-Everything) system made of roadside sensors and V2X base stations, despite 5G particular contraptions into vehicles, and other road customers (e.g., individuals by walking, cyclists, etc.). Approaching security essential conditions ahead, extending road prosperity and traffic viability exist for the future. Starting at now, cells set up together V2X correspondences are supported as for LTE organizes as a segment of the 3GPP Rel-14 and 15, while 5G-based V2X will be introduced as a significant part of 3GPP Rel-16 set to be released in 2020.

FIGURE 15.7   The 5G-based video surveillance setup by Samsung.

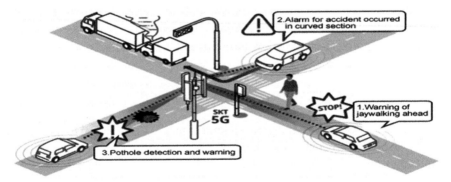

FIGURE 15.8   5G-enabled traffic safety service. Image credit: SK Telecom.

15.5   CONCLUSION

IoT is the extremely not so distant future idea that shapes our lives. It is one of the empowering advancements for 5G cell frameworks. To empower

IoT applications, a few prerequisites must be happy with every one of them utilizing certain advancements. These advances considered IoT empowering innovations that are for the most part used to empower 5G cell frameworks as well. This overview directs a near examination between a few IoT network alternatives to research which of them is most appropriate for IoT applications. So as to coordinate wireless sensor network with IoT using 5G abilities, we considered distinctive related work and will attempt to streamline the issues of existing innovation by supplanting it with 5G framework.

KEYWORDS

- **5G**
- **IoT**
- **wireless sensor network**
- **LTE**
- **low power wide area network**

REFERENCES

1. Akpakwu, G. A. et al., "A survey on 5G networks for the Internet of Things: communication technologies and challenges", IEEE Access, 6, 3619–3647, 2017.
2. BLE, "Smart Bluetooth Low Energy", http://www.bluetooth.com/Pages/Bluetooth-Smart.aspx, 2018.
3. Taylor, L.A., Zigbee, "Interconnecting Zigbee & M2M Networks", ETSIM2M Workshop, Sophia-Antipolis, 1–18, 2011.
4. Nokia, "LTE evolution for IoT connectivity", Nokia, Espoo, Tech. Rep., Nokia White Paper, 1–18, 2016.
5. SigFox, "SigFox", 2018, htpp://www.sigfox.com.
6. Vangelista, L., Zanella, A., Zorzi, M. "Long-range IoT technologies: the dawn of LoRaTM", In Future Access Enablers of Ubiquitous and Intelligent Infrastructures, pp. 51–58, Springer: Berlin, 2015.
7. Da Xu, L., He, W., Li, S. "Internet of Things in industries: a survey", IEEE Transactions on Industrial Informatics, 10, 2233–2243, 2014.
8. Kaplan, K. "Will 5G wireless networks make every internet thing faster and smarter?", 2018, https://qz.com/179794/will-5g-wireless-networks-make-every-internetthing-faster-and-smarter/
9. Hosek, J. Enabling Technologies and User Perception With Integrated 5G-IoT Ecosystem, Brno University of Technology: Brno, 2016.

10. Stephan, J., Krishnamurthy, K. "Understanding the industrial internet of things", 2018, http://usblogs.pwc.com/emerging-technology/understanding-theindustrial-internet-of-things/
11. Kumar, A., Salau, A. O., Gupta, S. and Paliwal, K., 2019. "Recent trends in IoT and its requisition with IoT built engineering: A review". In Advances in Signal Processing and Communication (pp. 15–25). Springer, Singapore.
12. Rana, A. K. and Sharma, S., "Enhanced energy-efficient heterogeneous routing protocols in WSNs for IoT application", IJEAT, ISSN: 2249-8958VOL. 9 ISSUE-1, 2019.
13. Kumar, K., Gupta, E. S. and Rana, E. A. K., Wireless Sensor Networks: A review on "Challenges and Opportunities for the Future world-LTE".
14. Rana, A. K., Krishna, R., Dhwan, S., Sharma, S. and Gupta, R., October. Review on Artificial Intelligence with Internet of Things-Problems, Challenges and Opportunities. In 2019 2nd International Conference on Power Energy, Environment and Intelligent Control (PEEIC) (pp. 383–387). IEEE, 2019.
15. Rana, A. K. and Sharma, S., Contiki Cooja Security Solution (CCSS) with IPv6 Routing Protocol for Low-Power and Lossy Networks (RPL) in Internet of Things Applications. In Mobile Radio Communications and 5G Networks (pp. 251–259). Springer, Singapore.
16. Rana, A. K., and Sharma, S. "Industry 4.0 manufacturing based on IoT, cloud computing, and Big Data: manufacturing purpose scenario". In Advances in Communication and Computational Technology (pp. 1109–1119). Springer, Singapore.

PART III

Attacks, Threats, Vulnerabilities and Defensive Measures for Smart Systems and Research Challenges

CHAPTER 16

Internet of Things (IoT): Vulnerability, Attacks, and Security

GURINDER PAL SINGH* and PARVEEN K. BANGOTRA

Department of Space, Semi-Conductor Laboratory, Mohali, Punjab, India

Corresponding author. E-mail: gps@scl.gov.in, gpshpr@gmail.com.

ABSTRACT

Internet of Things (IoT) is the buzz word in today's developing world. IoT devices are used in a multiple fields whether it is the industry, agriculture, defense, weather forecasting, or home automation. As IoT is spreading at an immense rate in various fields, the main concern is how reliable the security is? The data can be compromised as the devices are vulnerable to attackers/hackers. This can also compromise privacy and security. This paper examines the various vulnerabilities in IoT devices, whether it is machine-to-machine, device-to-device, or device-to-cloud. Discussed are the vulnerabilities in terms of devices, networks, back-end IT systems, communication protocols, and front-end sensors/actuators. An IoT device is cracked, the vulnerabilities are listed, and a few security solutions are discussed. Overall, this paper covers the attack surfaces associated with the vulnerability of IoT.

16.1 INTRODUCTION

The IoT concept was first introduced in 1990. IoT devices are interconnected with the help of the Internet, thus making them capable of interacting between the physical worlds (IoT device) and computing. Basically, this network paradigm is being called the Internet of Things (IoT) and there are many ways to define the IoT world. For example, smart devices that are connected to the Internet fall under the IoT category. IEEE describes IoT to be networks consisting of sensors and smart objects. The purpose is to interconnect "all" things, including everyday gadgets and industrial objects, in a way that makes them more intelligent, programmable, and more capable of interacting with humans [1].

Physical objects + controllers, sensors, actuators + Internet = IoT

Physical objects can be defined as a collection of a microcontroller (for intelligence), sensors that measure some parameters, and the internet (to transfer the data according to communication protocols). Many unsecured IoT devices connected to the internet come with potential danger to the applications associated with them. This is because IoT is used in many fields including education, healthcare, defense, agriculture, weather forecasting, smart homes, automation, etc.

The IoT market is growing very quickly. Naturally, the threats are also increasing. The IoT business is expected to hit $300 billion by 2020 [2] and Forbes reported that the annual revenue of IoT vendors could exceed $470B by 2020. Forbes also predicted that by 2025, there will be over 80 billion smart devices on the internet. This is because all kinds of household systems and equipment can be transformed to work on IoT systems. For example, home automation systems are already being designed to control refrigerators, smart TVs, microwaves, washing machines, IP cameras, smart light bulbs, home thermostats, motion control, and security locks, etc. Furthermore, more smart devices like wearable smartwatches are being used to monitor health parameters like blood pressure, heart rate, body temperature, and the number of calories burnt. All of these factors are very convenient, but they come with a price.

The main challenge now is to secure these IoT devices since they are so widely used in all fields. This may help heighten security measures in border areas between countries. It can also make pacemakers or health monitoring systems in a hospital more reliable and that could be life-saving for patients. Essentially, the main issue is protecting personal information from being hacked. There are two kinds of threats: threats against IoT and threats from IoT [9].

16.2   MAJOR ATTACKS ON IOT

In a F5 Lab Threat Analysis report [3], IoT attacks exploded by 280% in the first half of 2017. Billions of IoT devices are easily accessible (via Telnet) and easily hackable due to their default credentials and firmware vulnerabilities. In total, 83% of attacks are reported from Spain, on the

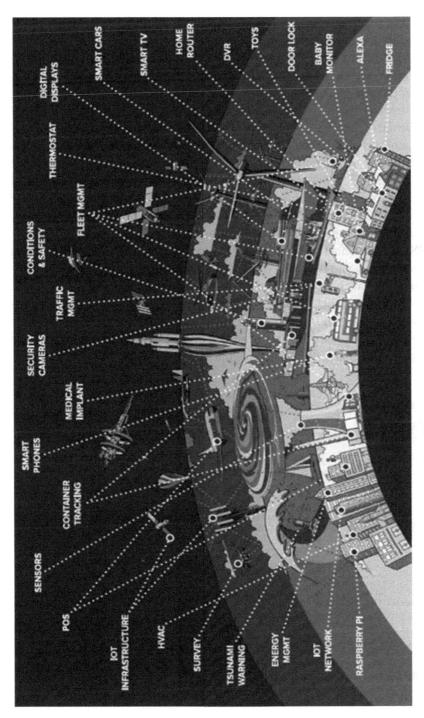

FIGURE 16.1 IoT connect the world around us. Photo Courtesy: www.f5.com.

hosting service provider, Solo Gigabit. The challenge is that there are no defined guidelines to implement security on IoT devices. However, Open Web Application Security Project, an online community in the field of application security, drafted some security guidelines for manufacturers, developers, and consumers.

In the past, there have been many attacks on the IoT. The largest Distributed Denial of Service (DDoS) attack was known as "Mirai Botnet." It works by scanning the Internet for vulnerable devices. Mirai is used in DDoS attacks and up to 1.2 terabytes of network traffic are generated every second [12, 18]. Mirai loaders are remote administration tools that take control of devices. As soon as vulnerable devices are detected, the login credentials, IP address, and an open port 23 are stolen (Telnet) [3]. Mirai has the capacity of performing various types of DDoS attacks like Domain Name System (DNS), User Datagram Protocol, Streaming Text Oriented Messaging Protocol, SYN, and ACK flooding [12]. Mirai DDoS attacks were possible because of weak default passwords on various IoT devices [9].

In 2017, the botnet named "Persirai" infected 1250 numbers of Wireless IP Camera (P2P) WIFICAM model. Total Infected hosts as of June 2017 are 600,000 [3]. This malware gained access to the IP camera web interface via TCP port 81. Persirai flow is depicted in Figure 16.2.

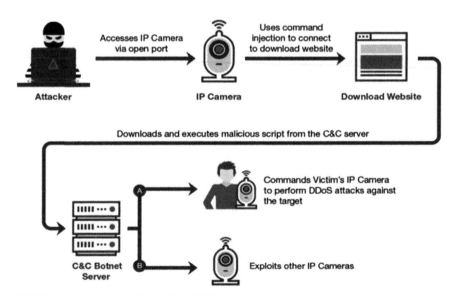

FIGURE 16.2   Infection flow of Persirai botnet.

Source: Reprinted from Ref. [6].

The next is "Bricket bot." It was released on April 4, 2017. In this attack, all the data on the internal storage of a device are wiped out and make the device permanently useless. This attack is also known as the Permanent Denial of Service (DoS) attack. In the TREND net Webcam hack, the attacker can have clear login credentials of the users, and anyone who knows the IP address of the camera can have access to the user's credentials.

In 2015, IBM Security Intelligence discovered "The Jeep Hack." By exploiting the firmware, they were able to speed up, slow down, or break the Jeep. Lastly, in 2014, hackers managed to break into Target's Financial Systems unit through a heating ventilation and air conditioning (HVAC) unit and were able to steal network credentials from an HVAC vendor.

Even airplanes are susceptible and can be hacked. Many software vulnerabilities have been identified in several commercial aircrafts, including Boeing 737-800, 737-900, 757-200, and the Airbus A-320. Chris Roberts, a security researcher at One World Lab, hacked into a United Airlines jet while onboard and modified its in-flight entertainment system [3].

Moving on, hospitals are the main target of hackers. Hollywood Presbyterian Medical Centre in Los Angeles was brought down by hackers for a week by demanding ransomware from the hospital administration. The healthcare industry is predisposed to security breaches because it is more connected to devices and sensors.

Likewise, smart industrial buildings like power grids are unsecured, making them more exposed to hackers. Cybersecurity experts have been warning that power grids and gas pipes are vulnerable for a while now. This is because wireless networks using video cameras for transmitting video signals are insecure. This made it possible for a steel mill in Germany to be hacked and allowed hackers to gain access to the production system.

Lastly, an article published in 2016 [13] showed that digital video recorders manufactured by more than 70 different vendors were vulnerable to remote code execution. Another report released by L3 Communications in 2016 suggested that some of the bots have infected more than 1 million infected devices and these devices were hosted in Taiwan, Brazil, and Colombia [13].

IoT devices are used by attackers for DDoS attacks. The DDoS attack in IoT devices remains undetected in an unattended device-to-device communication model until its services become unavailable [13]. The biggest attack on a website was through a DDoS of 665Gbps by hacking multiple IoT devices that were vulnerable and they were turned into DDoS botnet [14].

16.3   MAJOR SECURITY PROTOCOLS OF IOT

Many protocols are developed to ensure communication between IoT layers and IoT devices [13]. Different IoT layers, that is, edge technology layer, access gateway layer, middleware layer, and application layer use different protocols. The main protocols that are prominently used in IoT are Hypertext Transfer Protocol, Constrained Application Protocol (CoAP), Extensible Messaging and Presence Protocol, and MQ Telemetry Protocol [10][16]. CoAP is designed for machine-to-machine applications, so it is used in IoT devices because of its lightweight. These protocols are used in different layers of IoT. Those standard protocols are offered by the Internet Engineering Task Force, Institute of Electrical and Electronics Engineers (IEEE), International Telecommunication Union, and other standard organizations [4]. The Datalink layer connects two IoT elements; two sensors or the edge device and a sensor that connects a set of sensors to the Internet. It is important to note that threats exist in all layers of IoT and some of the built-in security mechanisms in the protocols are discussed below.

16.3.1   MAC 802.15.4

The media access control (MAC) enables the transmission of the MAC frame. It controls frame validation, guarantees time slots, and deals with node association. It is used for secure communication. Security includes confidentiality, authentication, integrity, access control, and secured time-synchronized communication [4].

16.3.2   6LOWPAN

This wireless technology uses 128-bit encryption and the data access is given to only authorized users. Reliability of the data transmitter is available, and it is capable of detecting malicious intrusion [5]. Cryptographic keys are used for secure communication. The 6LoWPAN private key cryptography is used because it consumes less energy [5, 17]. It provides two basic modes of security—secure mode and nonsecure mode. Further, in the secure mode of 6LoWPAN IEEE802.15.4 specifications, there are two more options:

1. Access control list (ACL) mode: each device in the 6LoWPAN network maintains its own ACL. This list (ACL) only allows the devices already entered in the list to communicate.

2. Secure mode: it is a complete secure mode that includes everything from data integrity to sequence checks.

16.3.3 RPL

The routing protocol is for low-power and lossy networks (RPLs). It offers a different level of security by utilizing a 4-byte Internet Control Message Protocol for the IPv6 (ICMPv6) message header. It consists of a header and a payload protocol. RPL protects data from replay attacks. RPL attacks include Hello Flooding, Blackhole, and DoS attacks.

16.3.4 APPLICATION LAYER

The application layer can provide an additional level of security using transport layer security (TLS) and secure socket layer (SSL). TLS is more secure than SSL, as it provides the data in a secure form. More security can be implemented by buying up to date TLS certificates with the option of elliptic curve cryptography, Ron Rivest Shamir and Leonard Adleman, or Digital Signature Algorithm encryption. routing protocol for low-power and lossy networks (RPL's). It offers a different level of security.

16.3.5 IOT EDGE DEVICES

IoT edge devices work in the perception layer. Hackers use its vulnerabilities to gain access and install malicious code/applications. Lightweight encryption algorithms must be used in edge devices to keep data protected from eavesdropping [15]. Hardware and software exploitations should be taken care of to secure IoT edge devices from malicious firmware or software vulnerabilities.

16.4 DIFFERENT PHASES OF IOT HACKING

16.4.1 RECONNAISSANCE

Look for the weak target, before we engage it. To find vulnerabilities, we look for open ports with the help of physical and online tools like Angry IP Scanner, HackRF One, websites like shodan, suphacap, thingful, censys, etc. Use PING command, doing a "Whois" Lookup, checking for Registrar for DNS.

16.4.2   *LOOKING FOR VULNERABILITIES*

To find the vulnerabilities in hardware or software, we use various vulnerability scanners to gather more information about the device. Port scanner is used to find which port is listening to Gateway; use various plugins for IoT for scanning. Bestrom tool can be used to find buffer overflow vulnerability; this tool worked on 15 different types of protocols. IoT inspector used to exploit IoT Firmware.

16.4.3   *ATTACKS*

Once know the vulnerability now deploy the attack. Different kinds of payloads are available as per the device make and model and the operating system (OS) used in the device. Dealing with rolling codes to know which code is transmitted out of the keys. Some of the tools like Jams, Scans, Replay Attacks, etc., are used to find the radio frequency. The Firmware Mod Kit tool is used to extract the image of the firmware and again reload it with the backdoor installed in it.

16.4.4   *ARCHIVE ACCESS*

The path to the device whether it could be via network, OS, or via an application, we get access of the device and can do whatever we want to.

16.4.5   *MAINTAINING ACCESS*

Remain anonymous after gaining access, so that security professionals don't trace you. Using various tools to clear the logs can use the compromised system/device as a pivot point to get into the other system. Exploit the firmware.

16.5   THE ATTACK SURFACE OF IOT

Hackers target different layers and exploit its vulnerabilities. Some of the basic attack surfaces of IoT devices are given below.

16.5.1 DEVICE MEMORY

Encryption keys credentials from the users and third party are stored in the memory of the device itself, so hackers tried to get access to the memory.

16.5.2 ECOSYSTEM ACCESS CONTROL

Trust between different IoT components is motion sensors and water sensors.

16.5.3 PHYSICAL INTERFACE

Command line interface and firmware.

16.5.4 WEB INTERFACE

The web interface of the device is not secure. Two-way authentication is required. Various attacks like cross-site scripting (XSS), injection attack, weak password, and numeration of user's accounts are managed through a web interface.

16.5.5 FIRMWARE

Hackers use various tools like firmware mod kit to extract the firmware. They then build the vulnerable image by building backdoor malicious codes/ scripts and deploy the same on the device.

16.5.6 NETWORK SERVICE

It is used for various network-related attacks like DoS attack. IoT devices come with USB and data card ports, so the use of USB Rubber Ducky is used to exploit the device.

16.5.7 ADMIN INTERFACE

As the two-factor authentication is not supported, so the admin interface is used to deploy attacks like SQL Injection, XSS, etc.

16.5.8   DATE STORAGE

User credentials and other important keys are stored locally on the device.

16.5.9   CLOUD WEB INTERFACE

It is used for XSS, request forgery.

16.5.10   UPDATING

Forget to update the OS as well as the firmware.

16.5.11   THIRD-PARTY BACKEND APPLICATION PROGRAMMING INTERFACE

Most of the mobile apps share information without your knowledge and no use to share your location while installing the English directory.

16.5.12   NETWORK TRAFFIC

IoT network should be separated from the existing network so that if it is compromised, your other devices would be saved.

16.6   IOT SECURITY

There are some common requirements for IoT security. These requirements are as follows:

1. Securing devices.
2. Communication security.
3. Data management security.
4. Service provision security.
5. Integration of various security policies.
6. Mutual authentication and authorization.
7. Security auditing.

It depends on the developer, service provider, and users to implement these requirements. IoT security implementation is the basic way to protect data and maintain user privacy. Some of the following technologies can be used to secure IoT.

16.6.1   IOT NETWORK SECURITY

These devices are connected to a network in order to communicate with each other. This can be seen as a threat, as the network layer is the layer where the majority of attacks are performed [17] so the first step is to secure the network layer in order to prevent this. The use of firewalls is also useful at this stage, as this allows intruder detection to be detected at an early stage. Next, the implementation of antivirus and the use of logs can be checked. IoT devices are not expected to perform payload verification and do integrity checks, so this makes the system even more vulnerable [7]. Trustchip [8] can be used for secure communication between network systems and edge devices. It provides a singular security architecture that operates as a security service for any application.

16.6.2   IOT AUTHENTICATION

Authentication is the second layer of security and is where the user's credentials are matched, in terms of username and password. Passwords should be of two-factor authentication. Two-factor authentication requires a pin number to be entered in order to login for more security. The authentication process may involve a biometric process for additional security.

16.6.3   IOT ENCRYPTION

To avoid data sniffing by the hacker's encryption, algorithms should be used. While transmitting data between edge devices, some standard encryption algorithms should be used to maintain data integrity. IoT security is an end-to-end approach.

16.6.4   IOT PUBLIC KEY INFRASTRUCTURE

In order to secure communication, public/private key generation, distribution, and implementation should be provided. The use of a digital certificate and cryptography should be implemented to safeguard the data. Digital certificates can be loaded securely by the manufacturers and will be invoked by the third-party public key infrastructure software.

16.6.5   *IOT SECURITY ANALYTICS*

Proper analysis of IoT data during communication and transferring should be analyzed. Login attempts, failed authentications, IoT-specific attacks, sniffing, identity theft, and excess data from a particular IP address should be monitored, and those reports should be analyzed. Logs can also be used.

16.6.6   *IOT APPLICATION PROGRAMMING INTERFACE SECURITY*

Application programming interface (API) security is also essential for safeguarding the data between edge devices and back-end systems. Access should be provided to authorize devices, and apps to communicate to APIs should be used so that potential threats can be avoided. Standard protocols should be followed for secure APIs.

16.6.7   *IOT ADMIN CREDENTIALS*

The main reasons for easy access to IoT devices are default usernames and passwords. Some of the easy to guess/default admin credentials are given in Table 16.1. Developers are aware of these default admin credentials and can effortlessly change them accordingly. The attacker can also find the default passwords via a brute force attack.

Security experts estimated that 63% of IoT devices use the default credentials and some of the devices are not designed to accept admin credential changes [3].

16.6.8   *IOT NETWORK MONITOR*

This tool allows users to pinpoint vulnerabilities in IoT devices and it has a user-friendly interface. It scans the network traffic analysis on the network that the IoT device is on and exploits it for a default user ID/password. Gudrun et al. [11] mentioned that it scans the devices for their IP-address, port number, and default login credentials. It changes the default passwords of the device to a randomly generated 12-character string and reports it back to the user.

TABLE 16.1 Most Commonly Attacked Admin Credentials

Username	Password
support	support
root	root
admin	admin1
user	user
guest	guest
test	test
oracle	oracle
ftp	ftp
git	git
ftpuser	ftpuser
nagios	nagios
ubuntu	ubuntu
tomcat	tomcat
1234	1234
default	default
testuser	testuser
monitor	monitor
apache	apache
backup	backup
webmaster	webmaster
hadoop	hadoop

16.7 CONCLUSION

IoT administrators should ensure that information to the user should not be denied. The three principles of information security, that is, availability, integrity, and confidentiality should be implemented. Ensure that any web interface did not accept the weak password, prompt for old and weak passwords. The security guidelines for manufactures, developers, and users should be implemented. In this paper, the IoT scenario is presented per the growing market and then major IoT attacks, and their vulnerabilities are presented. Common requirements for IoT security and IoT protocols defining security are also discussed. The aim of this technical paper is to elaborate on the vulnerabilities in IoT devices and make users aware of their threats.

16.8   FUTURE SCOPE

Future research can be carried out for the implementation of security patches which will automatically update the devices or throw a mail to the system administrator to change the password. Apart from the implemented security algorithms, new algorithms will be developed. As the threats and vulnerabilities discovered the login, data access and network communications will be taken care by a secure developed application. If the data transmission thresh-hold level reaches, the IoT device will collapse automatically. Some of the data handling scope and work of IoT devices proposed by the authors are as under:

1. With the help of general-purpose input/output ports system OS should be updated with the latest security patches.
2. Periodic updations of firmware should be updated.
3. Latest standards of encryption should be followed or taken into mind while accessing the IoT devices.
4. Develop more secure communication in transport layer encryption.

KEYWORDS

- **vulnerabilities**
- **communication protocols**
- **device-to-device**
- **device-to-cloud**
- **machine-to-machine**
- **security**
- **attacks**

REFERENCES

1. Folk, C., Hurley, D. C., and Payne, J. F. X., "The security implications of the Internet of Things," AFCEA International Cyber Committee, Cyber City, 2015.
2. Sharma, P., and Bangotra, P. K., "Internet of Things-scope, challenges & solutions from Indian perspective," in iNAC-2017, Bhimtal, Nainital, India.
3. Boddy, S., and Shattuck, J., "The hunt for IoT—the rise of thingbots," Threat Analysis Report, Volume 3, 2017.
4. Salman, T., and Jain, R., "Networking protocols and standards for Internet of Things" In: Internet of Things and Data Analytics Handbook, pp. 215–238, John Wiley & Sons, Inc.: Hoboken, 2017.
5. Vincent, A., Francis, F., and Ayyappadas, P. S., "Security aspect in 6Lowpan networks: a study," IOSR Journal of Electronics and Communication Engineering. (IOSR-JECE) e-ISSN: 2278-2834, p-ISSN: 2278-8735. PP 08-12 www.iosrjournals.org
6. https://blog.trendmicro.com/trendlabs-security-intelligence/persirai-new-internet-things-iot-botnet-targets-ip-`cameras (last accessed August 16 2018).
7. Ahamed, J., and Rajan, A. V., "Internet of Things (IoT): application systems and security vulnerabilities," 2016 5th International Conference on Electronic Devices, Systems and Applications, Ras Al Khaimah, United Arab Emirates, 2016.
8. Jiang, D. U., and Wei, C. S., "A study of information security for M2M of IoT," 2010 3rd International Conference on Advanced Computer Theory and Engineering, Chengdu, China, 2010.
9. Ling, Z., Liu, K., Xu, Y., Jin, Y., and Fu, X., "An end-to-end view of IoT security and privacy," 2017 IEEE Global Communications Conference, Singapore, 2017.
10. Andy, S., Rahardjo, B., and Hanindhito, B., "Attack scenario and security analysis of MQTT communication protocol in IoT system," 2017 4th International Conference on Electrical Engineering, Computer Science and Informatics, Yogyakarta, Indonesia, 2017.
11. Jonsdottir, G., Wood, D., and Doshi, R., "IoT network monitor," 2017 IEEE MIT Undergraduate Research Technology Conference, Cambridge, MA, USA, 2017.
12. Seralathan, Y., Oh, T. T., Jadhav, S., Myers, J., Jeong, J. P., Kim, Y. H., and Kim, J. N., "IoT security vulnerability: a case study of a web camera," 2018 International Conference on Advanced Communications Technology, Chuncheon-si Gangwon-do, 2018.
13. Firdous, S. N., Baig, Z., Valli, C., and Ibrahim, A., "Modelling and evaluation of malicious attacks against the IoT MQTT Protocol," 2017 IEEE International Conference on Internet of Things (iThings) and IEEE green Computing and Communications (GreenCom) and IEEE Cyber, Physical and Social Computing (CPSCom) and IEEE Smart Data (SmartData), Exeter, 2017.
14. Visoottiviseth, V., Akarasiriwong, P., Chaiyasart, S., and Chotivatunyu, S., "PENTOS: penetration testing tool for Internet of Thing devices," 2017 IEEE Region 10 Conference, Malaysia, 2017.
15. Kumar, S. K., Sahoo, S., Mahapatra, A., Swain, A. K., and Mahapatra, K. K., "Security enhancements to system on chip devices for IoT perception layer," 2017 IEEE International Symposium on Nanoelectronic and Information Systems, Bhopal, 2017.

16. Niruntasukrat, A., Issariyapat, C., Pongpaibool, P., Meesublak, K., Aiumsupucgul, P., and Panya, A., "Authorization mechanism for MQTT-based Internet of Things," 2016 IEEE International Conference on Communications Workshops, Korea, pp. 290–295, 2016.
17. Rghioui, A., Bouhorma, M., and Benslimane, A., "Analytical study of security aspect in 6LoWPAN networks," 2013 IEEE 5th International Conference on Information and Communication Technology for the Muslim World, Rabat, 2013.
18. Potluri, S., Mangla, M., Satpathy, S., & Mohanty, S. N. (2020, July). Detection and Prevention Mechanisms for DDoS Attack in Cloud Computing Environment. 11th International Conference on Computing, Communication and Networking Technologies (ICCCNT) (pp. 1-6). IEEE

CHAPTER 17

Latest Trend of IoT Threats and Defense

KOMAL SAXENA* and RIYA SHARMA

Amity Institute of Information Technology, Amity University Noida, Noida, India

Corresponding author. E-mail: ksaxena1@amity.edu

ABSTRACT

With the increasing influence of the Internet in almost every sphere of our lives, Internet of Things (IoT) threats have also increased. Recent studies of damage caused by malware and virus attacks are proofs to understand the threatening impact of IoT risks. Cybersecurity experts are trying their level best to find out the loopholes and provide top-notch security both in local and shared network systems. The IoT devices should be used with the latest updates to protect them from malware threats. The devices are designed in such a way that it helps in easy use by users. Be it a big enterprise or a small business, the devices should be protected. Therefore, it is recommended to set separate local network systems for IoT devices. Using complex credentials can prevent vulnerabilities. Also, using updated software, it is possible to prevent threats. Disable unwanted features on your device as these can give a way to serious threats on your device. Before sharing confidential information over a common network system, check the connected devices properly. With a suitable firewall system, it is possible to safeguard devices in enterprises. By leveraging firewalls, it is possible to prevent unwanted traffic that may be an attack on the site. So, cybersecurity is making strategic plans to cope up with challenges.

17.1   INTRODUCTION OF IOT THREATS AND DEFENSE

The Internet of Things (IoT) has transformed our lives by its huge influence in almost all spheres of life. It requires top-notch security, and the IoT devices need better protection due to its increased usage. To prevent the possibilities of hackers and attackers, installing better security is important. To prevent hackers from getting easy access to a private network and install malware, top-level security should be installed [15, 17].

17.2   THE KEY FEATURES OF IOT

17.2.1   INTELLECT

To have a better experience when using a product, algorithm, and compute are integrated in the best way possible. For instance, Misfit Shine which is a fitness tracker offers a better user experience that helps in easy task distribution between cloud and smartphone when compared to other software. Here, AI is used for the smooth functioning of the products [1].

17.2.2   IMPROVED CONNECTION

IoT offers better connectivity compared to a WiFi network. IoT offers easy connectivity with easy compatibility enabling better data consumption [1].

17.2.3   ENHANCED SENSING

Senses and ability help in a better understanding of the world around us. Through experience, people are able to have awareness of the world. In addition, it also helps in better knowing of the complex world and copes up with the changes easily [1].

17.2.4   METHODS OF EXPRESSION

Better expression and forms of interactivity help stay connected with the outer world. Be it a smart home technology or similar technological advancement in agriculture, the ability for better expression helps to get a better scope for the outer world. Therefore, it enables better interaction with the outer world and environment [1].

17.2.5 BETTER SYSTEM OF ENERGY

To make the best use of creativity, energy is one of the forms that are required. Some parts like power efficiency, harvesting, and charging infrastructure are included in setting up the design of a power ecosystem. Without suitable input, the ecosystem may lack the efficiency of an inadequate team [1].

17.2.6 SECURITY PROCESSES

Apart from IoT efficiencies and better user experience, it helps to maintain safety measures. It should be maintained as IoT is increasingly used in every spheres of life. It includes maintaining the safety of personal information that is shared over different networks. Therefore, it calls for a top-notch security paradigm that shall help to maintain the information [1].

Therefore, by framing the IoT with the latest features, it makes team works an easy affair. It incorporates better designing, software, and latest business models. The characteristics are also used in single service or products. The key features are incorporated depending on the environmental restrictions and other factors [1] (Figure 17.1).

17.2.6.1 EFFECTIVE DEFENSE STRATEGY CAN HELP LOWER IOT SECURITY RISKS

Enterprise IoT is vital to be secured. Leaked data problems can break the image of your brand or attacks on critical infrastructure, medical devices used, and the like. To reduce the chances of life-threatening risks, take a look at the strategies elaborated below.

17.2.6.2 BUILDING AN EFFECTIVE IOT SECURITY STRATEGY

When you include IoT, it is important to avoid the possibility of damaging impacts of different devices. By knowing about the proper responsibility of the IT security team, it will be easy for the enterprise to plan a solid security plan for safeguarding the enterprise.

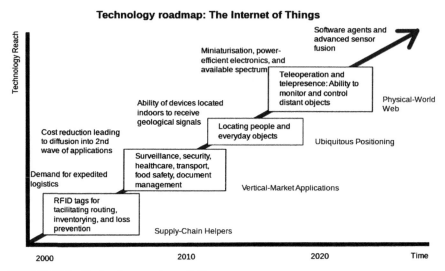

FIGURE 17.1   Technology roadmap: IoT.

Source: SRI Consulting Business Intelligence.

17.3   IOT SECURITY MECHANISM

To incorporate a secured IoT environment in an enterprise, the security tools should be well tested and tried for yielding better results. Here, checking new technologies, the encryption process is of immense importance, including threat detection devices. So, with the right mechanism set up for your enterprise, chances are better to fight against the security risks.

17.4   EVOLUTION OF THREATS DEFENSE

With technological advancement, hackers have taken better measures for hacking. The risk of hacking credit card details has also increased. For this risk zone, it is important to maintain the connected devices and update them regularly to defend the threats as much as possible. Also, the updates help to detect the possibilities of exploitation that the hackers can do. Therefore, it is becoming challenging for threat defense experts to find an appropriate solution that offers future protection to the networks. Identifying and blocking the known sources of attacks are common, but the connected devices used should be changed. It shall help to meet the complexity of malicious attacks. It will be easy to detect possible threats and block them with the right defense solutions (Table 17.1).

TABLE 17.1 Three Generation of IoT Security [3]

First Generation	Second Generation	Third Generation
• Test environment	• Real time	• IoT policy
• Security methods: confidentiality, integrity, availability	• Protocol should be standardized	• Industry and market driven
• Privacy of data	• IoT platform should be centralized	• Other technologies
• Standards are not required	• Confidence and trust control	• Customer privacy should me first priority
• Adopt the latest technology	• Authentication and proof of identity	• Transformed smart phone or BYOD
	• Lack of privacy	• Customer transaction

17.5 ARCHITECTURE IOT

The IoT is based on a concept that seems to be complex. Knowing about the elements that are assembled together in forming the structure shall help in a better understanding of each stage. There is a need for potential structure of the IoT, and there are three layers of architecture. The client-side, operators working on the server side, and a network for connecting clients and operators are the three layers of IoT. However, the four stages in the architecture are described below [4, 5] (Figure 17.2).

1. Sensors—in this stage, data collected by sensors are converted into useful data. This form of data is important for better analysis. For fastest response of the network, the data processing at the initial stage is useful [4, 5].
2. Internet getaways and data acquisition systems—Internet gateways work via WiFi connection, and data acquisition system is connected with sensor networking and the end results. For better understanding, it can be said that the data are better processed in this stage making it ready for further analysis through the IoT architecture.
3. Edge IT—here, the ready data are shifted to the digital form. The IT processing system is also available in some remote offices. Therefore, it helps to better understand IoT.
4. Datacenter and cloud—for in-depth processing of data, where it does not require immediate feedback, it is stored in the datacenter. The IT system can manage and securely store the vital data that are required for future use. So, only after meeting the required standard, the information will be stored in the cloud.

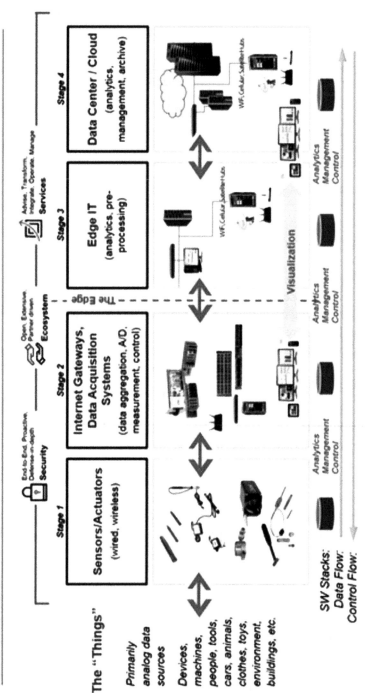

FIGURE 17.2 Architecture of IoT [5].

Some simple steps to follow in combating security risks are as follows:

1. Detecting and accordingly blocking the possible threats on the devices across different networks and the ones used via the cloud.
2. For better cybersecurity and managing it well, implementing the right and secured IoT solutions are required.
3. It is important to establish secure communication among different locations and have suitable control of any third-party access.
4. Providing proper protection of IoT devices that are used by the business.

17.6 COMPARISON OF THREATS AND ATTACKS

In information security, threat is the presence of a danger caused to the integrity of information stored. However, threats can be present in the form of a computer virus of person. Attacks are the act of exploitation done to the vulnerabilities of the security system containing vital information. Therefore, there is a number of ways to prevent the occurrence of attacks and the chances of threats in information security [17].

With the development of the IT system, it will be easy to prevent the information by means of firewalls and antimalware used in the systems. One such instance is the increasing use of video conferencing, where different features are used in the voice over Internet protocol. Though companies are adopting different ways of video conferencing it is still important to maintain safety measures when having important business discussions over the video conference.

17.7 ADVANTAGES AND DISADVANTAGES OF IOT

IoT has become an important part of the technology that is increasingly used these days. From managing our day-to-day activities, IoT plays a vital role. The IoT also helps other technologies and therefore, it brings in both benefits and disadvantages for other technologies [6].

17.7.1 ADVANTAGES OF IOT

1. Better tracking—IoT is able to keep a perfect track of the things that are required. Also, it will never run out of information when it is required even during the last moment [6].

2. Money—the IoT technology helps to replace human beings who are responsible for monitoring and maintaining the supplies.
3. Saves time—using IoT, it helps to save time, that is, required in monitoring to go through the task that otherwise would be tiresome.
4. Better data availability—for IoT, better data are available that helps in taking an informed decision. Knowing the right way to use the available data will help to save your time without wondering aimlessly.

17.7.2 DISADVANTAGES OF IOT

1. Complexity—the development, design, structure, and maintenance of IoT is a tough job. Even after giving a proper indication of the requirement, you may not be able to accomplish the task due to the complex nature of IoT [6].
2. Security—as many IoT systems are interconnected, very few security measures are adopted making the systems more vulnerable to threats and attacks.
3. Privacy—data must be well protected with IoT so that the data cannot be easily accessed that are stored in IoT.

17.7.2.1 BETTER USE OF TECHNOLOGY FOR IOT

There are many technologies where IoT is incorporated. The main purpose is to use its network to establish better communication among the devices that involve the use of IoT. Here, many wireless devices are included.

17.7.2.2 EASY ADDRESSABILITY OF IOT DEVICES

The Auto-ID center works via the Electronic Product Code and it can be used in devices that run on IP address or URI. These are also used by powerful servers for better human interaction. As most of the integrated devices are used via IP addresses, it can be easily identified. As there is limited space in IPv4, the devices in IoT will have to use the space offered under IPv6 protocol. Therefore, it can be said that to get access to the large space required for easy access to the IoT devices, IPv6 is the future of IoT. Thus, it can be said that for the successful development of IoT future, IPv6 will be adopted massively across different platforms.

17.8 LIST OF SHORT-RANGE WIRELESS NETWORKS

1. Bluetooth mesh networking—mesh network variant with more number of nodes and advanced application model.
2. Light fidelity—this wireless technology works similar to a WiFi network that makes the use of visible light communication to get better bandwidth.
3. Near-field communication—in this, two electronic devices can be communicated that are placed within a range of 4 cm.
4. Radio-frequency identification—this technology makes the use of magnetic fields that help in better data storage.
5. WiFi technology—this is the best networking for the local area that works on IEEE802.11 standard. Here, devices are connected through a shared point or via individual devices.
6. ZigBee—it works on personal area networking that works on the IEEE 802.15.4 standard. It offers low power consumption, low cost with the high outcome.
7. Z-Wave—it works on wireless communication that is mainly used for home automation and some security applications.

17.8.1 LIST OF MEDIUM-RANGE WIRELESS NETWORKS

1. LTE advanced—this network is suitable for mobile networks and enables high-speed communication. It offers low latency, better coverage, and higher output.

17.8.2 LONG-RANGE WIRELESS

1. Low-power wide-area networking (LPWAN)—this wireless network is suitable for low-range communication that is available at reduced power, easy cost of transmission consuming low data. LPWAN technology helps in better networking.
2. Very small aperture terminal—this is an excellent satellite communication technology in which small dish antennas are used for broadband data.

17.8.3 WIRED CONNECTIONS

1. Ethernet—this is a general-purpose network in which twisted pair and fiber optic links are used in switches.
2. Power-line communication—in this technological setup, power and data are transmitted through the help of electrical wiring.

17.9 MINIMIZING IOT SECURITY RISKS CAN BE ADVANTAGEOUS

With the growing popularity of the trend of IoT, cybersecurity risks are also facing increasing trouble. As it has already influenced most of the spheres of our lives, there is increasing use of voice assistants, improved infrastructure, and connected appliances. As of now, the use of connected devices is a must for running any critical management system, such as traffic control, environment management, and the like. IoT has both provided advantages and disadvantages in different spheres of life. It has resulted in the rise of cyberattacks, where hackers, including malicious parties, are exploiting different devices of business enterprises in which personal information are available. If the devices have poor security toward malware practices, there is a chance that the company may lose its essential information and confidential documents to third parties. Let us take a look at some of the steps to minimize cyber risk possibilities.

17.10 IDENTIFYING THE THREATS AND ATTACK

Security experts should understand the chances of cyberattacks and improve the vulnerabilities of the information system. By taking the right measures, it becomes easy to identify the venerable threats. Therefore, suitable identification measures should be adopted. Some of the steps to identify the attacks are as follows [18–20].

1. Cyber ecosystem—in the cyber ecosystem, both good and bad data are stored. But there is no such scope to discriminate between the data as the information is transferred without discrimination.
2. Discriminating threats—it is important to have discrimination within Information technology, and it should occur in different security layers.
3. Knowing between bad and good information—there is an urgent need for the identification of bad and good information contained in the security layers of IT infrastructure.

4. Checking attack surface—the cyberattacks take place when the vulnerable sources are exposed. Therefore, the vulnerabilities should be embedded in the software for preventing the surface attack.
5. Fast action—in case, cyberattacks have been identified at the security level, there is a possibility to protect the information system.
6. Data-sharing—this is a common way to identify the possibilities of threats and attacks. In these cases, with the help of elapsed time to identify threat measures can be used to find out the possible threat while sharing data [19, 20].

17.11 RISK IN IOT DEVICES

17.11.1 REDUCING THE CHANCES OF ATTACK SURFACE

If the surface attack is smaller, then the risks will be limited. There are some devices for which it is important to work on a WiFi network by connecting with the main server. But once the device has been configured while using it for the first time, it may not be required any further. Here, the IT managers can try to disable the features that can prevent any third-party threat when using IoT. Also, to reduce the risk possibilities, the technical team should try to limit the task to a single channel that will be negotiating just between the remote service and the device.

Therefore, arising from such a situation, it is better to limit the storage of information on the device which is vulnerable to third-party threats.

17.11.2 USE OF NO PLAIN TEXT

You should not take the risk of storing highly sensitive information in the form of plain text. The devices used can store the user information when used through a mobile app during proper configuration. The device that gets the personal information of the users will forward the data to the remote server with which it is connected. Here, it can validate whether the user is a valid one or not. So, it is of utmost importance that the data should be encrypted before they are sent via the remote server.

This is required in case of communication that takes place between devices. For secure and safe communication protocol, it is important that the hardware design should not restrict communication features.

17.11.3   TESTING POTENTIAL VULNERABILITIES

By keeping a frequent check on the probable vulnerabilities on the system, it is possible to prevent vulnerabilities. Vulnerabilities do not show up immediately after you buy the product. Plenty of devices are integrated and used in a company and therefore, the chances of weak points are also increasing. When certain code is changed, users provide feedback for it. At that time, it is possible to prevent the chances of risks from forming more. As developers cannot foresee the chances of risks, running updates of the system or devices can avoid the chances of risks.

17.11.4   ALLOWING THE UPDATES

So, it is of vital importance to address the chances of risks and try to find out effective means to mitigate the same. Here, allowing the required updates are important. Even after top-notch efforts, some flaws are found in the system related to security issues. With increasing the number of connected devices in the market, the chances of products getting more prone to cyberattacks are growing day-by-day.

17.11.4.1   COMMON IOT SECURITY THREATS TO AVOID BY ADOPTING LATEST METHODS

The IoT is security at a fast pace and exchange of information, connectivity between devices, transmitting, and receiving data are common through IoT. But in recent times, IoT has been connected with security problems and it is also increasing. From connecting people to smart machines, IoT has spread its influence in many spheres of life. So, it is important to question the security of modern IoT. Some of the common threats are elaborated in the following part of the article [8].

17.11.4.2   HACKING OF DEVICES THAT SEND SPAM EMAILS

Smear appliances used in the home such as refrigerators are run on the same computing power and similar functionality as that of a tablet. Therefore, it becomes easy to hijack the device and use it for different purposes in email servers. According to past findings, it can be said that the refrigerator has sent near about a thousand spam emails without the owner knowing about the problem [8].

17.11.4.3   USE OF UNSECURED DEVICES

Since the coming of IoT, there has been an increase in the use of unsecured devices. When IoT devices are shipped to customers, they are sure not to change the username and password of the device unless they are asked to do so by the manufacturer as per device instructions.

17.11.4.4   PRIVACY LEAKAGE ISSUES

For skilled hackers, an IoT device is enough to get access to its information and other details. Through the device, they can get the Internet details and use it for other different purposes. Therefore, the use of virtual private networking technology can help to secure IoT as per security experts. Through this, it is possible to protect traffic in your ISP by installing VPN technology with a router. Therefore, for protecting smart home devices, using the VPN shall help to protect your private information.

17.11.4.5   HOME INTRUSIONS OF IOT THREATS

This is one of the scariest threats possible as hackers will try to get through private information through the use of unsecured devices at your home. Hackers will try to hack the residential address and then sell personal information to other website operate through other Internet networks. Therefore, it is important to secure your network credentials and get it connected with VPN networks for better IoT security [19, 20].

17.11.4.6   METHODS TO HIJACKED SMART REMOTE VEHICLES

There are chances that smart driving cars can get hijacked by hackers. Before letting a hacker remotely control the access of your remote car, it is better that you look for its security. So, automakers are paying great attention to minimize the risks of the vehicle hijacking. As a sign of appropriate action, developers have come up with the use of wireless cars that can prevent hackers from getting access to its remote control [8].

17.12   SECURITY PRIVACY OF IOT

The new environment of Internet-connected devices is different from the traditional system structure. Through the newly connected devices, a massive exchange of data takes place everyday and it is important to encrypt it at the earliest for safeguarding confidential information [7].

17.12.1   MAINTAINING SECURITY IN IOT ECOSYSTEM

Malware, viruses, and hacking are the traditional forms of cyberattacks but in the case of IoT, the threats come through different connected devices used, identity theft, eavesdropping, and the like. In case, the IoT are broken or hijacked, it can cause great loss to different organizations and individuals. Through IoT, it is possible to get access to different sections of the work of an organization. The IoT flaws make this more easily accessible for the hackers.

17.12.2   THREE FORMS TO DEFEAT IOT SECURITY

17.12.2.1   THEFT

1.   There can be intellectual property theft.
2.   Stealing any organization or home device connected with other devices.
3.   Getting access to data stored in the device through eavesdropping.

17.12.2.2   MANIPULATION

1.   Manipulation is possible in the case of using devices, routers, or clients.
2.   Forcefully causing system crash and malfunctioning of the entire system.
3.   Modifying actions of different systems.

17.12.2.3   FRAUD

1.   Trying to identify theft to prevent access to user's devices.
2.   Protecting device credentials giving access to Internet servers and data stored.

17.12.3   WAYS TO SECURE YOUR DEVICE

17.12.3.1   STRENGTHENING SECURITY PROCEDURE OF IOT

There are different ways to strengthen the security procedure of IoT that requires adopting advanced security measures for the safe use of devices and data storage. Some of the ways are elaborated in the following part for a better idea.

17.12.3.2   EFFECTIVE DATA ENCRYPTION

Before the exchange of data through the devices, it is necessary to authenticate and encrypt it for better results. By encryption, it can be considered that the data are no more left in the accessible form by any third party. Even device authentication ensures that nobody can manipulate the functioning of the device. Thus, the machine cannot be controlled by the hacker and it will be possible to safeguard the data stored in the system.

17.12.3.3   SECURING THE DEVICE

Proper device encryption will prevent the data from being accessed by hackers. Therefore, security companies are ensuring to provide top-notch service in protecting the device. A centralized controlling system of the devices will be required to safeguard the devices end properly.

17.12.3.4   MAINTAINING SECURITY ON THE CLOUD

Data are stored in cloud which is one of the major traffic areas for IoT. Therefore, the cloud server should be checked after regular intervals to prevent hackers from getting access to the cloud and vast information stored in it. Innovative cloud security provisions are available in the market and you should deploy the efficient one that is suitable for the IoT environment. With the increasing use of the Internet, the security issues also need to be checked. It is important to look after the risk that is associated with cloud servers. As there is more chance of losing data and personal identity theft, the security measures should also be taken care of properly. So, IoT device users should be aware of the safety measures that shall help to immune the cybersecurity risks that are increasing at a fast pace.

17.12.3.5   MAINTAINING CODE SIGNING CERTIFICATES

The code signing certificate is similar to a digital signature that can be operated through a certain validated code. The code is required to run a particular device and the code cannot be corrupted by hackers. Only the editor can get access to the validated code. This has been done to add some extra layer of security for the IoT devices that are connected and used in different platforms.

17.12.3.6   IP CAMERAS—A NEW FORM OF MALWARE ATTACKS

IP cameras are also the sources of cybercriminal locators. According to the studies in recent years, it has been seen that some of the major vulnerabilities have been detected in devices like IP cameras that are installed in different public areas. However, in the list of new malware threats, DDoS attacks, Cryptocurrency mining, and data theft are common [21,22].

17.12.3.7   DDOS ATTACKS

As previously seen, the main purpose of IoT malware deployment is to find out the vulnerabilities of DDoS attacks. Through the use of Botnet, hackers can hack specific addresses where it can handle requests from real users of the devices. However, it has been seen that such attacks are common from Trojans. The worst scenario may crop up when an infected device gets blocked by ISP. In such cases, it is possible to get rid of the hacking problem just by rebooting the device.

17.12.3.8   PREVENTION FROM DATA THEFT

It has been seen that VPNFilter Trojan malware extracts data from username and passwords used and then send it to the cybercriminal servers. Some of the features of VPNFilter are given as follows.

1. Due to its robot resistant, it can modify the configuration setup of the device and change it to a nonvolatile memory of the device.
2. With its modular architecture, the malware can inject any JavaScript code in the web pages and hack the information.
3. The Trojan has the capability to self-disable the device when it receives such command. It can delete itself and then overwrite with

garbage data of the system and clean its presence just by rebooting the device.

17.12.3.9 *IMPORTANT WAYS TO REDUCE RISK CHANCES OF SMART DEVICES*

With the increasing rate of smart device infection, the following tips can help to overcome the hacking problem.

1. Unless it is not necessary or urgent, it is better not to connect the device with an external network as this gives access to the hackers to easily hack your smart device.
2. Check for new versions of firmware and try to keep the device updated to stay away from problems of malware.
3. Try to set a complex password of a minimum of 8 characters that include both lower-case and upper-case letters. Special characters and numerals for better protection.
4. During the initial setup of the device, try to change the factory password. This is important to prevent the hackers from getting access to your data on the device.
5. Block unused ports if you can. In case, there is an unused router address, it is better to delete or block it to prevent intruders from getting access to device data.

17.12.3.10 *IOT SECURITY BREACHES AND HACKS*

With the increasing use of the Internet, the risk of unsecured devices has also increased, and experts are trying to find out ways to combat the situation. This has started after IoT first came into being during the late 1990s. After a number of attacks have made headlines, people and experts have started to realize the consequences of the risks involved. In this regard, it should be known that the IoT devices are not the sole target of the hackers rather they consider the devices are the entry source to get access to the large network and data stored in it.

As of 2010, the Stuxnet virus came into being that can damage Iranian centrifuges. The initial attack by this virus took place during 2006, and this can be considered among the earliest attacks of the virus. The main target of the virus was supervisory control and data acquisition and others where malware can infect the instructions that are sent by different programs. Following this, different malware attacks on individual network continued, and it started to target the IoT systems.

17.12.4   IOT SECURITY TOOLS

Though there are many IoT security frameworks, there is no such industry-accepted framework to safeguard data in the devices. Therefore, adopting a suitable framework with the use of the right tool will help companies in protecting IoT devices. With more use of such frameworks, it will help to prevent vulnerabilities and risks. So, it is important to have a better security framework for IoT devices used in different industries.

17.12.4.1   THE INDUSTRIES PRONE TO IOT THREATS

The IoT security hacks can take place in different industries ranging from smart home devices to manufacturing plant to connected car industries. The severity of the hack depends on different systems and the data collected in each of the arrangements. When a connected car is hacked, the attack disables the breaks of the car. Even an attack in the refrigerator system which is regulated by the IoT system can ruin the medicines. In case temperature fluctuates, it can damage the medicines [18].

17.12.4.2   THE STEPS TO PROTECT IOT DEVICES AND SYSTEM

The security method that you wish to adopt varies depending on the IoT devices and applications that you use. From product manufacturers to companies dealing with semiconductor items, security should be given from the initial stage for better protection. Here, the hardware used should be made tamper-proof and using secured hardware. In addition, performing dynamic testing can also help and establishing secured integration between the machines. For operators, to prevent problems of security threats, it is important to keep the system updated, auditing, use of updated patches, protecting the infrastructure, and protection the vital credentials used to login to the systems. The main focus of the developer should be on proper software development and its secured integration. For the ones using IoT systems, some of the common IoT security measures are elaborated in the following part of the article.

17.12.4.2.1 Using Proper Security Measures at Design Phases

It is important for IoT developers to incorporate security measures at the initial stages of the enterprise, industrial devices, consumer, and the like. You cannot set default security but it is required to protect the devices from sudden malware attacks.

17.12.4.2.2 Use of Hardcoded Credentials

Hardcoded credentials cannot be used in the design procedure instead users can try to update device credentials before they start using it. When a device comes with a default credential, the users must change its username and password to prevent hackers from getting access to the device. For this, using a strong password is required including multifactor authentication if possible.

17.12.4.2.3 Use of Digital Certificates

Developing and maintaining secured IoT devices, using digital certificates and public key infrastructure is important. For secured exchange of data over networks, better protection is required.

17.12.4.2.4 Identity Management

The identity management is important to keep a track of details of the device. Through the unique identifier, it is possible to know how the device behaves, what are other devices it interacts with, the required security measures that should be taken for the device for safeguarding its data.

17.12.4.2.5 Application Performance Indicator Security

Application performance indicator (API) is required to protect the data integrity of the device when it is sent from IoT devices to other systems. For further security, it should be ensured that only secured developers, authorized devices, and secured applications can communicate with the API [16].

17.13   EFFECTIVE PREVENTIVE METHODS TO DEAL WITH IOT HACKING ISSUES

When living in a connected world, the number of connected devices is also increasing. The IoT is a big thing now that offers plenty of benefits when deployed in different industrial works. In addition to this, it brings in serious security threats that can result in great loss of confidential data and hacking of personal devices. As physical devices can be connected by means of IoT, its hacking can cause a great toll on human lives. But, with the rising chances of threats and vulnerabilities, it is time to make strategic plans that can help to prevent hacking problems. Some of the biggest IoT threat concerns are elaborated further.

17.13.1   USE OF UNSECURED NETWORKS

There are chances of vulnerabilities in network systems due to unsecured networks that give essay access to hackers. The intruders can get access to personal information stored in connected devices through the network used. In this way, intruders get access to confidential data which they may use for other forms of crimes. Some of the causes of unsecured networks are the use of open ports, user datagram protocol services, and the like. However, the situation calls for countermeasures to prevent hacking issues. Some of the preventions for this are as follows.

1. Only using the necessary ports available.
2. Do not leave any network ports open to UPnP.
4. Try to protect services from probable chances of DoS attacks through local and shared networks.

17.13.2   A POORLY PROTECTED WEB INTERFACE CAN BRING IN THREAT ISSUES

The web interfaces are interacting with IoT devices and therefore, a weak web can get hacked easily. To reduce its risk possibilities, it is important to take some preventive measures to deal with the situation better. Some of the causes are weak credentials, declaring credentials in networks, cross-site scripting or XSS, SQL injection, and others. To counter these situations, try to change the default set username and password and set a robust password recovery method [19].

17.14 BENEFITS OF DEVICE AND DATA ENCRYPTION

If IoT devices are not protected when used in local networks, it can bring in serious IoT threats. In case, data are transmitted without protection, it enables easy access to the confidential data. When data are not protected, it becomes vulnerable due to poor coding, it can go to wrong heads and result in misuse of data. To get rid of the situation, the proper use of SSL/TLS should be implemented at the initial stage of design.

Therefore, by following the above-said encryption methods, it is possible to safeguard confidential data. The IoT will bring in more threats in the coming years without the use of effective and robust preventive measures. It is important to become more cautious and concerned regarding the safety issues and try to properly address the threat issues in the initial stages itself for a better solution. Also, organizations and individuals should be careful when using IoT devices and look after suitable data encryption to prevent confidential data.

17.15 WEB OF THINGS

The Web of Things (WoT) is a special style or programming pattern through which real-world objects can be well accessed through World Wide Web (WWW). Similar to the equation between Web and Internet, the WoT and IoT works. These are capable of working across different platforms and domains making the task an easy one. It further focuses better on different layers of the network. Therefore, WoT helps in better connectivity between the devices and further helps in better building of applications. Due to all these reasons, there is an increased use of WoT in different platforms and social networks [9].

The WoT is an evolution in the way in which Web Protocols are connected with the outer world. It offers a better presence of WWW and its usage on different platforms. In other words, the WoT indicates suitable integration of smart things with Internet and the applications used [9].

17.15.1 ARCHITECTURE OF THE WOT

Similar to any multilayered architecture that organizes the protocols and suitable standards of Internet, the WoT architecture helps in better handling of the Web protocols. Thus, the framework formed helps in better device connection with the use of the web. The WoT Architecture is designed of multiple layers and these add better and advanced functionality to the applications in which the programing pattern is used. Therefore, each of the layers used helps in better functioning and efficient connection of the devices that are used by humans (Figure 17.3).

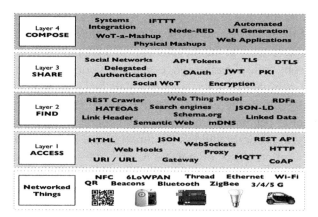

FIGURE 17.3   Architecture of WoT [9].

17.16   GREEN IOT

Green IoT indicates the efficiency in IoT principles. Therefore, it can be said that Green IoT is an efficient way to reduce the greenhouse effect in IoT devices. Thus, the IoT system is designed in such a way that it helps in maintaining a greener society [1] (Figures 17.4).

17.17   APPLICATIONS OF IOT

17.17.1   CONSUMER APPLICATIONS

Different IoT devices are introduced for consumer use such as wearable technology, home automation, remote control appliances, and the IoT is used in various applications like smart homes, eldercare.

17.17.2   SMART HOME

For effective use of home automation, IoT devices play an important part. It includes lighting, air conditioning, heating, media, and proper security systems. In this, it offers good benefits such as energy savings that help to ensure that the electronics and lights are turned off when not in use.

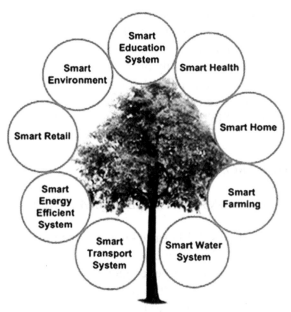

FIGURE 17.4   Green IoT.

Source: Reprinted with permission from Ref. [12]. © 2018 Springer Nature.

A smart home can be used on different platforms where different smart devices or appliances are connected to make it function efficiently. For example, by the use of Apple's Homekit, it is possible that home accessories will be accessed by applications on iOS device. The app of the iOS device should be an efficient one that can be controlled as Apple's Home application without the use of any WiFi connection. In addition, there are smart home hubs on which different products can be connected for effective functioning. Some of the connected products are Google Home, Echo, and the like. There are also some open source ecosystems including Home Assistant and Domoticz.

17.17.3   ELDER CARE

One of the key benefits of smart home products is to offer easy accessibility to elderly and the disabled ones. The home systems are installed with assistive technology that can work as per the user's disability. The users with sight and mobility issues can be used by voice control applications. It will alert the system by establishing an easy connection with cochlear implants that are worn by hearing-impaired users. The devices have safety measures including sensors for monitoring medical emergency situations. Therefore, it can be said that smart home technology appliances offer plethora of benefits to users along with the high quality of life.

In this relation, enterprise IoT (EIoT) refers to devices that are useful in corporate and business setups. However, it can be expected that by 2019, near about 9.1 billion EIoT devices will be used by different industries.

17.17.4 COMMERCIAL APPLICATION

17.17.4.1 APPLICATIONS USED IN MEDICAL AND HEALTHCARE SECTOR

Internet of medical things (IoMT) also known as the Internet of health things refers to the devices used in the medical and health industry for data collection, suitable data analysis for better monitoring, and research facilities. The IoMT is a type of smart healthcare with which it is possible to setup a digitized healthcare setup. It further helps to connect medical resources and other healthcare facilities [11].

In the healthcare industry, IoT devices help in better remote health monitoring and get fast emergency notifications. There are different monitoring devices such as blood pressure machines, heart rate monitors to other specialized monitoring devices such as pacemakers, electronic wristbands, hearing side, and the like. Even smart beds are also used by some hospitals that help to get an easy notification when a bed is empty or when a patient wants to get up from the bed. Also, it offers better support and adjusts the pressure of the patient without the need of any human influence.

Healthcare IoT devices have found several benefits. One such instance is the 2015 Goldman Sachs report that is an excellent instance where the devices can help the US save almost $300 billion. This is done by increasing revenue and decreasing the cost simultaneously. Other than this, mobile devices are also used for better medical follow-ups. It includes capture, transmit, and analyzing the statistics better by collecting the data from different sources.

Even for maintaining the general wellbeing of senior citizens, installing specialized sensors at home shall be of immense help. It further helps in proper treatment and helps patients regain lost mobility through means of therapy. With the use of sensors, it is possible to create a stable network that is capable of collecting, transferring, processing, and also analyze the information taken from different sources, such as in-home monitoring device, hospital-based systems, and the like. There are other consumer devices available that help better with the assistance of IoT. Even different health monitoring platforms are available for chronic patients. It helps in managing critical health problems that require frequent medications.

The low-cost and use and throw IoMT sensors are used, and this is possible due to advancement in plastic and fabric electronics methods. Even for using disposable sensing devices, the sensors along with RFID electronics can be made on e-textiles or paper for ease of usage. However, different latest technology applications have been introduced for providing medical diagnosis making the devices portable and simple functioning systems.

As of 2018, usage of IoMT devices has extended to the clinical laboratory industry and health insurance industries. Now, the IoMT is being used in healthcare industries, helping doctors, patients, nurses, families, and the like. Even for saving the huge amount of patients' records in the database, IoMT devices help the doctors and staff to have easy access to medical records of the patients as necessary.

Most of the IoT devices are patient-centered that enables flexible accessibility to patient records. Even in the insurance industry, IoMT helps in better access and creating dynamics of information. Here, sensor-based solutions are incorporated for ease of work such as wearable, biosensors, health-related devices, mobile apps for suitable tracking, and others. It helps in creating the latest pricing models.

Therefore, it can be said that IoT plays a vital role in the healthcare industry in dealing with chronic diseases and helps introduces better prevention and control measures. Remote monitoring makes it easy for establishing better wireless connections. It helps the practitioners in better and fast handling of patient's data and using the easy way of data analysis.

17.17.4.2 *IOT HELPS IN BETTER MANAGEMENT OF TRANSPORTATION SYSTEM*

With help of IoT, better integration of communication and information accessibility helps in a better transportation system. It can be said that IoT has extended its benefits to every aspect of the transportation system. From maintaining infrastructure to vehicles and maintaining driver information, IoT makes it a lot easier and quicker. It also enables easy interaction between different components of vehicular communication by offering smart traffic control, smart parking, electronic toll collection, suitable fleet management, vehicle control, road assistance, and adopting better safety measures. IoT plays an important role in fleet and logistics management for continuous and effective monitoring of vehicles and locations. For seamless connectivity, IoT devices are of immense help that offers advanced connectivity. Some sensors used are GPS, temperature, and humidity, which send data better through the use of IoT and facilities easy analysis of data. For checking the real-time status of vehicles and managing delay, theft and damage issues better, the IoT devices are of great help. Even for reducing traffic accidents, machine learning helps [11].

17.17.4.3   V2X COMMUNICATIONS

In a vehicular commination system, there are three components: vehicle to vehicle communication, vehicle to pedestrian communications, and vehicle to infrastructure communication [11].

17.17.4.4   BUILDING AND HOME AUTOMATION

For better management of mechanical, electrical, and electronics system, the IoT devices are beneficial to use. The systems are used in different public, industrial, residential, and institutional areas. In this regard, three main areas are mentioned below.

1. The combination of the Internet with energy management systems helps in creating an efficient energy system.
2. It helps in real-time monitoring by reducing energy consumption and enables easy monitoring systems.
3. The combination of smart devices and knowing the way of usage in the future applications have been made easier with IoT devices [11].

17.17.5   INDUSTRIAL APPLICATIONS

The IoT devices used in industrial applications are also known as IIoT that helps in better to analyze data from different equipment. In addition, it helps in better monitoring device, helps in data regulation, and managing industrial tasks efficiently [11].

17.17.5.1 MANUFACTURING

With the help of IoT, the connection of different manufacturing devices is possible that helps in better processing, identification, communication, and advanced network facilities. Through the use of such devices, it helps to think about new business ideas and using the latest market opportunities resulting in better manufacturing options. For the effective use of industrial applications, equipment manufacturing, situation management, and process control within the system can be done. In addition, the IoT system enables better creation of products, helps meet product demands better, using a control system, and handling the manufacturing better.

Even the digital control systems help in better process control, handling service information for optimizing plant's safety when using IoT devices. Here, it is also used for better asset management through statistical evaluation, suitable maintenance of data, and the like. Proper measurements, health management along with adopting safety measures, and plant optimization are offered from networked sensors used.

Therefore, industrial IoT helps to generate better business values that result in advancement in the industrial sector. However, by the use of IoT devices, it is possible to generate $12 trillion of GDP growth in the coming 10 years [11].

17.18 A CASE STUDY OF CISCO

With the increasing problem of IoT security issues, CISCO IoT threat Defense is aiming to resolve it with full-proof solutions. As many devices are connected to each other, it can pose challenges of preventing the network from cyberattacks and other threats. The experts and research surveyed managers said that to them the biggest challenge is the security of IoT [17].

While securing IoT devices, CISCO experts get to know the actual number of devices that are connected with the network. However, for many businesses, security vulnerabilities arise when they are unable to see some of the IoT endpoints and therefore, they cannot secure it. Having the right knowledge about the number of devices connected will help in maintaining security of the devices and prevent the chances of probable threats. Therefore, other than securing IoT devices, there should be any chances of the endpoint to communicate with other networks unnecessarily [17].

KEYWORDS

- **IoT**
- **threats**
- **attacks**
- **cybersecurity**
- **wireless technology**
- **IOT devices**

REFERENCES

1. https://designmind.frogdesign.com/2014/08/Internet-things-six-key-characteristics/ Carlos Elena-Lenz August 23, 2014.
2. https://en.wikipedia.org/wiki/Internet_of_things#/media/File:Internet_of_Things.svg.
3. Khan, L. "Big IoT data stream analytics with issues in privacy and security," in Proceedings of the Fourth ACM International Workshop on Security and Privacy Analytics, 2018.
4. https://www.edureka.co/blog/what-is-iot/#archit.
5. https://medium.com/datadriveninvestor/4-stages-of-iot-architecture-explained-in-simple-words-b2ea8b4f777f.
6. https://e27.co/advantages-disadvantages-Internet-things-20160615.
7. Gilchrist, A. IoT Security Issues by Alasdair Gilchrist, Walter de Gruyter GmbH & Co KG: Berlin, 2017.
8. https://www.iotforall.com/7-most-common-iot-security-threats-2019/.
9. https://en.wikipedia.org/wiki/Web_of_Things.
10. https://ieeexplore.ieee.org/abstract/document/8530550.
11. https://en.wikipedia.org/wiki/Internet_of_things.
12. https://link.springer.com/chapter/10.1007/978-3-319-60435-0_13.
13. https://www.kaspersky.co.in/resource-center/threats/Internet-of-things-security-risks .
14. Dehghantanha, A., Choo, K.-K. R. Eds, Handbook of Big Data and IoT Security, Springer: Berlin.
15. https://www.ibm.com/blogs/Internet-of-things/what-is-the-iot/.
16. https://www.sap.com/india/trends/Internet-of-things.html.
17. https://www.cisco.com/c/en_in/solutions/security/iot-threat-defense/index.html.
18. https://securitytoday.com/articles/2019/08/07/iot-security-current-threats-and-how-to-overcome-them.aspx.

19. https://www.kaspersky.com/iot-threat-data-feed.

20. https://www.securityweek.com/encrypted-threats-iot-malware-surge-past-2018-levels-report.

21. https://hackernoon.com/how-to-secure-healthcare-facilities-against-iot-security-threats-ab28dd284cac.
    Security Challenges and Approaches in Internet of Things by Salman Hashmi.

22. Potluri, S., Mangla, M., Satpathy, S., & Mohanty, S. N. (2020, July). Detection and Prevention Mechanisms for DDoS Attack in Cloud Computing Environment, 11th International Conference on Computing, Communication and Networking Technologies (ICCCNT) (pp. 1-6). IEEE.

CHAPTER 18

Latest Techniques Used to Detect the Botnet

KOMAL SAXENA* and AJAY

Amity Institute of Information Technology, Amity University, Noida, India

Corresponding author. E-mail: ksaxena1@amity.edu

ABSTRACT

Botnets originated in times of networking and growth of the Internet. The global threat bot in 2000 was the precursor to modern botnets. Internet currently is not just about browsing, communications, and applications but it is also about Internet of Things. This research Paper is precisely more focused on latest trends and security mechanisms to be used to prevent and detection of botnet.

18.1 INTRODUCTION

A botnet or "bot," as it is known, is a network of computers that have been hacked remotely by an unknown person or organization with malicious code that carries out predetermined and automated robotic functions. Individual systems may have individual bots that are remotely controlled and the remote operator can then use the network to carry out functions like Zues, DoS, Waledac, Conflickers, Mariposa, and click frauds [8]. Botnets can cost organizations millions in losses besides harm to their reputation [1]. The botnet is defined as a group of computer systems that are taken over by hackers who then use the network to carry out a variety of activities such as initiation DOS attacks, hacking host systems for data, and phishing activities (Figure 18.1).

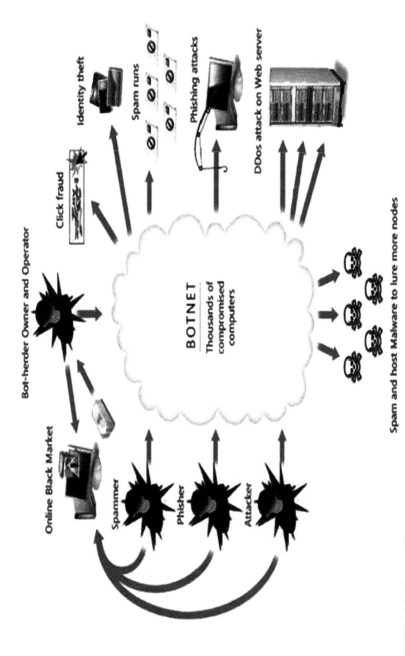

FIGURE 18.1 Botnet [9].

18.1.1 WORKING MODEL OF BOTNET

Botnets kept evolving over time ranging from when it was based on mIRC clients that enabled the running of custom scripts and access to user datagram protocol and transmission control protocol sockets. Fast forward to current times when the biggest attack was launched by reaper that affected the 1 million systems and organizations. Reaper affected Internet of Things (IoT) devices like cameras, servers, and networked attached storage. This calls for higher than normal security measures to detect attempts by botnet servers to take over control and to put in place systems for the prevention of such situations where systems become compromised thereby affecting a business organization (Figure 18.2).

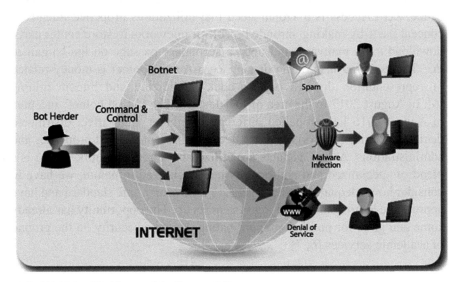

FIGURE 18.2   Working model of botnet [10].

18.2 LITERATURE REVIEW

Botnets originated in the times of Internet Relay Chat (IRC). A victim machine would connect to the IRC channel and malware would creep into the system. This started as far back as 1999 and gave rise to the global threat bot in 2000 based on mIRC client. In 2002, new bots emerged such as SDBot and Agobot. SDBot was based on C++ with the source code made available leading to the emergence of bot variants. Agobot delivered payloads sequentially during the attack from a back door. The year 2003 saw the rise of Spybot that had new functions like keylogging and data mining. Rbot handled SOCKS proxy and information stealing. Because most system ports did not open IRC and had better firewalls, bots moved away to use HTTP, ICMP, and SSL port protocols as well as peer-to-peer (P2P) networks. P2P is increasingly favored by bot master due to inherent difficulty in locating, monitoring, and shutting down such networks. Bagle and Bobax followed in 2004. ZeuS and RuStock arrived on the scene in 2006, and Zeus became a tool for stealing data. Stom botnet, Srizbi, and Cutwail made the scene in 2007 followed by Asprox and thousands of variants. Strict action against botnets led to their evolution with botnet developers adopting new techniques. Conflicted, for instance, could generate 50,000 alternative names each day. In 2013, Symantec is the biggest known botnet that uses a shared (P2P) component for correspondence. Zero Access is a Trojan steed that utilizations propelled intends to conceal itself by making shrouded record frameworks to store center parts, download extra malware, and open a secondary passage on the bargained PC. The essential inspiration driving Zero-Access botnet is money-related misrepresentation through pay-per-click publicizing and bitcoin mining [6]. In August 2017 in the area of IoT devices. The "Mirai botnet" incepted in August 2016 has propelled different prominent, high-affect distributed denial-of-service (DDoS) assaults affecting different Internet properties and administrations. As IoT gadgets are utilized by a general public which is a blend of specialized and additionally nonspecialized in nature, we have to consider how adequately IoT gadgets are following a safe standard and have appropriate logging and checking system set up. The opportunity has already come and gone for pondering coordinating the cybersecurity on the ground of academic services [6, 7].

18.2.1 LIFE CYCLE OF BOTNET

In general, the characteristic of the botnet is that it gives complete anonymity by using multitier command and control architecture and the bot master may be located in one country with a botnet in another country, making it difficult to track him.

Botnets have a lifecycle covering a stage1 initial infection followed by second stage secondary injection, Stage 3 connection, command, and control cycle stage 4 Malicious Activities and then final stage is to taking upgrading, prevention, maintenance, the last of which involves techniques like a migration of servers [2, 5].

In recent times, the Reaper botnet affected 1 million organizations. Mirai, before that, mostly target smaller systems such as those of homeowners. Reaper and its likes pose a greater threat since they now exploit IoT devices and can prove far more disruptive. The need for security has been increasing and so have been efforts aimed at detecting and eliminating botnets before they can inflict damage [3, 4] (Figure 18.3).

1. Prevention stage
2. Maintenance
3. Prevention

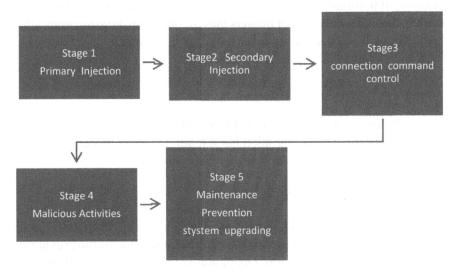

FIGURE 18.3   Life cycle of botnet.

18.2.2   DETECTION OF BOTNET

The risks are high due to botnet infection and detection is important. Over time efforts were made to detect and track botnets, which is an ongoing activity as bot masters evolve code and methods. The Honeynet is one of the earlier projects covering the study of the problem and setting up honeynets. The problem with honeynet is that it gives an understanding of botnet technology but may not detect infection. Some may make use of passive traffic monitoring and exploration to detect the existence of botnets. The techniques are signature-based detection, mining-based detection, DNS-based detection, and anomaly-based detection to be used to detect the botnet [22].

18.2.3   APPROACHES TO DETECT THE BOTNET

All these techniques have some weakness or the other. For instance, one method is to identify higher than usual activities of DDNS query but bot masters can easily evade this by using fake DNS queries. A more sophisticated approach is attributed to Van Helmond and Schonewille. It relied on higher than usual NXDOMAIN reply rates and hosts that repeatedly issue queries as being likely to be bot infected. This has a better chance of success since it refers to DDNS and enables DNSBL reconnaissance activity. Heuristics are involved to distinguish legitimate traffic from bot traffic and it gives early warning of bot-masters performing reconnaissance. The chance of success is high in detecting bots but bot masters may go one up by implementing countermeasures like reconnaissance poisoning or distributed reconnaissance.

18.2.4   ANOMALY APPROACH

Anomaly-based approach monitors DNS traffic, a method that is robust and helps detect C&C server migration but it required longer processing time.

18.2.5   MINING APPROACH

The mining-based approach is used in identifying C&C traffic but has not proved to be as effective as expected. This is because C&C traffic uses normal protocols leading to confusion. Goebl and Holz did propose Rishi in 2007 for monitoring of passive traffic but bot masters moved away from IRC, rendering this method ineffective. It is the same with machine learning techniques suggested by Strayer in 2008. Masud's approach is based on mining log files to detect C&C traffic independent of protocols and it is somewhat more effective. Bot miner approach based on data mining to detect traffic is an advancement on Bot sniffer with the ability to correlate clusters and capacity to work independently of protocols used by botnets (Figure 18.4).

A comparison shows that various methods and approaches were conceived and also implemented, they had some shortcoming or the other with the result that bot-masters, who kept one step ahead in technology, were able to and are still carrying on their activities. Two methods are employed. One is fast flux in which a set of IP addresses keep changing all the time. The second is domain flux in which a set of domain names are automatically generated to correspond with a unique IP address. These two techniques make it difficult to detect, trace, and identify the source [22].

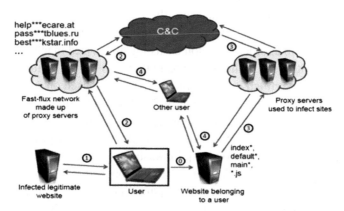

FIGURE 18.4   Approaches to detect the botnet [11].

18.2.6   STATIC ANALYSES AND BEHAVIORAL ANALYSIS TO DETECT THE BOTNET

There are two types of analysis: (1) static analysis and (2) behavioral analysis.

The first analysis is elementary, profligate, and resource approachable and the other behavioral analyses are not only more systematic but also more comprehensive [12, 13]

18.2.7   TECHNIQUES USED TO DETECT THE BOTNET

Techniques were developed such as the botnet fast flux detection technique claimed to be first developed by Holz that is based on three parameters such as IP domain mapping in DNS lookup, name server records in a single domain, and autonomous system in IP domain pairs [12]. There are others too such as Zhou who came up with the application of behavior analysis model [13], Caglayan who developed a real-time detection mold of fast flux service [14], and Perdisci who came up with a recursive DNS tracing methodology [15]. Yu went further in defining key metrics to distinguish between fast fluxing attack networks and benign fast fluxing service network so as to identify which one is malicious. This technique is also included the average online rate. The system comprised of a dig tool to garner information of new

IPs added to databases, robot agents to monitor HTTP requests, IP lifespan, and detector for FFAN and FFSN by IP lifespan [16].

Domain flux detection techniques had its pioneers such as Stone-Gross and others who tried reverse engineering, the domain generation algorithm and setting up an Apache web serve to log bot requests and record traffic [17]. Ma and others went in another direction by using supervised machine learning to detect and identify the malicious website that was rooted in automated URL classification and refined it further in 2009. They focused on suspicious URL identification [18]. Jiang and others, in 2010, thought an anomaly detection method using DNS failure graphs that captured the interaction between hosts and irresolvable domain names. All such approaches were primarily focused on identification and detection [19]. Prakash developed a PhishNet to protect systems from phishing attacks. PhishNet is supposed to detect automatically generated domain names in bot sent to spam. Such names are then blacklisted for future blocking. Even here, there are issues such as URLs not matching, for which a complex algorithm was developed to match a new URL against an existing URL in the blacklist. It used semantic and syntactic variations while keying into IP address, hostname, directory structure, and other parameters all of which were evaluated [20]. Yadav and others explored the possibility of using alphanumeric bigrams and unigrams to identify such algorithm-generated domains. This led to the implementation of a model that grouped DNS into top-level domains and IP addresses to which they were mapped. This was followed by examining the distribution of alphanumeric characters [21].

Recent methods like fast flux and domain flux detection have proved to be more effective but each has its strengths and drawbacks. However, the core of the matter of cybersecurity as regards botnets, which is to completely prevent such activity and trace the source, is still a work in progress thing. Due to the complexity of the bots network and difficulty in accessing such compromised systems and convincing owners to cooperate as well as the evolution of techniques by bot masters, security against bot attacks may not be as rock-solid and impenetrable as one expects. Witness the recent attack by Reaper. That botnets have evolved into not just attacking computer systems, launching DoS, and capturing data but also into targeting IoT is a matter of grave concern. Just how advanced, it can be seen from the fact that Reaper makes use of LUA, an embedded systems programming language. If IoT devices become the targets, the future implications are frightening. In many cases, IoT devices also gather data and one can infer what bots can do with such data.

18.3   USED TOOLS TO BE DETECT THE BOTNET AND ALSO PREDICT THE FUTURE OF BOTNET

Now the botnets have developed, and the tools have been used to spill on and eliminate them. Nowadays, we are more focused on open-source applications, which are similarly to Snort and extra complete, incorporated safety intelligence offerings from providers like AlienVault [23].

1. Define once the network is unfamiliar in predefined methods.
2. Classify it network source.
3. Investigate its nature and influence.
4. Directly isolation, limits, or remove local bots.
5. They provide a very fast and smart solution. There are three methods to resolve it.
6. TechCentric.
7. HumanCentric.
8. Combination of both methods.

18.3.1   THE OTHER TOOL WHICH WE CAN USE TO DETECT THE BOTNET IS DISTIL NETWORKS

Distil Networks is the only preemptive solution for moderating malicious bot movement or a traffic—blocking malicious website traffic (attacks after botnets) before it ever gets an opportunity to arrive at your application [26].

18.4   CHARACTERISTICS OF BOTNET

Most of the botnets at present feature DDos attacks in which different frameworks submit whatever number demands as could reasonably be expected to a single Internet PC or administration, overloading it, and keeping it from adjusting authentic request. A model remains an attack on a target server. The target server is shelled with demands through the bots, endeavoring to interface with the server, in this way, it is overloading.

Spyware is a type of software which refers data to its initiators about a user's actions—typically passwords, debit card, smart card numbers, credit card numbers, or any other digital card and further data that can be retailed on the black market. Machines that are placed inside a corporate network can be valued furthermore toward the bot herder, in place of they can frequently gain access to familiar organization data. Several targeted attacks on huge organizations targeted to steal important information, for example, Aurora Botnet [27].

18.4.1   E-MAIL SPAM

E-mail messages are imperceptible messages from individuals, yet they are promoting, infuriating, or malicious

18.4.2   CLICK FRAUD

The consumer's PC visit or click website without the knowledge of the user's to make fake traffic on the web for individual or for making a profit in the business [28].

18.4.3   BITCOIN MINING

Nowadays, it is using as the latest botnet for gaining more profit in the business [29, 30].

18.4.4   SELF-SPREADING

This is usefulness to look for predesigned command and control (CNC) strapped instructions comprises and focused on victim or network or devices, to go for more infection, and is likewise seen in a few botnets.

18.5   ARCHITECTURE OF BOTNET

Botnet architecture has advanced through the years with a view to avoid detection and disruption. Traditionally, bot packages are built as users which communicate through extant servers. This permits the bot herder (the individual monitoring the botnet) to carry out all manipulation from a far remote place, which obfuscates their website visitors [6]. Many latest botnets now depend on present P2P networks to chat. These P2P bot packages carry out equal actions as the client–server, they cannot communicate to the server for so long.

Botnet supported the following architecture:

1. Client–server model.
2. Peer–peer model.

The first methodology uses a naive back-and-forth algorithm to search for botnets (Figure 18.5).

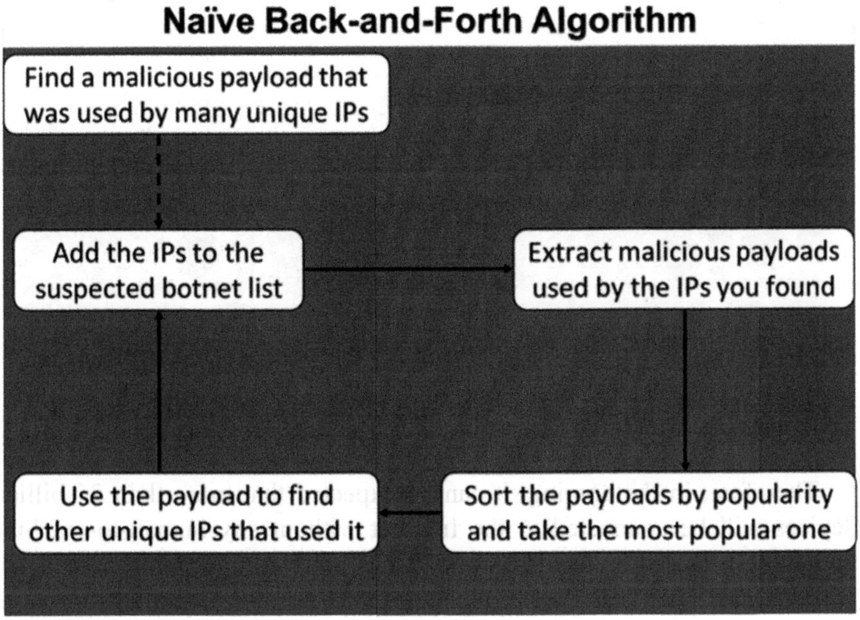

Naïve Back-and-Forth Algorithm

```
Find a malicious payload that
was used by many unique IPs

Add the IPs to the                    Extract malicious payloads
suspected botnet list                 used by the IPs you found

Use the payload to find               Sort the payloads by popularity
other unique IPs that used it         and take the most popular one
```

FIGURE 18.5 Naive back-and-forth algorithm [33].

The other methodology is used to detect the botnet, it is a client-classification facility to cluster clients that supported out various synchronized attacks (Figure 18.6).

18.6 IOT AND BOTNET

The IoT is commonly used in every part of life. In other words, it can be said to be a system in which different devices are interrelated. It involves digital machines, objects, mechanical devices, and people who have unique identifiers and the like. Through the interconnection, it makes possible, the easy transfer of data. Even from toys to watches, everything is connected online that is changing the way of data transmission.

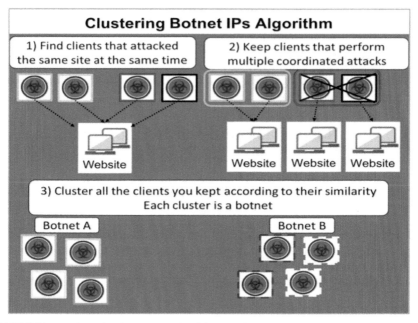

FIGURE 18.6   Clustering botnet IP's algorithms [33].

Therefore, in the coming, it can be expected that more than 25 billion devices will be connected to the Internet without any human-to-machine interaction. This rise in the number of connected devices that call for better security and top-notch connection measures as it becomes prone to cybercriminal attacks. For this, it is important to check the devices that are interconnected. As more data will be transmitted, it is required to steal the data and protect the system.

18.6.1   INCREASED PROBLEMS OF MALWARE ATTACKS

There have been increased malware attack problems in the past few years and has been the spread of mailing worms that more dangerous than the macro viruses and file infectors. By 2000, the use of the Internet has been increased, and it became easy for cybercriminals to plan for frequent attacks. This is when the use of botnets came into being. Therefore, it can be said that the influence of IoT will bring another change in the form of dealing with problems of thingbots.

Therefore, thingbots are botnets that are composed of IoT devices that are infected. The cybercriminals can use the device to attack machines, steal confidential data, and carry out other malicious activities on systems. These have increased in the last few years and enterprises are trying to use top-notch security measures to safeguard confidential data that are prone to cyber-attacks.

18.6.2   DISADVANTAGES OF THINGBOTS

As thingbots are commonly present everywhere, they easily get connected with an Internet connection, wireless routers connections including modems. In addition, the other targeted devices are network cameras, network storage systems, and the like. However, most of the devices run on Linux operating system in which attackers make use of Linux malware. Through this, it becomes easy to specify the architecture in which it wishes to attack.

It was very simple and easy for cybercriminals to attack the devices that could be accessed by Telnet default login details. As the devices were prone to attacks, there were infections in them. However, DDoS attacks are called to be the crucial use for the devices that are infected [78]. However, it can be expected that the impacts of IoT malware are going to increase in the coming years. The most important part is to find out protective measures from the easy malware attacks. Also, the actual potential of thingbots is yet to be revealed in the near future.

18.7   EFFECTS OF CYBERCRIMINALS ON BOTNET

The botnet is effective for use by cybercriminals as it enables them to execute the instruction on the devices easily. The botnet is run by commands that are created and sent by the cybercriminals.

The botnet can be collectively called a number of connected devices that are made by infected malware and it is operated on the same network. These days most companies are using a botnet. The origin of the word takes place by combining robot and network in which the robot is infected by some effective malware and then it is made a part of the network within which different devices are connected.

18.8 CORE COMPONENTS OF BOTNET

The originator of the botnet is called a "bot master" which can control the device remotely. This mechanism is called command and control. The operating program that is used to communicate with different devices via a covert channel with the victim's machine helps in making the task an easy one.

18.9 CONTROL PROTOCOLS OF BOTNET

For better communication protocols, the bot master creates an IRC channel that lets the infected clients join the communication network. The message that is sent to the network or channel will be shared with all its fellows. Here, the bot master can set the channel's subject to command the botnet to contaminate or infect the dissimilar devices. For instance, when bot master or bot herder receives the message—"herder!herder@example.com TOPIC #channel DDoS www.victim.com," it alerts the clients of the channels to get ready for the DDoS attack on the victim's website. As a response to this, the bot herder responses that it has begun with the cyber-attack as commanded.

In some botnets, customized versions of protocols are used that helps in better results. For instance, the advanced feature of botnets can help in better testing of spam capability of the device. Even, botnets are often installed with top-notch SMTP server for better functioning of the device.

18.10 FUNCTION OF THE ZOMBIE COMPUTER

This above-mentioned zombie computer (ZC) term is referred to as a computer that is linked with the Internet. This system can be used by hackers and different malicious activities can be performed in one direction on this system. In this regard, botnets of zombie PCs are to be used to spread spam e-mail to different recipients and start with the DOS attack. The user of ZCs is not aware of such usages of the computers and due to this, it is often called ZCs. A well-coordinated DDoS attack can be conducted on the botnet machines that also resemble a zombie attack on the devices. This way, computers are not always aware that the computer system is infected with bots. Therefore, this method of stealing system's resources and also connected the system with a botnet is referred to as "scrumping" [34, 35].

This table clarifies different kinds of botnets and the reason behind infusing those into a network system. The general reason behind such an attack is eventually, to upset PC frameworks or to take the information (Table 18.1).

TABLE 18.1 Types of Botnet with purpose

Type of Botnet	Persistence
DoSBot	DoS and Distributed DoS attack using Layer 3 to 7 protocols
SpamBot	Email spamming by collecting address books
BrowseBot	Gather user's browsing trends and feed into advertisement network
AdSenseBot	Same as BrowseBot but targeted to Google adsense
ChatBot	Collect chat transcripts to find user's chatting trends
idBot	Collect userid and password information
CCBot	Collect credit card information from e-commerce portal screens
PollBot	Manipulate online polls meant for products and services

18.11 CREATION OF BOTNETTO USED FOR MALICIOUS GAIN

The illustration is given below:

1. A hacker can build Trojan along with an exploit kit and by this hacker starts to infect the user's computer that has the malicious application of bot.
2. This way, the bot will instruct the user's computer to connect with the command and control system and get easy access to online credentials.
3. Following this, the bot master will get the keystrokes by using bots that shall further help in stealing the online login details. It may also sell the online credentials online making a profit from it.
4. The value of the bot will depend on its potentiality and quality.

However, the new bots have the potential to easily scan the environment in which it is used and easily gets spread using weak passwords. If the bot is able to scan more vulnerability and spread through it, the botnet controller system considers the bot to be more valuable.

If computers have malicious software, it can be used as a botnet. This can be done if users exploit the vulnerabilities of a web browser. In addition, the user can also be tricked into running a Trojan horse program that has originated from when the attachment of e-mail is opened. By running the attachment, it will install modules on the system, it becomes easy to get control of the computer system by botnet's user (person who operates the botnet). After the required application (software) has been copied on the computer, a reconnection packet will be sent to the host computer. It depends on the operator in what way they have written the command. Depending on this, the Trojan can either delete it or remain present on the system. Botnet is made by helper hacktivists such as enactments of Low Orbit Ion Cannon while creating the project [36].

18.12 SRIZBI BOTNET

The Srizbi botnet is arguably one of the largest botnets that send obtainable furthermost of the spam which is sent by major botnets that are shared together. The botnet devices involve computers that are affected by Srizbi Trojan wherever the spam mail has sent on command. During 2008, Srizbi suffered massive obstruction at the time of Janka Cartel. As a result of this, the global spam rate reduced to 93%.

18.12.1 SIZE OF SRIZBI BOTNET

The estimated size of the botnet is around 450,000 [38] that conceded of apparatuses with variances less than 5% from different sources [37, 40]. The botnet can send near about 60 trillion threats in a single day that is estimated to be more than half of the total of 100 trillion Janka threats that are sent daily. Thus, it can be concluded that the famous Storm botnet is able to send only 20% of the spam that is sent during the peak phase [39, 41].

Srizbi botnet shows a decline in the growth of number of spam that it can send during the middle of 2008. As of July 13, 2008, it was believed that botnet was able to send almost 40% of spam through the net. There has been a decline of almost 60% during May [42] in 2008.

18.12.2 ORIGINS OF SRIZBI BOTNET

In near about 2007, this botnet is very much famous in the reports with differences in detection dates from different dealers [43, 44]. Depending on the reports, it can be said that the first version was assembled in 2007 [45].

The above-said botnet is also considered the largest botnet on the Internet. Though, there are some controversies about the largest botnet with Kraken botnet [46–49].

18.12.3   DETAILS OF BOTNET COMPOSITION

The Srizbi botnet is made from computers infected by Srizbi Trojan horse. The Trojan horse is used on the victim computer through the use of Mpack malware kit [50]. However, the "n404 web exploit kit" malware kit has been used to spread the malware in victim's computer. But the use of "n404 web exploit kit" is preferred against the use of Mpack kit. [51]

The malware kits are distributed by the use of a botnet. The botnet is known to send spam that contains the links of fake videos of celebrities. In addition, it also includes a link indicating the malware kit. Such spams are also sent in case of other subjects like illegal software sales and personal messages. [52–54]. Other than this, the MPack kit has better potentiality in spreading spam among different websites as reported in June 2007 [55]. Pornographic websites are found in this domain, Gregg [56] forwards unsuspecting visitor website links that have the MPack program.

If a computer gets infected by Trojan horse malware, the system becomes a zombie. It is called so as it will be used for creating commands and executing them by botnet controller that is commonly referred to as botnet herder [57]. The Srizbi botnet is operated by a number of servers that control the use of individual bots in the whole network of a botnet. These servers are made identical to each other that helps in protecting the botnet from being destroyed when a fails functioning the server is taken down as a result of legal action by higher authorities.

18.12.4   REACTOR MAILER

The "Reactor Mailer" is a program that handles server operation of Srizbi botnet. Further, this program is Python-based which helps in better coordination of the spam sent to the separate bots into the botnet network. The program mentioned above has come into since 2004, and it is the third release that will control the Srizbi botnet. Even the application (software) is to be used for more *security We need to do secure* login [clarification needed] and allows easy access to numerous accounts simultaneously. Further, it can be said that Srizbi botnet is able to run concurrent batches of a spam run by IP addresses at the same time. If a user has access to a botnet, they can use the software to forming a message and send it. Following this, they can also opt for testing the message created for SpamAssassin score. After this, it will be sent to users from the list of e-mail addresses.

Further, it is often suspected that the same person has created the reactor mailer program and the Srizbi Trojan program, as the code fingerprint of the two programs is close enough. In case, this proves to be true, then the coder will help in setting the program for another botnet called Rustock. A similar situation cropped up that is based on Symantec is called the code in Srizbi Trojan is similar to the one in Rustock Trojan. In addition, it can be expected to be a radical version of the afterward [58].

ST is a program that sends spam messages from infected machines. Trojan is considered as extremely efficient in infecting machines. This is why it explains why this Trojan can send such huge volumes of spam irrespective of the number of infected machines.

Other than an effective spam engine, Trojan can hide itself from both users and within the system itself. It includes the Trojan being detected by antivirus programs installed on the system. The program is executed on the system in kernel mode. This mode uses rootkit technologies so that it does not fall into the trap of any detection [59]. By getting connected with NTFS system driver files, the Trojan program will make files invisible in the system. Therefore, the human user can easily detect the infected Trojan program present in the system. The program can also hide network traffic by attaching with NDIS and TCP drivers. However, this process helps the infected Trojan bypass any virus detection program that is located on the system [58].

As the bot is perfectly operational, it will get in touch with the hardcoded servers from the given list. The server is responsible to provide the bot along with a zip file that has a number of archives required intended for the spamming business.

18.13   STORM BOTNET

The other name of Storm botnet is Dorf botnet and Ecard malware [63] that is an automated controlled network by the zombie PC that is connected with Storm Worm. The Trojan horse is used to send spam through e-mail. In 2007, it is very familiar with the name of the Storm botnet and it was used universally from (1–50 million) computer systems [59, 60]. This accounted for nearly 8% of malware used on different Microsoft Windows computers

[61]. In 2007, its first identification, which was used to be spread through e-mail with subjects like "230 dead as storm batters Europe," was created by changed name. The use of botnet declined during late 2007 but again from mid-2008, it is known to infect almost 85,000 computers. This number is less than that it had infected earlier [77].

As a result of this, by December 2012, there has been an attempt to find the originators of the storm. However, this botnet has shown defensive actions indicating that controllers are active in defending the botnet for any operations like tracking. The controllers were also careful about disabling the botnet from being attacked by security software and researchers who tried to investigate it [63]. Based on expert comments in 2007, it is known that the operators of botnet started to handle operations better; therefore, it became difficult to sell off portions of the Storm botnet to others. Botnet was known to be more powerful compared to others as it was able to execute spam commands better within 1 s compared to the world's top supercomputers [64]. Therefore, the United States Federal Bureau of inspection thinks that botnet can pose a high hazard for other cybercrimes like bank scam, identity stealing, burglary, theft, and other activities [65, 66].

18.13.1   ORIGIN OF STORM BOTNET

In 2007, the inception on Internet, the Storm botnet, and worm named so because of the storm are to be found the main source to spread the infecting e-mail. Other sources said that the primary way of getting the victim was through alluring users by changing social engineering schemes [66]. As per Patrick Runald, Storm botnet had close connections with agents working to support the USA [67]. But others have the opinion that Storm botnet controllers were of Russian origin. This further pointed toward Russian Business Network and the dislike of storm software. the other name of this word is a bulldog in Russian [68].

18.13.2   COMPOSITION OF STORM BOTNET

The botnet consists of computers running on the Windows operating system [69]. After the compute is infected, it is known as a bot that is capable of functioning automated tasks. It varies from data collection to attacking user's websites and infecting e-mail without letting its owner know about the possible infection. As per estimates, about 5000–6000 computers help in the spread of the worm via e-mails in the form of infected attachments. In addition, 18.2 billion virus messages were sent by botnet in September 2007. However, this virus message counts to 57 million on August 22, 2007, alone [70]. In this relation, computer forensic Lawrence Baldwin commented that storm has been sending billions of messages in a single day. The number of messages can double up in billions, easily [59]. One of the ways to allure victims to access the infected websites is to offer free music for artists like Beyoncé Knowles, Foo Fighters, R. Kelly, Kelly Clarkson, Rihanna, The Eagles, and Velvet Revolver [70]. To protect botnet from signature-based detection, the defense software in the computer systems are infected by storm variants. [71]

The servers controlling the spread of Storm botnet can re-encode distributed infection software twice an hour. It enables new transmissions as a result of which the antivirus detection software cannot prevent virus spread in the system. The location of remote servers that controls the botnet also cannot be identified as it is frequently changing DNS technique that is known as fast flux, stopping the virus hosting sites, and other servers from functioning.

In other words, as the name and geographical location of the machines have been transformed rapidly, it becomes hard to detect the actual location or server used for Storm botnet. There is no such "command and control" point that can be shut down. [76]. Moreover, the botnet uses encrypted traffic [74]. However, for infecting other computers, it only requires convincing users to download some unknown e-mail attachments that contain the virus. In this instance, the National Football league's opening took advantage of the event and send out e-mails offering the tracking programs of the game. This was one of the ways to infect user's computer [75, 78] as soon as they wish to get access to the football tracking program through their system.

As per the statement of Matt Sergeant which is the chief antispam technologist at MessageLabs said that botnet utterly blows away even the supercomputers and infects it instantly. Due to this, it can be said that the situation is becoming frightening as the criminals are able to get easy access to the computer system despite protection. But there's little to almost no ways that users can do about it [72]. Despite all these, only 10%–20% Storm botnet is currently being used in the current scenario [73].

The seven biggest attacks of the 21st century are in Table 18.2 [77].

Botnets have been a constant threat to the IT infrastructure of the IT industry, and dealing with them requires a hostile, assertive, and skilled cybersecurity approach. It is to be pro in combating botnet attacks and other similar cybersecurity attacks, for that you should be a Certified Ethical Hacker (C|EH).

TABLE 18.2 Biggest botnet Attack

Name of botnet	Year	Functionality
EarthLink Spammer	2000	It is a first botnet which is recognized in 2000on public Website. The large no of phishing mails to be spread all over.
Cutwail	2007	It is used to send malicious Email on operating system like Windows
Grum	2008	This botnet was found in 2008 as enormous pharmaceutical spammer
Kraken	2008	This bot net target the infrastructure of fortune Industries or companies. Its is a peer to peer technique they spread more than 50 million messages each day.
Mariposa	2008	This botnet affect the pc in more than 200 countries The various methods, are as given below:- 1. Instant messages, 2. Credit Card Fraud 3. File sharing, 4. Hard disc devices etc.
Methbot	2016	It is the biggest bot ever digital ad malware that acquired thousands of IP addresses with US-based ISPs. And later on the send videos and advertisement more than a million each day.
3ve	2018	It is created by fake traffic as a bot on net. Most of the companies were infected by this the main aim of this botnet is to make money and earn money,

18.14 CONCLUSION

Currently, top-level antivirus companies are working on bot security and offer products that monitor ports on various network protocols to detect threats and attacks so users can take preemptive action for security. It is an ongoing process because security is not restricted in one place. In this, we also discussed the architecture of botnet, tools to use to detect and prevent the botnet. Furthermore, we also investigate some biggest attacks, their nature, origin, components to use, and to create the botnet and give more emphasis on tools to be used to detect the botnet and last not least the biggest famous botnet the year of origin and their nature. We cover all the aspects of botnet, thingbot IoT, etc.

KEYWORDS

- **botnet**
- **IRC**
- **PhishNet**
- **IoT**
- **honeypot**
- **global threat bot**
- **network**

REFERENCES

1. index-of.es/Denial-of-service/Botnet/BotnetDetection%20Countering%20the Largest Security Threat.pdf.
2. file:///C:/Users/0735/Downloads/Botnet_Evolution_Infographic%20(1).pdf.
3. engineering.purdue.edu/kak/compsec/ NewLectures/ Lecture29.pdf.
4. [Alparslan, E., Karahoca, A., Karahoca, D., "BotNet detection: enhancing analysis by using data mining techniques". https://www.researchgate.net/publication/265109518_ BotNet_Detection_Enhancing_Analysis_by_Using_Data_Mining_Techniques
5. Symantec.com/avcenter/reference/ the.evolution.of.malicious.irc.bots.pdf.
6. Snedaker, S., and McCrie, R., "The best damn IT security management book period". https://www.zdnet.com/article/what-is-the-internet-of-things-everything-you-need-to-know-about-the-iot-right-now/
7. Syngress, "Botnets, the killer web app". https://doc.lagout.org/security/Botnets%20 -%20The%20killer%20web%20applications.pdf
8. www.kaspersky.com/blog/botnet/1742/.
9. digitalcaffeinegroup.com/wp-content/uploads/2015/03/botnet.jpg.
10. s3.amazonaws.com/fedscoopwp-media/wp-content/uploads/2015/01/23154522/2014 _10_Screen-Shot-2014-10-22-at-4.34.19-PM.png.
11. media.kasperskycontenthub.com/wp-content/uploads/sites/43/2010/12/08124838/ How-the-Bredolab-botnet-was-created.png.
12. alienvault.com/blogs/security-essentials/botnet-detection-and-removal-methods-.
13. information-age. /how-detect-and-remove-botnets-your-network-.
14. Holz, T., Gorecki, C., Rieck, K., and Freiling, F. C., "Measuring and detecting fast-flux service networks", in Proceedings of the Network and Distributed System Security Symposium, San Diego, CA, 2008.

15. Zhou, C. V., Leckie, C., and Karunasekera, S., "Collaborative detection of fast flux phishing domains", Journal of Networks, 4(1), 75–84, 2009.

16. Caglayan, A., Toothaker, M., Drapeau, D., Burke, D., and Eaton, G., "Real-time detection of fast flux service networks", in 2009 Cybersecurity Applications & Technology Conference for Homeland Security, 285–292, 2009.

17. Perdisci, R., Corona, I., Dagon, D., and Lee, W., "Detecting malicious flux service networks through passive analysis of recursive DNS traces", in 2009 Annual Computer Security Applications Conference, 311–320, 2009.

18. Zhou, Y. S., and Wang, S., "Fast-flux attack network identification based on agent lifespan", in 2010 IEEE International Conference on Wireless Communications, Networking and Information Security, 658–662, 2010.

19. Stone-Gross, B., Cova, M., Cavallaro, L., Gilbert, B., Szydlowski, M., Kemmerer, R. A., Kruegel, C., and Vigna, G., "Your botnet is my botnet:analysis of a botnet takeover", in ACM Conference on Computer and Communications Security, 635–647, 2009.

20. Ma, J., Saul, L. K., Savage, S., and Voelker, G. M., "Beyond blacklists: learning to detect malicious web' sites from suspicious URLs", in Proceedings of the 15th ACM SIGKDD International Conference on Knowledge Discovery and Data Mining, 1245–1254, 2009.

21. Jiang, N., Cao, J., Jin, Y., Li, L., and Zhang, Z.-L. "Identifying suspicious activities through DNS failure graph analysis", in The 18th IEEE International Conference on Network Protocols, 144–153, 2010.

22. Kumar, P. M., Kompella, R., and Gupta, M., "PhishNet: predictive blacklisting to detect phishing attacks", in 2010 Proceedings IEEE INFOCOM, 1–5, 2010.

23. Yadav, S., Reddy, A. K. K., Reddy, A. N., and Ranjan, S., "Detecting algorithmically generated malicious domain names", in Proceedings of the 10th Annual Conference on Internet Measurement, 48–618, 2010.

24. Zhang, L., Yu, S., Wu, D., and Watters, P. "A survey on latest botnet attack and defense" in 2011IEEE 10th International Conference on Trust, Security and Privacy in Computing and Communications, Changsha, 2011.

25. alienvault.com/blogs/security-essentials/botnet-detection-and-removal-methods-best-practices.

26. distilnetworks.com/glossary/term/botnet-detection/.

27. "Operation Aurora—the command structure", Damballa.com. Archived from the original on June 11, 2010. Retrieved July 30, 2010.

28. Jim, E., "This is what it looks like when a click-fraud botnet secretly controls your web browser", November 27, 2013. Retrieved May 27, 2017.

29. Shaun, N., "Got a botnet? Thinking of using it to mine Bitcoin? Don't bother", June 24, 2014. Retrieved May 27, 2017.

30. Bitcoin Mining, "BitcoinMining.com", Archived from the original on April 30, 2016. Retrieved April 30, 2016.

31. Craig, A. S., Jim, B., David, H., Gadi, E., Tony, B., Carsten, W., and Michael, C., "Botnets Overview", pp. 29–75, Burlington: Syngress, January 1, 2007.

32. Simon, H., "Botnet command and control techniques", Network Security, 2007(4): 13–16, April 1, 2007. doi:10.1016/S1353-4858(07)70045-4.

33. https://www.imperva.com/ the-challenges-of-diy-botnet-detection-and-how-to-overcome-them/.

34. Troj/RKAgen-A Trojan (Rootkit.Win32.Agent.ea, Trojan.Srizbi)—Sophos security analysis. Sophos. 2007. Retrieved July 20, 2008.

35. Joe, S., "Inside the 'Ron Paul' Spam Botnet", Secureworks.com. SecureWorks. Retrieved March 9, 2016.
36. Gregg, K., "Porn sites serve up Mpack attacks", ComputerWorld. June 22, 2007. Archived from the original on May 16, 2008. Retrieved July 20, 2008.
37. Eduard, K., "Cybercriminals attempt to revive Srizbi spam botnet", SecurityWeek. August 28, 2014. Retrieved January 5, 2016.
38. "Spam on rise after brief reprieve", BBC News. November 26, 2008. Retrieved May 23, 2010.
39. Darren, P., "Srizbi botnet sets new records for spam", PC World. May 8, 2008. Retrieved July 20, 2008.
40. Bogdan, P., "Meet Srizbi, the largest botnet ever", Softpedia. April 10, 2008.
41. Kelly, J. H., "Srizbi botnet sending over 60 billion spams a day", Dark Reading. May 8, 2008. Retrieved July 20, 2008.
42. John, E. D., "Srizbi grows into world's largest botnet", CSO Online. May 13, 2008. Retrieved July 20, 2008.
43. "Spam statistics from TRACE", Marshall. July 13, 2008. Retrieved July 20, 2008.
44. "Trojan.Srizbi", Symantec. July 23, 2007. Retrieved July 20, 2008.
45. "Troj/RKAgen–A Trojan (Rootkit.Win32.Agent.ea, Trojan.Srizbi)—Sophos security analysis", Sophos. August 2007. Retrieved July 20, 2008.
46. Joe, S., "Inside the 'Ron Paul' Spam Botnet", Secureworks.com. SecureWorks. Retrieved March 9, 2016.
47. Jackson, H. K., "New massive botnet twice the size of storm", darkreading.com. London: UBM plc. April 7, 2008. Retrieved January 9, 2014.
48. Jackson, H. K., "Srizbi botnet sending over 60 billion spams a day", darkreading.com. London: UBM plc. May 8, 2008. Retrieved January 9, 2014.
49. "Internet reputation system", TrustedSource. September 17, 2013. Retrieved January 9, 2014.
50. "Kraken, Not New But Still Newsworthy?", F-Secure Weblog: News from the Lab. F-secure.com. April 9, 2008. Retrieved January 9, 2014.
51. Gregg, K., "Mpack installs ultra-invisible Trojan", ComputerWorld. Archived from the original on May 22, 2008. July 5, 2007. Retrieved July 20, 2008.
52. Joe, S.. "Inside the 'Ron Paul' Spam Botnet", Secureworks.com. SecureWorks. Retrieved March 9, 2016.
53. Blog, TRACE, "Srizbi uses multi-pronged attack to spread malware", Marshal Limited. March 7, 2008. Retrieved July 20, 2008.
54. Grey, M., "Srizbi botnet is largely responsible for recent sharp increase in spam", June 25, 2008. National Cyber Security. Archived from the original on August 28, 2008. Retrieved July 20, 2008.
55. "Srizbi spam uses celebrities as lures", TRACE Blog. February 20, 2008. Retrieved July 20, 2008.
56. Gregg, K., "Hackers compromise 10k sites, launch 'phenomenal' attack", June 10, 2007. ComputerWorld. Archived from the original on May 16, 2008. Retrieved July 20, 2008.
57. Gregg, K., "Porn sites serve up Mpack attacks", June 22, 2007. ComputerWorld. Archived from the original on May 16, 2008. Retrieved July 20, 2008.
58. "Spying on bot nets becoming harder", SecurityFocus. October 12, 2006. Retrieved July 20, 2008.

59. Kevin, S. "Worm 'Storm' gathers strength", Neoseeker. September 7, 2007. Retrieved October 10, 2007.

60. "Storm worm's virulence may change tactics", British Computer Society. August 2, 2007. Archived from the original on October 12, 2007. Retrieved October 10, 2007.

61. George, D., "Storm botnet storms the net", Institute for Ethics and Emerging Technologies. September 24, 2007. Retrieved October 10, 2007.

62. Gregg, K., "Top botnets control 1M hijacked computers", Computer World. April 9, 2008. Retrieved December 24, 2012.

63. John, L., "Storm worm retaliates against security researchers", The Register. September 25, 2007. Retrieved October 25, 2007.

64. Dennis, F., "Experts predict Storm Trojan's reign to continue", October 22, 2007. Search Security. Retrieved December 26, 2007.

65. Rick, C., "FBI: 'Botnets' threaten online security", Inside Bay Area. December 18, 2007. Retrieved December 27, 2007.

66. David, U., "Storm botnet driving PDF spam", July 13, 2007. Retrieved October 10, 2007.

67. Thorsten, H., "Measurements and mitigation of peer-to-peer-based botnets: a case study on storm worm", Usenix. April 9, 2008. Retrieved April 23, 2008.

68. Ryan, S., "Report: cybercrime stormed the net in 2007", Wired News. December 7, 2007. Retrieved December 27, 2007.

69. Erik, L., "The Internet's public enemy number one", PC World. December 3, 2007. Retrieved March 18, 2010.

70. Sharon, G., "Storm worm botnet more powerful than top supercomputers", September 6, 2007. Retrieved October 10, 2007.

71. Sharon, G., "After short break, storm worm fires back up with new tricks", InformationWeek. September 4, 2007. Retrieved October 10, 2007.

72. Bruce, S., "Gathering 'Storm' superworm poses grave threat to PC nets", Wired News. October 4, 2007. Retrieved October 17, 2007.

73. Chris, S., "Storm worm the 'syphilis' of computers", The Star. October 15, 2007. Retrieved October 17, 2007.

74. "Storm DDoS hits anti-scam sites", Virus Bulletin.com. September 10, 2007. Retrieved October 17, 2007.

75. Pedro, H., "Storm worm rewrote the botnet and spam game", Enterprise IT Planet. October 4, 2007. Retrieved October 17, 2007.

76. Joe, S., "Storm worm DDoS attack", Secureworks.com. SecureWorks. Retrieved March 9, 2016.

77. https://blog.eccouncil.org/9-of-the-biggest-botnet-attacks-of-the-21st-century/.

78. Potluri, S., Mangla, M., Satpathy, S., & Mohanty, S. N. (2020, July). Detection and Prevention Mechanisms for DDoS Attack in Cloud Computing Environment, 11th International Conference on Computing, Communication and Networking Technologies (ICCCNT) (pp. 1-6). IEEE.

CHAPTER 19

SDN-Enabled IoT Management Architectures and Security Solutions: A Review

SARABJEET KAUR[1*], AMANPREET KAUR[1], and ABHINAV BHANDARI[2]

[1]University Institute of Computing, Chandigarh University, Gharuan, Chandigarh Group of Colleges, Landran, Mohali, Punjab, India

[2]Department of Computer Science and Engineering, Punjabi University, Patiala, Punjab, India

*Corresponding author. E-mail: mca.sarabjeet@gmail.com

ABSTRACT

Software-defined networking (SDN) is an upcoming technology which is replacing the traditional networking from past few years. SDN is a software approach to control the network equipment. It has separated the control plane and data plane. IoT is Internet of things which connects the objects over Internet. Recent advancements in network design and implementation have enabled the fusion of secure networks and IoT devices. Emergence of SDNs has further increased the possibility to control and implement the secure and reliable communication between different sensors and machines. The main emphasis in IoT is given on interconnecting various objects and further extends its limits over the Internet. As the number of objects to be interconnected is increasing exponentially, there erupts a need for a well-managed network with a higher grade of efficiency due to its complexity. The SDN provides a better solution due to its flexibility in programming the network without any major changes in existing architecture design. In this chapter, a study of different architecture available for SDN in IoT management is presented. Further, a review of some of the SDN-based security solutions is also covered in this chapter. A broad coverage of SDN architectures for wireless sensor networks has been emphasized along with

SDN-based IoT device security solution study. The comparison analysis provides the view of different SDN-enabled IoT architectures and security solutions as upcoming trends.

19.1   INTRODUCTION

Internet of things (IoT) is a system of inter relating the objects or computing devices which share the data over the Internet without any interaction. It means connecting everything through Internet. Software-defined networking (SDN) is a new era that controls the network devices as and when required through software approach [42]. The main strength of SDN over traditional networks is the separation of its control plane and data plane. As the congestion in complex networks is increasing, the SDN technology adoption is becoming much popular [3–5]. There is a possibility of fusion of software-defined networks and IoT. Some of the application areas of IoT are shown in Figure 19.1. IoT has three-layered architecture, one among three is the network layer which is responsible for data sharing. The network layer implementation using SDN technology provides flexibility to network architectures in IoT.

The IoT network is formed by some physical devices, wireless communication devices, and sensors, and so forth [6,7]. There are various frameworks available for the architectural management of SDN and IoT systems. Out of these available and designed architectures, some are discussed in this research. These architectures enable the complexity to be implemented over the network in the view of multiple sensor nodes of a wireless network which is being designed to provide the pathway of data transmission at a higher speed and of a big volume. The architectures have been designed in view of the availability of the bandwidth type of controller programmability of systems. Section 19.2 covers the study of various SDN-based architectures. These architectures are for wireless networks. Section 19.3 covers the security solutions for SDN-based framework. Section 19.4 finally discusses Conclusion.

19.2   SDN-BASED IOT ARCHITECTURES

This section is basically about the architectures that could be implemented to use the SDN-based networking of IoT devices. These frameworks are for wireless sensor-based networks. This section covers the management, control and data decoupling, protocols used, scalability, benefits, and limitations of these architectures. SDN architecture uses different available controllers such as OpenDaylight [9] and Nox/POX [11].

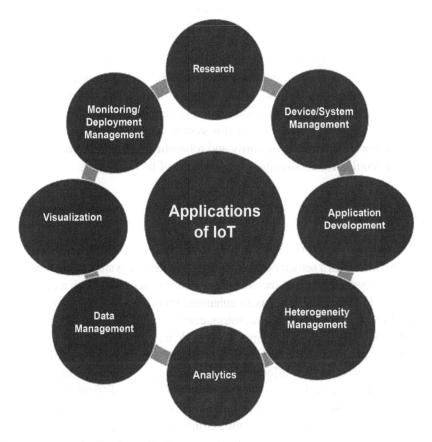

FIGURE 19.1 Applications of IoT.

19.2.1 SDN-WISE

SDN-WISE stands for SDN wireless sensor networks. It is a software-defined network specially designed for implementation of IoT devices [23]. It comprises of a distributed network of sensors which has been localized to get efficiency in power consumption. This enables the architecture to provide a better management of power consumption hands to improve the efficiency of the devices and their life. For example, if the sensor nodes are being distributed over a wide area in the sea where the sensors are battery powered and have a limited amount of electrical energy for their operation. If a better energy solution is provided by a network as it is provided by this network, it helps in increasing the life of sensor operations. One of the major advantages of this type of architecture is that it has Openflow flow table for a controller with the dumb sensor node. The floor rules are already embedded in IT software which helps in proper tracking and maintaining the flow of the network system. The backbone of this system is a separated centralized controller and dumb data plane which uses Openflow protocol with medium scalability. One of the major benefits of SDN-WISE is its state full approach which reduces the information exchange. The mobility and localization of the domain controller also add to some of the benefits of this system. But while using this architecture a compromise between security and reliability is generally thought of. The missing details of the assignment are also one of its limitations.

19.2.2   *WSN-SDN*

Wireless sensor network (WSN-SDN) is also one of a widely accepted architecture which uses a sensor network flow management system. The main property of the system is use of the wireless sensor cluster along with a centralized controller [24]. This system has an enhanced monitoring by installing a central controller which controls and monitors continuously the flow operation. The architecture makes the use of open flow or distance aware routing protocol. A major advantage of the system is its benefit in selection of the optimum path which manages the flow effectively and efficiently. A major limitation of the WSN-SDN framework is lower scalability, that is, it is difficult to extend the pre-existing network or to add a distant node. It also provides the adjustment of the routing strategy. This enables the setting of a proper path in network flow. Although the benefit of having a central controller enhances the management yet the placement, implementation, and organization of the central controller is not clear. The hazy picture of this also has certain validation issues hence hinder its authenticity and make it un-understandable for some while troubleshooting any hardware or software problems.

19.2.2.1   *SD-WSN*

The SD-WSN has its benefits such as the implementation of the infrastructure management over the other systems [25]. The main benefit of using this is that the reconfiguration of the infrastructure is possible that extends the horizon of its use. SD-WSN architecture also has few limitations such as dependency on devices and hardware being used for its implementation.

19.2.2.2 INTEGRATED WIRELESS SENSOR DEFINED NETWORK (WSDN)

It manages the platform using machine (intermediate network node, INNP). It also has a localized controller in each sensor node which interacts with a centralized controller [26]. The main characteristic of this system is that INNP being used here is done through a virtual machine in node platform. Integrated WSDN uses the centralized and local controller. The protocol being used here is Contiki OS on each local controller. The scalability of integrated WSDN is low. Though it lacks in behavior evaluation and performance, yet it is flexible enough and reduces the cost of commodity off the shelf devices.

19.2.2.3 SOF

Sensor Openflow (SOF) is a framework about flow management. INNP is implemented in data plane and flow based packet forwarding [27]. SOF has a centralized controller and distributed data plane, which makes it different from other protocols. The protocol being used here is SOF. It also has low scalability. The benefits of SOF are handling of peer compatibility and address classification. The major drawback of SOF is that it is just a theoretical idea which has not yet been experimentally proved. Another aspect of the research is to have a view on security solutions available for SDN-based IoT.

There is always a risk of security aspects for IoT devices in a heterogeneous network. There are few approaches of security aspects for SDN-based IoT networks. This could be implemented as controller authentication in IoT devices as in Figure 19.2. In this case of a wireless object when a connection is being established, the controller blocks other ports.

Then the controller finds the authenticated user to allow the flow. These are taken as security controllers. There are few security solutions for SDN-based IoT devices discussed here.

19.3 SECURITY OF SDN ARCHITECTURE

One among various approaches is the security of SDN architecture. The main security parameter of this approach is the authentication. It uses the

Ad hoc network for communication. In this approach, the centralized SDN controller stops all of the switch ports to receive the flow from the new device after authenticating it. Still, the major drawback of this approach is its nonexperimentation. Apart from its theoretical and overview of expected advantages of this approach, the practical implications of implementation are yet to be encountered. The security solutions are also required to prevent the various Internet attacks like distributed denial of service attack [42, 43].

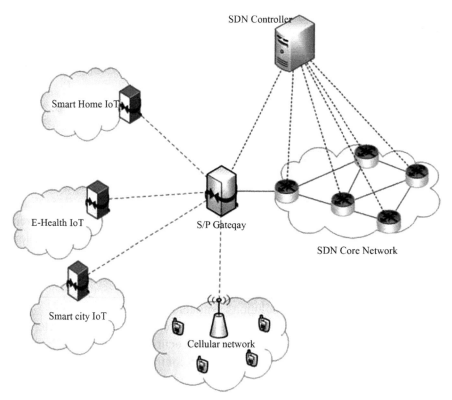

FIGURE 19.2   IoT network.

19.3.1 *DISFIRE*

Another approach for security check is DISFIRE which is being based upon authentication and authorization. This approach uses the grid network for flow management [27]. It is a hierarchical cluster network which has multiple SDN controller implementations. The approach uses dynamic firewall to ensure authorization. It lacks in framework evaluation which makes it inefficient. Another drawback is the protocol being used is Opflex which is not tested or implemented yet.

19.3.2 BLACK SDN

Black SDN approach of the security solution is another add-on. It has secure controller architecture. Black SDN provides the location security. The major benefits of black SDN are counted as its confidentiality and integrity [29]. It is a secure and authenticated approach which supports the privacy of the system. Black SDN uses Generic IoT/machine to machine communication network for the flow management. It secures the meta-data by using TTP SDN controller. It also provides the link-layer encryption and implements a secure network. Apart from various merits, there exist certain limitations such as low scalability issues. Due to its low scalability, it is unable to provide complete security. To implement the secure communication it shares a key which provides the authenticity.

19.3.3 SOFTWARE DEFINED PROTOCOL (SDP)

SDP is one of the approaches used for SDN-based IoT security solutions. It also provides a secure network by implementing the authentication over the network [35]. It collects the IP addresses of all machine-to-machine devices being capable for communication. These IP addresses are then stored in a logical network. SDP authenticates the user on the basis of stored information. Again the scalability issue affects the performance of SDP.

19.3.4 SOFTWARE DEFINED INTERNET OF THINGS (SDIOT)

It uses the generic IoT network for authenticating the network. It uses SD security network authentication [25]. As the limitation of the SDIoT approach, it is hard to manage the large networks with a single SD sec element. This is again a theoretical concept that lacks experimental evaluation.

19.4 CONCLUSION

The way of communication between humans and machines is taking a new turn with the emergence of IoT. Rather than connecting every traditional physical device with the Internet, the IoT is changing the trend. Although IoT is rising, yet it lacks in managing the data, security, and programmability as per the requirements of the customer. These limitations of IoT raise the need of combining it with a centralized control as implemented in SDN. In this chapter, the details of SDN architectures based on IoT are discussed. Some of the security solutions are being summarized along with some of the issues yet to be resolved. The combination of SDN with IoT may lead to a better networking era in near future.

KEYWORDS

- **IoT**
- **Openflow**
- **SDN**

REFERENCES

1. Cisco Visual Networking Index: Global Mobile Data Traffic Forecast Update, White Paper, Cisco (2015–2020).
2. Nunes, B., Mendonca, M., Nguyen, X., Obraczka, K., and Turletti, T. 2014. A Survey of Software-Defined Networking: Past, Present, and Future of Programmable Networks. IEEE Communications Surveys & Tutorials. 16, 1617–1634, 3 (2014). DOI: 10.1109/SURV.2014.012214.00180.
3. Kreutz, D., Ramos, F., Esteves Verissimo, P., Esteve Rothenberg, C., Azodolmolky, S., and Uhlig, S. 2015. Software-Defined Networking: A Comprehensive Survey. Proceedings of the IEEE. 103, 14–76, 1 (2015). DOI: 10.1109/JPROC.2014.2371999.
4. Benzekki, K., El Fergougui, A., and Elbelrhiti Elalaoui, A. 2016. Software-Defined Networking (SDN): A Survey. Security and Communication Networks. 9, 5803–5833, 18 (2016). DOI: 10.1109/COMST.2016.2618874.
5. Karakus, M. and Durresi, A. 2017. Quality of Service (QoS) in Software Defined Networking (SDN): A Survey. Journal of Network and Computer Applications. 80, 200–218 (2017). DOI: 10.1016/j.jnca.2016.12.019.
6. Haque, I. and Abu-Ghazaleh, N. 2016. Wireless Software Defined Networking: A Survey and Taxonomy. IEEE Communications Surveys & Tutorials. 18, 2713–2737, 4 (2016). DOI: 10.1109/COMST.2016.2571118.
7. Agadeesan, N. and Krishnamachari, B. 2014. Software-Defined Networking Paradigms in Wireless Networks: A Survey. ACM Computing Surveys. 47, 1–11, 2 (2014). DOI: 10.1145/2655690.

8. Braun, W. and Menth, M. 2014. Software-Defined Networking Using OpenFlow: Protocols, Applications and Architectural Design Choices. Future Internet. 6, 302–336, 2 (2014). DOI:10.3390/fi6020302.

9. Medved, J., Tkacik, R., and Gray, K. 2014. Opendaylight: Towards a Model-Driven SDN Controller Architecture. A World of Wireless, Mobile and Multimedia Networks (WoWMoM), 1–6, 2014. DOI: 10.1109/WoWMoM.2014.6918985.

10. Floodlight, S. D. N. OpenFlow Controller. Web: https://github. com/floodlight/floodlight.

11. Gude, N., Koponen, T., Pettit, J., Pfaff, B., Casado, M., McKeown, N., and Shenker, S. 2008. NOX. ACM SIGCOMM Computer Communication Review. 38, 105, 3 (2008). DOI: 10.1145/1384609.1384625.

12. Evans, D. 2011. The Internet of Things, Evol. The Internet Is Chang. Everything Whitepaper Cisco Internet Bus. Solutions Group IBSG, Vol. 1, pp. 1–12, 2011.

13. Li, J., Altman, E., and Touati, C. 2015. A General SDN-Based IoT Framework With NVF Implementation. ZTE Communications, 13, 42–45, 3 (2015).

14. Mazhar, M.M., Jamil, M.A., Mazhar, A., Ellahi, A., Jamil, M.S., and Mahmood, T., 2015. Conceptualization of Software Defined Network Layers Over Internet of Things for Future Smart Cities applications. In Wireless for Space and Extreme Environments (WiSEE), IEEE International Conference. 1–4, 2015. DOI: 10.1109/WiSEE.2015.7393104.

15. Liu, J., Li, Y., Chen, M., Dong, W., and Jin, D. 2015. Software-Defined Internet of Things for Smart Urban Sensing. IEEE Communications Magazine. 53, 55–63, 9 (2015). DOI: 10.1109/MCOM.2015.7263373.

16. Desai, A., Nagegowda, K., and Ninikrishna, T. 2016. A Framework for Integrating IoT and SDN Using Proposed OF-Enabled Management Device. International Conference on Circuit, Power and Computing Technologies (ICCPCT), 1–4, 2016. DOI: 10.1109/ICCPCT.2016.7530127.

17. Li, L. E., Mao, Z. M., and Rexford, J. 2012. Toward Software-Defined Cellular Networks. In Software Defined Networking (EWSDN), 2012 European

18. Gudipati, A., Perry, D., Li, L., and Katti, S. 2013. SoftRAN: Software Defined Radio Access Network. Proceedings of the Second ACM SIGCOMM Workshop on Hot Topics in Software Defined Networking, 2013. DOI: 10.1145/2491185.2491207.

19. Jin, X., Li, L., Vanbever, L., and Rexford, J. 2013. Softcell: Scalable and Flexible Cellular Core Network Architecture. Proceedings of the Ninth ACM Conference on Emerging Networking Experiments and Technologies, 163–174, 2013. DOI: 10.1145/2535372.2535377.

20. Cho, H. H., Lai, C. F., Shih, T., and Chao, H. C. 2014. Integration of SDR and SDN for 5G. IEEE Access. 2, 1196–1204, (2014). DOI: 10.1109/ACCESS.2014.2357435.

21. Akyildiz, I., Wang, P., and Lin, S. 2015. SoftAir: A Software Defined Networking Architecture for 5G Wireless Systems. Computer Networks. 85, 1–18, (2015). DOI: 10.1016/j.comnet.2015.05.007.

22. Namal, S., Ahmad, I., Saud, S., Jokinen, M., and Gurtov, A. 2015. Implementation of OpenFlow Based Cognitive Radio Network Architecture: SDN&R. Wireless Networks. 22, 663–677, 2 (2015). DOI: 10.1007/s11276-015-0973-5.

23. Galluccio, L., Milardo, S., Morabito, G., and Palazzo, S. 2015. SDN-WISE: Design, Prototyping and Experimentation of a Stateful SDN Solution for WIreless SEnsor Networks. IEEE Conference on Computer Communications (INFOCOM), 513–521, 2015. DOI: 10.1109/INFOCOM.2015.7218418.

24. Gante, D., Aslan, M., and Matrawy, A. 2014. Smart Wireless Sensor Network Management Based on Software-Defined Networking. 27th Biennial Symposium on Communications (QBSC), 71–75, 2014. DOI: 10.1109/QBSC.2014.6841187.

25. Miyazaki, T., Yamaguch, S., Kobayashi, K., Kitamichi, J., Guo, S., Tsukahara, T., and Hayashi, T. 2014. A Software Defined Wireless Sensor Network. International Conference on Computing, Networking and Communications (ICNC), 847–852, 2014. DOI: 10.1109/ICCNC.2014.6785448.

26. Leontiadis, I., Efstratiou, C., Mascolo, C., and Crowcroft, J. 2012. SenShare: Transforming Sensor Networks Into Multi-Application Sensing Infrastructures. European Conference on Wireless Sensor Networks, 65–81, 2012. DOI: 10.1007/978-3-642-28169-3_5.

27. Luo, T., Tan, H., and Quek, T. 2012. Sensor OpenFlow: Enabling Software-Defined Wireless Sensor Networks. IEEE Communications Letters. 16, 1896–1899, 11 (2012). DOI: 10.1109/LCOMM.2012.092812.121712.

28. Qin, Z., Denker, G., Giannelli, C., Bellavista, P., and Venkatasubramanian, N. 2014. A Software Defined Networking Architecture for the Internet-of-Things. Network Operations and Management Symposium (NOMS), 1–9, 2014. DOI: 10.1109/NOMS.2014.6838365.

29. Wu, D., Arkhipov, D., Eskindir, A., Zhijing, Q., and McCann, J. 2015. UbiFlow: Mobility Management in Urban-Scale Software Defined IoT. IEEE Conference on Computer Communications (INFOCOM), 208–216, 2015. DOI: 10.1109/INFOCOM.2015.7218384.

30. Boussard, M., Bui, D., Ciavaglia, L., Douville, R., Le Pallec, M., Le Sauze, N., Noirie, L., Papillon, S., Peloso, P., and Santoro, F. 2015. Software-Defined LANs for Interconnected Smart Environment. 219–227, 2015. DOI: 10.1109/ITC.2015.33.

31. Jararweh, Y., Al-Ayyoub, M., Darabseh, A., Benkhelifa, E., Vouk, M., and Rindos, A. 2015. SDIoT: A Software Defined Based Internet of Things Framework. Journal of Ambient Intelligence and Humanized Computing. 6, 453–461, 4 (2015).

32. Sahoo, K., Sahoo, B., and Panda, A. 2015. A Secured SDN Framework for IoT. International Conference on Man and Machine Interfacing (MAMI), 1–4, 2015. DOI: 10.1109/MAMI.2015.7456584.

33. Gonzalez, C., Charfadine, S., Flauzac, O., and Nolot, F. 2016. SDN-Based Security Framework for the IoT in Distributed Grid. International Multidisciplinary Conference on Computer and Energy Science (SpliTech), 1–5, 2016. DOI: 10.1109/SpliTech.2016.7555946.

34. OpFlex: An Open Policy Protocol White Paper. (n.d.). Retrieved November 22, 2016, from http://www.cisco.com/c/en/us/solutions/collateral/data-center- virtualization/application-centric-infrastructure/white-paper-c11-731302.html, (2016).

35. Chakrabarty, S. and Engels, D. 2016. A Secure IoT Architecture for Smart Cities. 13th IEEE Annual Consumer Communications & Networking Conference (CCNC), 812–813, 2016. DOI: 10.1109/CCNC.2016.7444889.

36. Flauzac, O., Gonzalez, C., Hachani, A., and Nolot, F. 2015. SDN Based Architecture for IoT and Improvement of the Security. 29th International Conference on Advanced Information Networking and Applications Workshops (WAINA), 688–693, 2015. DOI: 10.1109/WAINA.2015.110.

37. Olivier, F., Carlos, G., and Florent, N. 2015. New Security Architecture for IoT Network. Procedia Computer Science. 52, 1028–1033, (2015). DOI:10.1016/j.procs.2015.05.099.

38. Han, Z. and Ren, W. 2014. A Novel Wireless Sensor Networks Structure Based on the SDN. International Journal of Distributed Sensor Networks. 10, 874047, 3 (2014). DOI:10.1155/2014/874047.

39. Acobsson, M. and Orfanidis, C. 2015. Using Software-Defined Networking Principles for Wireless Sensor Networks. 11th Swedish National Computer Networking Workshop (SNCNW 2015) Karlstad, Sweden, 2015.

40. Robert, E. 2015. Building the Internet of Everything (IoE) for first responders. Systems, Applications and Technology Conference (LISAT), 1–6, (2015). DOI: 0.1109/LISAT.2015.7160172.

41. Singh, B., Saluja, K., and Bhandari, A. (2015). Simulation Study of Application Layer DDoS Attack. 893–898. 10.1109/ICGCIoT.2015.7380589.

42. Kaur, A. and Bhandari, A. (2017). Detection and Mitigation of Spoofing Attacks by Using SDN in LAN. 10.1007/978-981-10-3325-4_24.

43. Potluri, S., Mangla, M., Satpathy, S., & Mohanty, S. N. (2020, July). Detection and Prevention Mechanisms for DDoS Attack in Cloud Computing Environment. 11th International Conference on Computing, Communication and Networking Technologies (ICCCNT) (pp. 1-6). IEEE.

CHAPTER 20

A Survey of DDoS Defense Mechanisms in Software-Defined Networks (SDN)

JASMEEN KAUR CHAHAL* and ABHINAV BHANDARI

Department of Computer Science and Engineering, Punjabi University, Patiala, Punjab, India

Corresponding author. E-mail: jasmeenkaur2592@gmail.com.

ABSTRACT

Software-defined networking (SDN) has been claimed to be a revolutionizing paradigm shift in networking that gives assurance to make the networks programmable, flexible, and dynamic in order to provide a relatively easier management and reduce complexity. As SDN influence has been increasing, the security of SDN technology is becoming a major concern. Distributed denial of service attacks are one of the potential attacks against the SDN environment. This chapter shows the survey of the research in a comprehensive way, relating to distributed denial of service defense mechanisms (detection, mitigation) in SDN.

20.1 INTRODUCTION

Due to the emergence of trends like clod, mobile computing, social networking, big data, and so forth, Internet is growing at a high pace and demanding high speed and bandwidth than ever. Software-defined networking (SDN) has been claimed to be a revolutionizing paradigm shift in networking that gives assurance to make the networks programmable, flexible, and dynamic in order to provide a relatively easier management and reduce complexity. The major idea of SDN is to separate the network's control logic (control plane) from the network routers and switches (data plane). The network switches change to simple forwarding devices responsible for the packet forwarding based on the rules installed by the centralized controllers. The controller supervises the whole network; provide feedback with better decisions based on the global network view.

According to Open Networking Foundation [1], SDN's definition is–"In the SDN architecture, the control and data planes are decoupled, network intelligence and state are logically centralized, and the underlying network infrastructure is abstracted from the applications." SDN reference model (shown in Figure 20.1), consists of three layers [2]:

- *Infrastructure layer (also known as data plane):* This layer consists of networking devices (e.g., switches, routers, and so forth) that are responsible for forming underlying network to forward network traffic. These devices store the information of network status (e.g., network topology, traffic statistics, and so forth) and send it to the controller. Also, it processes the packets based on the rules provided by the controller.

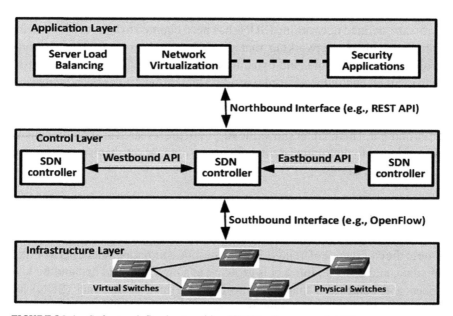

FIGURE 20.1   Software-defined networking (SDN) reference model [1].

- *Control layer (also known as control plane):* This layer consists of one or more software-based SDN controllers for providing the control functionality through application programming interface (API). The

APIs control the network, forwarding behavior of devices through an open interface. A controller interacts with infrastructure layer using southbound interface and with application layer using northbound interface. For longer network domains, multiple controllers exist and these controllers interact with each other using an east–west bound interface to coordinate their decision-making processes and sharing of network information.

- *Application layer:* This layer mainly consists of end-user business applications. The end-user business applications access and control the switching devices in the infrastructure layer by using the programmable platform provided by the control layer. Examples of such applications include server load balancing, network virtualization, security applications, and many more.

To protect the network from threats and anomalies, SDN has been used to enhance the network security to monitor, analyze, and response. The controller acts as the brain of the system. The detection methods deployed in the network send the under supervision data to the centralized controller on a regular basis. The various applications are used by the network administrators to analyze and correlate this feedback from the complete network. The new flow rules are propagated to the security system which contains the new security measures according to the analysis. This consolidated approach can efficiently speed up the control and containment of network security threats [3]. Although, same attributes of centralized architecture of SDN introduce many security challenges. Being a crucial part of the network, literally, "brain" of the network which is required to be stable, secure, and steady in order to direct and manage the network traffic flowing throughout the network. There are many security threats and challenges [4]:

- Unauthorized access, for example, unauthorized controller access or unauthenticated application access
- Data leakage, for example, flow rule discovery or forwarding policy discovery
- Data modification, for example, flow rule modification to modify packets.
- Malicious applications, for example, fraudulent rule insertion or controller hijacking
- Configuration issues, for example, lack of TLS adoption policy enforcement.

- Denial of service, for example, controller-switch congestion or switch table overflow.

Among these threats, distributed denial of service (DDoS) attacks in SDN are one of the notorious security threats that can both degrade and disrupt the control layer and infrastructure layer, causing the denial of network services.

20.2   DDOS DEFENSE MECHANISMS IN SDN

By analyzing the various defence mechanisms, we divide these into two broad categories:

- *SDN-supported*: The centralized architecture of SDN can be utilized to detect and mitigate DDoS attacks.
- *SDN-self*: The controller of the network is itself vulnerable to DDoS attacks, and becomes a single point of failure.

Wang et al. [5] found that the SDN and cloud computing can enhance the DDoS attack defense. They proposed an anomaly-based DDoS detection and reaction mechanism called DaMask. DaMask mechanism is made up of two modules, DaMask-D for detection and DaMask-M for mitigation. The detection is based on probabilistic inference graphical model. In DaMask-M, mitigation mechanism is a set of common APIs, where a defender can customize their own defense mechanism. DaMask is implemented on a hybrid cloud, made up of public cloud (Amazon Web Service EC2) and private cloud (lab setup) using Mininet.

Mausavi et al. [6] proposed a lightweight DDoS detection mechanism based on entropy calculation of destination IP of incoming packets to the controller. The chosen threshold is set to the lowest possible rate of attack traffic with a detection rate of 96%. They used Mininet emulator to evaluate the detection technique and POX controller to collect the destination IPs of the new incoming packets by adding a function of entropy computation.

Cui et al. [7] proposed a mechanism, SD-anti-DDoS, for detection, traceback, and mitigation of DDoS attacks in SDN. They propose a DDoS detection trigger module to achieve a quick response of detection. The detection module is based on back propagation neural network. Mininet is used as an experimental platform to simulate the mechanism with the RYU controller. The results show that the detection mechanism starts quickly and accurately trace the attack source.

Dong et al. [8] proposed a detection method based on a statistical tool to detect the novel DDoS low-traffic flows and locate the potential interfaces that are compromised. The detection approach is based on sequential probability ratio test. They choose DARPA intrusion detection data sets to evaluate the detection algorithm. In comparison with percentage method, count method, and entropy method, the proposed method showed outstanding properties.

A deep learning-based multivector DDoS detection model is proposed by Niyaz et al. [9]. They detected various spoofed attacks including TCP, user datagram protocol (UDP), and Internet Control Message Protocol (ICMP) vectors. They used traffic collector and flow installer to extract the headers for TCP, UDP, and ICMP traffic. The feature extractor module triggered using a timer function. Then, deep learning-based technique Stacked Autoencoder is used for traffic classification. By using this technique, they classify the traffic in eight classes, one normal and seven types of DDoS attack classes based on TCP, UDP, or ICMP vectors launch either separately or in combinations. For the evaluation of the proposed technique, they used a real network and a private network test bed. Hping3 tool is used as a DDoS attack traffic generator.

On-demand mitigation framework "ArOMA" has been proposed by Sahay et al. [10] with an aim to make possible the collaboration between the ISP and their customers. The respective work is concentrated only on the mitigation of suspicious traffic. The controllers are deployed at customer and ISP side, and they communicate with each other using a secured channel. The detection mechanism generated alerts in the presence of suspicious traffic, and the customer controller sends alert information to the ISP controller. Based on alerts, the mitigation mechanism further requests the path lookup module to infer the best path to enforce the mitigation actions on the flows of concern. They evaluate the performance of the proposed framework using both Mininet-based simulations and test bed-based experiments.

Phan et al. [11] combined the two machine learning techniques support vector machine (SVM) and self-organizing map (SOM) and took advantage of both for flow classification and accurate decisions. The whole proposed mechanism is located at the controller. Also, policy enforcement module is used to mitigate the attack traffic. The experimental results show higher accuracy rate than the original SVMs and SOM, that is, 98.13%.

Hu et al. [12] proposed a detection and mitigation module based on entropy and machine leaning, against DDoS attacks in real-time. Entropy is used to extract the current network features from the collected traffic information and SVM classifier has been used to classify the attack traffic and normal traffic. Mitigation mechanism is made up of mitigation server (deployed at controller) and mitigation agent (deployed at host).

Mohammadi et al. [13] proposed a prevention and detection technique named SLICOTS, to defend against TCP-SYN flood. The proposed technique is implemented on the controller. The technique detects the attack based on the MAC addresses of the destination host stored in the pending list to handle illegitimate requests. When the stored malicious requests for a particular host exceed the threshold, SLICOTS obstructs it based on the MAC address. Emulated platform has been used to evaluate the technique performance implemented on ODL controller. SLICOTS outperforms the normal SDN under different scenarios.

A two-layer DDoS detection is used by Yang et al. [14]. First, the course-grained DDoS detection at data plane, where the flow monitoring algorithm captures the characteristics of DDoS attack by polling the values of counters in OpenFlow switches. Second, fine grained DDOS detection at control plane, where fine grained detection takes place on the anomalous flows filtered by the data plane. Further authors extended the defense mechanism and include the attack classification and botnet tracking functionality in Han et al. [15]. They proposed a DDoS defense framework called Overwatch, where the DDoS attack sensors (attack detection) and actuators (attack response) are deployed at data plane and DDoS attack classifier and botnet tracking functionality is carried out at control plane.

A queuing-based technique has been used by Bhushan et al. [16] to detect and react against DDoS attacks in SDN-enabled cloud environment. The mitigation approach is applied to eliminate flow-table overflow DDoS attacks. To resist the attack at a particular switch, authors used the free space of other switches and redirect the attack flow from the victim switch to other switch or switches. Mininet emulator has been used to evaluate the performance of the proposed defense mechanism with a POX SDN controller.

Ye et al. [17] believed that there exists some similarity and regularity in attack flows. On the basis of this rationale, they classify the normal and attack traffic using an SVM classifier. The experimental setup is created by

Mininet with Floodlight controller. Hping3 tool is used to generate attack traffic (ICMP flood, UDP flood, and TCP-SYN flood). An average detection accuracy and false alarm rate is 95.34% and 1.26%.

Nam et al. [18] proposed two approaches to classify the normal traffic and DDoS attack traffic. One is the hybrid technique with the collaboration of SOM + k-NN and second is a SOM distributed-center algorithm of classification. In case of both approaches, trained SOM has been used for classification stage. Entropy has been used to build the representative features in order to measure the degree of divergence. By deploying a test bed environment, they evaluate the proposed algorithms using "DDoS Attack 2007" dataset. The technique reduces the computational time as well as maintains the suitable detection accuracy.

Chen et al. [19] built a detection mechanism based on XGBoost algorithm, improved version of gradient boosting decision tree. The authors highlighted the SDN controller vulnerabilities against DDoS attacks, that is, mainly two attacks—controller resources consumption and control channel congestion. POX controller has been used as SDN controller and topology has been emulated using Mininet. Also, they used a famous KDD Cup 1999 dataset as a train set of the detection model. The emulation results show the high XBoost classifier accuracy (98.53%) with low FPR (0.008%) in comparison to various machine learning algorithms.

The comparison of different DDOS defense mechanisms in SDN is shown in Table 1.

20.3 CONCLUSION

The programmable and centralized architecture of SDN, improves the scalability and manageability of the network, but, SDN architecture itself introduces potential DDoS attack vulnerabilities across the SDN platform. Therefore, the security of SDN infrastructure is becoming a major challenge in the forthcoming years and DDoS attack is a major obstacle for the uninterrupted functioning of SDN infrastructure. In this article, we have presented a comprehensive review of the research work on DDoS defense mechanisms in SDN to date. Although, we consider that still there is a strong need of state-of-art SDN infrastructure to accurately detect and mitigate highly flooded DDoS attacks.

TABLE 20.1 The Comparison of Different DDoS Defense Mechanisms

Year	Ref.	Conference/Journal proceeding	SDN-Supported/ SDN-self	Detection	Classifier	Simulated/ Real	Controller	Dataset	Performance Metric
2015	[5]	Journal proceeding	SDN-supported	Probabilistic inference graphical model	Graphical Model	Simulated	Floodlight	UNB ISCX dataset	DR—89.30%
	[6]	Conference proceeding	SDN-self	Entropy	—	Simulated	POX	—	DR—96%
2016	[7]	Journal proceeding	SDN-self	Inspecting flow entries	BPNN	Simulated	Ryu	—	—
	[8]	Conference proceeding	SDN-self	Sequential probability ratio test	—	—	—	DARPA	FPR—2.26% FNR—1.01%
	[9]	Journal proceeding	SDN-supported	Inspecting flow entries	Deep learning based SAE	Real	POX	—	CA—95.65%
	[11]	Conference proceeding	SDN-self	Based on flow information	SVM and SOM	—	POX	CAIDA dataset	DR—98.13% TPR—96.03% TNR—98.17% FPR—3.96% FNR—1.83%
2017	[10]	Journal proceeding	SDN-supported	—	—	Simulated/ Real	Ryu	—	AG—550 KB/s
	[12]	Conference proceeding	SDN-supported	Entropy	SVM	Simulated	POX	—	DR—99.9%
	[13]	Journal proceeding	SDN-self	Based on flow information	—	Simulated	ODL	—	ADT—3.03 s
	[20]	Conference proceeding	SDN-supported	Snort IDS	—	Simulated	ODL	—	T—467.16 Mbps

TABLE 20.1   *(Continued)*

Year	Ref.	Conference/Journal proceeding	SDN-Supported/SDN-self	Detection	Classifier	Simulated/Real	Controller	Dataset	Performance Metric
	[14]	Conference proceeding	SDN-supported	Based on flow characteristics	–	Real	Ryu	–	–
2018	[16]	Journal proceeding	SDN-self	Queuing theory	–	Simulated	POX	–	HTSDN—480s PER—254 packets/s
	[15]	Journal proceeding	SDN-supported	Based on flow information	Autoencoder-based classification	Real	Ryu	–	–
	[17]	Journal proceeding	SDN-supported	Based on flow characteristics	SVM	Simulated	Floodlight	–	DR—95.24% FPR—1.26%
	[18]	Conference proceeding	SDN-supported	Entropy	SOM & kNN	Real	POX	DDoS Attack 2007	DR—98.24% FPR—2.14% PT—2.810 ms
	[21]	Journal proceeding	SDN-supported	Correlative analysis	–	Real	Floodlight	–	DR—90%
	[22]	Journal proceeding	SDN-supported	–	Fuzzy SOM	–	NOX	–	TPR—94%
	[19]	Conference proceeding	SDN-self	–	XGBoost	Simulated	POX	KDD Cup'99	CA—98.53% FPR—0.008%

D—detection, M—mitigation, DR—detection rate, CA—classification accuracy, TPR—true positive rate, TNR—true negative rate, FPR—false positive rate, FNR—false negative rate, A—accuracy, T—throughput, AG—average goodput, ADT—average detection time, PT—processing time, HTSDN—holding time of SDN, PER—packet exchange rate, BPNN—backpropagation neural network

KEYWORDS

- **software-defined network**
- **distributed denial of service attack**
- **detection**
- **mitigation**
- **defense**

REFERENCES

1. "OpenFlow. Open Networking Foundation (ONF)." [Online]. Available: https://www.opennetworking.org/. [Accessed: 01-Mar-2018].
2. Xia, W., Wen, Y., Foh, C. H., Niyato, D., and Xie, H., "A survey on software-defined networking," *IEEE Commun. Surv. Tutor.*, vol. 17, no. 1, pp. 27–51, 2015.
3. Scott-Hayward, S., O'Callaghan, G., and Sezer, S., "SDN security: A survey," in *Workshop on Software Defined Networks for Future Networks and Services*, 2013.
4. Yan, Q., Yu, F. R., Member, S., Gong, Q., and Li, J., "Software-defined networking (SDN) and distributed denial of service (DDoS) attacks in cloud computing environments : A survey, some research issues, and challenges," *IEEE Commun. Surv. Tutorials*, vol. 18, no. 1, pp. 2–23, 2015.
5. Wang, B., Zheng, Y., Lou, W., and Hou, Y. T., "DDoS attack protection in the era of cloud computing and software-defined networking," *Comput. Netw.*, vol. 81, pp. 308–319, 2015.
6. Mousavi, S. M. and St-hilaire, M., "Early detection of DDoS attacks against SDN controllers," in *IEEE International Conference on Computing, Networking and Communications, Communications and Information Security Symposium*, 2015, pp. 77–81.
7. Cui, Y. et al., "SD-anti-DDoS: Fast and efficient DDoS defense in software-defined networks," *J. Netw. Comput. Appl.*, vol. 68, pp. 65–79, 2016.
8. Dong, P., Du, X., Zhang, H., and Xu, T., "A detection method for a novel DDoS attack against SDN controllers by vast new low-traffic flows," in *IEEE ICC 2016 Communication and Information Systems Security Symposium*, 2016, pp. 1–6.
9. Niyaz, Q., Sun, W., and Javaid, A. Y., "A deep learning based DDoS detection system in software-defined networking (SDN)," *arXiv Prepr. arXiv1611.07400.*, 2016.
10. Sahay, R., Blanc, G., Zhang, Z., and Debar, H., "ArOMA: An SDN based autonomic DDoS mitigation framework," *Comput. Secur.*, vol. 70, pp. 482–499, 2017.
11. Phan, T. V., Bao, N. K., and Park, M., "A novel hybrid flow-based handler with DDoS attacks in software-defined networking," in *IEEE Conference on Ubiquitous Intelligence & Computing, Advanced and Trusted Computing, Scalable Computing and Communications, Cloud and Big Data Computing, Internet of People, and Smart World Congress (UIC/ATC/ScalCom/CBDCom/IoP/SmartWorld)*, 2016, pp. 350–357.
12. Hu, D., Hong, P., and Chen, Y., "FADM: DDoS flooding attack detection and mitigation system in software-defined networking," in *EEE Global Communications Conference*, 2017, pp. 1–7.

13. Mohammadi, R., Javidan, R., and Conti, M., "SLICOTS: An SDN-based lightweight countermeasure for TCP SYN flooding attacks," *IEEE Trans. Netw. Serv. Manag.*, vol. 14, no. 2, pp. 487–497, 2017.

14. Yang, X., Han, B., Sun, Z., and Huang, J., "SDN based DDoS attack detection with cross plane collaboration and lightweight flow monitoring," in *IEEE Global Communications Conference*, 2017, pp. 1–6.

15. Han, B., Yang, X., Sun, Z., Huang, J., and Su, J., "OverWatch: A cross-plane DDoS attack defense framework with collaborative intelligence in SDN," *Secur. Commun. Networks*, vol. 2018, pp. 1–15, 2018.

16. Bhushan, K. and Gupta, B. B., "Distributed denial of service (DDoS) attack detection in software defined networking with cloud computing," *J. Ambient Intell. Humaniz. Comput.*, vol. 3, pp. 1–13, 2018.

17. Ye, J., Cheng, X., Zhu, J., Feng, L., and Song, L., "A DDoS attack detection method based on SVM in software defined network," *Secur. Commun. Netw.*, vol. 2018, pp. 1–8, 2018.

18. Nam, T. M. et al., "Self organizing map-based approaches in DDoS flooding detection using SDN," in *2018 International Conference on Information Networking (ICOIN)*, Chiang Mai, 2018, pp. 249–254. doi: 10.1109/ICOIN.2018.8343119

19. Chen, Z., Jiang, F., Cheng, Y., Gu, X., Liu, W., and Peng, J., "XGBoost classifier for DDoS attack detection and analysis in SDN-based cloud," in *IEEE International Conference on Big Data and Smart Computing (BigComp)*, Shanghai, 2018, pp. 251–256. doi: 10.1109/BigComp.2018.00044.

20. Chowdhary, A., Pisharody, S., Alshamrani, A., and Huang, D., "Dynamic game based security framework in SDN-enabled cloud networking environments," in *Proceedings of the ACM International Workshop on Security in Software Defined Networks & Network Function Virtualization SDN-NFVSec '17*, Scottsdale, AZ, USA, 2017, pp. 53–58.

21. Zheng, J., Li, Q., Gu, G., Cao, J., D. K. Y. Yau, and J. Wu, "Realtime DDoS defense using COTS SDN switches via adaptive correlation analysis," *IEEE Trans. Inf. Forensics Secur.*, vol. 13, no. 7, pp. 1838–1853, 2018.

22. Pillutla, H., and Arjunan, A., "Fuzzy self organizing maps-based DDoS mitigation mechanism for software defined networking in cloud computing," *J. Ambient Intell. Humaniz. Comput.*, pp. 1–13, 2018.

23. Bhandari, A., Sangal, A. L., and Kumar, K. "Characterizing flash events and distributed denial of service attacks: an empirical investigation." *Secur. Commun. Netw.*, vol. 9, no. 13, pp. 2222-2239, 2016.

24. Kaur, A. and Bhandari, A. "Detection and mitigation of spoofing attacks by using SDN in LAN." *Proceedings of Sixth International Conference on Soft Computing for Problem Solving*. Springer, Singapore, 2017.

25. Singh, B., Kumar, K., and Bhandari, A. "Simulation study of application layer DDoS attack." *2015 International Conference on Green Computing and Internet of Things (ICGCIoT)*. IEEE, 2015.

CHAPTER 21

Internet of Things: Challenges and Research Opportunities

MANDEEP KAUR[1*] and MANMINDER SINGH[2]

[1]Computer Science and Engineering, SLIET Longowal, Punjab, India

[2]Department of Computer Science and Engineering, SLIET Longowal, Punjab, India

*Corresponding author. E-mail: mandeepkaur472@gmail.com

ABSTRACT

Internet of things (IoT) is a widely used technology based on sensors. The main idea behind IoT is the machine-to-machine communication in which every device is connected and collects or sends information using sensor technology. IoT is implemented in various scenarios like healthcare, environment monitoring, motion monitoring, agriculture, home automation, and so forth. In this chapter, we present the basic knowledge on IoT its architecture, technologies, protocols, and challenges related to security that IoT will encounter. We will also focus on research directions that could be the future work for the solutions of open security issues for IoT in the real world.

21.1 INTRODUCTION

The advancement in the area of electronics and the deployment of wireless communication systems, ubiquitous services (providing anywhere-anytime-anything connectivity to the users), and mobile devices expand quickly over the past decades. Ubiquitous computing, pervasive computing, sensors, embedded devices, communication technologies, and Internet protocols are combined to form a system where the real and digital world meet and continuously in a symbiotic interaction [1]. The Internet of things (IoT) applications are develop daily because the usage of the Internet is varied with time. IoT is the approach to integrate the Internet into professional, personal, and societal life. This chapter examines the IoT architecture and existing technologies, various possible future applications of these technologies, and how these technologies are going to change the lifestyle in the future.

21.2 INTERNET OF THINGS

The term "Internet of things" refers to an interconnected network of physical devices connected to each other via Internet. The things refer to the digital machines, physical devices, or object in the network that has its own unique identifier and are able to exchange data over a network. The physical devices can be mobile phones, PCs, headphones, vehicles, and so forth.

The purpose of IoT has been illustrated in Figure 21.1. IoT allows objects to be controlled remotely across existing network infrastructure. IoT is the technique which we can use it to easily access physical objects and it reduces human efforts. This technique also has an independent control feature by which any device can be controlled without requiring manual intervention and it will make the impact of the Internet still more personal and close in everyday life. The rising prevalence of IoT technology is facilitated by devices linking the Internet with different technologies such as an actuator, sensor networks, ZigBee, radio frequency identification (RFID), and throughout location-based technologies.

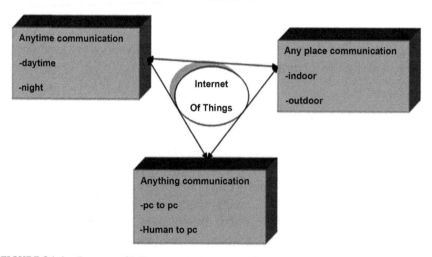

FIGURE 21.1   Purpose of IoT.

21.2.1   ARCHITECTURE OF IOT

The layered architecture of IoT has been represented in Figure 21.2 which consists of the following layers:

- Sensor/perception layer
- Gateway and Internet layer
- Management and service layer
- Application/business layer

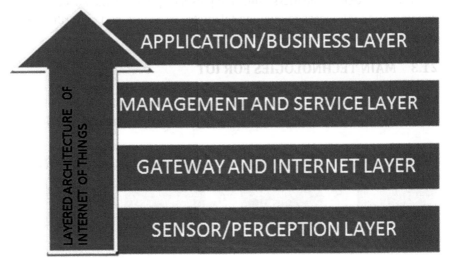

FIGURE 21.2   Layered architecture of IoT.

Sensor/Perception Layer: Sensor layer is also called the lowest abstraction layer or perception layer. This layer contains sensors, RFID tags, actuators which are wireless devices and form the wireless sensor networks (WSNs). This layer gathers data from sensors or gives out to the actuators. It interconnects the real world with the digital world and collects and processes the real-time information. Sensors which are used for different applications are—motion sensor, environment and humidity sensor, water sensor, soil sensor, and so forth [8, 9].

Gateway and Network Layer: This layer is responsible for routing and sending data to the management and service layer which is coming from the sensor layer. This layer requires a large amount of storage capacity to store data collected by RFID tags and sensors. Various protocols are used on this layer for routing.

Management and Service Layer: Management and service layer is used for managing the IoT services like security examination of devices and information. This layer enables the communication between heterogeneous objects. This layer is also responsible for data mining (handle the huge amount of data), and so forth. [11].

Application/Business Layer: Application layer provides a user interface. It is responsible for the effective utilization of data collected. Different IoT applications include government retail, health care, transportation and agriculture, and so forth. Protocols on application layer are constrained application protocol, extensible messaging and presence protocol, advanced message queuing protocol, message queuing telemetry transport, and so forth [11].

21.3 MAIN TECHNOLOGIES FOR IOT

Major IoT networking technologies are RFID, nanotechnology, near field communication technology, intelligence embedded technology WSNs.

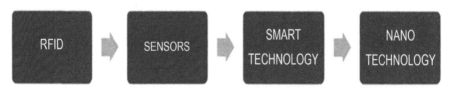

FIGURE 21.3   Technologies in IoT.

RFID technology plays an important role in IoT. It contains two components-tag (also called transponder) and reader. RFID uses radio waves to gather information stored on a tag which is attached to the object (animal, people, and devices) and send that information to other devices through a wireless network [1]. It is used at the place of bar code and does more as compare to bar code [2]. RFID technology is also used to track devices to get information, for example, location tracking. RFID tags are of two types—active or passive. Active tags use a tiny battery and cover a large area for communication and to perform difficult operations, whereas passive tags are small and the area for reader transmission is limited [1,6].

Another technology is WSN which is used to collect and process data in different areas. WSNs consist of large amount of sensor nodes established in different regions to sense a definite event for example, humidity, motion sensor, and so forth. Sensors have a limited lifetime because they are powered by small battery and scarce memory capabilities [1].

Nanotechnology is used to make small devices to interact and connect with each other. Nanotechnology is used in the medical area and also developed for application to a variety of industrial and purification processes.

Other technologies are *Bluetooth* and *near-field communication* technologies used for small distance communication. Using near-field communication technology devices enable us to send or receive data less than 4 cm, example– smart phones [1].

All the above technologies come under the collection phase of IoT.

21.4 OPEN SECURITY ISSUES AND FUTURE DIRECTIONS

In this section, we focus on the main security issues and future research areas in IoT. Security and privacy are major issues by the public. At the very beginning of the Internet, there is no requirement of security but with the growth of the Internet, a number of privacy and security issues are occurring. The main security challenges in IoT are from scalability, reliability, and heterogeneity of the objects. The author describes the object identification as the major security issue which comes before any security issue for example, domain name system which causes DNS cache positioning attack, Man-in-The-Middle (MiTM) attack.

MiTM attack is defined as the communication between two parties that is secretly monitored and modified by an unauthorized third party. Examples of MiTM attacks are session hijacking, replay attacks. Authentication and authorization of objects is an important research area. Authentication is achieved by passwords or public-key cryptosystems but because of heterogeneity of objects authentication is not applicable to all objects. The fast growth of objects makes management of crypto key task complex [4].

In previous papers, authors describe the security threats layer by layer. On the perception layer, natural disaster and environmental threats like earthquakes, floods, and inappropriate value of temperature destroy the physical infrastructure of IoT. On the communication layer, different attacks have occurred—jamming attacks and, sinkhole attack.

Selecting forwarding attacks, hello flood attacks, Sybil attacks, and so forth. In jamming attack attacker occupies the communication channel. The media access control protocol authorized the nodes to send out packets only when the channel is free but in constant jamming, attack attacker uses the path by emitting radio signals and in deceptive jamming, attack attacker sends packets without any pause. Jamming attack targets the availability of information and resources. On business layer, social engineering attacks have occurred example of this type of attack is phishing attack. Phishing attack is that attack in which an attacker gets the trust of the user by sending messages and mails to the user to lose the authentication and integrity of data [5]. Centralized architecture of IoT in which devices relate to server on cloud with large capacity can cause many security threats:

Distributed denial of service attack if a centralized server is damaged then the whole network will fail. To overcome this issue, blockchain technology is used to provide IoT security [7,13]. The other security threats are buffer overflow and botnets, rootkit (install a program on computer to get administrator level rights), advanced persistent threats, and so forth [5]. Large volume of IoT applications data is stored on the cloud which causes storage issues if only useful or sensitive information is stored on the cloud then storage issue will not occur in IoT [12].

21.4.1   COUNTER MEASURES

Open Web Application Security Project describes that physical security comes under the top 10 risks of IoT. First step toward physical security is to ensure that only authorized users can access the information. Protocols to provide security on different layers of IoT are IEEE 802.15.4 protocol. IEEE 802.15.4 protocol is used for short-range communication and control the transmission at the physical and MAC layers. Some limitations of this protocol are: it cannot protect ACK messages and vulnerable against jamming attacks. Future research work is possible in this area [5].

ZigBee provides security at the network and application layer. Other security mechanisms are Bluetooth low energy security, firewall, z-wave, and so forth.

With the growth of IoT, a large amount of sensor nodes and workstations are used so storage and congestion issues arise. To overcome this, artificial intelligence is used in IoT to manage the large amount of data [10].

21.5   CONCLUSION

The rapid growth of IoT brings us into a new epoch in which things can exchange information and make decisions without human intervention. In this chapter, we describe open issues in IoT and future research directions in the IoT security field. Besides IoT security, architecture, communication, discovery, data mining are open research areas in IoT. But the security is the major concern. Centralized IoT security model is very difficult to manage and scale and will be easily targeted by distributed denial of service attack by single-point failure to overcome this blockchain technology (decentralized architecture) in IoT appears.

KEYWORDS

- **Internet of Things**
- **M2M**
- **RFID**
- **ubiquitous computing**
- **WSN**

REFERENCES

1. Borgia, E. (2014). The Internet of Things Vision: Key Features, Applications and Open Issues, *Computer Communications*, 54:1–31.
2. Tan, L. and Wang, N. (2010). Future Internet: The Internet of Things. *2010 3rd International Conference on Advanced Computer Theory and Engineering (ICACTE)*, 5: 376–380. Available at: https://ieeexplore.ieee.org/abstract/document/5579543.
3. Li, B. and Yu, J. (2011). Research and Application on the Smart Home Based on Component Technologies and Internet of Things, *Procedia Engineering*, 15:2087–2092. Available at: https://www.sciencedirect.com/science/article/pii/S1877705811018911 (Accessed: 2011).
4. Zhang, Z., Cho, M., Wang, C., Hsu, C., Chen, C. and Shieh, S. (2014). IoT Security: Ongoing Challenges and Research Opportunities, *2014 IEEE 7th International Conference on Service-Oriented Computing and Applications.*
5. Radoglou Grammatikis, P., Sarigiannidis, P. and Moscholios, I. (2019). Securing the Internet of Things: Challenges, Threats and Solutions. *Internet of Things*, 5:41–70. Available at: https://www.sciencedirect.com/science/article/pii/S2542660518301161 (Accessed: March 2019).
6. Joung, Y. (2007). RFID and the Internet of Things, Taiwan University.
7. Gupta, H. and Varshney, G. (2017). A Security Framework for IOT Devices Against Wireless Threats. *2017 2nd International Conference on Telecommunication and Networks (TEL-NET)*. Available at: https://ieeexplore.ieee.org/abstract/document/8343548.
8. Opentechdiary.wordpress.com.
9. www.slideshare.net.
10. Osuwa, A., Ekhoragbon, E. and Fat, L. (2017). Application of Artificial Intelligence in Internet of Things, 2017 *9th International Conference on Computational Intelligence and Communication Networks (CICN)*. Available at: https://ieeexplore.ieee.org/document/8319379.

11. Al-Fuqaha, A., Guizani, M., Mohammadi, M., Aledhari, M. and Ayyash, M. (2015). Internet of Things: A Survey on Enabling Technologies, Protocols, and Applications. *IEEE Communications Surveys & Tutorials,* 17(4):2347–2376.

12. Jindal, F., Jamar, R. and Churi, P. (2018). Future and Challenges of Internet of Things, *International Journal of Computer Science & Information Technology (IJCSIT)*, 10(2): 13–25.

13. Banerjee, M., Lee, J. and Choo, K. (2018). A Blockchain Future for Internet of Things Security: a Position Paper. *Digital Communications and Networks*, 4(3):149–160.

Index

9781771889612